MUSIC IN WESTERN CULTURE. A SHORT HISTORY

MUSIC IN WESTERN CULTURE. A SHORT HISTORY

JOHN D. WHITE *Kent State University*

Wm. C. Brown Company Publishers. Dubuque, Iowa

MUSIC HISTORY AND LITERATURE

Consulting Editor
Edith Borroff
Eastern Michigan University

Contents

Credits

Foreword

This book is designed to meet the needs of undergraduate college and university students of music. Although directed primarily toward courses in music history or music literature, it is both concise enough and comprehensive enough to be valuable to graduate students taking survey courses in music literature, history, or musicology, and it should be particularly helpful in preparation for candidacy exams. It can well be used in courses at the freshmen and sophomore level which combine the study of music literature and music theory, and it can also serve as a reference or supplemental text in virtually any aspect of the study of music. I hope, of course, that it will be used by all who love music and its history.

There are a number of eminent scholars, students, and other helpful people who have been involved in the preparation of this work. They include Professor Guy Marco, musicologist and Dean of the School of Library Science at Kent State University, for his valuable suggestions; Professor F. Joseph Smith, musicologist of Kent State University, for his careful reading and criticism of the chapters on the Middle Ages; and Professor Edith Borroff of Eastern Michigan University for her suggestions on the entire manuscript. In particular I would like to thank Mrs. Leanne Fazio, my graduate assistant at Kent in 1970–71, for her diligence and discrimination in carrying out her bibliographical and discographical tasks. And I must remember my wife for her patience during the years of work on the book.

Miss Peg Bissler and Miss Donna Fitzgerald devoted much time and energy to the preparation of the manuscript, as did also my secretaries, Mrs. Betsey Poole and Mrs. Grace Mason. Freshest in my mind at this time are Professor Ken Rosenberg and the students of our Honors Colloquium in Twentieth Century Music, spring quarter 1971, from whom I drew renewed excitement and energy for the final three chapters dealing with the twentieth century.

J. D. W.

Prologue

In the dim corridors of prehistoric time music probably began with singing—not in words, but in vowel sounds within a narrow pitch range, perhaps no wider than a perfect fourth. Conceivably, this kind of vocal expression predated the origins of language, and may have served as a means of communication for early man. The melodic lines were mainly stepwise, perhaps with larger intervals used occasionally in descending passages. These prehistoric pitch patterns may have evolved toward the pentatonic scale which is thought to have been used commonly in the ancient cultures of Europe and Asia. Then, as music became more complex, two or more voices may have been combined in devices such as the *drone* (long sustained tones above or below an active melody), *parallelisms* at various intervals, and *heterophony* (differently ornamented versions of the same melody performed simultaneously). Since music was used with the magic and dance of tribal ritual, it was natural that responsorial practices developed in which one voice or group of voices would alternate with another. Instrumental music probably began to evolve from the practice of striking sticks and rocks together to add rhythmic emphasis to vocal music.

Unlike modern man for whom music has not often served a utilitarian purpose, early man found music to be a useful thing. He used his voice and rudimentary percussion instruments for signaling; when working in groups he found that music miraculously lightened his burden; he used it to cure disease; and music was an integral part of his religious and magical rituals. Over the centuries the relationship between music and magic evolved toward the concept of music as an art, though vestiges of the ancient practices are found, for example, in the present-day use of music in religious services.

In some highly developed Oriental cultures, music still retains its aura of magic. In the Shinto religion of Japan, the mysterious tones of the bamboo flute and the koto (a large plucked stringed instrument) play an important role in prayer rituals. In the older Chinese culture, very large groups of instruments were used in religious ceremonies, and in the pre-Buddhist epoch of India (before 600 B.C.), sacred texts were sung to a primitive chant.

Although we do not consciously associate magic with today's concert music, vestiges of early man's relationship to music can be found in our own responses. A single tone of unique timbre or a simple persistent rhythm can evoke powerful images or create strong emotional states in the listener. Our present-day reactions to music—often both primitive and sophisticated—manifest our lineage with early man.

Until very recently, all theories about the genesis of music were entirely speculative. It is only in this century that practitioners of the young sciences of comparative musicology and ethnomusicology have begun to approach the music of ancient times in a scientific manner. These scholars have formed hypotheses based on archeological findings and on the study of present-day tribes in the South Pacific Islands, Africa, and Asia, whose cultures are believed to have changed very little for thousands of years.

Mesopotamia

The earliest culture of which musical scholars have some knowledge is that of Mesopotamia, which was controlled successively by the kingdoms of Sumer (3500–2000 B.C.), Babylonia (2000–1000 B.C.), and Assyria (1000–500 B.C.). The evidence is scanty, but excavations in this area located between the Tigris and Euphrates rivers have uncovered a few preserved instruments as well as pictorial evidence of musical instruments of various types. These flutes, drums, rattles, horns, and numerous varieties of harps and other stringed instruments are thought to have been used in religious ceremonies by the Sumerians and to some extent by the Babylonians. The Assyrians were influenced by Egyptian music, and probably used music in more secular ways. The oldest preserved example of musical notation is a piece of music from the kingdom of Sumer known as the "Hymn of Creation." Its notation has not been deciphered and very little is known of the sound of the music of these peoples.

Egypt

The main sources of knowledge of music in the ancient Egyptian civilization are found in sculpture and pictorial relics from as early as 3000 B.C. and instruments from as early as 1800 B.C. The music of the Middle and Old Kingdoms (4000–1580 B.C.) is thought to have been quiet and reserved in character, performed chiefly on flutes and harps. The remarkable preservation of two flutes from this period suggests that the melodies moved in intervals of major seconds and thirds.

The New Kingdom (from 1580 B.C.) ushered in a marked change in musical practices due to the influence of the instruments and music of Asia. During this period, large groups of many kinds of instruments performed together in groups similar to those of the ancient Chinese. Examination of the numerous preserved instruments from this time reveals that the music utilized small intervals. Pictures of performing groups indicate that singers and instrumentalists performed together, perhaps with the aid of conductors.

During the New Kingdom it is thought that Asiatic influences led to excessive emotion and lack of restraint in music. This, plus a decay of morals around 600 B.C., caused a reaction and reform in Egyptian music which resulted in a return to the more dignified, less passionate techniques of the Old Kingdom. A similar conflict existed somewhat later between the Apollonian and Dionysian elements of Greek culture. Indeed, it is very likely that Egyptian music exerted a strong influence on that of Ancient Greece—on music theory as well as on the ethical and moral attributes of music.

Hebrew Music

Until this century there was little documentation of ancient Hebrew music, partly because Jewish music had not been written down with any precision until the sixteenth century. Studies conducted by comparative musicologists on the semitic tribes of Arabia, Babylonia, Persia, and Syria revealed a striking similarity among the chants of these peoples, even though they had been isolated from each other since the Roman conquest and the destruction of the Second Temple of Jerusalem in 70 A.D. From this it is concluded that the cantillations (chanting) of these modern Semitic tribes must be very similar to the Jewish chant of the pre-Christian era (c. 500 B.C.).

The performance practices of these chants were handed down by word of mouth for nearly 1,000 years. In performance, hand signs were used and accent symbols were written above the words of the chant to indicate pitch inflections. The three basic types were (1) cantillation of Biblical texts, (2) responsorial singing, and (3) hymn singing. With their simple stepwise lines in a relatively narrow range, these chants directly influenced the early chants of the Christian church. The Jews of Yemen, for example, used the chant shown in figure 1 to recite the Pentateuch and certain of the psalms. The remarkable similarity of this and other chants to the Gregorian psalm settings supports the theory that the chants used in this century by these widely dispersed semitic tribes predate the beginnings of the Christian era.

Figure 1. Hebrew Chant Used by the Jews of Yemen.

A wide variety of musical instruments was used in the Temple during the reigns of David and Solomon (c. 1000 B.C.), including instruments imported from other countries such as double oboes, harps, and percussion instruments. King David gave great support to both vocal and instrumental music and a class of professional musicians known as Levites was established in the Temple. Extensive use of instruments in the Temple continued up to 70 A.D., especially for signaling important occurrences in the service such as the entrance of the priests. These included instruments mentioned in the Bible such as the *kinnor* (lyre), the *tof* (small drum), and the *shofar* (ram's horn), the trumpet, and assorted percussion instruments. The only one of these signaling instruments which survived the ban on instrumental music in 70 A.D. is the shofar, which is used even today in certain sacred services of the temple. Hebrew music is of special significance to the study of music in Western civilization because of its influence upon musical practices in the early Christian Church. Aside from the scientifically proven influence of early Jewish chant upon Gregorian chant, liturgical traditions of the Temple exerted a traceable influence upon the liturgy and music of the early Christian Church.

Greece

Of music's role in ancient Greece much is known. We know of its function in drama and of the ethical and moral properties attributed to the various musical modes. We have specific data on the use of music in religious ceremonies, and we can trace certain present-day musical concepts and terminology back to Greek sources. Music was important to Greek society and men such as Plato, Aristotle, Pythagoras, Aristoxenus, and many others devoted considerable attention to it in their writings.

And yet, paradoxically, we don't really know what Greek music sounded like. There is much scholarly speculation on the subject, but it is founded almost entirely upon writings *about* music; and our scholars have yet to agree on the interpretation of the handful of extant examples of Greek notation. To all appearances, it is an unlikely area for study; yet the history of musical thought in Western culture begins in ancient Greece.

In philosophy, law, politics, science, and the fine arts, the Greeks made significant and often germinal contributions to the future. Medieval and Renaissance artists and men of letters were influenced by the sculpture, architecture, and writings of the Greeks. Since many Greek art objects and writings survived the ravages of time, later artists and philosophers gained direct knowledge of the work of their ancient counterparts. They could study and, if they wished, emulate the models of antiquity.

Such was not the case with music. Greek musical practices were, to some extent, passed on to the Romans, but with the beginnings of the early Church and the fall of the Roman Empire, much knowledge of Greek music was lost. This was partly because the early Church fathers strove to remove all traces of paganism from their religious services as well as from their daily lives. Music had been associated with pagan ritual and with revelry. By removing the old music, with its evil associations, from the Church, the early Christians hoped to purge their minds of sinful influence. The result was that nearly all knowledge of the traditions and practices of Greek and Roman music was erased from human memory. Yet we do have considerable theoretical knowledge and information abut the role of music in Greek society simply because many writings on these subjects survived.

Homer and Hesiod referred to music in their epic poems, but the earliest definite knowledge comes from the writings of Terpander (c. 675 B.C.), a poet-musician of Sparta famous for his drinking songs, which he accompanied on the lyre. The combination of voice and instrument in such music would be classed as heterophony—that is, the instrument probably played almost the same thing as the voice. The few variations between the voice and the instrument might have added musical interest, but the two lines were not sufficiently different in pitch and rhythm to create genuine counterpoint. Most Greek music falls into the class of heterophony, with melodies constructed from short melodic patterns called *nomoi*. It is believed that counterpoint and chords were not used, although there is some evidence (e.g., in the writings of Aristoxenus) that polyphony did exist. Since poetry and music were viewed as a single indivisible entity by the Greeks, it is natural that the melodic and rhythmic inflections followed the patterns of the language.

The metrical organization was based on a poetic meter using quantitative rhythmic modes. The names for these modes (iamb, trochee, anapest, etc.) were later applied to a medieval rhythmic system that is similar but not identical to the Greek system. Each metric foot in the Greek system consisted of two or three syllables, depending on the mode (see fig. 2). The short syllable (indicated by a dot) is called the *arsis* and the long syllable (indicated by a dash) the *thesis.* The number of poetic feet in each line of poetry is indicated by the terms *dimeter* (two feet), *trimeter* (three feet), *quatrimeter* (four feet), *pentameter* (five feet), and *hexameter* (six feet). Thus, iambic pentameter describes a line of five iambic feet. Obviously this is similar to the system used today to describe metrical structure in poetry.

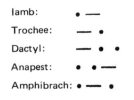

Figure 2. Rhythmic Modes of the Greeks.

In the earliest period, Greek music was closely linked with mythology. Indeed, the very word "music" is derived from a Greek word meaning the art of the muses, sister goddesses who, according to mythology, presided over music and the other arts. The god Apollo was the giver of music to mankind. By the time of Terpander, however, music had gone beyond its association with mythology and ritual magic and had become an art. It nevertheless continued to play an important role in religious ceremonies, as seen in the fact that the kithara and lyre were strongly associated with the religious cult of Apollo, and the aulos with that of Dionysus. The lyre is an instrument of three to seven strings stretched on a frame extending over a sounding bowl, while the kithara is simply a larger, somewhat modified version of the lyre. Both instruments were used to accompany the singing of epic poems, and they were also played alone. The aulos was a double pipe reed instrument, a kind of double oboe. Its shrill, penetrating tone was used in connection with the reading of a type of poetry called the *dithyramb* in worshipping Dionysus. It is thought that Greek drama developed from this practice and that the aulos was used in the musical portions of the great dramatic works of Aeschylus, Sophocles, and Euripides.

As to secular music, the great athletic events often included musical competitions as a part of the festivities. A famous piece for aulos illustrating the combat between Apollo and the dragon was performed by a musician called Sakadas at the Pythian games of 586 B.C. Such contests became increasingly prevalent after the fifth century B.C. and Greek music reached its height during the Periclean period or "Golden Age" (500–400 B.C.).

Plato, in his *Republic,* gave great importance to music in the ideal state and argued that the traditional (Apollonian) music should be preserved. So strong was the belief in the ethical and moral attributes of music that Plato advocated a ban on tragedy partly because it included music for aulos, the Dionysian instrument of revelry. The emphasis on secular music and the increasing popularity of the aulos was believed by many philosophic writers to have led toward the downfall of the ancient art of music. The Apollonians felt that only through vocal music, wherein words played a redeeming role, could man transcend the demonic aspects of music.

In the sixth century B.C. Pythagoras, a philosopher and mathematician of Samos, conducted important experiments with a single stringed instrument called the *monochord.* He proved that the string vibrated in segments and devised a table of frequency ratios known as the Pythagorean scale. Among other things, he experimented with a device known as the spiral of fifths, with which he discovered that if twelve Pythagorean fifths (interval found between the second and third partial of the overtone series) are projected upward from C (C-G-D-A-E-B-F#-C#-G#-D#-A#-E#-B#), the final B# will be about 1/8 of a tone higher than its enharmonic C. The difference between the resultant and the original C is known as the Pythagorean comma. This phenomenon led to many experiments with tuning systems in succeeding centuries, one of which is our present-day system of equal temperament.

Pythagoras' experimentation exemplifies the Greek view of music as a microcosm in which the laws of nature rule sound and rhythm just as they rule the universe; and each different kind of music could affect man in its own specific way. This helps explain the Greek doctrine of *ethos* and its relationship to the conflict between the Apollonian and Dionysian aspects of Greek culture. Writers disagreed on the ethical character or *ethos* of the various modes, but in general the dorian and phrygian modes were considered strong and manly, the hypodorian exciting, the lydian immoral or effeminate, and the mixolydian sad.

Although these modes correspond in name to the modes used later in Gregorian chant, the actual scales or patterns of intervals in Greek music are different from the later Church modes. The Greek scales were built of tetrachords, as shown in figure 3. (They are shown in descending form in accordance with the Greek feeling that scales go down rather than up.)

Figure 3. Tetrachords Used in Greek Scales.

Further refinements of the tetrachords are described by the terms *diatonic, chromatic,* and *enharmonic* (no connection with modern meanings of these terms). The tetrachords were joined to form scales in one of two systems, the greater perfect or the lesser perfect. The greater perfect system was made up of four dorian tetrachords, as shown in figure 4, with an added A at the bottom called the *proslambanomenos.* The middle A in this scale is called the *mese* (from the "middle" string of the kithara). The two middle notes of each tetrachord were movable, while the outer tones were fixed, thus allowing for modification of the quality of the tetrachord.

Figure 4. Greater Perfect System.

The lesser perfect system, shown in figure 5, was made up of only three dorian tetrachords, all conjunct (i.e., each added tetrachord beginning with the last tone of the preceding), plus the *proslambanomenos.* A later scale system was invented by Ptolemy in the second century A.D. in which seven keys or *tonoi* were possible.

Greece became a Roman province in 146 B.C. and any musical practices indigenous to the Italian peninsula were replaced or absorbed

Figure 5. Lesser Perfect System.

by the imported culture of the Greeks. Perhaps certain military brass instruments of the Romans originated in the Etruscan culture which preceded the Roman Empire, but little is known of this. Most significant to the history of musical thought is the fact that the Romans passed on to the Middle Ages certain musical concepts and philosophies which were essentially Greek. These are (1) a scientific approach to musical sound—theory of music and acoustics, (2) a basic musical terminology, (3) the concept of scales built of tetrachords, (4) the linkage of words with melody, (5) the concept of music as pure melodic line, and (6) the philosophy of music as a phenomenon possessed of strong ethical and moral attributes, and as an integral part of the cosmic system of man and nature.

I. THE MIDDLE AGES

1. The Early Middle Ages

Music in the Early Church—Gregorian Chant and the Liturgy—Chant Notation—The Church Modes and the Hexachord System—Secular Music

Music in the Early Church

Although secular music certainly existed during the early Middle Ages, the main stream of musical thought in this period is reflected in the liturgical music of the early Church. This music exerted a strong influence upon later medieval music and upon the Renaissance. Indeed, the development of new polyphonic techniques in the Gothic and pre-Renaissance periods found its melodic foundation in the plainsong *(cantus planus)* of the early Christian liturgy. The mystique surrounding these thousands of finely wrought melodies hearkens back to music's primitive link with magic. This, of course, was far from the intention of the early Church fathers, who strove to eliminate all vestiges of paganism from the service. Even so, the melodic beauty of plainsong cuts across all sectarian lines and appeals to the listener in a way that is both mystical and deeply musical.

The earliest Christians in Palestine established a simple service which retained certain features of the Jewish musical service including responsorial singing of the psalms and hymn singing. Psalm singing was passed almost intact from the Temple to the Church, for the psalms are written in characteristic Hebrew style with pairs of phrases in which the second phrase poetically amplifies the idea stated in the first, a structure ideally suited to responsorial or antiphonal treatment.

In Rome the early Christians found it necessary, because of persecution, to hold secret services, such as weekly night-long prayer vigils which culminated in a meal commemorating the Last Supper. The hours of prayer during these vigils were derived from the Jewish daily prayer hours and developed into the canonical hours or divine offices —Matins, Lauds, Prime, Terce, Sext, Nones, Vespers, and Compline. The commemorative meal was known as the Eucharist, the earliest

3

form of the sacrament of Communion and ancestor of the Mass. It was not until the third century A.D. under Emperor Constantine that Christians could worship in public, and with this came the establishment of temples and increasingly elaborate church services.

Constantine reunited the Roman Empire following recurrent political problems in various dominions and in 330 designated Byzantium (later Constantinople, now Istanbul) as the capital of the Roman Empire. This became a center of art and learning blended of Oriental, Hebrew, and Grecian elements—a flourishing culture contrasting sharply to the "dark ages" of medieval Western Europe. As the two cultures grew, so also developed two churches, the Eastern in Byzantium with its Patriarch, and the Western in Rome with its Pope. This division finally culminated in the great "Schism" of 1054 when two separate and independent ecclesiastical organizations were formalized.

The music of the two churches developed separately but with some cross-influence, for many sources of Christian liturgical song are found in the Eastern provinces of the Empire. Jewish and Greek influences were mingled from the outset and for 300 years Greek was the language of the new faith. The Roman Mass, which became fully developed by the eleventh century, is mostly in Latin, with only the Kyrie remaining in Greek. Byzantine chant is quite different from that of the Roman Church, yet certain chants of the Eastern Church were incorporated into the Roman liturgy. The most important of these are the Byzantine hymns, which developed from short responses between verses of the psalms into longer chants known as *canticles.* Of these, all but one were taken into the liturgy of the Roman Catholic Church. The best known is the *Magnificat,* Canticle of the Blessed Virgin, which figures prominently in music history.

Of the many diverse influences which contributed over the centuries to the Roman Catholic liturgy, the most important chant types are the *Ambrosian* of Milan, the *Gallican* of France, and the *Mozarabic* of Spain. Some of these are used today in the regions of their origin, but the Roman or Gregorian chant eventually dominated the liturgy of the Western Church.

Gregorian Chant and the Liturgy

Ancient tradition holds that the Roman chants were codified during Gregory the Great's reign as Pope (590–604) and that through his guidance and inspiration the Church was left with a vast body of Christian song known as *Gregorian chant.* Little is known of the true role played by Gregory I in assembling and organizing these chants. Indeed, there is evidence to suggest that what is today called Gregorian chant actually developed in Germany and France during the eighth and ninth centuries. Perhaps an early type of Roman chant was codified by Gregory, but if so, it was replaced in Rome by the later chant. Thus, the term Gregorian chant, though useful as a label, is probably not historically accurate.

The chants and the liturgy developed concurrently and are almost inseparable. The first of the two large divisions of the liturgy is the series of eight services (actually seven, since Lauds and Prime were usually performed as one service) throughout the day known as the Canonical hours or Divine Offices. As mentioned, these developed in the early Church from the Jewish hours of prayer. In the Middle Ages this was the most important part of the liturgy, but today the Divine Offices are not observed in their entirety except rarely in cloisters such as monasteries, seminaries, and the like. The other and more important division of the liturgy is the Mass. The term comes from the word *missa* in *"Ite, missa est,"* final section of the Mass which functions simply to tell the congregation to leave. Derived from the early service of the Eucharist, the Mass was originally performed only after the canonical hours of Terce and Sext. Today it is performed independently of the Divine Offices as the basic service of the Catholic Church.

The Mass is divided into two sections: (1) the *Ordinary* with the same texts used throughout the Church year, and (2) the *Proper* with texts and chants which vary according to the occasion of the Church year. Certain parts of both Ordinary and Proper are sung, while others are simply read. The chart in figure 6 shows the sequence of the complete Mass.

The sung section of the Ordinary is of most concern to music history because this part of the Mass remains invariable throughout the Church calendar (with some exceptions such as the omission of the *Gloria* during seasons of penitence). Thus, from a purely musical standpoint, the Mass consists of the *Kyrie, Gloria, Credo, Sanctus* (with *Benedictus*), and *Agnus Dei* (omitting the *Ite, missa est* since it is really nothing more than a means of termination). It is these five sections of the Mass that were given musical settings by many composers from the Gothic period to the present.

The Mass is performed in several ways. The "low Mass" is a Mass without music, while the "high Mass" or *Missa Solemnis* is performed by a choir and priests who chant the liturgy. Between these two extremes is the *Missa Cantata* or "sung Mass" which is performed almost entirely with music but with less elaborate ritual than the high Mass.

The Mass

Sung (Concentus)		Recited (Accentus)	
PROPER	ORDINARY	PROPER	ORDINARY
1 Introit			
	2 Kyrie		
	3 Gloria		
		4 Collects, prayers etc.	
		5 Epistle	
6 Gradual			
7 Alleluia, or Tract (in Lent) with Sequence			
		8 Gospel	
	9 Credo		
10 Offertory			11 Prayers
		12 Secret	
		13 Preface	
	14 Sanctus (including Benedictus)		
			15 Canon
			16 Pater Noster
	17 Agnus Dei		
18 Communion			
		19 Post-communion	
	20 Ite, missa est or Benedicamus Domino		

Figure 6. The Mass.

When a specially composed Mass such as one by Palestrina is used, the service invariably takes the form of a high Mass. Within this framework there are several special kinds of Masses, such as the Requiem or the Nuptial Mass, each with appropriate modifications in the content of the Proper. There are many different Gregorian Masses appropriate for various occasions of the church year. Indeed, if one includes the chants for the Divine Offices as well as the Mass, there are nearly 3,000 different Gregorian chants. The texts for most of the liturgy are drawn from the psalms. (It should be remembered that the numbering for the psalms in the Catholic Church does not correspond to the psalm numbers in the Protestant Bible.)

There are basically three classes of chant as well as three distinct melodic styles. The three classes are (1) *Strophic*—meaning that the various stanzas of the text are set to the same chant. This class is most characteristic of the hymns but also includes the Kyries and portions of the Agnus Dei. (2) *Psalmodic*—meaning that the chants are used in antiphonal or responsorial settings. Since most of the texts of the liturgy are drawn from the psalms, this is the most abundant class of chant. (3) *Through-composed* or *Free*—meaning that the melody continues to flow freely without repetition for the various sections of the text, though melodic sequences and repetition of patterns are typical. This class of chant is the least well defined but is characteristic of the Gloria, Credo, and Sanctus.

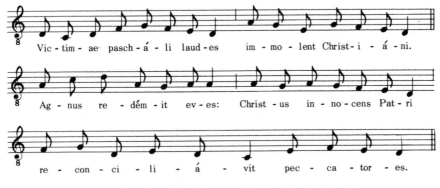

Figure 7. Opening of the Sequence Victimae Paschali Laudes.

The three melodic styles are (1) syllabic, (2) neumatic, and (3) melismatic. Figure 7 shows the opening of the sequence *Victimae Paschali Laudes* from the Easter Mass, which is a good example of the syllabic style in which, for the most part, there is only one note to each syllable of text. The final section of the antiphon *Gloriosa et Beatissima* (shown in figure 8) by Hermanus Contractus exemplifies the neumatic style of melody. Neumatic chants frequently use several tones to a single syllable of text but are not as predominately melismatic as the third melodic style.

Figure 8. Antiphon: Gloriosa et Beatissima, *final section.*

Figure 9 is a Gregorian setting of an Allelulia which serves well to illustrate the melismatic style. This example demonstrates the frequent practice of setting the final syllable of the Allelulia to an unusually long and florid melisma called the *jubilus.*

Al - le - lu - - - ia - - - - - - - - - -

Figure 9. Gregorian Alleluia *with a Jubilus.*

The Hebrew and Byzantine influences upon Gregorian plainsong resulted in an early chant that was predominately stepwise, with skips of thirds and fourths used only rarely. Then in the eighth and ninth centuries a resurgence of scholarship in the Frankish countries and England began to exert a strong influence upon the music of the Church. New musical centers developed such as the Monastery of St. Gall in Switzerland. Chants composed there (notably by the Monks Notker and Tuotilo) utilized larger intervals more frequently, and began to be more individualistic and humanly expressive—contrasting to the subjective impersonality of earlier times. This was accomplished in part through the increased use of skips. In particular, the interval of the third began to be used more often, a portent of the later development of triadic harmony and the diatonic tonal system.

Another innovation stemming from the northern influence was the practice of "troping" of which Tuotilo at St. Gall was one of the earliest masters. A trope is an embellishment or addition to a previously composed chant. At first these took the form of melismas added to the original chant; but words also were added, either to newly composed additions or to existing melismas in the original chant. These new texts amplified or explained the meaning of the original text and were added at any point in the chant. This practice became so prevalent, particularly in the Kyries, that by the time of the Council of Trent (1543–63) it was necessary for a ban to be placed on the use of tropes. The Kyries, however, continued to be known by the names of the tropes that were used with them.

One of the most frequently used melismas for troping was the jubilus, the name given to melismas occurring on the final syllable of the Allelulia. So many tropes were written for the jubilus melismas that the distinguishing label *"sequence"* was applied to this variety of trope. Sequences were originated by Notker at St. Gall around 870, and were written for almost every Mass. All except four were banned by the Council of Trent. The four which were retained in the liturgy are the *Dies Irae* (a famous melody used in the Requiem Mass), the *Lauda Sion,* the *Veni Sancte Spiritus,* and the *Victimae Paschali* (shown in fig. 7).

The performance practices for Gregorian chant owe much to the psalmody of the ancient Jewish liturgy. Psalm singing was used very early in the history of the Christian Church—certainly it was well established by the end of the third century. Since the psalms are built in unmetered verses of two lines, a natural manner of performance was to alternate one voice with another voice or group of voices. Hebrew psalm singing, then, set the precedent for the responsorial and antiphonal chants of the Roman Church.

The psalms using responsorial chants were originally sung by a cantor (soloist), with the congregation responding with an *Allelulia, Amen, Gloria Patri,* or other chant after each verse of the Psalm. As this manner of performance evolved, the responses became longer and more elaborate, and began to be performed by the choir rather than by the congregation. At the same time, the Psalm chant itself began to be abbreviated so that certain of the responses began to dominate this part of the liturgy. In performance the response is begun by a soloist singing a short section called the *incipit* (beginning), with the choir joining in at the point where an asterisk is found in the text. In the Mass the Allelulia and Gradual are typical chants of this type.

The antiphonal chants developed later than the responsorial and were also related to Jewish psalmodic practices. At first, the antiphon was a refrain used to separate the verses of the psalms but, as in the case of the responsorial chants, the antiphon soon became more important than the psalm itself. Essentially, the antiphonal method of performance consists of a divided choir singing verses in alternation.

Complete psalms are sung as a part of the Divine Offices, and each of the church modes has its own characteristic psalm-tone, a particular pitch which is used in that mode for intoning the text of the psalm in speech rhythm. A short stylized melodic formula called the *intonation* leads up to the psalm-tone, while the psalm-tone itself functions as the reciting tone. Other short melodic formulae called *mediants* are used as cadences to separate the verses of the psalm. Following the recitation, another melodic formula called the *differentia* leads downward to the final of the mode. The similarity between this manner of performance and the Hebrew chant shown in fig. 1 shows that this too is a vestige of ancient Jewish psalmody.

Chant Notation

Gregorian chant is notated on a four line staff with notational symbols called *neumes*—Predominantly square characters which indicate pitch and, to some extent, nuance. They are derived from accent signs in Greek and Latin literature used to indicate voice inflection for reading aloud. The acute (/) accent told the reader to raise the pitch level, while the grave (\) accent indicated descent in pitch. The acute developed into the neumatic symbol called the *virga,* while the grave became the *punctum.* Figure 10 shows the ancient inflection symbols and the simple neumes which developed from them.

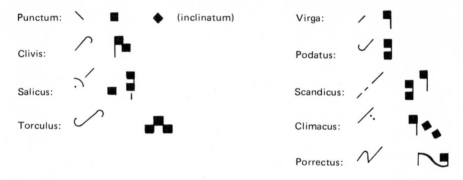

Figure 10. Early Inflection Symbols and Gregorian Neumes Which Developed from Them.

The earliest complete manuscript with neumes dates from the ninth century. The early neume notation was called *cheironomy* (hand direction), because a conductor led the singers by means of hand motions. The neumes were placed above the text to indicate higher and lower pitches but without exact pitch notation. The conductor's cheironomic motions probably served simply as reminders to the singers who undoubtedly had a large repertory of chants committed to memory.

In the eleventh century, perhaps as early as the year 1000, neumes began to be placed higher or lower above the text to indicate more or less specific pitch levels. Manuscripts of the time reveal that the neumes were placed in relation to one or more real or imaginary horizontal lines representing specific pitches. This type of notation, called *diastemic* notation or "heighted" neumes, is the earliest ancestor of our modern notation.

By the thirteenth century the neumes had evolved to the square notation shown in figure 10; and the four-line staff, which had been used as early as the eleventh century, became the norm. The musical theorist Guido of Arezzo (b. 995) is generally credited with the development of the four-line staff. Like our modern staff, the four-line staff indicates intervals of seconds between adjacent lines and spaces. The C or F clef placed at the left of the staff was the key to the specific pitches indicated by the lines and spaces. Compound neumes of two to four notes developed, as well as special neumes such as the *quilisma*, which indicated further subtlety of nuance. A description of all the conventionally used neumes is found in the *Liber Usualis,* a one-volume collection of the most frequently used chants.

There remains today some controversy about the rhythmic interpretation of Gregorian notation. All concede the importance of the rhythm of the words, but there is disagreement in regard to durations, groupings of notes and accents. The Benedictine Monks of Solesmes advanced what was once the most widely accepted theory—namely, that, for the most part, the neumes indicate notes of equal duration, like eighth notes, and that the first note of recognizable groups of two or three notes receives a slight, almost imaginary accent called an *ictus.* The ictus may or may not coincide with the word *accent,* but when viewed in longer units such as phrases, the rhythm of words and music are in agreement.

Figure 11 shows the opening of the Credo from the Gregorian Mass for Easter realized in both Gregorian and modern notation. In this case the C clef is used, designating the top line as middle C. Quarter-, half-, and full-bar lines in Gregorian notation indicate pauses or "breaths" of indefinite length, the quarter bar being the shortest pause, the half bar somewhat longer, and the full bar the longest. Double bars usually indicate the end of a sentence of text. The symbol found on a line or space at the extreme right of each staff is the *custos,* which tells the singer in advance what the first note will be on the next line.

The Church Modes and the Hexachord System

The medieval Church modes used for Gregorian chant are identified in ecclesiastical writings only by number. The Greek mode names, however, were applied to the Church modes in the tenth century and continue to be used today as common terminology among musicians. The modes are shown in figure 12 and it is apparent that the Greek names were misapplied, for there is little relationship between the Church modes shown here and the ancient Greek modes.

The "final" of each mode is the tone used (almost always) as the

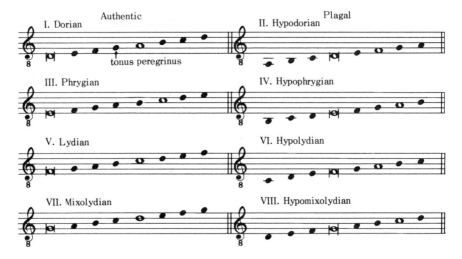

Figure 11. A Credo *Realized in Both Gregorian and Modern Notation.*

Figure 12. The Medieval Church Modes.

ending note for a chant composed in that mode. The finals are indicated in figure 12 by |o|. Note that the authentic mode and its related plagal mode have the same final. The essential difference between the plagal and authentic modes is their ranges, the plagal modes having generally lower ranges than their corresponding authentic modes.

For psalm recitation, each of the eight modes has its own psalm-tone—also called the *reciting tone, tenor,* or *dominant.* In the authentic modes, except for the Phrygian, the psalm-tone is a fifth above the final, which accounts for the later use of the term *dominant* as the fifth tone in the diatonic scale. In the Phrygian mode, the psalm-tone is on C. In the plagal modes, except for the Hypomixolydian, the psalm-tones are a third below the psalm tones in the corresponding authentic modes. In the Hypomixolydian mode, the psalm-tone is on C. The seeming irregularities in the Phrygian and Hypomixolydian modes are the result of the traditional avoidance of B as a psalm-tone. A rarely used psalm-tone called the *Tonus Peregrinus* is sometimes used in the Dorian mode (on G instead of A in the second half of the verse only). The psalm-tones are indicated in figure 12 by white notes.

The only accidental properly applied to the untransposed modes is B flat, which is used to avoid tritones and also as a descending passing tone between C and A in the Dorian and Lydian modes. B flat may also occur in a transposition such as a Dorian mode beginning on G. An occasional E flat may also be found in chants using transposed modes.

There are no church modes on A and C because the Dorian and Lydian modes with B flat added form patterns of intervals identical to the patterns on A and C, respectively. The Renaissance theorist Glareanus in 1547 added four modes to the original eight by adding authentic and plagal modes with finals on A and C, calling them *Aeolian, Hypoaeolian, Ionian,* and *Hypoionian.* These were never formally adopted into the liturgy, and to this day only the original eight modes are authorized by the Church. A mode on B was never used because of the diminished fifth between the first and fifth degrees, although the term *Locrian* was later applied to this hypothetical mode. Obviously, the Ionian and Aeolian modes are identical to the major and natural minor scales in the diatonic system.

As an aid to the performing music written in the Church modes Guido of Arezzo devised a hexachord (six-note scale) system using the syllables *ut, re, mi, fa, sol, la* to represent the first six pitches of the scale. These syllables were derived from the Hymn *Ut Queant laxis* by extracting the first syllable from each of its first six phrases, which happen to be arranged in regular stepwise-ascending order (see fig. 13).

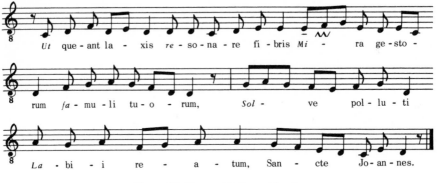

Figure 13. Hymn: Ut Queant Laxis.

It can readily be seen that these are the ancestors of our modern sol-feggio syllables in which *do* is substituted for *ut* and *ti* is added as the seventh scale degree.

The six syllables represent pitches arranged in an intervallic pattern identical to the first six tones of the diatonic scale and were used not only for convenient sight singing of chant, but also as an aid to reading other modal music, including polyphony. Seven such hexachords beginning on G, C, and F (with B flat) were arranged in a scale system extending from the G on the bottom line of our bass staff to the E on the top space of our treble staff (see fig. 14). Pitches in specific octaves were identified by the letter name and the syllable for all hexachords that included that pitch, for example, a *la mi re* for the A below middle C, or c *sol fa ut* for middle C. The lowest pitch in the system was called G *ut* or Gamma *ut,* and from this came the term *gamut,* meaning the entire scale, a word which has come down to us with a similar though not exclusively musical meaning.

In each hexachord the interval between mi and fa is a semitone, while all other intervals are whole steps. To accomplish this, the hexachord on G used the B natural indicated by the sign ♮ (a "hard" or square b), while the hexachord on F used B flat indicated by the sign ♭ (a "soft" or round b). These symbols are the ancestors of our modern sharp, natural, and flat signs. The hexachord on C was called the *natural* hexachord because it needed no distinguishing symbol, while the hexachords on F and G were called, respectively, *molle* (soft) and *durum* (hard) because of the symbols used to distinguish between B and B flat. These symbols, however, should not be viewed as accidentals in the modern sense.

In order to perform melodies that spanned more than one hexa-

e''						la
d''					la	sol
c''					sol	fa
b'						mi
b-flat'						
a'				la	fa	
g'				sol	mi	re
f'				fa	re	ut
e'			la	mi	ut	Durum
d'		la	sol	re	Molle	(Hard)
c'		sol	fa	ut	(Soft)	7.
b			mi	Naturale	6.	
b-flat		fa		(Natural)		
a	la	mi	re	5.		
g	sol	re	ut			
f	fa	ut	Durum			
e	la	mi	Molle	(Hard)		
d	sol	re	(Soft)	4.		
c	fa	ut	3.			
B	mi	Naturale				
A	re	(Natural)				
G	ut	2.				
	Durum					
	(Hard)					
	1.					

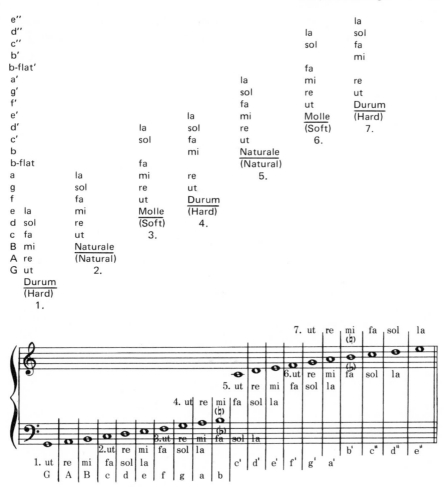

Figure 14. The Hexachord System.

chord it was necessary to shift from one hexachord to another. This process was called *mutation* and was usually accomplished at *re* of the new hexachord when ascending or at *la* when descending. *Mi* and *fa* were never separated in the mutation process, and they alone could be used to denote the semitone.

The process of sight singing by means of the syllables and the hexachord system was called *solmization* and was used well into the sixteenth century. Guido devised a teaching aid called the "Guidonian hand" in which the joints of the fingers of the left hand represented the twenty pitches of the scale system. Virtually every music textbook from Guido's time through the Renaissance included a picture of this hand.

Secular Music

Although medieval music history centers upon music for the church, a flourishing secular* art also began to grow. The first notated examples date from the seventh century, but secular music obviously had existed from the earliest times. From the tenth to the thirteenth centuries itinerant students and minor clerics, collectively known as *Goliards,* roamed throughout Europe playing a significant role in the secular culture of the time. Of their music little is known, for although some of it was notated in staffless neumes, only one manuscript has been deciphered. It is known, however, that among the Goliards were some of the intellectual elite of the time, and the texts of their songs touched every sphere of human activity.

Numerous Goliard song texts are found in a collection called *Carmina Burana,* named after the monastery *Benediktbeuern* where they were discovered. (*Beuern [Burana]* is a cognate of *Bayern* or Bavarian.) These Burana songs, written in Latin with some German and French mixed in, include satires on the Church, State, and human behavior, as well as numerous earthy lyrics on the joys of food, drink, and sensual love. The German composer Carl Orff in 1937 used a number of these texts in an attractive work for chorus and orchestra entitled *Carmina Burana.*

The twelfth and thirteenth centuries was a time of plagues, wars, and general suffering; a mood of almost fanatical penitence pervaded Europe and was manifest in strong popular religious movements. As a result of this zeitgeist, colonies of penitents and flagellants sprang up, particularly in Germany and Italy. These groups, who traveled from place to place whipping themselves and singing religious songs, were known in Italy as *Laudisti* after the songs of praise *(Laude)* they sang, and in Germany as *Geissler.* A few of their monophonic strophic songs are preserved in plainsong notation. The Geisslerlieder possess a remarkable similarity to the Lutheran choral tunes of the sixteenth century, while the *laude,* which were made possible by St. Francis of Assisi's efforts to allow the laity to create their own hymns, were precursors of the Baroque oratorio.

---

*As applied to medieval music, a better term might be "music in life." "Secular" is retained here because of its common usage in this sense.

The *conductus* is another type of monophonic song which, like the laude and geisslerlieder, falls into a gray area between liturgical music and secular song. Originally *conductus* probably meant "introduction," but it was also sung as walking music to "conduct" a celebrant in the Mass or an actor in a liturgical drama from one place to another. The metrical Latin texts were set to newly composed melodies rather than being adapted from chant. By 1300 the term conductus was loosely applied to any serious nonliturgical Latin song, whether sacred or secular.

Of great significance to the history of secular music are the troubadors, trouveres, and jongleurs. The troubadors were poet-musicians of southern France, knights and commoners who, in the period of 1100–1300, developed a type of stylized courtly poetry which they set to music. They were assisted by jongleurs (jugglers), professional entertainers who played the viele, the most important stringed instrument of the twelfth and thirteenth centuries. The jongleurs exemplified the strong secular currents that were awakening in the period. Dating from the tenth century, they traveled from place to place, patching together their livings with acrobatics, dancing, singing, and fiddling. The more fortunate ones were taken into the households of the nobility, thus gaining the status of minstrels. One of the types of monophonic songs that they performed were the *chansons de geste,* narrative epic poems with vernacular texts, of which the most famous is the Song of Roland. The jongleurs undoubtedly assisted the troubadors and trouveres in the more technical aspects of composition as well as accompanying and singing their songs.

The language used by the troubadors was the Provencal *langue d'oc* (*oc* was the word for yes) of southern France. Much of their poetry is based on the theme of courtly love, particularly of the unrequited variety. The stylized poems fall into categories such as *sirventes* (songs of fealty), *plaintes* (mourning songs), *albas* (morning songs warning lovers of approaching dawn), *pastourelles* (songs of the knight repulsed by the shepherdess), and various types of love songs. Their music was monophonic, with heterophonic accompaniments which may have included instrumental introductions and interludes. Notated on staves like plainsong, these modal melodies show the influence of melismatic chant. Modal rhythms using the poetic meters were probably used in some of the songs, particularly those intended for dancing. The two basic musical forms utilized by the troubadors are (1) the *canzo,* a form with six or seven verses with a resultant AAB form, and (2) the *vers,* a strophic form.

About fifty years later than the troubadors were the trouveres, aristocratic poet-musicians of northern France. Their music is of particular interest for its variety and sophistication of form. Like the troubadors', the trouveres' works were performed by the jongleurs, who must have contributed much to the shape of the tunes invented by their masters, finding musical solutions to the formal problems presented by the elaborate and highly varied poetic structures. These forms fall into four general types: (1) hymn—a through composed form; (2) litany—a strophic form; (3) sequence—a variable form derived from the liturgical sequence; and (4) refrain—dance songs in a variety of forms including the rondeau, virelai, and ballade (an AAB form). The refrains in this last category were usually sung by the audience or chorus while a soloist or dance leader sang the stanzas in various formal patterns. This type of form remained popular for centuries.

The trouveres used the language of northern France, the *langue d' oil* (with *oil* for yes) from which modern French developed, but the southern influence is seen in their use of many of the same stylized poetical subjects used by the troubadors. In particular, they favored the pastourelle, which they developed into a dialogue with incidental songs and dances—actually a musical play. The most famous of these is the *Jeu de Robin et de Marion,* written around 1284 by Adam de la Halle, who can be viewed as the progenitor of poetic music-drama. Adam was the last and most distinguished of the trouveres, but also included in their number were Blondel de Nesle, King Richard the Lion Hearted, and King Thibaut of Navarre.

The principal instrumental form of the thirteenth and fourteenth centuries was a type of dance music called the *estampie.* Derived from the sequence, it consisted of three to seven sections called *puncta,* each repeated. The earliest known example is *Kalenda Maya,* shown in figure 15, containing three *puncta.* This is the only example of an estampie with a text; all of the others are purely instrumental dances. This example serves well to illustrate the tendency among the troubadors and trouveres toward the use of modes which closely approximate our major and minor scales, for it seems to be very clearly in the key of C major.

It is generally believed that the rhythm of the troubadors and trouveres was controlled by the rhythmic modes (see fig. 16). These modes are similar to the Greek quantitative poetic meters (fig. 2) but are really not descended from them, for many differences will be noted. Their rhythm corresponds to modern triple meter with agogic accents accounting for the differences among the various modes. A system of *ordines* determined the number of times a modal pattern was repeated without a break; the second ordo indicated one repetition; the third ordo, two repetitions; and so on.

Figure 15. Kalenda Maya *Raimbault de Vaqueiras.*

The secular art of the jongleurs and their noble masters existed side by side with the profoundly beautiful and highly developed liturgical music of the time. The ideals of the crusades furnished the minstrels with a new source of inspiration, but the real genesis of secular music was found in the monasteries where troping and sequencing was practiced with such loving care—St. Gall, of course, but also St. Martial at Limoges in the South, for it was the area of Limoges that

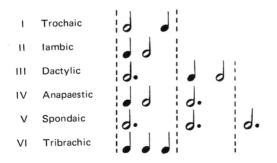

Figure 16. Medieval Rhythmic Modes.

produced the first troubadors. At the height of this courtly art the jongleurs played a most important part in its music, and through them the art was carried to later ages by their less illustrious descendents, the ballad singers and itinerant players.

A later counterpart of the troubadors and trouveres is found in the German minnesingers (love singers) who flourished in the thirteenth and fourteenth centuries. Their poetical subjects and musical forms were similar to those of the troubadors and trouveres, but their texts were generally more serious in nature. They made frequent use of duple meter, and used the bar form which followed the AAB shape of the *canzo* and the ballade. From them descended the meistersingers of the fifteenth and sixteenth centuries. Members of both groups were made famous in the nineteenth century by Wagner's use of them as characters in his music dramas. Names such as Tannhäuser and Hans Sachs mean much to the opera lover, but are of only passing interest to the student of early music. Nevertheless, some attractive music was produced by the minnesingers, while the meistersingers gave us the concept of musical guilds.

Of the music and poetry of the troubadors and trouveres, we have numerous examples, since much of it was copied professionally. There are about 300 extant melodies and 2,500 poems of the troubadors, while the trouveres left about 1,400 melodies and nearly 4,000 poems. Undoubtedly some of this was actually composed by the jongleurs, but this is conjectural since they could not afford copyists and their position in society did not entitle them to the privileges of authorship. Concurrent with this flowering secular art, music for the Church was experiencing profound changes through the beginning development of polyphony, to which we shall now turn our attention.

2. The Beginnings of Polyphony

Organum—Conductus—Motet—British Polyphony

Music in two or more distinct voice lines must have existed much earlier than historical documentation shows. Primitive man might well have stumbled upon the happy idea of adding a sustained stationary pitch to an existing melody, or of adding a moving voice starting on a different pitch than the original voice and maintaining a parallel relationship to it. Indeed, the drone and parallelism may have been the first forms of polyphony; and their earliest use undoubtedly was a source of strange delight to primitive man.

Aristoxenus of Tarentum (c. 354 B.C.), from whom we received much of our knowledge of Greek music, is one of the earliest authors whose writings suggest the existence of polyphony. Although the generally accepted theory is that Greek music was monophonic and heterophonic, some of Aristoxenus' comments on consonance and dissonance suggest that polyphony may have been practiced. Other later writings, such as those of Boethius in the sixth century A.D. and Joannes Scotus in the ninth century, allude to what might be part-singing, and a treatise by Cambrensis in the twelfth century describes two-part singing which may have existed for centuries among the musical folk of Wales.

Organum

The earliest tangible evidence of polyphony in the church is found in the *Musica Enchiriadis* (manual of music) dated around 850, questionably attributed to the monk Hucbald. The *Schola Enchiriadis*, dating from about the same time, but probably by a different author, amplifies and explains the *Musica Enchiriadis* by means of dialogue technique. The term *organum* is applied to the polyphony of the period from 800–1250, consisting in its simplest form of a "tenor" (principal or original melody) from plainsong with a second contrapuntal part added.

The examples in *Musica Enchiriadis* are written in two-part organum in which the perfect fourth and fifth are consonances which may move in strict parallel motion, while the intervals of the second and third may occur near the beginning or end of a phrase in the process of moving from a unison (in the case of a unison opening) or moving to a unison to close the phrase. The practice of ending a phrase on a unison produced the earliest form of the *clausula vera* (true close), in which the interval of a third closes in contrary motion to a unison. A cadence of this type is found in the example in figure 17. Note that the example proceeds in strict simple organum at the fourth (diatessaron) until arriving at the occursus (cadence), where the two voices converge through a third to a unison. The upper voice is the plainsong tenor beginning on the first psalm tone (*Tonus Protus*) in a transposed mode, while the lower is called the *organal voice.* Simple organum in this discussion refers to counterpoint consisting of two undoubled voices, but there are examples in *Musica Enchiriadis* of "composite" organum in which a semblance of four voices is created by doubling the *vox principalis* (plainsong tenor) at the octave below and the *vox organalis* at the octave above. Figure 18 is such an example and would be described as strict composite organum at the fifth (diapente).

Figure 17. Two Part Simple Organum.

Guido of Arezzo figures prominently in the history of organum, principally for his *Micrologus,* a short treatise on the organal practices of the early eleventh century. Probably written around 1040, it allows greater contrapuntal freedom than the *Musica Enchiriadis.* One notable distinction from the earlier treatise is that in Guido's strict organum, parallel fifths are considered less satisfactory than parallel fourths. All intervals smaller than the fifth are permitted between two voices except the diminished fifth, tritone, and half step. The perfect

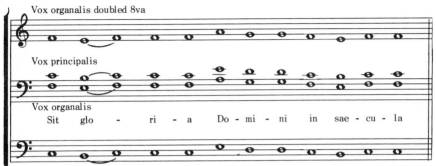

Figure 18. Two Part Composite Organum.

fifth itself is avoided in Guido's free organum. Greater freedom is found also in the fact that the organal voice may be sustained while several notes occur in the principal voice. Crossing of voices is also permitted and the two voices need not end at the same time. Figure 19 is an example of free organum from the *Micrologus.*

Although the *Musica Enchiriadis* and the *Micrologus* were the only written discussions of organum up to 1100, we may conclude that it was practiced widely, particularly as improvisation. Evidence of this is found in the fact that two treatises dated around 1100, *De Musica* of John Cotton (also called *Affligemensis*) and the anonymous *Ad Or-*

Figure 19. Free Organum from the Micrologus.

ganum Faciendum, contain substantial descriptions of free organum. In *De Musica* several notes may occur in the organal voice to one note in the principal voice—the reverse was found in the *Micrologus.* But the most significant innovation in both *De Musica* and *Ad Organum Faciendum* is that now the organal voice is sometimes found above the principal voice, a phenomenon important to the later development of polyphony. An earlier example of this is found in the *Winchester Troper,* an important English collection of two-part organa dating from the early eleventh century.

In France the abbey of St. Martial at Limoges was as important to polyphony as it was to troping and the development of secular music. The St. Martial organum of the early twelfth century used the early note-against-note style, but in a metrical framework. The example in figure 20 shows the typical modal rhythm of the St. Martial School. This metrical note-against-note style later became known as the *conductus style* after the nonliturgical monophonic conductus from which it developed (see chap. 2). This example is typical of the conductus style in that the organal voice is on top, and that the vox principalis is not a plainsong melody.

Another innovation of the St. Martial School is the development of *organum purum* or *organum duplum,* shown in figure 21. The upper voice (vox organalis) was known as the *duplum* and became more elaborate and rhythmically free, while the notes of the vox principalis were so prolonged that the lower voice became, essentially, a cantus firmus. The conductus style shown in figure 20 and the purum or duplum of figure 21 were sometimes combined in a single work to create forms with contrasting textures, as in the *Viderunt Hemanuel* of the St. Martial School shown in figure 22. The use of soloists seen in this example was typical also of organum composed at the cathedral of Chartres in the eleventh century. Other centers during the early stages of organum existed in Spain, England, and Germany.

The rhythmic modes discussed in the preceding chapter (see figure 16) were essential to the development of polyphony—more so than to monophonic music simply because music in two or more voices required the rhythmic coordination furnished by the modes. Unlike the Greek quantitative poetic meters, a feeling of triple meter was always present regardless of the mode, each unit of three beats being called a *perfectio.* The system developed gradually and with it grew a rhythmic notation in which ligatures were added to the Gregorian notation to tell the singer which mode to use. These ligatures are the ancestors of the stems used in present day rhythmic notation. Developing during the twelfth and thirteenth centuries, the rhythmic modes were of great

Figure 20. Mira Lege, Miro Modo, *Strophic Hymn of the St. Martial School.*

Figure 21. Organum Duplum of St. Martial.

Figure 22. St. Martial Organum Using Duplum and Conductus.

importance to organum composers associated with the cathedral of Notre Dame in Paris.

In the Notre Dame School, two composers are of particular significance in that they are the first composers of polyphony whose names are known to us. They are Leonin, who was active during the latter half of the twelfth century, and his successor Perotin, who died in the early thirteenth century. Leonin, who was called the *"optimus organista"* (greatest composer of organum), composed a monumental collection of organa for use in the Mass and divine offices called *Magnus Liber Organi de Graduali et Antiphonario.* This collection no longer exists in its original form, but there are several extant manuscripts containing music from it. Many of the organa in the *Magnus Liber* combine the two styles which had been used earlier at St. Martial. They are (1) the melismatic style, which is like the organum purum or duplum of the St. Martial School, and (2) clausulae in discant style, which is like the note-against-note conductus style except for the use of chant tunes (fragments from melismas) and that occasionally the upper voice would carry two or three notes to a single note in the lower voice. A "clausula" is a section composed in discant style, while the term organum is often applied restrictively to the first type to distinguish it from the clausula.

The tenors of Leonin's melismatic organum, because of the inordinate length of each tone, may have been performed by instruments rather than by voices, or perhaps by both. At any rate, the words of the original chant were given in the tenor even though, due to the excessive augmentation of each tone, both words and melody would have been unrecognizable in performance. Many of these drone-like tenors use only two or three syllables of the original syllabic chant.

Perotin, who was called *"optimus discantor"* (greatest composer of discant), revised parts of Leonin's *Magnus Liber* by composing new upper parts (clausulae) in two-part discant style and, in some instances, by expanding the organa to three or four parts. From the two-part clausulae, composed in great numbers by Perotin and his contemporaries, developed the medieval motet.

The tenors of the clausulae of the Notre Dame school were derived from fragments of melismas in Gregorian chant, while the tenors of organum (as distinct from clausulae) were from those portions of the original chant which were predominately syllabic (usually solo sections). The composers, in making a polyphonic setting of a chant, would choose to compose a clausula or an organum according to the melodic style in the various sections of the original chant. The tenors of the clausulae, since they moved faster than those of organum, were well suited to presenting the slow-moving words of melismatic chant, while the drone-like organum tenors could set forth more words by utilizing syllabic chant. The tenors in clausulae, as seen in figure 23, were in modal rhythm, and often moved in a pattern equivalent to a series of dotted quarter notes. The upper voice, also in modal rhythm, frequently utilized smaller note values.

Perotin's three- or four-part organa were known as *organa tripla* or *organa quadrupla,* depending upon the number of parts. The organum quadruplum excerpt shown in figure 24 illustrates a number of features of Perotin's style. An important innovation is the frequent use of triadic sonorities, although the empty perfect intervals were still considered to be the strong consonances in that they were invariably used at the ends of phrases. In addition to showing Perotin's characteristic use of modal rhythm, the *Viderunt* illustrates a number of his contributions to the development of polyphony, including his rudimentary use of canon (triplum measures 7-8 answered by quadruplum measures 9-10). The *Sederunt Principes,* another famous organum quadruplum by Perotin, is notable for its rhythmic freedom and striking dissonances.

Because of the modal rhythms in Perotin's organum, the melodies in the upper voices often have a lilt that is almost dance-like, while the tenors, as in Leonin's organum, are nearly stationary. Thus, there are essentially two textural strata—the two or three upper voices with their unified rhythm, and the drone-like tenor. Although triadic

Figure 23. Beginning of Clausula from Haec Dies.

Figure 24. Viderunt, *Perotin.*

sonorities occur, the harmonic movement cannot be equated with eighteenth-century harmony, which functions in relation to a tonal center. Rather, there is a static feeling of harmonic "hovering" over each sustained tenor tone (some of which continue through a hundred or so measures of the upper voices), so that one might describe the sections as harmonic "successions" but certainly not as harmonic progressions, for the concept of modulation is totally foreign to this music.

Conductus

Another type of thirteenth-century polyphony, sometimes included under the general heading of organum, is the polyphonic conductus, mentioned earlier as originating at St. Martial during the twelfth century. These were composed by Perotin and other composers of the Notre Dame school, generally in a simpler style than organum. Like the monophonic conductus, they used nonliturgical texts, usually on sacred or serious secular subjects. Aside from the fact that they did not use preexisting chant tunes, their most significant musical distinction is that, unlike the liturgical organa of the Notre Dame school, all of the voices (usually three) move in equal rhythm. This characteristic note-against-note syllabic texture became known as "conductus style," and is a predecessor of the Renaissance "familiar style."

The musical effect of conductus style was that of chords moving in modal (triple) rhythm, with occasional modest embellishments in melismatic style called *caudae.* The caudae were most frequent at cadences but also occurred occasionally at the beginning.

As in much of the organum of this time, the voices crossed and recrossed frequently, all within a relatively narrow pitch range. A favorite polyphonic device in conducti is the repetition of a passage with interchange of contrapuntal material among the various voices, a technique that is of interest to the history of polyphony even though it cannot properly be called double counterpoint since all of the voices are equal. More important is the fact that the conductus is the first instance of a polyphonic work composed entirely of new material without the use of preexisting melodies such as chant tunes. Figure 25 is an example of a conductus of the Notre Dame school to a text on the death of Thomas a Becket.

Motet

The history of the motet can be divided into three large periods: the medieval motet (1220–1450), the Renaissance (originally Flemish)

Figure 25. Novus Miles Sequitur, *An Example of Conductus.*

motet (1450–1600), and the Baroque motet (1600–1750). We are concerned here with the medieval motet, which was described by Johannes Grocheo in his treatise *Theoria* (c. 1300) as being a "song composed of several texts, in which two voices at a time are consonant." He goes on to say that "this type of song, however, is not fitting for the common people because they neither sense its subtleties nor are delighted when listening to it. But it is suitable for the educated and those who seek the refinements of the arts." Thus, the medieval motet is an early example of "art music" and was recognized in its own time as possessing esoteric qualities.

Just as sequences developed in the ninth century by the addition of texts to the jubili, so the motet originated in the early thirteenth century by the addition of texts to the dupla (upper parts) of the two-voice clausulae composed by Perotin and his contemporaries. The term *motet* or *motetus* comes from the French word *mot* (word), and is related to the fact that "words" (*mots*) were added to the dupla. Indeed, the term motetus was at first used to indicate the duplum voice, and only later came to be applied to the entire composition. After 1250, motets began to be composed in two, three, or four voices without being derived from preexisting clausulae.

The motet composer began by selecting a melismatic chant tune (typically a gradual, allelulia, or responsory), taking a fragment from it to use as a tenor, and then casting it in a pattern using one or more of the rhythmic modes. One, two, or three voices were then added over repetitions of the original pattern in the tenor to form a two-, three-, or four-voice motet. The number of repetitions of the tenor were controlled by the ordo system discussed earlier.

The text of the duplum amplified or explained the meaning of the original chant. When additional voices existed, the triplum and quadruplum at first carried the same text as the duplum, this type of composition being quite suitable for church performance in the manner of a clausula. But later, new texts were added to the upper voices, sometimes on subjects totally unrelated to the original chant, such as the text of a dance song or trouvere melody. The languages of the texts also began to vary among the separate voices so that in a given motet one might find a Latin tenor and a French duplum and triplum, each on a different subject. In a few instances German or English texts were used.

After 1275 three-voice motets were most common, with the triplum as the dominant voice. With the increasing secularization of the motet, even the tenors began to be taken from non-liturgical sources such as tropes, trouvere melodies, estampies, and even Paris street cries. Also, the tenors began to move more freely, with the ordines being applied less strictly. Undoubtedly the tenor parts were often performed on instruments, for even when a Gregorian tenor was used, only the first syllable (*incipit*) was included in the text. Composers of the late thirteenth century began to think in a more truly contrapuntal manner and the voices began to have greater rhythmic independence, as illustrated in the example of figure 26. Motets with the degree of rhythmic independence found in this example are sometimes called Franconian motets after Franco of Cologne, a late thirteenth-century composer and theorist whose treatise *Ars Cantus Mensurabilis* is important to our knowledge of the rhythmic practices of his time. Franco's description of rhythmic notation is more of a codification of thirteenth-century practices than an outline of a new system, but it is significant to music history in that it contains the main ingredients of modern rhythmic notation. The system, which was based on the rhythmic modes, provided a means by which more or less exact durations of tones could be indicated in the notation and measured in performance. In the fourteenth century Phillippe de Vitry (c. 1290–1361) used Franco's system as a point of departure from which to develop the mensural notation of the *Ars Nova* (to be discussed in the next chapter).

While rhythm is a vital element of all music, whether for one voice or many, the task of coordinating the various voices in the early polyphonic compositions brought rhythmic problems to the fore. Thus, the earliest significant events in the history of rhythm in Western music occurred during the beginnings of polyphony—most of all during the thirteenth and fourteenth centuries. Aside from developments in notation, this is seen in a breaking away from the domination of the ponderous, slow-moving tenors. Also, smaller note values began to appear in the upper voices, particularly in the triplum, and a more lively contrapuntal texture began to develop. Pierre de la Croix of Amiens is known for his utilization of the smaller note values (he is sometimes given credit for inventing them). Around the beginning of the fourteenth century he, and composers who wrote in his style, composed motets of considerable rhythmic interest, even utilizing rests in unusual and expressive ways.

The use of rests in the thirteenth century is also seen in a device known as the *hocket* or *hoquetus* in which the melodic flow of one of the upper voices is interrupted by a rest which is filled in by another voice. (Apparently the brief sporadic stoppages of the singer's breath sounded like hiccups, for the term "hocket" comes from the Latin *ochetus,* literally "hiccup.") In the early thirteenth century the voice part using this device was called the *hoquetus;* but the term was also

Figure 26. Motet: Pucelete–Je Languis–Domino.

applied to complete compositions which used hockets frequently. Figure 27 is an excerpt from such an example. In this hocket, note that rests occur in all four voices, but that only the uppermost voice has a complete text. One may conclude that the three lower parts were intended for instruments. The *In Seculum* tenor used here, a fragment of the Easter Gradual *Haec Dies,* is one of the most popular tenors of thirteenth-century clausulae and motets.

Figure 27. Hocket: Ja N'amerai Autre—In Seculum.

In the quotation from Grocheo cited earlier, note his statement that in the motet "two voices are consonant." Franco says essentially the same thing in his treatise when he says that the tenor should be written first, then the duplum, and that a third voice, if added, should agree with either the tenor or the duplum. The composer's procedure, then, was one of adding voices to a previously composed two-voice texture, taking care that the added voice be consonant with one of the other voices. This caused some rather startling incidental dissonances in the nonconsonant voice. It should be remembered, however, that much less attention was given to the vertical dimension of music than in modern times. Musicians and audiences did not really think and hear harmonically, in the modern sense, until perhaps 1600. Thus, as long as the consonances occurred at the proper points, the ear accepted what happened in between. These consonances, as in organum, were still the perfect fifth and octave, with thirds and sixths being accepted as imperfect consonances. Most medieval motets begin and end with perfect consonances without thirds, although a gradual trend toward triadic harmony can be seen.

Many questions about performance practices in thirteenth-century polyphony remain yet to be answered. Although there is no doubt that motet tenors were derived from Gregorian chant and that performance in the Church service could have been possible for many motets, it is not definitely known that they were, in fact, used in the service. Certain motets, because of secular, even salacious texts in the upper parts, could not have been used liturgically. Yet the larger portion of the motet literature utilized texts that were thoroughly appropriate to the service, and it is quite possible that they were performed in church in the same manner as clausulae.

Of the instruments in use during this period, the vielle is the most important. This bowed stringed instrument was popular until the fifteenth century, when it began to be supplanted by the viols. Played in a manner similar to the violin, it had four fingered strings plus a drone string. A fifteenth-century mechanical variety of vielle called the *hurdy-gurdy* utilized a rosined wheel in place of the bow. The rebec was a less popular type of medieval fiddle. Also in use during this time were plucked stringed instruments including the lute; percussion instruments of many kinds including bells, drums, tambourines, cymbals, etc.; winds such as flute types, the shawm (a double reed), brass instruments; and the organ and stringed keyboard instruments.

There is pictorial and written evidence that instruments were used with voices in motet performance. Certainly they were used to reinforce or substitute for the voice on the tenor line, and it is quite possible that they were used in the upper voices as well. The absence of texts in some upper parts supports the latter theory, and it may be that some motets were performed as solo songs with instrumental accompaniment, the voice performing the triplum with instruments on the other parts. The choice of one instrument over another was made by the performers, since the practice of assigning specific instruments to the various parts of the music did not begin until the late sixteenth century.

The medieval motet, partly because of its increasing secularization, declined in importance during the fourteenth century. Nevertheless, its linear structure, formal clarity, rhythmic interest, and contrapuntal innovation laid the groundwork for many future developments. It represents a peak of achievement in pre-fourteenth century music.

British Polyphony

Free organum existed in England as early as the eleventh century. As mentioned previously, the *Winchester Troper,* an early eleventh-century manuscript, contains organa for the mass and offices in which the vox organalis is above the vox principalis, one of the earliest examples of this important development. A type of English organum called *gymel* was probably practiced as improvisation much earlier than historical documentation indicates. It consisted of two voices moving in parallel thirds and/or sixths. Manuscripts from the thirteenth century contain examples of gymel with liturgical as well as secular texts. There are also English manuscripts of conducti from the thirteenth century and motets from the early fourteenth century.

English composers of the fourteenth century composed a type of polyphony called *English discant,* which could be described in modern terms as first inversion triads in three voices moving in parallel motion, one of the voices serving as a cantus firmus derived from a chant melody. The fifteenth-century French device known as *fauxbourdon* can be described in exactly the same way. The distinction between them is found in the position of the cantus firmus. In English discant it is in the lower voice, while in fauxbourdon the cantus firmus is on top. The term fauxbourdon is also used today in a somewhat different sense to describe passages in keyboard music in which first inversion triads move diatonically in parallel motion, usually over a pedal point.

Perhaps the most famous piece of English music from this time is a rota or round called "Sumer is icumen in" (c. 1300). The round in this case is a four-part canon at the unison sung against repetitions of an eight-bar accompaniment figure in two voices called a *pes.* The pes of "Sumer is icumen in," shown in figure 28, utilizes a technique known as *stimmtausch,* in which the two equal voices exchange parts. Note that the first four bars in the upper voice are identical to the last four in the lower, and vice-versa. Stimmtausch was used also by the composers of the Notre Dame school.

The period in music history from about 1150 to 1450 is sometimes called the Gothic period to correspond to the Gothic era in architecture,

Figure 28. An Example of Stimmtausch: Pes of Sumer is Icumen In.

painting, and sculpture. The period from 1250 to 1300, is known as the *Ars Antiqua* or "old art," to distinguish pre-fourteenth century French music from the music of the *Ars Nova.* The term *Ars Nova* is sometimes loosely applied to all music of the fourteenth century, but in the strictest sense should be used only for French music of the period from 1300 to 1350.

3. Pre-Renaissance Music (1300-1450)

*Mensural Notation—The Ars Nova in France—
The Italian Trecento—Musical Instruments—English
Music—Burgundian School*

The term *Ars Nova* was coined by Phillipe de Vitry around 1320 as the title of a treatise in which he described musical developments which were recognized, even in their own time, as being highly innovative. The period of the early 1300's was indeed a major turning point in musical thought and, as a result of the new developments, composers began to look upon themselves more self-consciously as artists—manifesting the increasing secularism and humanism that would come to flower in the Renaissance. The growth of a culture quite separate from the Church also produced remarkable results in literature and the other arts. Boccaccio, Chaucer, and Dante are examples of fourteenth-century writers who produced great works based on secular themes. In painting, Giotto (c. 1266–1337) began to break away from Byzantine formalism toward a more naturalistic representation of objects perceived, though he continued to use sacred subjects. Humanism, the guiding spirit of the Renaissance, found its beginnings during this period as seen in a renewed interest in ancient Greek and Roman literature.

A gradual movement away from the stable, Church-centered viewpoint of earlier periods gained momentum in all aspects of European culture. At the same time there were divisions within the church. The papal center moved to Avignon, and at one point there were as many as three rival claimants to the papacy. High ecclesiastical leaders were accused of corruption, often with good reason, and criticisms of the church and the clergy were expressed in writings as well as in movements away from the church—portents of the Protestant reformation to come in the sixteenth century.

The inharmonious state of affairs within the Church was paralleled by unrest in secular society; it was a time of economic and political chaos. Plagues and wars swept through Europe leaving poverty and despair behind and causing insurrection among the lower classes. Medieval chivalry, a vestige of aristocratic feudalism, continued as a mere formality, and a strong middle class began to grow. In Italy many small independent states were established, each with its own ruler who frequently patronized the arts and letters by establishing his own coterie of poets, artists, and musicians. In France there was a movement toward a centralized absolute monarchy, even though the general trend thoughout Europe was toward political disunity.

These changes, some of which had appeared in beginning form prior to the fourteenth century, were reflected in music by extremes of rhythmic subtlety which required a better system of rhythmic notation, as well as by innovations in harmonic and structural principles. Melody began to be treated more expressively, there was a new interest in secular polyphony, and the ordinary of the Mass for the first time was used as a matrix upon which to build a single complete composition. Parallelisms continued to be used, but more often in thirds and sixths than in fourths and fifths. Also thirds and sixths were used more often on the strong beats as consonances, although the final sonority continued to be a fifth, octave, or unison. The motet continued to be developed in the fourteenth century, but its popularity began to give way to new secular forms, typically in the general category of the accompanied solo song. The music of this time showed diversity, innovation, and a new kind of human expressiveness—traits which are curiously typical of the early Baroque period three centuries later and again of the early twentieth century. These three chronological points in music history, separated as they are by regular periods of three hundred years, suggest a kind of cycle in the development of musical thought—a period of discontent, diversity, and innovation followed by a longer period of stylistic stability and unification, which in its turn is upset by a new cycle of unrest and reaction.

Mensural Notation

Shortly after de Vitry's *Ars Nova*, other writers began to refer to the previous period of 1250 to 1300 as the *Ars Antiqua*, clearly illustrating that French musicians of the time were well aware of the significance of these new developments.* The increased rhythmic freedom and smaller note values appearing in the upper parts of late

*Jacques de Liége (c. 1270–c. 1330), more than any other writer, congealed this terminology for us.

thirteenth-century motets (such as those by Pierre de la Croix) anticipated the developments described by de Vitry. By 1300 the lunga, breve, semi-breve, and minim were in common use, to which were added in the early fourteenth century the semi-minim, the fusa, and the semi-fusa (see figure 29). Composers striving to increase the lightness and flexibility of the upper parts found themselves hampered by dependence upon the rhythmic modes. Aside from the question of smaller note values, the modes imposed the restriction of triple meter, which was thought to be associated with the "perfection" of the trinity (hence, the term *perfectus* for triple meter). Because of this, duple or "imperfect" meter held strong secular, if not profane, connotations and was slow in coming into common use. Its increased use by *Ars Nova* composers, then, is another indication of the greater prominence given to secular art.

A major contribution of the *Ars Nova* composers was the reorganization of rhythmic notation into a system called mensural (measured) notation which used Franco's late thirteenth-century system as a point of departure. Although Franco had described both triple and duple divisions of the lunga, the duple division had been rarely used. Phillipe de Vitry and his contemporaries placed duple meter on an equal basis with triple meter—a great step away from the shackling influence of the modes. In the new system the choice of dividing the long (lunga) into two or three breves was indicated by the mode or mood (not to be confused with the rhythmic modes). *Modus Perfectus* denoted a triple division of the long, while *modus imperfectus* indicated a division into two parts. The next metrical level was known as *tempus* or *time* and referred to divisions of the breve into semi-breves. Again, the terms perfectus or imperfectus indicated the triple or duple division. Finally, *prolatio* or prolation referred to the divisions of the semi-breve into

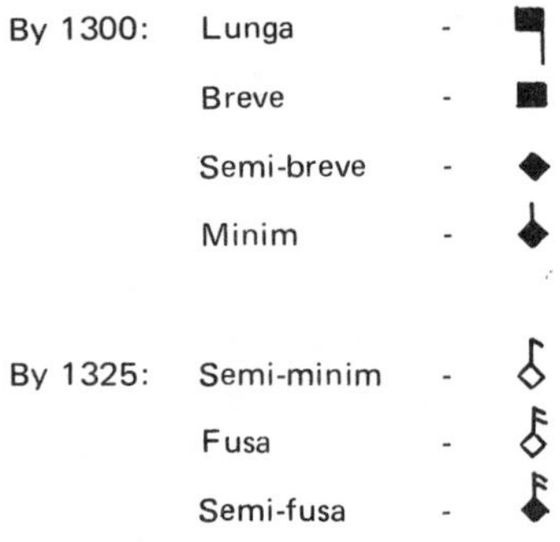

By 1300:	Lunga	-	
	Breve	-	
	Semi-breve	-	
	Minim	-	
By 1325:	Semi-minim	-	
	Fusa	-	
	Semi-fusa	-	

Figure 29. Thirteenth and Fourteenth Century Note Values.

two or three minims, major prolation indicating the triple division, minor prolation the duple. In actual practice, mood was rarely used, and then only to indicate a kind of phrase mensuration. Figure 30 shows the symbols used to indicate time and prolation, along with their equivalents in modern meter signatures. For the most part, note values smaller than the minim were used in multiples of two.

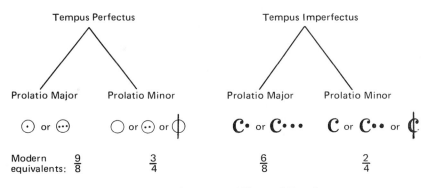

Figure 30. Meter Signatures of Mensural Notation.

It should not be assumed that all composers immediately adopted the new system, for some held to the precepts of the *Ars Antiqua* or wrote in both styles. Indeed, there ensued a confusion in musical notation that was not cleared up until nearly a century later. The dot (punctus), for example, was used in a variety of ways, sometimes to lengthen a note by half, as in modern notation, sometimes as a bar division, as well as for other purposes. Colored notes were sometimes used to indicate changes in note value; and we have already seen the variety of ways to indicate meters. Out of this confusion there developed over several centuries the notational system that has remained in use up to the present.

The Ars Nova in France

The earliest documented source of French music of the fourteenth century is found in a manuscript dated from 1316 containing about 130 compositions of various types including motets, alleluias, antiphons, and a variety of secular songs utilizing refrain forms. These were interpolated among the various verses of a satirical poem written by

Gervais de Bus in 1310 and 1314 entitled *Le Roman de Fauvel,* an allegorical attack on abuses against the Church by religious and semi-religious orders such as the Knights Templar. Fauvel is an imaginary animal in the poem, an allegorical ass whose name was invented from the first letters of the six vices: *Flaterie, Avarice, Vilanie, Variete, Envie,* and *Laschete.*

The motets in the Fauvel manuscript contain some of the earliest uses of a technique known as *isorhythm* ("same rhythm"). The essence of the system is that the tenors of isorhythmic motets were written as a series of repetitions of a preestablished rhythmic pattern called a *talea.* As the fourteenth century progressed, isorhythm began to appear in the upper parts as well as in the tenor (e.g., in the works of DeVitry, and Machaut), and a similar organization began to be applied to melodic patterns, a preestablished series of pitches being called a *color.* The juxtaposition of *talea* and *color* created interesting effects. When they coincided, the melody would have its original rhythm, but when repetitions of the talea overlapped the beginning of the color, the melody would appear in a changed rhythm.

Obviously the system was not entirely new. It can be viewed as a further development of thirteenth-century modal rhythm, for taleae are very like the ordines of the earlier period except that the taleae became longer and more complex than the ordines. The main difference between isorhythm and the older ordo system was the isorhythm achieved overall structural unity rather than rhythmic organization alone. Its use in the fourteenth century showed that composers of the *Ars Nova* were becoming increasingly concerned with the intricacies of their craft—were beginning to view themselves as artists with their own identity and personal expression rather than as anonymous purveyors of song. One manifestation of this is that a larger number of composers in the fourteenth century are known by name and are associated with specific compositions than in any previous century.

The outstanding example of such a composer is found in the person of Guillaume de Machaut (1304?–77), the leading composer of the French *Ars Nova.* Born in northern France in the province of Champagne, he was educated as a priest, and at the age of twenty became secretary to King John of Bohemia. In 1346, upon the death of King John, he entered the service of the French court and, in his retirement, became canon of the cathedral at Rheims. As a man of letters he wrote poetry as well as music, and in his secular music, which makes up the bulk of his output, he utilized his gifts in both areas to produce numerous monophonic songs called *lais* and *chansons balladees.*

The *lais* are in a form derived from the sequence and developed by the trouveres. The forms are variable, but in the case of Machaut often follow a double versicle pattern. The chansons balladées are in a refrain form known to the trouveres as the *virelai* and are invariably built of repetitions of an AbbaA pattern, the large A referring to the refrain section which occurs at the beginning and end of each stanza. In these works Machaut displays an extraordinary degree of rhythmic subtlety, particularly in his use of syncopation, a favorite device.

Although a few of the chansons balladées are in two parts with an instrumental tenor (one with an instrumental countertenor as well), the bulk of Machaut's polyphonic output is found in his motets, liturgical music, and in a vocal-instrumental form called the *rondeau*. Machaut's rondeaux are typically in eight lines, utilizing poetical subjects of sophisticated content and with music intended to appeal to the connoisseur. The eight lines can be diagrammed as AB a A ab AB, each stanza following this pattern. Complexity in the rondeau reaches its height in one entitled *"Ma fin est mon commencement et mon commencement ma fin."* The poem whimsically describes the techniques which are used in the music: the instrumental top part has the same melody as the tenor, but in retrograde, while the countertenor, also instrumental, goes to the middle of the piece and then reverses itself to present the retrograde version of its own first half. This is a good example of the medieval musician's propensity for musical symbolism and highly organized, though often obscure, structures. Just as composers of the Gothic period persisted in using a fragment of liturgical chant as a tenor, even though its tones were prolonged beyond possible recognition by the listener; so Machaut delighted in *cancrizan* (retrogression), diminution, and the mathematical abstractions of isorhythm. Obviously such devices exist in part on a purely contemplative level in the mind of the composer, for they are often beyond the conscious grasp of the listener. Yet they can and do lend a kind of inner organization to the sound of the music, even though the specific techniques are often too obscure to identify by ear. Such devices were also used in later periods. Bach certainly did not expect his listeners to hear all the extra-musical allusions in his chorale preludes or to follow every contrapuntal device applied to the subject in contrapuntal works such as *Art of Fugue*. (Nor did twentieth-century composers such as Alban Berg and Arnold Schoenberg expect their audiences to hear every permutation and combination of their tone rows or to perceive the obscure symbolism in some of their works.) *Augenmusik* (eye music) has always appealed to a certain kind of introspective composer, its abstract notational patterns furnishing an additional level of meaning while often mysteriously contributing to the actual sound of the music as well.

Machaut's motets are good examples of the kind of sophisticated, often abstract structure just discussed. There are twenty-three of them known; and most of them use isorhythm, some in such concentration that they are almost completely controlled by this single technical device. The motets in which isorhythm is most strictly applied are those in which it is applied to all of the voices. Others are comparatively free in rhythm, but it is important to note that this freedom was possible only because of the abandonment of the rhythmic modes; and one of the causative factors in the development of the isorhythmic principle was that a new organizational system was needed to fill the vacuum left by the abandonment of the rhythmic system of the thirteenth century. The new-found freedom required a different rhythmic discipline, and isorhythm met this need.

In ten of the motets the tenor melody, after a complete statement in the original time values of the talea, is repeated in a diminution divided by two or three, or even diminuted irregularly to create greater rhythmic interest. In some instances a tenor has two different taleae which are both applied to the same color.

The texts of the *Ars Nova* motets are on varying subjects. Many are religious, some point a moral, and others deal with political subjects. The tendency away from the liturgical texts toward subjects of current interest is found, to mention one example, in the motet entitled *"Plange republica regni"* in which Machaut calls for an end to civil chaos, and in the triplum outlines the duties of the king. One of his motets, entitled "David" after the text of the alleluia fragment from which its isorhythmic tenor was built, is for instruments alone. This motet is of interest because Machaut calls it a hoquetus, the only example of a piece with this title in his output, although he used the hocket technique in many of his works.

Machaut's best-known composition is his setting of the ordinary of the Mass (plus the *Ite, missa est*), which is notable for the fact that it is the first known setting of the complete ordinary by one composer. This work established the precedent for numerous Masses written in later periods, although the practice of setting the complete ordinary did not become common until the end of the fifteenth century. Called the *"Messe de Notre Dame"* (Mass of Our Lady), it may have been written around 1364, perhaps for the coronation of Charles V of France in that year, though this has not been proven. For the first time the composer regarded the five large divisions of the Mass as a single entity rather than as five isolated pieces. The various parts of the ordinary had, of course, been set previously, but never all at once with the intention of having them performed together as a single large composition. The unification of the five major divisions can be seen in the recurrence throughout the Mass of the motive shown in figure 31; also there is a similarity of style and mood among the various movements.

Figure 31. Motive of the Machaut Mass.

Machaut was perhaps the first musician to enjoy the kind of creative freedom that we today associate with the art of musical composition. Though he did not completely shake off the fetters of medieval liturgical tradition with its dependence upon preexisting chant tunes, he did invest the chanson balladée, motet, and Mass with a new artistry that helped establish the tradition of free melodic invention as the essence of musical composition. He is known to have said that the ear should be the final test of the worth of a piece of music, and he believed that a song must come from the heart—artistic attitudes which, though not completely new, were uncommon in his time.

From the papal center at Avignon in 1324, Pope John XXII issued a decree in which he deplored many contemporary practices in liturgical music, forbade certain practices, and prescribed penalties for what he believed to be musical abuses of the liturgy. In particular he decried the use of smaller note values and other rhythmic innovations characteristic of the *Ars Nova.* He advocated preservation of the original chant tunes, and, although he did not completely rule out the use of simple polyphony above plainsong melodies, he spoke against hocketing, motets (particularly of the polylingual variety), and discant. The decree tells us something about the musical practices in the Church of the time, and it may be that it had the effect of inhibiting the composition of polyphonic church music; certainly these practices did not completely cease. Yet his action probably prevented the development of a distinctive Church style in the fourteenth century at the same time that it may have helped the cause of secular art music. For the Pope was speaking against secularism in the church, and by legislating against music in the church for any purpose except devotion, he effectively encouraged composers to move art music into the secular world. Liturgical music continued to be written in France during the fourteenth century, but the typical composer of this period wrote much more secular music than sacred.

Strangely enough, the papal court at Avignon became one of the major centers for secular music during the fourteenth century. Here and at other centers in southern France composers such as Jacob de Senleches and Antonella da Caserta wrote polyphonic ballades, virelais, and rondeaux which were notable for their melodic fluidity and rhythmic interest. Most of these were solo songs with two additional instrumental parts, similar in texture to three-part motets. The forms were inherited from the monophonic patterns of the troubadors and trouveres, the texts dictating the formal patterns. Like the troubadors and trouveres, these fourteenth-century composers probably wrote many of their own texts and were really both poets and musicians.

Many of these works contain some rhythmical devices that were not equaled in complexity until the present century. In addition to abundant use of syncopation, it was not uncommon to find different meter signatures in the various voices as well as frequent changes of meter. Harmonically, the trend was toward increasing use of triads, although the practice of beginning and ending on an open perfect sonority persisted. The texts of these works, designed for the brilliant aristocratic society of the time, were usually on the subject of courtly love, with an occasional text on a subject of current interest.

The Italian Trecento

Nothing better describes the wide interest in art, letters, and music in fourteenth-century Italy than Boccaccio's *Decameron.* This delight in the fine arts was particularly strong in the city of Florence, where the *Decameron* is set. This work, like Chaucer's *Canterbury Tales,* is really many stories in one, and begins with a group brought together in Florence to avoid the plague of 1348. Each evening they told stories to each other, concluding the night's entertainment by singing and playing instruments:

> ... the tables having been cleared away, the queen ordered musical instruments to be brought, for all the ladies knew how to dance, as also the young men, and some of them could both play and sing excellently. Accordingly, by her command, Dioneo took a lute and Fiammetta a viol and they began softly to sound a dance; whereupon the queen and the other ladies, together with the other two young men, having sent the servants to eat, struck up a round and began with a slow pace to dance a brawl; which ended, they fell to singing quaint and merry ditties.

Although counterpoint may not have been included in their pleasurable pursuits, it is just possible that Boccaccio's *trecento* characters were playing and singing polyphonic music, for fourteenth-century Italian composers, like their French contemporaries, began to cultivate secular polyphonic forms. Chief among these were the madrigal, the *ballata,* and the *caccia.* Unlike French secular polyphonic works of the time, which often were polyphonic equivalents of troubador and trouvere forms, Italian secular polyphony developed more or less independently of earlier forms.

The madrigal originated as a poetic form of which Petrarch and other medieval Italian poets were masters. As a musical form it was most popular among the members of the early fourteenth-century Italian school such as Jacopo da Bologna and Giovanni da Cascia. The musical form follows rather closely the form of the poetry, so that a musical setting of a typical two stanza, eight line madrigal is similar to the bar form and the French ballade (AAB). Most of them were in two voices, some in three, and the style is closely related to that of the polyphonic conductus discussed in chapter 2 in that there is little real rhythmic independence among the voices. A notable feature of the bulk of Trecento polyphony is the lack of cantus firmus technique, which had been so important to the development of French polyphony. The texts, as in many sixteenth-century madrigals, frequently deal with the pursuit of the pleasures of love. The music of the Trecento madrigal, however, has nothing in common with its later counterpart.

The ballata (from *ballare,* to dance) is the chief form of fourteenth-century Italy, and is practically identical in form to the French virelai (called chanson balladée by Machaut). Because the virelai was originally a dance song with a soloist singing each six-line stanza preceded and followed by a choral refrain, it is generally assumed that the ballata was used to accompany round dances. There is, however, no definite evidence for this conclusion and most ballate do not contain dance-like rhythms. Probably the ballate, like many refrain forms, were derived from dance forms but came to be used as independent songs separate from the dance.

As its name implies, the texts of the caccia (chase) frequently dealt with hunting. Other texts were, of course, on the subject of love, as well as on such varied subjects as market scenes with street cries, sailing, fishing, and fires. The musical realization of these remarkable texts were highly depictive, for the caccia is one of the earliest examples of programmatic music. Both form and technique were highly stylized. They are in two sections, the first section being a strict unison canon with the second voice entering at least eight measures after the first. This canon occurs in the two upper parts, while an instrumental tenor proceeds in free rhythm below. The second section was also in canon between the two upper parts to form a kind of AB structure. There are a few examples in triple canon.

The French mensural notation discussed earlier in this chapter was an important step in the development of our modern notation. The Italians also found it necessary to develop a new system of rhythmic notation and though it did not have the evolutionary importance of the French system, it did meet the needs of their new musical expression. Italian notation is based on a system of dividing the breve into many different smaller note values. It utilized a "point of division" which divides the breve into as few as two or as many as seven semi-breves. Other aspects of the system permitted triple divisions up to twelve, and duple divisions up to eight. There were so many possible divisions of the breve, and consequently so many different values of semi-breves, that, with the increasing complexity of the music, the new notation, was quite confusing, and by the beginning of the fifteenth century became obsolete.

The outstanding Trecento composer was Francesco Landini (1325–97) who, though blinded in early youth from smallpox, nevertheless became one of the great artistic figures of fourteenth-century Italy. He played most of the musical instruments of his time and was particularly known for his skill on a small portable organ called the organetto. The main source of his music and that of other trecento composers is a magnificent collection, now in Florence, known as the Squarcialupi Codex after its first owner, a Florentine organist of the fifteenth century. Landini's extant works consist of 12 madrigals, one caccia, 87 two-part and 54 three-part ballate. One of his madrigals, entitled "Sy dolce non sono" is exceptional among trecento music in that it contains an isorhythmic tenor, Landini's only known use of this technique.

Landini's music and that of his contemporaries is characterized by some of the traits that have distinguished Italian music for centuries, even up to the present. This is seen in a melodic spontaneity that seems to be unique to the Italian spirit. Beautiful melodies designed for immediate communication through the human voice and clarity of form and texture have always been part of the Italian muse; these traits are found in the music of Dallapiccola, Pergolesi, and Palestrina as well as in Puccini and Verdi.

In Landini we hear this in the grace of his vocal lines and in the smoothness of his harmonies. He used fewer parallelisms than did earlier composers, and only on consonant intervals such as the fifth and octave, frequently avoiding parallelisms by means of passing tones. Triads abound in his music, although the empty perfect consonances continue to be used for beginnings and endings. In both French and Italian music of the fourteenth century, chromaticism began to be increasingly prevalent and it was during this time that the term *musica ficta* began to be used. The term (literally, "false music") refers to performers' application of accidentals to certain tones when the notation itself does not specify their use. In the dorian mode, for example, a C moving to D at a cadence might be raised to C sharp by the performers in order to create a leading tone. As shown in figure 32, musica ficta might also be applied to a G in a dorian cadence formula. Musica ficta was frequently used to change a B to B flat for various reasons—sometimes to avoid the diminished fifth or tritone (the *diabolus in musica*) and sometimes simply to enhance the beauty of the line.

Figure 32. Musica Ficta *in Cadences of the* Trecento.

Figure 33 (from a Landini ballata) is an example of a cadence which was characteristic of the Trecento composers. Its essential trait is the melodic formula in the top voice with its descent from the seventh scale degree to the sixth followed by the upward leap of a third to the unison cadence. Although this cadence formula has come to be known as the "Landini cadence," it was certainly not invented by him, for it was used by some of his predecessors, including Machaut.

Figure 33. Landini Cadence.

Key signatures of this time continued to be based upon Guido's hexachord system. That is, the B flat would be used to indicate the soft hexachord on F, but beyond that no accidentals were found in the key signature except an occasional E flat in a transposed mode. Landini, however, in about one fifth of his music, used conflicting key signatures in the various voices, for example, a B flat indicated in one voice but not in others. The purpose was often to create tension between a downward leading B flat and an ascending B natural, as well as to emphasize the near-tonal structure of the music at cadences.

Musical Instruments

There is no doubt that instruments were used in great abundance in both France and Italy during the fourteenth century. Pictures and literary sources indicate that polyphonic music was commonly performed with one voice or instrument to a part, and the presence of texts in the top part but not in the lower parts of some motets suggest that they were performed as vocal solos with instrumental accompaniment. Beyond this, very little is known of the use of instruments, for until the late sixteenth century, composers left the choice of instruments to the performers' discretion, with no instrumental indications in the score.

Forms of the harpsichord and the organ were used during the fourteenth century, but did not really come into their own until the Renaissance. The vielle continued to be popular, as did lutes, flutes, psalteries, and shawms. Various percussion instruments, and brass instruments such as horns and trumpets were used for outdoor entertainment. Because of their loud tone they were called "high" instruments, while the softer instruments were called "low." The viol-type instruments, which were to reach a peak of popularity in Elizabethan England, slowly began to replace the medieval fiddles such as the vielle and rebec.

English Music

There is ample evidence of the existence of singing in two or more parts at a relatively early date in England (see chap. 2). Medieval polyphony in the British Isles is distinct from that of continental Europe for its frequent use of thirds and sixths as seen in gymel and English discant. Undoubtedly this accounts for the predisposition toward tertian harmony that is apparent in the English pre-Renaissance period. During the twelfth and thirteenth centuries, English music had followed the trends of continental music, particularly those of France. Music of the Notre Dame School was known in England and three-part motets and conducti were being composed in the British Isles during the thirteenth century. Although an English school of composition existed at Worcester Cathedral during the fourteenth century, this was apparently a time of diminished musical activity in England. Influences from the continent were seen in the use of isorhythm and other techniques, but the most important feature of fourteenth-century English music was the beginning development of triadic harmony growing out of English discant. Figure 34 is an excerpt from an English Mass of this period. Although parallel fifths are found in the passage, there are also several passages in strict discant style which appear to us as first inversion triads moving in parallel motion. From near-tertian music of this type there gradually developed the triadic system that became the harmonic basis for music of the Renaissance.

Figure 34. From an English Mass of the Fourteenth Century.

The first examples of true triadic harmony as used in the Renaissance are found in the music of composers represented in several fifteenth-century English manuscripts (Bodleian and Old Hall manuscripts and the Trent Codices), most of all in the music of England's greatest pre-Renaissance composer, John Dunstable (c. 1370–1453). While Phillippe de Vitry can be credited with codifying the system of rhythmic notation that became the basis for rhythmic concepts and notation from the Renaissance through the Romantic era, Dunstable must be viewed as the first truly triadic composer, the man who first utilized a system of counterpoint and part writing based on a triadic substructure, and made possible the establishment of the tonal system in use from the early Baroque well into the twentieth century.

Dunstable was a uniquely gifted individual, famous as a mathematician and astrologer as well as a musician. So great were his abilities and achievements as a composer, during a time when there were few distinguished musicians in England, that he stands out as the most important English composer up to the Elizabethan period. His influence was felt on the continent, especially on the music of Dufay but also on other composers of the Burgundian school. His melodies use ideas based on triads, and his rhythms evolve naturally and charmingly from the rhythms of the words. The full sonorous harmonic textures, with their smooth voice leading, often create the aural impression of homophonic chords functioning in relation to each other around a tonal center, a harbinger of functional triadic harmony. Indeed, he might be called the father of modern part-writing in that he was the first to consistently treat dissonances in terms of meter, placing the consonances on the strong beats and the dissonances on the weak, as in sixteenth-century polyphony. Also, he treated the harmonic interval of the fourth as it was to be treated in the Renaissance—as a dissonance that resolves to a consonance.

Figure 35 shows the opening of the motet *Sancta Maria* by Dunstable. Aside from the frequent triadic outlines in the melodies, there is a general feeling of triadic harmony, almost of C major, and the cadence before the syllable "*cta*" sounds very much like a half cadence except, of course, that the melodic formula surrounding the F sharp in the top voice is that of the "Landini cadence." Also, this is an example of a motet with a single text, showing the trend away from the polytextual motets so popular around the beginning of the fourteenth century.

Almost all of Dunstable's compositions are sacred choral works, and in many of his motets there can be seen a beginning metamorpho-

Figure 35. Motet: Sancta Maria, *Dunstable.*

sis toward the Renaissance concept of the motet—that is, the motet as an unaccompanied polyphonic choral work with a sacred though not necessarily liturgical text, intended for incidental church performance. Although some of Dunstable's motets are similar to those of thirteenth- and fourteenth-century composers, with isorhythmic tenors, etc., others, such as the one in figure 35 and the famous motet *Quam Pulchra Es,* apparently evolved from conductus style and are quite different from other medieval motets in that they do not utilize chant fragments, do not use isorhythm, have only one text (usually Latin), seldom use complex or esoteric technical devices, and are clearly intended for church performance. In composing motets of this type, Dunstable reversed the secular trend seen in the early fourteenth century and pointed the way toward the Renaissance motet.

The Burgundian School

The most important composers of the Burgundian School are Guillaume Dufay (c. 1400–71) and Gilles Binchois (1400–60). While the Duchy of Burgundy can be geographically located in the Lowlands (Luxembourg, Belgium, and Holland), the Burgundian school was in fact an international school of composition including composers of many regions and nationalities throughout Europe. Patronage of the arts by the nobility was at a high level during the fourteenth and fifteenth centuries, and at courts throughout Europe chapels were being established and staffed with composers, singers, and instrumentalists who supplied the chapels with sacred music and the courts with music for entertainment.

The court of Burgundy at Dijon was the most important center for the arts at this time, and both Dufay and Binchois were associated with it. Philip the Good was Duke of Burgundy from 1419 to 1467, succeeded by Charles the Bold, who reigned from 1467 to 1477. Charles was defeated and killed at the Battle of Nancy in 1477, giving control of Burgundy back to France under Louis XI. Later the Duchy reverted to Mary of Burgundy, daughter of Charles the Bold. She married Maximilian of Austria, which brought the Germanic element into the picture and helped establish the international Flemish school of the early Renaissance with its profusion of influences from the Lowlands, France, and Germany.

The principle manuscript sources for Burgundian music are a large number of *chansonniers* or collections of *chansons,* some of the best of which are the Canonici manuscripts, the LaBorde Chansonnier, and the Mellon Chansonnier. The chanson, which is a generic term for rondeaux, ballades, and virelais, was the most popular type of secular music during the first half of the fifteenth century. Sacred works such as Masses, motets, and Magnificats were also written in considerable number, although complete settings of the ordinary of the Mass were rare until after 1450. The Burgundian composers used the Dorian, Ionian, Aeolian, and Mixolydian modes a great deal, but since Musica Ficta was applied to the leading tones, they were actually using major and minor scales. Conflicting key signatures similar to those of Landini continued to be used, often because of the need for a B flat at the cadence in only one of the voices. Figure 36 shows a commonly used cadence which, though clearly derived from the so called "Landini cadence," came to be called the "Burgundian cadence."

Figure 36. Burgundian Cadence.

Figure 37. Fifteenth Century Cadence with Crossed Voices to Avoid Parallel Fifths.

A newer type of cadence harmonically like the authentic cadence (V-I) is shown in figure 37. The octave leap in the lowest voice was used to avoid parallel fifths. Crossing of voices in itself is not remarkable, since the two lower voices commonly crossed and recrossed frequently during the course of composition. Many other types of cadences were found in Burgundian Music, some of which were significant to the development of the harmonic style of the Renaissance, but many of which were quite experimental. The rhythmic style of the Burgundians tended toward greater simplicity than that of the *Ars Nova* composers although some syncopation was used.

Prior to 1460, polyphonic textures were almost always in three voices, the top voice being called the *cantus, discantus,* or *Superius.*

The melodic style of the *discantus* was particularly appealing in Burgundian music; it moved gracefully above the two accompanying voices with delightful melismas in smaller note values at the approach to the cadence. The practice of writing all of the voices in such a way that they were harmonically and contrapuntally compatible began after 1450 at the beginning of the Renaissance, and with this new concept came the establishment of part-writing in four voices. This was done by adding a voice below the tenor which was called the *contratenor bassus* or simply *bassus,* while the voice above the tenor was called the *contratenor altus* or *altus* (hence, the modern terms alto, tenor, and bass). With the new four-part texture, the Renaissance concept of consonance and dissonance came into its own, and there gradually developed (in large part due to the influence of Dunstable) a stylized use of dissonance controlled by rhythm and harmonic intervals. Devices such as the suspension, passing tones, neighboring tones, and various types of cambiata figures began to be used in the mid-fifteenth century, all of which were significant to the Renaissance. Imitation, a device that was of prime importance to Renaissance polyphony, had been used at least as early as the twelfth century in rudimentary form, but now it began to be used more frequently, particularly in a succession of interlocked points of imitation.

Guillaume Dufay, the outstanding composer of the Burgundian school, rivals Dunstable for the distinction of being the greatest composer of the early fifteenth century. Born in Hainault, he was ordained as a priest around 1420 and became one of the more learned men of his time. He held clerical posts at the Papal chapel of Rome, was variously employed throughout his life at Savoy, Florence, and Bologna, and spent his retirement years at Cambrai, where he had been appointed canon of the cathedral in 1436. He was known in his time not only as a great musician but also as an influential and highly respected clergyman.

There is considerable contrast between the works of his early years, many of which were secular, and those composed around the middle of the century. In the earlier period, the influence of Machaut and the *Ars Nova* was apparent in angularity of line and complexity of rhythm that is in direct contrast to the precepts of the *Ars Nova.* It is believed that he was the first composer to use *fauxbourdon,* a technique very similar to English discant although its historical development is quite different (see chap. 3). The first known use of *fauxbourdon* is in a Dufay Mass composed around 1428. Quite possibly it had the same developmental effect upon Dufay that the English discant had upon Dunstable. In any case, it is in the sacred works of Dufay's later period that we see the progressive style that established a distinct liturgical manner of composition and led toward the polyphonic style of the Renaissance. Dufay is credited with being the first to add the fourth voice part, the bassus below the tenor (around 1450), and is also one of the first to compose Masses using secular tunes as *canti firmi.* A cantus firmus Mass is a type of Mass popular in the fifteenth and sixteenth centuries in which several or all of the movements are based on the same tune, usually presented in fairly long tones in the tenor. Two of the most secular tunes which were used for this purpose are *"L'Homme Armé"* (a folk tune) and *"Se la Face ay Pale"* (one of Dufay's own chansons), both of which were used by Dufay as the basis for Masses. The first phrase of the tune *"Se la Face ay Pale"* is presented in figure 38, and the opening of the Dufay Mass in which it serves as the cantus firmus is shown in figure 39.

Figure 38. First Phrase of Se La Face Ay Pale.

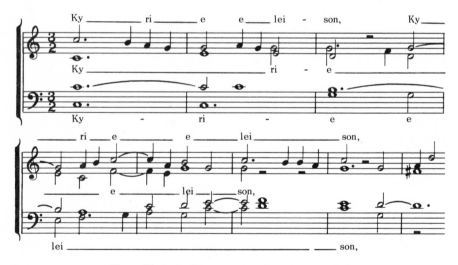

Figure 39. Dufay Mass Based on Se La Face Ay Pale.

The cantus firmus, which is found in the tenor, has approximately the same proportionate lengths as the original tune; and, unlike the incipits of twelfth century organum, is not so excessively augmented as to be totally unrecognizable. Nevertheless, the medieval influence must be acknowledged, not only in the agumentation of the cantus firmus, but also, in some Masses, by the occasional use of a kind of isorhythmic technique in the tenor. Cantus firmus Masses also used chant tunes and newly composed tunes for the cantus firmus, although these types were more popular in the sixteenth century than in the fifteenth.

Another type of Mass based on a preexisting musical source was the parody Mass, also popular in the fifteenth and sixteenth centuries. It is distinct from the cantus firmus Mass in that an entire section with all the voices of a polyphonic work is simply reset with the words of the Mass.

Oddly enough Gilles Binchois, Dufay's most distinguished contemporary who served at the Burgundian court for a period of about thirty years, apparently did not use the cantus firmus technique at all. Although Binchois composed a respectable amount of church music, the bulk of his output and his most characteristic style, is found in his fifty or more chansons. Most of his chansons are of the rondeau type and are usually in the typical three-voice texture. Here the likeness to medieval styles ceases, however, for his charming folk-like melodies with frequent triadic patterns, his simple rhythms and clear-cut cadences, and his rhythmic flexibility are far removed from the highly organized polyphonic structures of the *Ars Nova.* In his chansons the main melody is usually in the top part and is the only one supplied with a text. Instruments were known to have been used a great deal in the Burgundian court, and probably these secular works were performed as vocal solos with instruments on the lower parts. The instruments in use at Dijon included the harp, recorder, lute, shawm (an ancestor of the oboe), portative organ, sackbut (trombone), and *douchaine* (an ancestor of the bassoon). By this time the medieval fiddles such as the vielle and the rebec had all but disappeared from use and were being replaced by various forms of viols.

Standing as it was, on the threshold of the Renaissance world, the Burgundian school is one of the richest and most interesting periods in music history. For convenience we arbitrarily divide music history into blocks of time, but we do so with the recognition that a clean dichotomy seldom exists between any one period and the next. The secular and humanistic currents that were to shape the Renaissance were already moving during the time of the Burgundian court and even earlier, and our understanding of the ideas that came to flower in the Renaissance is enhanced by our knowledge of their slow germination in earlier times.

II. THE RENAISSANCE

4. The Renaissance: The International Flemish School

The Early Flemish School to Josquin—Josquin des Prez—Later Flemish Composers—Orlando di Lasso

The term "Renaissance," like "Gothic," was first used to designate the painting, sculpture, and architecture of a specific time in history. Gradually the term began to be applied to all cultural phenomena of the period of 1450–1600; and, in particular, became associated with the movement known as humanism. At its narrowest, humanism denotes the revival of interest in the ancient Greek and Roman cultures—their philosophy, sculpture, architecture, and drama. But in a broader sense it indicates a renewed general interest in human and secular matters, in man's activity for its own sake rather than for the glory of God. The beginning currents of humanism extend well back into the middle ages, perhaps most of all into fourteenth-century Italy, where men such as Petrarch, Giotto, Boccaccio, and Landini were producing works of art which, though frequently on religious subjects, dealt much more with man's earthly activities than with his immortal soul. The same was true of Chaucer in England and, to some extent, of Machaut in France. This exciting pre-Renaissance activity began to bear more fruit in the fifteenth and sixteenth centuries in the work of artists such as Botticelli, Raphael, Michelangelo, and Leonardo da Vinci, philosophers and writers such as Erasmus, More, Machiavelli, and Shakespeare, and scientists such as Galileo, Vesalius, and Copernicus.

"Renaissance" means literally "rebirth," and, indeed, it was a time of new ideas and renewed intellectual energy. But the "dark ages" were not nearly as dark as they were once thought to have been, nor were the ideas of the Renaissance, in many instances, quite as new as they appeared to be. As we have seen, this was particularly true of the art of music, where the evolution of Renaissance ideas began centuries before the year 1450, though that date was an important point of arrival and the ensuing period enjoyed great richness of musical activity. It is difficult to point to clear-cut causes for the Renaissance, but among many significant factors was the capture of Constantinople by the Turks in 1453, the year of Dunstable's death, thus terminating the Eastern Roman Empire, the last vestige of the ancient world, and sending many Byzantine scholars fleeing to Italy where their presence stimulated interest in scholarship in the classical languages and contributed much to the humanistic movement. The invention of printing toward the end of the fifteenth century helped to disseminate knowledge among larger numbers of people, and at about the same time men such as Christopher Columbus were beginning explorations which would ultimately extend Western man's frontiers to the farthest corners of the earth. Perhaps most important of all were the demise of the Holy Roman Empire, and the division of the Church into its Catholic and Protestant branches. The resultant weakening of the authority of Church and state kindled new fires of creativity in all areas of human endeavor.

Musically, the Renaissance is one of the most complex periods in history. As in medieval times, musicians continued to rely upon patronage, particularly from the Church. Nevertheless, secular music continued to increase through the activities of both professional and amateur musicians, though music as an independent profession did not really come into its own until later. Music printing developed shortly after the invention of printing, and in 1501 the first collection of polyphonic music printed from moveable type was published in Venice by Ottaviano dei Petrucci (1466–1539) under the title *Harmonice Musices Odhecaton*. At this time a double- or triple-impression process was used for music printing. That is, the staff lines and other constant features were printed in the initial process, the notes in a second process, and, when required, the text in a third process. A single-impression process for music printing was invented around 1525, and in 1528 Pierre Attaignant began to publish French chansons using the new method. Obviously music printing made it possible for many more people to be involved in musical performance. In particular it encouraged amateurs to perform secular music. Vocal ensemble pieces such as madrigals and chansons, and instrumental pieces were published in "part books." That is, rather than publish the full score, each individual part was printed by itself, a complete set of part books being required for performance. At the same time, instruction books for amateur musicians, explaining how to read and perform music, became fashionable. The most famous of these "how-to" books is *A Plaine and Easy Introduction to Practicall Musick* by the Elizabethan composer Thomas Morley (1557–1602).

The great diversity in Renaissance music makes it difficult to draw meaningful generalizations about the style of the period. There are, however a few features that are generally typical. A characteristic texture of the period consisted of four or more voice lines of similar quality and equal importance in the musical fabric. Vocal music predominated and, until recently, it was thought that authentic performances of Renaissance vocal music should be without instruments (i.e., a cappella). Today it is believed that, although the composer's "ideal" conception of a vocal work may have been without instruments, in actual practice instruments were almost always used, often to support a voice line or to substitute for a missing voice. Much instrumental music evolved from this practice; the *ricercar* and *canzona,* for example, originated as transcriptions of vocal pieces.

The homogeneity of texture achieved in Renaissance four-part polyphony led composers to think increasingly in terms of vertical sonorities. The compositional process for the earlier medieval motet has consisted of successively adding parts to the tenor, an accumulation which often started with a preexisting melody, then became a two-part texture, and finally a three-part motet. This process predisposed medieval composers to think horizontally rather than vertically, without much concern for the resultant vertical sonorities except at certain crucial points. Composers of the Renaissance, however, began to compose all of the parts at once, with careful control of dissonance in terms of the strong beats (tactus) of the meter. The basic units of harmony were the triad and its first inversion, although the latter was not thought of as an inversion since its evolution as a sonority came through fauxbourdon and English discant rather than through a vertical rearrangement of triad tones. Some feeling of diatonic harmony, the tonic-dominant concept, and even tonality began to be apparent in the music, though these things had not yet been expressed as concepts and were, indeed, not even consciously present in the composers' minds. Gradually the bass began to function as the harmonic foundation, though this too came about slowly and apparently not as a deliberately new concept. This is not to suggest that Renaissance polyphony was unattractive from the linear standpoint, for the period is a time of supreme achievement in melodic writing in contrapuntal textures. But for the first time composers began to give attention to consonance and dissonance in terms of the vertical sonority, at the same time producing horizontal melodic lines which were of great beauty, both in their relationship to each other and individually. By the end of the Renaissance, the trend toward vertical sonorities reached a juncture, and with the development of continuo the concept of vertical chords became an important distinguishing feature of the Baroque style.

There are two basic Renaissance vocal styles which, though sometimes combined in the course of a composition, nevertheless retain clear and separate identities. The first is the typical polyphonic texture in which the voices have considerable rhythmic independence, written by means of techniques such as canon and free imitation as well as free counterpoint, and which creates an effect of great fluidity of rhythm. The other is best represented by "familiar style," referring to a texture derived from the medieval conductus style in which all of the voices move in approximately the same rhythm without imitative devices, producing the effect of progressions of block chords. The term *familiar style* refers specifically to sacred vocal music, but the same type of thing also occurs in secular and instrumental music, particularly in instrumental dance pieces and in secular part songs such as the French polyphonic chanson.

Among the important innovations of the Renaissance were the development of a genuine instrumental style and the emergence of the concept of idiomatic instrumentation. The latter occurred at Venice toward the end of the sixteenth century and is perhaps more a precursor of the Baroque than a phenomenon of the Renaissance. Yet instrumental styles did develop, and in Elizabethan England there appeared a group of composers who produced a sizeable body of literature of uniformly high quality for keyboard instruments, the lute, and for groups of viols. Though instrumental music flourished, vocal music dominated the Renaissance. One major change in the manner of performance was that sacred vocal music began to be performed by choruses or choirs rather than by solo voices as in the middle ages. The relationship between poetry and music became stronger than ever before, finding an ideal union in the English and Italian madrigals as well as in the solo songs of the Elizabethans.

In spite of the recent upsurge in the popularity of "old" music, Renaissance music continues to be the earliest body of literature maintaining a permanently popular place in the repertory of the Western world. This may be because so many technical features of music of more recent periods, even up to the present day came into their own in the fifteenth and sixteenth centuries. Vocal textures, the concept of consonance and dissonance, the basic triadic sonorities, the union of words and music, the importance of secular art music, idiomatic instrumental writing, and contrapuntal devices such as canonic imitation are all Renaissance phenomena which, though modified in succeeding centuries, continued to significantly influence the art of music well into the twentieth century. In a sense, then, the Renaissance can be viewed as the beginning of modern music history. Its music communicates directly and meaningfully to twentieth-century audiences. But the period is equally important to general cultural history, for the precepts of rationalism, humanism, and idealism embodied in the Renaissance continue to exert their influence even to the present day.

So diverse is the musical activity in Europe and England during the Renaissance that it is difficult to deal chronologically with the many concurrent developments. Accordingly, this chapter will deal with the international school of Flemish composers, the next with the French, Italian and Spanish Renaissance, and chapter 6 with Renaissance Germany and England.

The Early Flemish School to Josquin

The dominating school of European composers of the late fifteenth and early sixteenth centuries has been variously titled the Flemish, Franco-Flemish, French-Netherlands, and the Netherlands school of musical composition. The nomenclature is of no real consequence as long as it is remembered that these terms all indicate the region from which most of the distinguished composers of this time originated—that is, in terms of modern geographical boundaries, Belgium, Holland, and the northern part of France adjacent to Belgium. These lowlanders dominated the musical life of Europe during the period of 1450–1550, holding down most of the important musical posts among the many courts of Europe.

Growing out of the Burgundian school with its various national influences, theirs was truly an international art, and one which composers and performers from other countries willingly accepted as the ideal. The school is first represented in the later works of Dufay and in the music of Johannes Ockeghem (1430?–95). Little is known of Ockeghem's early life, but we do know that in 1452 he was appointed to the chapel of the King of France and in 1465 was made master of the King's chapel music *(Maitre de Chapelle),* a post he held until his death. Though not extremely prolific, he was one of the most distinguished composers of his time and a highly successful teacher, for a number of the leading Flemish composers of the next generation were his students.

There are twelve Masses, ten motets, and about twenty chansons in his known output. During the period of 1450 to 1500, the Mass became a very popular vehicle of composition, and began to be viewed as the form in which composers were expected to demonstrate their prowess as musical creators. Ockeghem's Masses are similar in texture to those of Dufay in that most of them are written in polyphonic textures of four similar voices (a few in three or five voices). One difference is that the range of the bass part extended downward in some cases as far as the low F to create a four-voice texture very similar to that of modern times except that the range of the superius (top voice) did not extend as high as that of the modern soprano range. The extension of the bass range had the effect of producing a fuller and more homogeneous texture than that of the Burgundians, who rarely extended the bass more than an octave below middle C.

Ockeghem's use of canon represents a tendency on the part of early Flemish composers toward highly sophisticated contrapuntal devices. Their virtuoso techniques in canonic writing were demonstrated by the use of inversion, retrogression (crab or *cancrizan*), augmentation, and diminution in the answering voices. Two or more of these devices might be used in combination, and some compositions even involved the use of double canon, two canons (each with two or more voices) occurring simultaneously. The techniques of augmentation and diminution occurred in pieces called mensuration canons, so titled because mensural meter signatures were affixed to a single written melody in such a way as to indicate that its imitation should be at a different rate of speed, either faster or slower, than the original voice. The most famous example of this is Ockeghem's *Missa Prolationum* in which every movement is a *double* mensuration canon with various intervals of imitation and different combinations of time signatures.

Figure 40 is an excerpt from the opening of the *Sanctus* of the *Missa Prolationum.* The example has been transcribed to modern notation, but the symbols at the extreme left are original, indicating the manner in which the unnotated voices were indicated. Note that the meter (tempus) of the two voices not shown is imperfect (duple), while the notated voices are in perfect (triple) meter. Also, the prolation of the

Figure 40. Sanctus from the Missa Prolationum, *Ockeghem.*

two voices on the lower staff is major (triple), while the absence of the dot in the upper staff indicates the minor prolation (duple.) (See fig. 30 for the meter signatures of mensural notation.) The interval of imitation is also indicated by the signatures. Devices such as this in the music of Ockeghem and his contemporaries are not simply notational abstractions (as was sometimes the case during the *Ars Nova*), but in fact contribute significantly to the expressiveness of the music.

The foregoing may suggest that the technique of imitation was an all-important compositional device to the early Flemish composers; on the contrary, Ockeghem and his contemporaries made relatively little use of it in their Masses. Imitative passages are found, but usually involve only two of the voices in a four-part texture and are *not* used as a basic structural device to produce compositions built substantially of series of points of imitation as in the sixteenth century. Ockeghem wrote cantus firmus Masses, parody Masses, and freely composed Masses. Some of the cantus firmus Masses were of a special type in which each movement uses a cantus firmus that is drawn from the corresponding section of the appropriate plainsong Mass. Others use canti firmi derived from sources such as the rondeaux of Binchois, or the popular song *"L'Homme Armé."* One of the striking features of the Masses is their great rhythmic diversity and independence among the various highly ornamented parts, the result of a style that is, for the most part, nonimitative.

Ockeghem's chansons, mostly in three parts, show his lineage with the Burgundian school. Though not of the stature of Josquin, he is the most important composer in the transition from the early fifteenth century to the Renaissance. Called the "Prince of Music" by his contemporaries, his artistic evocation of the moods and emotions of words set important precedents for later composers.

The most important composers of the generation immediately following Ockeghem are Jacob Obrecht, Heinrich Isaac, and the greatest composer of the early Renaissance, Josquin des Prez. All three were born around 1450, and all had their early training in the Netherlands. Lesser Franco-Flemish composers of about the same time include Antoine Busnois (?–1492), who was of the same generation as Ockeghem, Pierre de la Rue (c. 1460–1518), and Loyset Compere (c. 1450–1518). The latter two were students of Ockeghem.

Obrecht (1452–1505), like Ockeghem, used free nonimitative counterpoint a great deal, and also wrote canons of the type described in the preceding section. In other works he used free imitation, but, like Ockeghem, did not rely upon it as a structural device. In general, his style is simpler than that of Ockeghem, and is marked by frequent passages in familiar style and by clear cut interior cadences, often suggesting IV-I or V-I. In some of his imitative passages, all four voices are equally active, anticipating the kind of polyphony to be found during the high Renaissance in the works of composers such as Lassus and Palestrina.

One of the most modern features of Obrecht's music is the clear-cut phrase structure created by the frequent cadences. The choice of final intervals or chords at these cadences tended to emphasize certain pitches, almost suggesting tonal centers, although at that time this could not have been done consciously. The result is that much of Obrecht's music has a very "modern" harmonic quality, often suggesting a tonal center defined by a tonic and dominant. This can be seen in the three-voice motet *Parce Domine* (readily available in modern editions), where a strong feeling of A minor is created by cadences on A and E. Two of the cadences on A, one of which is the final cadence, unquestionably create the progression of V to I in A minor, provided that musica ficta is utilized to create the G sharp leading tone.

There is a new kind of expressiveness to be found in the warmth and freshness of Obrecht's melodic lines. The feeling of ebb and flow created by the frequent cadences contrasts sharply to Ockeghem's long, intense melodic lines. In general Obrecht seems to have been more inclined to experimentation than was Ockeghem, for there is a spontaneous quality in his Masses and motets that suggest impatience with tradition and an intense desire to try new things. The result is that the old and the new are interestingly combined in his works, marking him as an important transitional figure of great originality.

The principal work of Heinrich Isaac (c. 1450–1518) is his *Choralis Constantinus,* commissioned by the Cathedral of Constance in 1508. The three-volume work consists of motets based on texts from the ordinary and proper of the Mass and the Divine Offices, covering nearly every occasion of the entire church year. Capable of composing in all the national styles of his time, in these motets Isaac demonstrates his skill with the Flemish polyphonic style in its most abstract form. Most of his church music, including his Masses, are in the four-voice style developed in the late fifteenth century.

Isaac was an important figure in the development of the polyphonic lied, the German counterpart of the Italian and English madrigals and of the French polyphonic chanson. It is in these works that his Germanic spirit is most fully expressed. His most famous lied is *"Innsbruck ich muss dich lassen,"* which later furnished the tune for the chorale *"O welt ich muss dich lassen"* harmonized by J. S. Bach. Isaac is also known for his secular compositions in the Italian and French styles.

Josquin des Prez

Josquin (c. 1450–1521) is one of the few composers in music history who, during his own life, achieved true international fame as the greatest composer of his time. Known as the "Father of Musicians," Martin Luther said of him, "He is the master of notes, others are their slaves." He was born near the French-Belgian border and is presumed to have been a student of Ockeghem. A part of his career was spent in Italy in the Papal choir and at Milan, while the latter part of his life was spent in Burgundy. Little else is known of his life, though his international reputation is well documented. Many of his works were published by Petrucci, and there are numerous laudatory references to Josquin by writers throughout the sixteenth century.

Josquin represents both the culmination of the musical art of the middle ages and the true genesis of Renaissance polyphony. The music of Ockeghem and Obrecht had reached a point where little further development was possible. Theirs was an art of rigorous, though at times free contrapuntal thinking in a four-voice fabric of equal intertwining voices. It was mystical and profound music, perhaps more medieval than Renaissance, but it left no room for further development, opened no doors for the future. To Josquin fell the task of setting the style for the bright new art of the Renaissance, and this came about in part through the Italian influence.

His earliest works, which form a body of music in the tradition of Obrecht and Ockeghem, demonstrate great contrapuntal skill and expand to the limits the expressive possibilities of the late fifteenth-century style. His sojourn in Italy brought about marked changes in his style, the most important aspects of which are a new emotional expressiveness, a greater interest in contrasting textures, a different kind of polyphony, and an overall lightness and clarity that was in contrast to the predominantly serious expression of Ockeghem and Obrecht.

In his motets, more than a hundred of which were published between 1501 and 1564, imitation became the chief structural device, setting the precedent for the important Renaissance technique of linking consecutive points of imitation. This technique, which was used by virtually all Renaissance composers after Josquin, consisted of setting each phrase of text in a free imitative fabric and connecting them by allowing the new point of imitation to begin before the final voice or voices in the previous phrase was finished. It is distinct from canon in that it is not strict imitation and because the linkage between phrases was so consistently utilized as to become a significant aspect of the formal structure.

In Josquin's motets, as in those of many later composers, each point of imitation was built of its own unique melodic material and covered one phrase of the text. The motet *Ave Maria,* an excerpt of which is shown in figure 41, is an excellent example of a work built almost entirely by means of this technique.

Figure 41. Motet: Ave Maria, Josquin.

The opening of the *Ave Maria* chant which served Josquin as the point of departure in the motet is shown in figure 42. Note that the opening line in the tenor of the motet follows the pitches of the opening phrase of the chant, except for the fact that the skip from G to D in the chant is filled in with stepwise motion in the motet. The first point of imitation, then, is built out of the first phrase of the chant; and successive points of imitation follow a similar pattern. Compare measure 11 of the motet, for example, with the *gratia plena* section of the chant, measure 16 with the *Dominus tecum,* and measure 21 with the *benedicta tu.* Thus, Gregorian chant melodies continued, as in the Middle Ages, to furnish melodic material for motets and other religious choral works. With characteristic freedom and flexibility, Josquin departs from the strict use of this technique at several points in the motet.

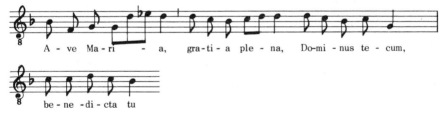

Figure 42. *Chant Upon Which Josquin's Motet* Ave Maria *is Based.*

Josquin also used the point of imitation as a structural device in his chansons, though not as fully as in his religious choral works. One notable innovation in his chansons is the expansion of the choral texture in some cases to as many as six voice parts, although there are also many examples in three or four parts. Their forms vary, some of them being derived from medieval forms such as the ballade. Most of the texts are based on the conventional themes of unrequited love, morality, and occasional humorous incidents. The most striking characteristics of these works is the consistency with which he musically expresses the mood of the text, a foretaste of the admirable text painting to be found in the madrigals of the later Renaissance.

His thirty Masses are all in four voices and, like the motets, consistently utilize the point of imitation as a structural device, though many also use canti firmi. The vocal ranges are somewhat wider than in earlier music and in many ways the voices begin to be used in the typical high Renaissance manner. The contrast of textures in these works is one of the important contributions to later Renaissance practices. Textural changes such as a pair of voices imitating another pair, or contrasts of familiar style to free imitation, manifest a new concept of vocal orchestration.

Josquin's most important contribution is not easily defined and is even less easily expressed, for it lies in the area of esthetics—of emotion and meaning in music. He seems to have been the first composer to have consistently thought and worked in terms of a "subjective" or emotional musical expression. Not only the rhetorical meaning of the text but also the composer's subjective interpretation of that meaning is consistently and beautifully expressed in his vocal music. This concept, which we associate with humanism, was typical of much vocal music of the later Renaissance. It became an important aspect of virtually all vocal music from that time to the present.

Later Flemish Composers

Nicholas Gombert (c. 1490–1556), one of Josquin's most famous pupils, was instrumental in disseminating the philosophies and musical practices of his great teacher. In his travels throughout Europe as a singer in the court of Charles V, Gombert had ample opportunity to absorb the influences of various national styles. The newer fashions are reflected in the fact that he wrote primarily in five or six voices rather than in the traditional four-voice texture and utilized both free counterpoint and imitation of the highest quality. By 1540, five and six voices became the rule rather than the exception, although compositions in as few as two and as many as eight parts can be found throughout the century. Nevertheless, Gombert also used a conservative four-voice imitative texture very much like that of Josquin, and in so doing, spread Josquin's influence throughout Europe. The four-voice motet *Super Flumina* is a good example of this.

A prolific composer, Gombert's output of sacred music included ten Masses and nearly two hundred motets and incidental composi-tions. Eight of his Masses are based in large part upon borrowed material, a manifestation of the increased popularity of the parody technique which had been used only tentatively by Josquin and his contemporaries. Usually the borrowed material was a motet, each movement of the Mass beginning with a form of this material, but soon departing into a freer texture. (The term "parody Mass" has no connota-tion of humor or satire, but simply indicates the use of preexisting music in an altered form, sometimes nothing more than the substitu-tion of a new text.)

The motet *Super Flumina*, mentioned above, exemplifies the typi-cal motet style of Gombert. It is built, for the most part, of interlocking points of imitation, with one short section in triple meter which, with its fauxbourdon harmonies, affords a point of contrast in an otherwise smooth and unchanging imitative texture. The use of rests at different points in the various voices adds textural contrast to his music, and his syncopations and varied note values create a unique rhythmic quality.

Jacobus Clemens (c. 1510–56) or Clemens non Papa (he adopted the latter name probably to distinguish himself from a contemporary poet named Jacobus Papa) employed the parody technique even more exten-sively than Gombert, for fourteen of his fifteen Masses are based on preexisting material. Most of them are for five voices and the textures show an increase in the proportion of chordal writing to contrapuntal. In addition to the masses, his compositions include more than two hundred motets, many polyphonic chansons, and four volumes of sim-ple psalm settings in three parts.

Clemens' psalm settings were based on the *Souterliedekens* ("little psalter songs"), a Dutch translation of the psalter published as early as 1540 and used until 1568 when Netherlands Protestants adopted the Genevan Psalter of John Calvin. The Huguenot Church, based on Cal-vin's teachings, was founded in 1559 and adopted musical practices quite different from those of Martin Luther. The only music allowed in the church were psalm settings of metrical translations of the psalms made by Beza and Marot. The most famous of these hymns is "Old Hundredth" by Louis Bourgeois, which was originally a setting of Psalm 134 in the Genevan Psalter. (The name "Old Hundredth" stems from the fact that the music was used in Sternhold and Hopkins Psalter [1562] as a setting of Psalm 100.)

One of Clemens' Latin Motets, *Vox in Rama*, serves well to illus-trate a theory about the "secret chromatic passages" of Flemish com-posers of the sixteenth century. According to this theory a special kind of musica ficta was applied by flatting certain notes, adding much chromaticism and, therefore, greater emotional intensity to the music. The practice, if the theory is correct, was kept a closely guarded secret and was used by only a few composers of the mid-sixteenth century. The technique resulted in unusual modulations and was used as a text-painting device on words of exceptionally strong emotional feeling. There is evidence to substantiate the theory, although the application of the secret musica ficta was not essential to a sensible reading of the music. That is, if the performers were not aware of the hidden cues to indicate the use of the additional flats, the music still made sense in its unaltered diatonic form.

The textures of Clemens' motets are notable for their smooth, homogenous textures—far different from the fifteenth-century practice in which extreme rhythmic contrasts were found among the various voices. Indeed, the voices in sixteenth-century polyphony became so nearly equal that it began to be almost impossible to find a principal or leading voice in the texture.

One of the most influential Flemish composers of the middle sixteenth century was Adrian Willaert (c. 1490–1562), who, though born in Flanders, spent most of his life in Italy. As director of music in the Cathedral San Marco at Venice from 1527 until his death, he is viewed as the founder of the influential Venetian school of composition of the second half of the sixteenth century, which was important for the development of instrumental styles and for antiphonal choral techniques.

Willaert's teacher, Jean Mouton (c. 1470–1522) and Antoine de Fevin (c. 1474–1512) are also worthy of mention. Both were followers of Josquin (perhaps pupils) and both composed in the prevailing style of the time. Ludwig Senfl (c. 1490–1543), a student of Isaac working chiefly in Germany, was more conservative in style. Although a composer of Masses and motets, Senfl's chief contributions were a large body of secular songs to German texts and some compositions with German texts for the Lutheran church.

Orlando di Lasso

Possessed of a universal musical gift unparalleled in the Renaissance, Orlando di Lasso (1532–94) composed in all national styles of the time. Born at Mons, Belgium, he spent most of his early years in Italy as a singer. A portion of his career was spent in Antwerp and in Venice, and he traveled in France and England. In 1556 he was employed by the Bavarian court at Munich under Duke Albert V, where he remained for the rest of his life. A listing of his compositions illustrates his tremendous productivity and versatility, for he composed around 1,200 motets, more than 50 Masses, 100 Magnificats, and about 650 secular works, including Italian madrigals, French chansons, and German polyphonic lieder.

The motets, above all his other works, demonstrate his great musical expressiveness and ability to unify verbal and musical meanings. In addition to the more obvious kinds of text painting in which the music contains a literal representation of the word (such as an ascending melodic line for the word *ascendit*), he also employed a more subtle kind of musical imagery in which rhythms and textures subtly evoke the essence of the verbal meanings. The well-known motet *Tristis est anima mea* serves well to illustrate some of these more sophisticated kinds of text painting. In the excerpts from this motet shown in figure 43 a feeling of stark, even death-like simplicity is evoked by the use of the empty fifth on the cadence for the word *"mortem,"* all the more because by this time the use of a sonority without a third at a cadence was quite unusual. Likewise, in the second excerpt, the words *"quae circumdabit me"* ("that will surround me") are set at a close-time interval of imitation with many closely knit repetitions to create the effect of an overwhelming multitude. The substitution of the eighth note for the quarter note on some of the imitations of the word *"quae"* adds to this effect. In the course of the motet certain phrases are given special emphasis by being set in familiar style to contrast to the more prevalent imitative texture.

Among Lasso's finest works are the *Seven Penitential Psalms,* a set of 132 motets, most of which are settings of the individual verses of the Psalms; though each Psalm also closes with two additional motets set to the texts *Gloria patri* and *Sicut erat in principio.* Lasso's many and varied stylistic devices are well represented in this impressive work. In some of the motets his tendency toward harmony based on the fifth relation can be seen in leaps in the bass voice from the root of one triad to that of the next, quite often connecting two triads with roots a fifth apart. This obvious anticipation of the harmonic practices of the Baroque period is perhaps more typical of Lasso than of his contemporaries. Probably the most unusual aspect of his textures is the frequent use of extremely florid lines in all of the voices, creating a smoothly fluctuating and contrapuntally interesting effect. Most of the motets of the *Seven Penitential Psalms* are in five voices, although they vary from as few as two voices to as many as six.

The gift for evocative text painting can also be seen in Lasso's secular works, which include Italian madrigals, French chansons, and German part songs or polyphonic lieder. His ability to assimilate the

Figure 43. Excerpts from the Motet Tristis Est Anima Mea, *Lasso.*

technique and compose authentically in these three distinct national styles is truly remarkable. This ability can be seen to a lesser degree in the music of some of the other members of the international Flemish school such as Phippe de Monte (1521–1603), who composed more than 1,200 madrigals in the Italian style, many of which are of the finest quality. The stylistic characteristics of these secular part songs vary from one nationality to the other and will be discussed in detail in subsequent chapters.

The international school of Flemish or Netherlands composers was at its height during the period of 1450–1550. Although Flemish composers dominated European music during this period, distinct national styles in Italy, France, Germany, and England existed concurrently with the learned art of the Netherlanders. But it was only in the latter half of the sixteenth century that these national styles began to supersede the Flemish in importance. This occurred in all European countries, but was most apparent in Italy where a national musical style gained such supremacy after 1550 that it became the most influential style of Europe for a period of nearly two hundred years.

5. The Renaissance: National Styles of France, Italy and Spain

The French Chanson—The Italian Madrigal— The Roman School of Church Music—The Venetian School—Spanish Music—Instrumental Music

The French Chanson

The use of the term "chanson" to indicate secular songs of various types extends back to the time of Machaut. But in sixteenth-century France its meaning narrowed to denote a new type of French part song distinctly different from its predecessors. The first examples of the new chanson style, sometimes called the French polyphonic chanson, appeared in the initial publications of the French printer and music publisher Pierre Attaignant, who was the first to use the single impression process of music printing. Between 1528 and 1552 he published over fifty collections of chansons, for a total of more than 1,500 works. Chansons became so popular that they were widely transcribed for other media, particularly as lute solos and solo songs with lute accompaniment.

Although French is the language of the chanson, its most immediate ancestor is the Italian *frottola,* a type of four-part strophic song popular in Italy during the late fifteenth and early sixteenth centuries. Frottole, with their homophonic textures and strong regular rhythms in syllabic settings, may have represented an Italian reaction to the sophisticated contrapuntal style of Flemish polyphony. Popular in the Italian courts, they were probably performed with a solo voice on the top part and instruments taking the three lower voices as accompaniment. In addition to furnishing the model for the French chanson, the frottola was one of several popular Italian forms which led to the Italian madrigal.

The traits of the frottola which most strongly influenced the chanson are (1) the division into short sections according to the structure of the text, (2) the homophonic or chordal harmony, and (3) the simple, well-defined rhythmic character. In the typical chanson texture, a light imitative style was contrasted to chordal writing. Frequent cadences delineated the text and the appealing tunes of the chansons were cast in strong lively rhythms. Repeated notes were used frequently in the subject, particularly in the following pattern: ♩♩♩ So often was this dactylic pattern used in the opening measure, that it became a hallmark of the chanson style and was later carried over into the Italian instrumental *canzona* which descended from it. Chansons in simple two- or three-part forms were most frequent, the sections clearly defined by cadences, though in some instances a strophic form was used in which the same music was repeated to a new text.

The two most important composers of chansons were Claudin de Sermisy (c. 1490–1562) and Clement Janequin (c. 1485–1560), both of whom are well represented in the chanson collections published by Attaignant. Janequin, a pupil of Josquin, is particularly noted for his near-literal depictive techniques. In *Les Oiseaux,* one of his most famous works, he emulates the sounds of many different varieties of bird calls, while in other chansons he imitates such things as battle sounds and street cries. As might be expected, affairs of the heart often furnished the material for the texts of the French chansons, although some of them dealt with more serious subjects.

Many chanson composers, particularly those who were not French, relied more heavily upon Flemish contrapuntal techniques than did Sermisy and Janequin. Among these were Italian madrigal composers such as Willaert and Jacob Arcadelt (c. 1505–c. 1560) as well as Gombert, Clemens, Thomas Crequillon (d. c. 1557), and Orlando di Lasso. Most chansons are in four or five voices, with the five-voice texture becoming almost standard after 1550. The chanson style is similar to the motet, except that the textures are simpler, with more frequent chordal passages, and more regular rhythms. Figure 44 presents an excerpt from a four-voice chanson of Crequillon entitled *Pour ung Plaisir.* Note the use of imitation in a rather simple texture as well as repeated notes and chordal passages. As we shall see later, this type of chanson led to the Italian instrumental canzona. Indeed, this very piece was used by Andrea Gabrieli (c. 1510–1586) as the basis for a four-voice instrumental canzona with the same title.

A somewhat artificial poetical and musical development known as the *vers mesuré* led to another, less important type of chanson. Concurrent with the freely polyphonic chanson, vers mesuré was a manifestation of the humanistic movement, for its adherents—principally the poets Ronsard and Baif—strove to imitate the quantitative rhythms of classic Greek and Roman poetry. The *Academie de poesie et de musique* was founded in 1570 by Baif for the purpose of setting vers mesuré poetry to music. The resultant compositions, which may be

Figure 44. Bars 16 to 27 of Crequillon's Chanson Pour Ung Plaisir.

called measured chansons, were theoretically to use only short and long tones in a ratio of one to two. The most successful composers of measured chansons were Claude le Jeune (1528–1600) and Jacques Mauduit (1557–1627), both of whom found it impossible to restrict themselves to so rigid a rhythmic plan. Its historical significance is found in the fact that, because it was a predominantly chordal style, it was another step toward the establishment of the diatonic tonal system.

The Italian Madrigal

The sixteenth-century madrigal is without doubt the most significant artistic achievement in the genre of secular part songs. Although its name originated in the fourteenth century it has little in common with the Trecento madrigals written by Landini and his contemporaries.

Nowhere in music history can a finer fusion of poetry and music be found than in the Renaissance madrigal. It was stimulated by an innovative movement in Italian poetry during the second quarter of the sixteenth century which began as a reaction to the frivolity of the frottola texts. Under the influence of models furnished by Cardinal Pietro Bembo (1470–1547), many short lyric poems of dignified character were written by Italian poets of the time. Designed to be set to music, their form was free, with lines of seven or eleven syllables in varied rhyme schemes. They were usually cast in a single strophe or stanza, often ten lines in length.

Poems of this type were then set to music by madrigal composers in a musical style very similar to the motet. At first, from about 1520–50, they were most often set in four voices—after 1550 in five voices, though six-voice madrigals are found, as well. Although present-day madrigal singers try to preserve the purity of one solo voice to a part, in the actual practice of the sixteenth century the performers probably used whatever was available, so that instruments undoubtedly doubled or substituted for voices quite commonly.

As in the motet, contrapuntal textures alternated with homophonic, and overlapping points of imitation were often found. The madrigal style is notable for its progressiveness during the late sixteenth century, suggesting that late Renaissance composers were more inclined to be innovative and experimental when writing secular vocal music than when composing music for the Church. The reverse was true in the early sixteenth century when the motet, and before that the Mass, had been the most important vehicles for musical innovation.

The texts, as in so much secular music up to this time, were most often on the subject of love, sometimes quite erotic in character, while some of the more serious ones pointed a moral. Much of the poetry was stereotyped and stilted, perhaps because it was so often read or sung at courtly social gatherings. Some composers, however, used texts of greater artistic merit by poets of considerable stature such as Petrarch, Tasso, and Ariosto. Madrigals were published and republished in great profusion well into the seventeenth century, a total of as many as 2,000 collections being printed between 1530 and 1600 alone.

For convenience, the history of the madrigal can be divided into three periods, (1) the early madrigal (1520–40), characterized by a three- or four-part texture and in a style not far removed from the frottola; (2) the classic or middle period madrigal (1540–80) in five, occasionally six parts, with considerable use of polyphony and imitation and more text painting; and (3) the late madrigal (1580–1620) in a more elaborate style with varying textures, increased dissonance and chromaticism, occasional separate instrumental accompaniments, and with greater emphasis upon vocal virtuosity. Madrigalists of the late period were more innovative than their predecessors, and often strove to illustrate the meaning of the text by highly dramatic effects and daringly innovative harmonies. Some of the madrigals of this period prepared the way for the development of opera in the early seventeenth century. Indeed, in the madrigals of Claudio Monteverdi (1567–1643) there can be seen the evolution from the sixteenth-century polyphonic style to the accompanied solo madrigal with continuo accompaniment, a development that led to the seventeenth-century operatic aria and accompanied monody.

Most significant among the early group of Italian madrigalists were Philippe Verdelot (c. 1480–c. 1540), Costanzo Festa (c. 1490–1545), Willaert, and Arcadelt. With typical Flemish versatility, Arcadelt and Verdelot wrote French chansons as well as madrigals. All of the early group are Flemish except Festa, who was Italian. Employed by the papal chapel during the early sixteenth century, Festa was one of the first Italian composers of the Renaissance to offer real competition to the Netherlanders. In addition to his many madrigals he was also noted for his motets and Masses.

Willaert, with his pupil Cipriano de Rore (1516–65), standardized the five-voice madrigal texture, and did much to alter the early homophonic frottola type of madrigal—mainly by increased use of imitative textures and free counterpoint. After 1540 the madrigal acquired greater musical expression and a closer relationship of text to music. In Willaert's madrigals of the middle period, word painting plays an increasingly prominent part, leading toward the classic concept of the madrigal as a piece of music devoted to the evocation, expression, or description of a poetic text—the essence of madrigalism.

Although Cipriano de Rore worked for a short time at St. Marks in Venice, Andrea Gabrieli, also a student of Willaert, more clearly represents the Venetian school in the second half of the sixteenth century in that he worked at St. Marks from 1566 until his death twenty years later. Though best known for his sacred and instrumental music, Gabrieli composed many madrigals, some of which are comic in nature. Other composers of the middle period include Phillippe de Monte and Giaches de Wert (1535–96), with whom the line of great Flemish composers in Italy came to an end. De Monte, a conservative composer of the first order, produced more than a thousand madrigals in which all of the essential aspects of the middle period style can be seen. Lasso and Palestrina (c. 1525–94), both best known for their compositions in other areas, also contributed to the madrigal repertory on the middle period. Lasso, though perfectly capable of writing in any of the styles of the time, composed madrigals which are somewhat less striking and certainly more conservative than his motets and chansons. Palestrina's modest contribution to the madrigal literature includes a number of madrigals with spiritual texts which are indistinguishable in style from his church music.

The most important composers of the late period of the Italian madrigal are Luca Marenzio (1553–99), whose works represent the culmination of the Italian madrigal, Carlo Gesualdo (c. 1560–1613), who was undoubtedly the most radically innovative, and Claudio Monteverdi, who bridges the transition period from the Renaissance to the Baroque. Figure 45 is an excerpt from the opening of the madrigal *S'io parto, i'moro* by Marenzio. Note the contrast of polyphonic and homophonic passages as well as the rhythmic flexibility seen in the varying number of metric units per measure. Marenzio's skill in expressing texts, sometimes by means of chromatic harmonies, and his prodigious polyphonic technique mark him as one of the most significant Renaissance composers. His deft evocation of the poetic image through musical sound perhaps marks him as the greatest of the Italian madrigalists.

Gesualdo, Prince of Venosa and one of the most colorful figures in music history, carried Renaissance versatility to the extreme of distinguishing himself as a murderer as well as a composer. His music seems somehow in keeping with his remarkable life style, for in his late madrigals he reaches extremes of chromaticism and uses unusually sharp contrasts for the sake of dramatic effect. His many dissonances and cross relations in a highly advanced harmonic fabric serve the text

Figure 45. Madrigal: S'io Parto, I'moro, *Marenzio.*

well for the most part, although occasionally his penchant for vivid text painting resulted in a series of more or less unconnected images. The exerpt from his madrigal *Io pur respiro* shown in figure 46 illustrates not only his extravagantly expressive chromaticism but also his resourceful use of textural contrast.

Orazio Vecchi (c. 1550–1605), a less famous member of the late madrigal group, is known particularly for his "madrigal comedy" *Il Amfiparnasso*. The characters in the musical play are those of the classical French comedy—Columbine, Pantaloon, and Harlequin. The plot unfolds in a series of five-part madrigals preceded by a prologue. The work represents an important step in the transition toward music drama.

Figure 46. Madrigal: Io Pur Respiro, *Gesualdo.*

Monteverdi's seven books of madrigals span his entire career, and in them can be seen the evolution of the *Seconda prattica,* one of the important steps in the emergence of the Baroque style. His earlier madrigals (books 1 to 4) are in the polyphonic style of the Renaissance *(Prima prattica)* but in the preface to Book Five (1605) he declared his adoption of the new style of modern music. The new style emphasizes solo vocal virtuosity, still in the service of the text but no longer in the unaccompanied polyphonic style of the Renaissance. In Book Seven much use is made of the solo voice accompanied by *basso continuo,* an accompaniment group consisting of a keyboard instrument plus a bass instrument—the medium which was to become the all-important accompaniment group of the Baroque period. The use of the continuo in the early seventeenth century is an important milestone in the history of musical thought. It exemplifies the movement away from the practices of the Renaissance, for continuo is based on a purely vertical conception of harmony in which chords are constructed of intervals above a bass tone. Renaissance polyphony was conceived horizontally as a fabric of several strands of melody whose relationship to each other produced a harmonic texture. This is not to say that Renaissance composers ignored the vertical sonorities that resulted from their multivoiced textures. Indeed, they calculated them very carefully. But Renaissance polyphony is heard primarily in terms of the interrelation of horizontal voice lines, while Baroque music, for the most part, is organized in vertical sonorities.

The Roman School of Church Music

Giovanni Pierluigi da Palestrina, the chief representative of the Roman school, was born around 1525 in the town of Palestrina (Praeneste); he later added the name of his birthplace to his own name. Though not an ordained priest, he spent much of his career in the service of the Church, mostly in various chapels of Rome. From 1571 until his death in 1594 he served as *Maestro di capella* of the Julian Chapel in Rome, a position he had held for a brief time twenty years earlier. Nearly all of his music was written for the church service, including more than a hundred Masses, about 260 motets, and a large number of incidental sacred works such as Magnificats and hymns. His few secular works, such as the madrigals mentioned earlier, are among his less distinguished compositions.

Palestrina worked primarily in a choral texture of four to eight parts, occasionally in as many as twelve parts, infusing his music with a profoundly emotional feeling in which the human voice is revealed as an instrument of deeply sensuous beauty. Much of his music is contemplative and reserved, well suited to the expression of profound religious faith. His most characteristic texture is imitative, the various voices weaving their way through a conservative harmonic fabric in a predominantly stepwise melodic style. The stepwise character of Palestrina's melodic style causes his music to have a very smoothly flowing effect, eminently suited to the human voice. Although he used conventional musica ficta, mostly at cadence points, he did not indulge in the kinds of expressive chromaticism and dissonance used by some of his contemporaries. In his masterful text settings, the natural rhythms of the words influence the rhythm of the music, stressed syllables usually being set to longer note values, in the usual practice of the Renaissance. So clear and consistent is Palestrina's musical style that rules and principles have been extracted from his music which are used traditionally as the basis for the study of sixteenth-century counterpoint. Following the general practice of Flemish and Italian composers of the sixteenth century, he treated dissonance in relation to rhythmic stress and intervals above the lowest voice. It should be remembered, however, that his is only one of several polyphonic styles of sixteenth-century vocal composers, and for this reason, the study of sixteenth-century counterpoint should encompass much more than merely the style of Palestrina.

The Roman Catholic Church reacted to the Reformation movement of the first half of the sixteenth century by a Counter Reformation. One manifestation of this was the formation of a famous council which met irregularly over a period of eighteen years (1545–63) in the city of Trent. The "Council of Trent," as it was called, was formed of Catholic churchmen who were concerned, among other things, with the increasing secularization of the church service. Parody masses based on secular tunes, instruments in the church, complex polyphony which hindered understanding of the text, carelessness in carrying out the services, and even irreverent attitudes on the part of the church musicians became subjects of discussion by the Council. Although the Council of Trent made no really specific pronouncements on musical matters, it undoubtedly did influence Church composers of the time, particularly in Rome, toward a simpler, smoother and clearer style, and led toward the distinctive practices of the composers of the Roman School of church music, culminating in the works of Palestrina. The story that Palestrina was asked by certain members of the Council of Trent to "save" polyphonic music for the Church, though interesting, is untrue.

Perhaps the best way to understand the style of this great Renaissance composer is through an examination of one of his works. Figure 47 presents two excerpts from one of his most famous works, the Pope Marcellus Mass, around which grew the legend of Palestrina as the "savior" of polyphonic music for the Church. In many ways this work exemplifies the precepts of the Council of Trent, for its texture is smooth and homogenous, and although it contains much imitation, it also has numerous passages in which several voices sing the same words at the same time (familiar style), thus making the words more readily understandable.

As in most musical settings of the Mass, the Pope Marcellus Mass deals only with the five sections of the ordinary of the Mass, but because there are two settings of the *Agnus Dei*, the work is actually in six movements. Although written for a basic chorus of six parts, certain sections are in only four or five parts and the second Agnus Dei uses a seven-voice texture. Canonic imitation can be seen in the opening of the Kyrie shown in figure 47. Note in this excerpt the smooth stepwise motion of the melodic lines as well as the overlapping of phrases at the beginning of the second phrase.

The Kyrie serves well to demonstrate the evolution toward diatonic tonality taking place in the sixteenth century. The movement is in three sections corresponding to the three sections of the text—*Kyrie eleison, Christe eleison, Kyrie eleison*—and each of the three sections ends with a complete cadence, the first on C, the second on G, and the third on C. Although Renaissance composers were still consciously using the system of Church modes, this type of clear indication of a tonic-dominant relationship was quite common in sixteenth-century music, presaging the firm establishment of the fifth relation as the basic concept of tonal structure in the seventeenth century.

The *Gloria* opens with a line of Gregorian chant to the words *"Gloria in Excelsis Deo,"* followed by the chorus presenting the words *"Et in terra pax"* in familiar style. The text of the *Gloria* is second only to the *Credo* in length, so that both become very substantial movements in musical settings of the Mass. It is worth noting, in view of the concerns of the Council of Trent about the treatment of the text of the Mass, that the more complex sections of the Mass *(Gloria* and *Credo)* are set in predominantly homophonic textures, thus making the words more easily understandable, while the other movements, with their shorter simpler texts, are rendered in more complex polyphonic settings with considerable repetition of words.

The second excerpt in figure 47 illustrates the kind of rhythmic freedom characteristic of the Roman School and of Renaissance polyphony in general. A microrhythmic analysis of the excerpt has been made by means of brackets, each of which indicates a unit, usually beginning with a long note followed by successively diminishing note values. It should be remembered that bar lines are added in most modern editions of Renaissance music corresponding to the "tactus" or strong beat which was used in the fifteenth and sixteenth centuries in place of bar lines as an aid in performance and to furnish an orientation point in the handling of dissonance. The number added above each bracket indicates the number of quarter note values in each unit. The rhythmic freedom in Renaissance music is, in part, a side effect of the careful treatment of the text. The actual rhythm of each voice in the music rarely corresponds to the bar lines or tactus; and, because of their varying lengths, the units frequently overlap among the various voices, creating a beautiful effect of rhythmic freedom and subtle fluctuation in the flow of the music.

The *Credo* of the Pope Marcellus Mass, like the *Gloria*, opens with a line of Gregorian chant followed immediately by the next lines of text sung by the chorus. Because of the several distinct theological concepts expressed in the text, the *Credo* is quite sectional in form, frequently with contrast in the texture or number of parts between sections. Musical symbolism and subtle word painting are heard throughout the *Credo* on such phrases as *"ascendit in coelum," "descendit de coelis,"* and *"Crucifixus."*

The *Sanctus*, serene in its beauty, encloses the *Benedictus* by means of the following pattern: (1) basic text of the *Sanctus* up to (2) *"Hosanna in excelsis"* followed by (3) *Benedictus*, and (4) concluding with an exact repetition of the *"Hosanna in excelsis."* The first *Agnus Dei* which follows is very similar to the opening *Kyrie*, providing thematic unity in the Mass as a whole. The second *Agnus Dei*, with its seven-part texture, furnishes the richest and strongest web of sound heard up to this point in the Mass, concluding the work on a note of confidence and affirmation.

Other members of the Roman School of church music include Marcantonio Ingegneri (1545–92), Giovanni Nanini (c. 1545–1607), and Felice Anerio (1560–1614). The latter two, in addition to composing in the style of Palestrina, wrote in the so called "colossal style," scoring for very large groups of choruses, soloists, and instruments. Anerio, in fact, rearranged the Pope Marcellus Mass of Palestrina in a polychoral setting not unlike the Venetian style to be discussed in the next section.

Tomas Luis de Victoria (c. 1540–1611), although of Spanish birth, ranks second only to Palestrina among the composers of the Roman School. He worked in Rome for a period of about thirty years from 1565 and was ordained a priest in 1575. His teacher was Cristobal Morales

Figure 47. Two excerpts from Palestrina's Pope Marcellus Mass. The Second Excerpt Shows the Microrhythmic Structure Characteristic of Much Renaissance Polyphony.

(c. 1500–53), also a Spaniard, who sang in the papal choir in Rome. Victoria's style is similar to Palestrina's, although he was more daring in his use of chromaticism and dissonance.

The conservatism and consistency of style in the music of the Roman school, and the pure a cappella manner of performance in the Roman chapels epitomize the ideals of polyphonic church music of the Renaissance. It remained, however, for the more progressive composers of sixteenth century Venice to infuse the music of Renaissance Italy with ideas which led toward the new practices of the Baroque.

The Venetian School

The splendor, power, and wealth of Venice had reached its peak in the fifteenth century, but in spite of economic decline, wars, and other misfortunes during the Renaissance, she continued to maintain her cultural dominance in European civilization well into the seventeenth century. As a city she maintained an attitude of aloof superiority, for she was the chief European port for trade with the East, and while she was nominally part of Italy, she was also separated—geographically by her system of lagoons and canals, and politically through her status as an independent city-state. The combination of her cosmopolitan atmosphere, wealth, and independence created a fertile environment for artistic endeavor.

The musical culture of Venice centered in the magnificent eleventh-century cathedral of St. Mark (San Marco). Situated on the spacious piazza San Marco, it is a most impressive structure, with brilliant mosaics below sumptuous Byzantine domes, and with a vast interior drenched in filtered green-gold light. It furnished the setting for the majestic ceremonies of both Church and State which often required every possible resource of musical sound. Like the city, the cathedral also enjoyed considerable independence; for its clergy and musicians were responsible primarily to the Doge of Venice rather than to Rome. ("Doge" is a cognate of duke and is the name given to the chief magistrates of the cities of Venice and Genoa.) Thus, the music in the cathedral was the responsibility of state officials who spared no expense to maintain the time-honored standards and traditions of Venice.

The position of choirmaster at St. Mark's, the most coveted musical position in all Italy, was held during the sixteenth century by Willaert, the founder of the Venetian school, by Rore, Gioseffo Zarlino (1517–90), and Baldassare Donati (1530–1603). Because of the fact that there were two organs in the cathedral, there were also two positions for organist. These were held during the sixteenth century by Jacques Buus (d. 1565), Padovano, Merulo, Andrea Gabrieli, and his nephew Giovanni Gabrieli (c. 1557–1612). The cathedral is constructed in such a way that the two organs were placed on opposite sides of the church in two separate choir areas. Although the divided choir did not originate in Venice, the structure of the cathedral was a contributing factor to the Venetian practice of composing for multiple choirs of voices and instruments. The typically Venetian use of massive chordal harmonies in preference to intricate polyphonic textures may in part have been a result of the acoustics of the vast sanctuary. Thus, the situation in the city and the architecture of the church significantly influenced the musical style of the Venetian school.

In a more general way the atmosphere of Venice was quite different from that of Rome, and this too had its impact upon musical style. Rome, with its religious, even ascetic aura, had little of the extroverted, flamboyant, and cosmopolitan quality of Venice. The hedonistic life style of the Venetians eschewed excessive seriousness, and this can be heard in the rich full textures (predominantly homophonic), and in the highly varied and colorful harmonies of the Venetian composers. The use of instruments in St. Mark's added to the pageantry as well as to the variety of timbres. Not only the organs but also trombones, cornets, viols, and other instruments were used in combination with the voices.

Indeed, the instrumental practices at St. Mark's set precedents that were of the great importance for the development of instrumental practices of the Baroque and subsequent periods in music history. Chief among these were (1) the beginning development of *idiomatic* composition for instruments, (2) the development of the *concertato* style, and (3) the use of dynamic markings. All three are vividly illustrated in a famous piece of music by Giovanni Gabrieli entitled *Sonata pian'e forte.* As the name implies, it utilizes the contrast of loud to soft and thus is the earliest known piece to make use of specific dynamic markings. It is also the first piece known to have its exact instrumentation specified in the score—the beginning of idiomatic writing for instruments. Finally, scored for two instrumental choirs (cornetto or Zink and three trombones, and viola and three trombones), it makes use of striking contrasts of instrumental groups—an important innovation of the Venetian school which came to be known as the *concertato* style.

The concertato style, which was to become so important to the development of the Baroque concerto, is a generic term for the contrast of two instrumental or vocal groups, usually one large and one small, within a single piece of music. In a sense, the Venetian polychoral motet, with its echo effects and sharp contrasts, exemplifies the concertato style, although the term is most typically associated with purely instrumental music. Giovanni Gabrieli's use of the concertato style, with his broad masses of choral sound and progressive writing for the instruments, won him the title of "Father of Orchestration."

Among the other innovations of the Venetian school is the daring chromaticism and free use of modulation practiced by Willaert, the founder of the Venetian school. In the area of instrumental writing, Antonio Gabrieli and Merulo composed pieces called *toccatas,* a title later used for virtuosic keyboard pieces of the baroque. Zarlino is best known as a theorist, conducting investigations of tuning systems including just intonation and, to some extent, equal temperament. Less well known is Nicola Vicentino (1511–72), whose daring speculations on the use of microtones led to the development of a fantastic keyboard instrument called the *Arcicembalo* which had six keyboards with 31 tones to each octave and was able to play in all of the ancient Greek enharmonic genera. Vicentino described the instrument in his *L'Antica Musica* (1555).

Students of Giovanni Gabrieli and others influenced by him were scattered throughout Austria and Germany in the late sixteenth and seventeenth centuries. In particular, mention should be made of Michael Praetorius (1560–1629), Handl (1550–91), also known as Gallus, and Hans Leo Hassler (1564–1612), all of whom in their music showed a strong influence of Venetian polychoral writing. Although in the shadow of Florentine monody during the early seventeenth century, the progressive and innovative spirit of the Venetian school exerted a significant influence upon the stylistic developments of the Baroque.

Spanish Music

A number of Spanish composers and musicians achieved distinction through their association with the school of Church music in Rome during the sixteenth century. Chief among these were Morales and Victoria, mentioned earlier in the discussion of Roman Church music, but there were a number of other Spanish composers and theorists of importance working in their own country during the Renaissance. Earliest among the composer-theorists is Bartolome Ramos de Pareja (c. 1440–92), who in his *De Musica Tractatus* laid the foundation for our harmonic system and established the frequency ratios of several of our harmonic intervals. His experiments with the monochord came close to achieving equal temperament. He can be viewed as a forebear of the nineteenth-century acoustician Heinrich Helmholz, whose research, though more precise than that of Ramos, was in the same general area. Francisco de Salinas (1513–90), another composer-theorist, made the earliest collection of Spanish folk music to illustrate passages in his *De Musica Libri Septem* (1577), a work which is most notable for its description of mean tone temperament.

The development of instrumental styles and idioms owes much to the Spanish masters of the Renaissance. In addition to organ music, they composed for instruments native to Spain such as the guitar and *vihuela,* a lute-like instrument which used a tablature notation similar to Italian lute tablature. In 1535 and 1536 the composer Luis Milan (1500–61) produced the first published Spanish tablature book, a volume entitled *El Maestro* which includes directions for tuning the vihuela and for reading tablature. In addition to purely instrumental pieces, it contains some of the earliest examples of solo songs with vihuela (or lute) accompaniment. These songs, which were called *villancicos* or romances, were important to the development of instrumental variation forms.

Antonio de Cabezon (1510–66), blind organist and harpsichordist to Charles V and Philip II and the greatest sixteenth-century Spanish instrumental composer, contributed much to the development of variation forms. In his travels he exerted a strong influence upon composers throughout Europe, notably upon Sweelinck in Holland. Cabezon's *diferencias* are among the first true examples of the theme and variations, and undoubtedly influenced Diego Ortiz (born c. 1529), another Spaniard who composed some excellent early examples of variation forms for the bass-viol and cembalo.

The influence of the Netherlanders was felt very strongly upon the sacred polyphony of Renaissance Spain as it was throughout continental Europe, though little is known of the history of Spanish polyphony prior to the fifteenth century. A characteristic avoidance of complex contrapuntal devices combined with a typically Spanish fervency of religious expression lends a unique flavor to the sacred choral music of the Spanish Renaissance, Morales' motet *Emendus in melias* is a good case in point, though other examples can be found among the works of both Victoria and Morales.

Instrumental Music

Some of the Renaissance instrumental developments of France, Italy, and Spain have been discussed earlier, but because there are so many cross-influences and simultaneous developments, a summary is in order. Until 1550 the Renaissance had been primarily concerned with vocal polyphony, but at the same time there were a number of serious composers who evidenced considerable interest in the development of idiomatic instrumental styles. Obviously instrumental music existed prior to the Renaissance but, as we have seen, its role in ensemble performances was primarily supportive—to reinforce a weak voice or substitute for a missing one. Since the music was written first of all for voices rather than for instruments, there was little opportunity for the development of musical styles unique to specific instruments. In many instances there is evidence to suggest that certain medieval polyphonic works were intended to be performed by a solo voice, with instruments taking the lower parts even though this was rarely, if ever, specified in the score.

At the beginning of the sixteenth century instrumental music was still closely linked with vocal style, but the publication of books which described instruments or gave instructions for playing them indicated a growing regard for instrumental music. The first of these was Sebastian Virdung's *Musica getutscht und ausgezogen* (1511), which contains pictures of a wide variety of wind instruments, followed a century later by Michael Praetorius' *Syntagma Musicum* (1618), which more fully covered the field of Renaissance instruments.

A notable feature of these books is that the instruments are consistently arranged in sets or families of similar types in order that one instrumental timbre could be achieved throughout the overall range of the various sizes of instruments from bass to soprano. The homogeneity of sound in this arrangement was in keeping with the Renaissance ideal of a uniform mass of sound as seen, for example, in the typical choral texture of the music of the Roman school. The complete sets of instruments were called "chests" or "consorts." A piece of music written for a "complete" consort included enough parts for all of the instruments in a particular family (viols or recorders, as the case might be), while a "broken" or "mixed" consort indicated that the music was written for selected instruments from a chest or for a mixture of families.

The wind instruments in common use during the Renaissance included the family of recorders, ancestors of our modern flute; the shawm, a double reed instrument from which our oboe and bassoon descended; the crumhorn, with its double reed enclosed in a box; and the cornetti, trumpets, and trombones (sackbuts). The stringed instruments included many types of lutes and viols. The viols differed from the instruments of our modern violin family in that they were not tuned in fifths but usually followed a lute tuning in which the strings were tuned a fourth apart except for the two middle strings, which were a major third apart (i.e., A-D-G-B-E-A). Also, the viols used frets, which greatly influenced the technique of the instrument; only a slight vibrato was possible with frets and then was probably used only in special instances, almost as an ornament.

Known for centuries in Europe, the lute was by far the most popular household instrument as well as the virtuoso instrument of the Renaissance. It was used for solos, for ensembles, and for accompaniment to voices. Built in sundry shapes and sizes (e.g., the vihuela with its guitar-like body, and the theorbo with its oddly shaped neck), the standard lute body was pear-shaped with a flat-fretted finger board and a peg box set perpendicular to the neck. With skillful plucking of the strings it was possible to play not only chords, but also melodies, scales, ornaments, and simulated contrapuntal passages. Lute music was notated by means of tablature, a system in which the strings were represented by lines, and the pitches indicated by finger positions on the lines. Similar tablature systems were used to some extent for keyboard notation as well.

The keyboard instruments included the organ, the harpsichord, and the clavichord. By 1500 the large church organs were very similar to the organs of today, although the pedal board was adopted in Germany and the Netherlands long before it became popular in the other European countries. The harpsichords were built in many forms and sizes and went by various names such as virginal, clavecin, clavicembalo, spinet, etc. The harpsichord is distinguished from the clavichord primarily by its manner of tone production. The clavichord tone is produced by a metal tangent striking the string when the key is depressed so that, within narrow limits, its volume could be controlled by the performer who could also impart a slight vibrato to the tone by manipulation of the key. Its tone was very soft and was used primarily for private solo performance in small chambers. The harpsichord tone is produced by a mechanical plucking action activated by the depression of the key. Although its volume could not be appreciably altered by varying the pressure, it nevertheless was a much more useful concert instrument than the clavichord because of its larger volume of sound and its ability to achieve contrasts (though not gradations) in dynamic level by the use of different stops and manuals. As an accompaniment instrument, the harpsichord was second only to the lute in the Renaissance, and was the most popular keyboard instrument of the Renaissance and Baroque periods.

For the most part, Renaissance instruments were softer in dynamic level than their modern counterparts. The recorders were softer and mellower than our modern flutes; the viols were pale in sound in comparison to the violin-type instruments in use since the seventeenth century; and even the trumpets, trombones, and cornetti did not have the brilliance made possible by modern technology of brass instrument making. (A notable exception is the crumhorn, which usually sounds more penetrating, rougher, and more awkward than our modern oboe.) It may very well be that the relatively lower dynamic levels and delicate contrasts to which Renaissance listeners were accustomed enabled them to hear more perceptively and discriminate more intelligently among the subtle details of Renaissance line, color, and ornament than modern audiences conditioned by two centuries of symphony orchestras.

Renaissance instrumental music can be divided into three general classes: (1) transcriptions, arrangements, or imitations of vocal music; (2) idiomatic instrumental music written for specific solo instruments or ensembles; and (3) music for dancing, either newly composed or transcribed. The most important types of instrumental music in category one, those derived from vocal music, are the *ricercar* and *canzona.* The practice of substituting instruments in the pieces written originally for voices can be viewed as an extension of the medieval and pre-Renaissance practice of performing vocal motets as solo songs, with instruments taking the lower parts. Gradually the concept of adapting vocal pieces to instruments led toward the composition of instrumental pieces which, though not derived from specific vocal works, were based on vocal prototypes. The meaning of the word *ricercar* is illuminating in this regard, for it means to "search out" or "look back," a cognate of "research." One interpretation of its connection with the instrumental form is that a ricercar was originally based on a preexisting vocal form which was unearthed or "searched out" from the music of the past. Another interpretation is that the word should be translated as "study" and that a ricercar is a study in contrapuntal writing for instruments. The latter theory is borne out by the sobriety and scholarly nature of many ricercari, including the famous examples in J. S. Bach's *Musical Offering.*

The imitative or contrapuntal ricercar is the instrumental counterpart of the Renaissance motet; in some instances the instructions in the scores actually stated that the works could be either sung or played on instruments. Constructed in a series of points of imitation, frequent tones of relatively long duration add to the prevailing mood of seriousness. Many were written for ensembles, but imitative ricercars written specifically for organ began to appear around the middle of the sixteenth century. After 1550 these began to be based on one theme or several slow themes in succession—the beginning development of the baroque organ fugue. There are, however, many pieces inappropriately called ricercari written for lute, organ, other instruments, and even voices, none of which are related to the motet. At its height, the ricercar utilized contrapuntal devices such as augmentation and inversion—as in a fugue; and, though originally conceived in imitation of a vocal style, it gradually began to use idiomatic instrumental techniques and increasingly varied rhythms.

In its simplest form a canzona is an instrumental transcription of a French polyphonic chanson, for the word "canzona" is simply the Italian word for "chanson." The terms *canzon da sonar* (chanson to be sounded or played) and *canzona alla francese* are both common terms for the Italian instrumental *canzona,* examples of which were written for solo instruments as well as ensembles. The several types of canzone include (1) an ornamented version of a chanson, (2) works very similar to the first type but composed of new material rather than being derived from a chanson and (3) the "quilt canzona" or "sectional canzona." Figure 48 is an example of the first type. A. Gabrieli is the composer and it is an embellished version of the Crequillon *chanson* excerpted in figure 44. A comparison of the measures cited here with the original vocal work will reveal how closely the composer of the instrumental work followed the original, for the two are harmonically identical, and Gabrieli did little more than fill in many of the leaps with instrumentally conceived scale passages and broken thirds.

Figure 48. Bars 16 to 27 Canzona Francese Deta Pour Ung Plaisir, *A. Gabrieli.*

Examples of the second type are numerous and differ from type one in that many of them were a bit more sophisticated in their contrapuntal textures—more similar to the ricercar; although the opening dactylic motive continued to be found in all types of *canzone* as a hallmark of the form and a vestige of the French chanson. The sectional *canzona* consisted of as many as eight or more sections of contrasting tempi and texture, all separated by well-defined cadences. This type can be viewed as one of the ancestors of baroque sonata forms, for in the seventeenth century its sections gradually expanded to form individual movements. Changes of meter from section to section, even in some of the earliest sectional canzone, forecast the meter changes that were to appear in sonatas of the Baroque.

The second general class of Renaissance instrumental music includes many types of solo and ensemble music—preludes and toccatas for the keyboard, variation forms such as those mentioned in the section on Spanish music, and improvisatory works with or without a given cantus firmus. The keyboard works included organ preludes for use in church services, but the works in the toccata category for organ or harpsichord are more significant. These include the *Intonazio d'organo* of G. Gabrieli and culminated in the brilliant polyphonic toccatas of Claudio Merulo. The Spaniards Cabezon and Ortiz are the most important composers of variation forms, contributing to the development of the theme and variations as well as to the passacaglia and chaconne.

Sixteenth-century performers improvised in two basic ways: (1) by embellishing a given melodic line; or (2) by adding contrapuntal parts to an existing cantus firmus. The first of these methods is seen in the widespread practice of ornamentation which was to become so important to the performers of the seventeenth and eighteenth centuries, and which today is the subject of so much scholarly speculation. The second is a vestige of medieval practices and was considered an important discipline in a composer's training. The Latin term for this practice, *Discantus supra librum,* led to the modern meaning of our term "descant." Other works in free improvisatory style, but without the use of canti firmi included *praeambula, fantasias,* and even works which were mistakenly called ricercari. It should be remembered that, since the sixteenth century was the period in which music for specific instruments was first "written down," much of the early notated instrumental music was the written representation of improvisational practices that may have existed for centuries.

Dance pieces, those in our third general class of Renaissance instrumental music, include pieces for lute, keyboard, and ensembles—a sizeable portion of sixteenth-century instrumental music. They owed little to vocal forms, were not improvised as in the Middle Ages, and developed because of the widespread practice of social dancing. Many of them were written in tablature or part books and are found in collections published by various music printers including Petrucci and Attaignant. Because they were designed for dancing, the rhythmic patterns are clear, regular and quite repetitious, with homophonic textures predominating. The practice of grouping the dances in pairs, as in the *pavane* and *galliarde* or the *basse danse* and *tourdion,* led to the instrumental dance suite of the Baroque.

6. The Renaissance: National Styles of Germany and England

German Vocal Music and the Reformation—
German Instrumental Music—The Reformation in
England—Elizabethan Secular Vocal Music—
Elizabethan Instrumental Music

German Vocal Music and the Reformation

Polyphony developed later in Germany than in the countries of southern Europe. Its real beginnings came after 1450 with the influence of the Flemish composers, particularly Heinrich Isaac, teacher of Ludwig Senfl. Though born in the Netherlands, and employed for a time in Italy, Isaac's art is most closely associated with Germany. Like most Flemish composers, his versatility encompassed all of the European national styles of the early Renaissance, but he is particularly well known for his secular German part songs, the polyphonic lieder.

In the fifteenth century the two most important collections of German secular song are the *Locheimer Liederbuch* (c. 1450) and the *Glogauer Liederbuch* (c. 1460), both of which contain music bearing some relationship to the earlier art of the minnesingers as well as examples of polyphonic songs. Some of them are in chordal style, while others are in three parts with a slow-moving folk song used in the middle voice as a cantus firmus. The Glogauer collection also contains some instrumental dance music as well as examples of the *quodlibet,* a novel kind of polyphonic song made up of tunes or fragments from various sources put together in such a way as to make musical sense. Senfl composed many quodlibets and, though the juxtaposition of miscellaneous texts produced some incongruous or deliberately humorous effects, the musical results were sometimes quite artistic.

Isaac, Hassler, Senfl, and Lassus are the most significant composers of polyphonic lieder with German texts. These are musically distinguishable from the chanson and the madrigal by their folk-like quality and generally simpler chordal textures. However, the late sixteenth-century domination by Italian styles, particularly that of Venice,

103

caused the fading out of a distinct German vocal style, so that the late Renaissance polyphonic lieder are, except for the German texts, very much like the chansons.

Martin Luther's famous statement of principles presented in the year 1517 to the church authorities of Wittenberg started a chain reaction that led to a century of religious strife and to the establishment of several Protestant churches. Significant among the musical aspects of Luther's reforms were (1) the removal of the *Credo* and *Agnus Dei* from the ordinary of the Mass, and (2) the substitution of German hymns for certain sections of the proper. The first of these led to the composition of numerous short Masses for use in the Lutheran Church, while the second led to the development of the Lutheran chorale. The chorales rapidly grew into a large body of literature—the communal songs of the Lutheran church.

The chorale tunes came from a number of sources. As mentioned earlier *"O Welt ich muss dich lassen"* was derived from Isaac's *"Innsbruck ich muss dich lassen,"* and the famous passion chorale "O Sacred Head" comes from a *Lied* by Hassler entitled *"Mein G'muth ist mir verwirret,"* originally a tavern song. Some were adapted from Gregorian chant tunes; others came from folk tunes; and a number of chorales were composed originally, many to texts translated or written by Martin Luther. Luther himself was not without musical ability. He knew the music of his time, particularly esteeming the works of Josquin, and it is likely that he composed the music for a number of chorales, including *Ein' feste Burg.*

The first polyphonic works based on the Lutheran chorale tunes were composed by Johann Walther (1496–1570) in a collection called the *Geystlich Gesangk Buchleyn* published at Wittenberg in 1524. The thirty-eight pieces in the collection are for three to six voices, with most of the melodies in the tenor in the old motet style. Toward the middle of the sixteenth century the practice of playing the melody in the tenor—a vestige of cantus firmus technique—declined in favor of chorale harmonizations with the melody in the soprano. This trend was seen also in the Calvinistic psalm settings by composers such as Claude Goudimel, discussed earlier. The practice was firmly established in a collection of fifteen psalms and chorales by Lucas Osiander (1534–1604) published in 1586. Many German composers continued to write Catholic church music throughout the sixteenth century, and the influence of the Venetian school was spread throughout Germany, most of all by Hassler, who had been a student of Andrea Gabrieli.

German Instrumental Music

Virdung's *Musica Getutscht und ausgezogen* of 1511, discussed in the preceding chapter, is a manifestation of the thriving interest in instrumental music in sixteenth-century Germany. In the same year another book, also in German, was published under the title *Spiegel der Orgelmacher und Organisten.* Written by the blind organist and lutenist Arnold Schlick (c. 1460–c. 1517), the book offers a detailed description of the early Renaissance organ in Germany. The organ had developed early in Germany. Indeed, primitive pedal boards had been in use as early as the fourteenth century, and in the sixteenth century, German organs had two or three manuals, a fairly complete pedal board, and an assortment of stops to achieve a variety of timbres. Such instruments were ideally suited to the performance of polyphonic music, a fact that is most important to the later development of organ music by the great composers of the German baroque. The pedal board was almost unknown in Italy during the sixteenth century and was not used in England until after the time of Handel.

Although German Renaissance organ music is not the most distinguished body of literature for the instrument, it is of importance in the overall history of organ music since it exemplifies the earliest music specifically notated for the instrument. The *Buxheimer Orgelbuch* (c. 1470) contains about 250 pieces, some in organ tablature, including arrangements of Burgundian chansons. Conrad Paumann is the first distinguished organist composer of Germany and is also the author of one of the first textbooks of composition and improvisation, *Fundamentum Organisandi* (1452). A number of later Renaissance organ composers studied with Paulus Hofhaimer (1459–1537), a famous organist and composer of songs and organ pieces.

Henricus Glareanus (1488–1563), though Swiss rather than German, is mentioned here for his important theoretical work, the *Dodecachordon* (1547). The title means literally "twelve strings," but the volume is directed toward the discussion of modes. Using many musical examples, including some by Josquin, Glareanus advocated the use of twelve modes instead of the eight traditional Church modes. The major contribution of the book is the recognition of the Aeolian and Ionian modes, even though, in actuality, they had been in use for some time through the application of musica ficta to the eight Church modes.

The Reformation in England

The Tudor period ushered in one of the great eras in English music. The name comes from Owen Tudor of Wales who married the widow of Henry V of England, and the period extends through the reign (1558–1603) of Queen Elizabeth I up to the time of James I in the early seventeenth century. Musical developments in England during this time seemed to follow those of the continent with a lag of twenty-five to fifty years, but this is not meant to suggest that the English merely imitated Italian and French styles. On the contrary, though the styles of the continent furnished points of departure, this is perhaps the greatest and most productive period in English music.

The English reformation movement began around 1530 and, as in Germany, wielded a strong influence upon music for the church. The real separation of the English church from the Roman took place in the year 1534 under Henry VIII and, though the reasons for the King's action were political and personal rather than doctrinal, a new liturgy began to take shape which became official in 1549 under Edward VI. Latin was abandoned and the English Book of Common Prayer was adopted as the only permissible liturgy. There was a brief return to Catholicism under Mary I ("Bloody Mary"), who reigned from 1553–58, but when Elizabeth I took the throne in 1558 the Church of England was reestablished in essentially the same form that it retains today. John Taverner (c. 1495–1545) was the first outstanding Tudor composer and, although he wrote nothing for the Anglican Church, his Catholic church music demonstrates his mastery of the polyphonic techniques of the Netherlands composers.

The three most important parts of the Anglican liturgy are the services of Morning and Evening Prayer and the communion service. The communion is the English version of the Mass, while the other two services are adapted from the canonical hours of the Roman liturgy. The first musical setting of the Book of Common Prayer was composed in 1550 by John Marbeck (1523–c. 1585) and was called *The Booke of Common Praier Noted.* The setting consisted simply of tunes for congregational singing, but choral settings of the services were composed soon after by Christopher Tye (c. 1500–72) and Thomas Tallis (c. 1505–85). The English counterpart of the Latin motet was the anthem with English text, which began to be composed around 1560 and, except for the services, was the most important musical form of the Anglican Church. The anthem differed from the Latin motet in that it was predominantly syllabic, less contrapuntal in texture, and utilized short symmetrical phrases with great emphasis on the text.

Using the English anthem as a point of departure, William Byrd (1543–1623), the greatest composer of the English Renaissance, developed the verse anthem. This form, which survived well into the Baroque period in the compositions of Henry Purcell (1659–95), consists of alternating passages for solo voice or voices with sections for full chorus, all accompanied by instruments. Orlando Gibbons (1583–1625), another great Elizabethan composer, wrote verse anthems as well as anthems in the older motet style. One of his outstanding works is the anthem in motet style entitled *"Almighty and Everlasting God"* in which the text painting lends to the work the same kind of expressiveness that is found in the English madrigal. Gibbon's admirable setting of text is particularly apparent in the fourth of the five sections on the words "Stretch forth thy right hand."

It should not be presumed that church music of the Renaissance English composers was written solely for the Church of England. William Byrd, like his teacher Thomas Tallis, and like Christopher Tye, composed music to Latin texts for use in the Roman church as well as settings of the Anglican liturgy. Indeed, some of Byrd's greatest works are those written for the Catholic Church, and he remained a Catholic throughout his life. These include three Masses for four, five and six voices respectively, and a number of motets.

Elizabethan Secular Vocal Music

In the year 1588 the Italian madrigal came to England in a publication called *Musica Transalpina,* a volume including madrigals by most of the outstanding Italian madrigalists—all with English translations. This and a similar publication in 1590 strongly influenced the English madrigalists, who followed the Italian models in their use of imaginative text painting and musical symbolism, but were somewhat less inclined than the Italians toward polyphonic and chromatic complexity.

As indicated in Thomas Morley's *A Plaine and Easie Introduction to Practicall Musicke,* and other writings of the time, musical activity was a vital part of many Elizabethan households. Madrigals were often performed as entertainments by amateurs, which suggests that the ability to sing a vocal part at sight from a "part book" was a fairly common talent. Much Renaissance music in Europe as well as England was published in individual parts, although in most modern editions the part book has been abandoned in favor of full score. Probably the most difficult polyphonic madrigals were beyond the reach of most amateurs, but there is no doubt that many of the light homophonic part songs were sung frequently and enthusiastically in Elizabethan households.

Elizabethan part songs can be divided into two basic categories: (1) light homophonic pieces of the "fa-la" variety, strophic in form, also called ballets, and (2) madrigals with more serious poetic texts and more polyphonic textures. Those of the first type were composed in great abundance by many Elizabethan composers including Morley, whose "now is the Month of Maying" and "Sing we and Chant it" are famous examples. In most of these short pieces each verse concludes with a fa-la refrain. Easily performed by nonprofessionals, they typify the lightest and freshest side of Elizabethan music.

Those of the second type are more properly called madrigals and were composed in great numbers by Thomas Weelkes (c. 1575–1623), John Wilbye (1574–1638), Morley, Byrd and others. A representative collection is found in the *Triumphs of Oriana,* published by Morley in 1601 after an Italian anthology entitled *Il Trionfo di Dori* (1592). The *Oriana* collection contains twenty-five madrigals, each by a different composer, and each concluding with the words "Long live fair Oriana," a name poetically applied to Queen Elizabeth I. Pastoral poems, most of them anonymous, were highly favored as texts, others pointed a moral, while others were (of course) on the subject of unrequited love. The elegance of expression and nicety of sentiment in English madrigals suggests that intense emotion was less important than finesse in musical expression, although there are some notable instances of the use of chromaticism to express grief, pain, or death. Figure 49 presents such an example from the five-part madrigal "The Silver Swan" by Gibbons. Typifying the more serious madrigal, the text points a moral, is realized in a polyphonic texture, and uses musical devices to subtly describe the meaning of the text. A poignant bit of text painting is found in the second measure of the example in the top voice on the word "death." The five parts at this point form an augmented triad to evoke the feeling of death, a mood which is enhanced by the rarity of this sonority in sixteenth-century music.

The air, or "ayre," another form of secular Elizabethan vocal music gaining popularity around the end of the sixteenth century, is essentially nothing more than a solo song with instrumental accompaniment. So popular did this type of song become that during the first quarter of the seventeenth century it began to supersede the madrigal as a form for musical entertainment. Among the numerous composers of airs, the two most noted are John Dowland (1563–1626) and Thomas Campion (1567–1620). The typical example shown in figure 50 is the first phrase of a Dowland song entitled "My thoughts are wing'd with hope." Its simple, clean phrase structure typifies the style, with most of the four-bar phrases ending with clear-cut cadences on the tonic or dominant—a manifestation of the increasing tendency toward chordal diatonic harmony based on the relationship of two sonorities with roots a fifth apart.

Elizabethan Instrumental Music

The excerpt in figure 50 is also of interest to the development of instrumental music in England, for it appears as an instrumental piece

Figure 49. Excerpt from The Silver Swan, Gibbons.

in Dowland's *Lachrimae, or Seaven Teares Figured in Seaven Passionate Pavans* for viols or violins, and is also found as a lute solo. As on the continent, English instrumental music developed first of all as transcriptions of vocal music. Books of English lute songs or lute ayres were often published in two versions and placed on facing pages, the version on the left being a polyphonic transcription of the song on the right page. Thus four different versions were possible and in the performance practices of the time any one of the following might have

Figure 50. Air: My Thoughts Are Wing'd With Hope, Dowland.

been used: (1) the original solo song version with lute or harpsichord accompaniment; (2) as a solo song accompanied by an instrumental ensemble, perhaps a group of viols reading from the transcribed version on the left; (3) as a vocal ensemble with unaccompanied voices reading from the polyphonic version like a madrigal; and (4) as a purely instrumental ensemble reading from the polyphonic version.

The fourth of these methods follows the same developmental pattern as the Italian ricercar and canzona. The Elizabethan counterpart of these two continental forms is the fantasia or "fancy," ensemble pieces for recorders, viols, or broken consorts, usually in six parts. These were written in great number by Dowland, Byrd, Morley, Gibbons, and John Bull (c. 1562–1628). A related instrumental ensemble form of Elizabethan England is the *In nomine,* a cantus firmus form which takes its name from the fact that the cantus firmus is a tune taken from the setting of the words *in nomine Domini* from the benedictus of the Taverner Mass *"Gloria Tibi Trinitas."* A number of *in nomines* were composed by William Byrd.

Keyboard music also flourished, the most popular instrument being the virginal, a small version of the harpsichord mentioned in Virdung's *Musica Getutscht.* The leading composers among the Elizabethan virginalists were Byrd, Bull, Morley, Gibbons, and Giles Farnaby (c. 1560–1640); and one of their major contributions was the development of the variation form during the late sixteenth century. Numerous sets of variations are found in a compilation dating from about 1620 entitled *The Fitzwilliam Virginal Book.* The tunes used for these variations were usually short, simple songs or dance tunes with clear cadences setting off the phrases, often in binary or ternary form. These are the ancestors of the *theme and variations* of the late eighteenth century and, like their counterparts of the classic period, each variation preserves the structure of the theme as to cadences and harmonic plan. Even the theme itself might be retained with some ornamentation throughout the set of variations. Unlike the later theme and variations, the texture was continous and unbroken with no pause between variations. In order to compare theme to variations in a typical example, figure 51 presents the first two phrases of the theme, and two phrases of the first variation from Farnaby's variations on *Loth to Depart.*

The *Fitzwilliam Virginal Book,* which is the largest collection of English keyboard music, also contained a few organ pieces, dance pieces, and miscellaneous harpsichord pieces, such as arrangements of popular songs. Another collection of virginal music, *My Lady Nevell's Book* (1591) contains forty-two compositions written by William Byrd for Lady Nevell, one of his pupils.

Figure 51. Variations on Loth to Depart, *Farnaby.*

In this and the two preceding chapters covering the Renaissance, we have seen the development of musical style in a particular period brought to the highest level of technical consistency and expressive power in the works of composers such as Lassus, Palestrina, and Byrd. But even while Renaissance styles were arriving at their culmination, the new styles of the Baroque period were in the process of formulation. This was seen most of all in the works of the Venetian composers at the end of the sixteenth century—a pre-indication of the fortuitous domination of the early and middle Baroque by Italian composers. The early seventeenth century saw the use of the terms *stile antico, prima prattica, stile moderno,* and *seconda prattica*—an indication that Renaissance styles were slow in succumbing to the new esthetic of the seventeenth century. This transitional period has been compared to the *Ars Nova* of the Trecento as well as the early twentieth century, for in all of these periods innovative composers were attempting to overthrow the domination of the preceding era.

III. THE BAROQUE PERIOD

7. The Early Baroque

*The Beginnings of Opera—Secular Vocal Music
Other Than Opera—Sacred Vocal Music—Growth
of Instrumental Styles—Ricercar Types—Canzonas
and Sonatas—Variation Forms—Dance Music—
Improvisatory Pieces*

Music of any period reflects, in its own way, some of the same influences, tendencies, and generative impulses, that are found in the other arts of that time. Thus the word "baroque," originally used disparagingly by eighteenth-century art critics to describe the art and architecture of the seventeenth and early eighteenth centuries, came to be applied also to the music of the seventeenth and early eighteenth centuries. The term has in the past, and to some extent in the present, carried implications of absurdity, grotesqueness, or abnormality. But as applied to the music of the period of 1600–1750 the term "baroque" has no such pejorative connotations, for much of the music of this time is of the finest quality.

The ornamental aspects of the Baroque, those elements which eighteenth-century art critics decried as being excessive, are perhaps most apparent in the many Baroque churches of Europe which incorporate lavishly beautiful ceiling and altar paintings, ornate carving and metal work, and highly expressive sculpture—all somehow unified in their religious milieu. It is understandable that opinion of a certain time might have found these things excessive, and parallels can be found in the music of the seventeenth century. The flamboyance, spectacle, and emotionalism of some early Italian operas, the use of dramatic techniques in religious music, and the massing together of large groups of instruments and voices are among the elements in Baroque music which bear traits in common with the other arts of the time. As in any period of reaction and transition, some innovative efforts fell short of artistic excellence. Nevertheless, the musicians of the Baroque period left a vast heritage of musical works which in their diversity and quality merit our close attention and admiration.

The rather arbitrary dates of 1600–1750 have been generally accepted by historians as a convenient approximation of the limits of the

Baroque period in music, even though it is recognized that many traits of Baroque music were apparent before 1600 and were being gradually supplanted well before 1750 by some of the new ideas of classicism.

Indeed, in the early seventeenth century the older Renaissance practices existed side by side with the new techniques of the Baroque. Monteverdi, as we have seen, declared his adoption of the new practices and coined the terms *prima prattica* and *seconda prattica* in the foreword to Book Five of his madrigals (1605). But earlier beginnings of Baroque styles were found in the instrumental and polychoral music of the Venetian school. Giovanni Gabrieli's use of double chorus, his opposing instrumental and vocal groups, and his beginning efforts in idiomatic writing for instruments led to the concertato style and laid the groundwork for Baroque instrumental forms such as the concerto grosso.

The harmonic experiments of Gesualdo, along with those of Monteverdi, did much to break down modality and firmly establish the chordal harmonic concept that had slowly been gaining ground throughout the sixteenth century. Along with this came the firm establishment of regular metrical rhythm, and by 1650 the use of regular accents set off by barlines was the common practice. Free unmeasured rhythm continued to be used, however, as seen in recitatives and improvisatory solo instrumental pieces. In the late Baroque, a regular persistent rhythmic pattern was frequently used throughout a movement of an instrumental piece in order to consistently maintain a single basic mood or "affection."

The term "affection" in this context means a passion or emotion, and was manifest in early Baroque vocal works by the use of elaborate text painting and musical symbolism, particularly in the accompanying instruments. In a sense, the Baroque doctrine of affections is an extension of the Renaissance concept of madrigalism in which the poetic images of the words are depicted by carefully conceived text painting devices. In the Baroque, however, the affections were depicted in much more highly stylized ways, and with more vehemence and intensity, quite different from the tasteful word painting of the madrigalists. Indeed, Baroque composers developed an actual vocabulary of musical figures and devices with which to communicate extra-musical ideas. In J. S. Bach's choral music, for example, jubilation was characteristically expressed by the use of fast triplet rhythms, death by an ostinato figure, sadness by sigh figures, and so on. It should be added that the devices themselves do not necessarily enhance the quality of the music, for in all music there is a purely musical meaning that is usually more important than any extra-musical association.

As pointed out earlier, a significant difference between the styles of the Renaissance and Baroque is found in their concepts of polyphonic texture. The Renaissance ideal was a texture of equal voices which moved in rhythmic independence of each other, and although the vertical pitch relationships were carefully calculated, the texture was heard as a web of several equal voices moving in horizontal motion. The typical Baroque texture, on the other hand, was heard as a series of vertical sonorities with similar rhythms in all of the parts, the horizontal motion existing primarily in the firmly moving bass and florid soprano. This Baroque concentration on the outer parts, and indifference to the inner voices, was manifest most of all in a system of musical shorthand called figured bass in which only the bass line and solo voice were notated on the staves, with the actual harmonies indicated by numbers and symbols placed above the bass tones. The keyboard player read from the figured bass, "realizing" the full harmonic texture by means of the numbers and symbols above the bass tones, while the bass line itself was played by a bass instrument such as a cello, viol, or bassoon. Although it varied according to the inclinations and the improvisatory skills of the keyboard player, a realization of a figured bass might include appropriate arpeggiations, motives from the melody, or perhaps simply a chordal accompaniment. This combination of keyboard player and bass instrument was known as the *basso continuo* or simply *continuo,* and was used as the accompaniment group in much Baroque music. The figures above the bass were arranged vertically to indicate the intervals above each bass tone that were to be added to the harmony. Figure 52 presents an example of figured bass from an eighteenth-century edition of the Corelli violin sonatas. In most modern editions of Baroque music, the figured bass is fully realized in conventional notation. The emphasis on vertical chord structure, so obvious in music utilizing continuo, is of prime importance to Baroque styles, both instrumental and vocal.

If all Baroque textures had consisted exclusively of the kind described above—a solid bass line and a florid solo part with harmonies realized from the figured bass—it would imply a total rejection of the linear counterpoint practiced by composers of the Renaissance and earlier. But Baroque composers continued to write music in several parts, for voices as well as for instruments. The kind of counterpoint practiced in these multivoiced works however, was quite different from that of Renaissance polyphony, for it was governed by vertical sonorities, and subordinated to a harmonic scheme that was dictated by the concept of continuo. But like Renaissance polyphony, it was still a blending of several melodic lines into a single texture. At first the use of bar lines and the restrictions of the harmonic system tended to limit contrapuntal freedom. The early seventeenth century had seen some

Figure 52. Opening Page of an Eighteenth Century English Edition of Corelli's Violin Sonatas.

daring chromaticism in the music of late Renaissance and early Baroque composers such as Gesualdo and Monteverdi, and a good deal of chromaticism was found in improvisatory instrumental pieces of the Baroque (for example, in the toccatas of Froberger and Frescobaldi), but until the time of J. S. Bach, Baroque composers rarely used dissonance and chromaticism in contrapuntal textures. It was not until the eighteenth century that the new harmonic system was perfected and worked out to the point that real contrapuntal freedom was impossible.

To speak of a new harmonic system is perhaps misleading, for progressions of triads with roots separated by a fourth or fifth had been used throught the Renaissance. Yet the major-minor system of tonality which evolved from this practice was a baroque phenomenon, its most important feature being the definition of a key or tonal center by means of the tonic and dominant triads. Much of the aural effect of the music, indeed its form, was governed by the quality of the relationship of the various cadence points to the home tonality, the key center of the piece. This system, which is so familiar to the twentieth century and which dominated all Western music of the eighteenth and nineteenth centuries, was not clearly articulated until 1722 in Rameau's *Treatise on Harmony,* even though it had been in common practice for at least fifty years before.

The Beginnings of Opera

The true beginning of opera coincides with the beginning of the baroque period, but there were in the sixteenth century a number of vocal forms, some discussed in chapter 5, which are immediate predecessors of opera. Among these are continuo madrigals such as those by Monteverdi, madrigal comedies like *Il Amfiparnasso* of Orazio Vecchi, and musical entertainments which were inserted between the acts of stage plays. The last category includes *intermezzi* (also called *intermedi*) and other short dramas with more or less continuous music. They took varied forms and often included dancing and other entertainment. Many of them were pastorales, a favorite poetic vehicle of the time. More distant predecessors of opera include Adam de la Halle's *Play of Robin and Marian,* a work which has been called the progenitor of modern music dramas, liturgical dramas such as the mystery and miracle plays of the middle ages, and classical Greek drama of which it is believed that the choruses and perhaps some of the dialogue were performed as song. Thus, the idea of combining music with drama was by no means new to the seventeenth century, but the modern idea of opera as a unified drama with a more or less continous musical texture was indeed new—a Baroque development which has remained a significant area of creative endeavor in Western culture up to the present time.

One of the prime agents in the early development of opera was a group of poets and composers calling themselves the *Camerata* who met at the home of Count Bardi in Florence. From what they knew of the lyrical qualities of classical Greek drama they developed a new monodic style which came to be known as *stile rappresentativo*. This "representative style," to translate it literally, was the first form of recitative, and one of the main requirements was that the words should be clearly understood and sung in speech rhythm. The music was also supposed to express or "represent" the true sentiments of the text and strongly communicate these emotions to the audience. The Camerata included Jacopo Peri (1561–1633), Giulio Caccini (c. 1546–1618), and Emilio del Cavalieri (c. 1550–1602), all of whom made contributions to the development of vocal music. The most significant poets of the Florentine group were Tasso and Rinuccini, but the earliest and most persuasive spokesman for their philosophies was Vincenzo Galilei (c. 1520–91), father of the famous astronomer, who in 1581 published his *Dialogue About Ancient and Modern Music* in which (though something of a madrigalist himself) he attacked the practices of the madrigal composers. Following the doctrines of Girolamo Mei, a classical scholar who had earlier advocated solo singing in imitation of the Greeks, Galilei argued that solo song was superior to polyphony because it was better able to convey the true inflection and meaning of speech. In madrigals, he pointed out, the various voices in the polyphonic texture did not even sing the words at the same time, much less attempt to find the ideal rhythm and pitch inflection for presentation of the text. Apparently missing the point of subtle musical evocation of mood and emotion—one of the great beauties of the madrigal—he said that the correct way to set words (and there could be only one ideal setting of any text) was to utilize the solo melodic line in such a way as to enhance and magnify the natural speech inflections of an accomplished orator. The awareness of the poetic image as distinct from the literal word meaning, a vital trait of madrigalism, is absent from this philosophy. In its place the words were to be set in realistic speech rhythm with pitches emphasizing the natural pitch inflections of speech, all in an intensely emotional declamatory style.

As in most musical theories which came before the fact of the music itself, Galilei's ideas needed to be treated with great flexibility in actual practice. Although Galilei made a few attempts, Peri and Caccini, both singers themselves, developed a monodic style which, though influenced by Galilei's ideas, by no means followed the theory strictly. The earliest examples of Florentine monody are found in *Le nuove musiche* (1602), a publication of solo songs written by Caccini in the 1590s. The volume contains twelve solo madrigals and ten strophic arias, all with continuo accompaniment designated for performance on a large lute called the *chitarrone*. These works serve well to represent the new monodic style, and Caccini's preface sheds much light on the vocal technique of the time, covering such matters as proper breath support, the avoidance of sliding to pitches, vocal embellishments (called *gorgia*), and the use of rubato. Caccini, because he was a singing teacher as well as a performer and composer, was able to bring a three-way insight to the art of musical performance, and it is apparent in his preface that he is speaking sometimes as teacher, sometimes as performer, and sometimes as composer.

The short excerpt in figure 53 is from the madrigal *Amarilli mia belli* from *Nuove Musiche,* notated (except for the use of modern clefs and note-shapes) as in the edition of 1602. Note that, although the piece is clearly in the key of G minor, only the B flat is indicated in the key signature, making it necessary to indicate the E flats as accidentals. This practice, which persisted well into the eighteenth century, is a vestige of the modal system in which only the B flat was indicated in the key signature, with other sharps and flats being applied as musica ficta. This and other evidence suggest that composers still thought in terms of modes, and that in this instance the composer viewed the key of G minor as a transposed dorian on G, with E flats as well as F sharps occurring as accidentals.

Figure 53. Amarilli Mia Belli, *Accompanied Madrigal, Caccini.*

The first opera, a joint product of Peri and Caccini to a libretto by the poet Rinuccini, was written for the festivities of the wedding of Henry IV of France with Marie de'Medici in 1660. Entitled *Euridice,* it dealt with the Orpheus myth, but in this version for this happy occasion, Rinuccini allowed Euridice to remain in the world of mankind with her beloved rather than return to the underworld as in the original myth. In the following year each composer published his own complete separate version, the two earliest complete extant operas. Although they are of little real musical interest, their historical significance is enhanced by the presence of occasional passages of melodic character in contrast to the austerity of the stile rappresentativo, thus foreshadowing the use of alternating recitatives and arias in later opera.

Up to this point the new stage medium served only for the delectation of a small audience of connoiseurs at the Medici court. Opera might indeed have reached an untimely end with the rather pale efforts of Peri and Caccini had it not been for the work of a man of true musical genius, Claudio Monteverdi. His first opera, *Orfeo,* produced at Mantua in 1607, is notable for its brilliant use of the orchestra to evoke the intense passions of the drama. The work contains twenty-six separate instrumental pieces such as *sinfonie, ritornello,* interludes, and the first operatic overture (a fanfare entitled "Toccata"). The forty instruments listed in the score are divided into two categories, those capable of playing chords (called *fundament* instruments), and melodic instruments. The specific instrumentation is given only in a few places (for definite dramatic situations), but Monteverdi must be credited with establishing in the drama a place for instrumental music— a place which it soon lost and did not fully regain until the operas of Gluck and Mozart, for throughout the Baroque period the standard opera orchestra consisted only of strings and continuo.

Monteverdi's *Orfeo* is in five acts, with a prologue sung by "La Musica." The composer's masterful setting of the poem by Striggio realized the full dramatic power of the Orpheus myth. The wide variety of forms includes variations, madrigals, vocal pieces in concertato style, and recitatives, all carefully balanced as to overall structure. Adult male sopranos (castrati), were used in Orfeo for the first time in opera. Their powerful and flexible voices must have contributed much to seventeenth-century performances of the work. The most elaborate aria in the opera, *Possente Spirito,* sung by Orfeo in Act III, is a set of five strophic variations concluding with a short accompanied recitative (one of the first uses of recitative accompanied by more than continuo). Of Monteverdi's next opera, *Arianna,* a few fragments have survived including one complete number, a famous song entitled "Lament" which was regarded in the seventeenth century as the finest and most expressive example of the monodic style.

Little else occurred in the early development of opera until fifteen or twenty years later when a school of Roman opera began to develop. The Roman operas of this time were less intensely dramatic but more spectacular than the earlier efforts of the Florentine composers. Many of the libretti were on sacred subjects, but comic episodes were also included in Roman opera for the first time in the short history of opera. Another innovation was the frequent use of chorus, and the opera orchestra became standardized as an ensemble of strings and continuo. The clear separation of recitative and aria began to appear in the Roman opera, forecasting the basic formal plan of the later Neapolitan opera.

The most significant opera of the Roman school is *Sant'Alessio* (1632) of Stephano Landi (c. 1590–1655). Based on the legend of St. Alexis, its libretto was written by Giulio Rospigliosi, the man responsible for the first comic scenes in opera. (He later became Pope Clement IX.) The recitatives in this and other Roman operas began to be nothing more than a vehicle for delivery of the dialogue, very much as in the operas of the late eighteenth century. Of particular interest in *Sant'Alessio* are the instrumental pieces preceding Acts I and II. Both are derived from the canzona, but their contrasts of slow and fast tempi anticipate later operatic overture forms. The slow-fast pattern of the first *sinfonia* was later to be used as the basic form of the French overture, while the fast-slow-fast pattern of the second became the basic shape of the Italian overture, the accepted overture form of the later seventeenth century. Another important composer of the Roman school is Luigi Rossi (1597–1653) whose *Orfeo* (1647), though not as dramatically effective as Monteverdi's, has many moments of great musical worth.

The center of opera soon shifted from Rome to Venice, and with the opening of Venice's *Teatro San Cassiano* in 1637, opera for the first time became available to large public audiences. Before long Venice became the operatic center of Europe, a position which it retained until the end of the seventeenth century when the focus shifted to Neapolitan and French opera. Composers associated with Venetian opera were responsible for spreading the influence of Italian opera to southern Germany during this period.

By later standards, seventeenth-century Venetian opera was ridiculous as drama, a drawback that was offset by scenic splendor and some very excellent music. The improbable plots and absurd mixtures of incongruous scenes and characters served only as pretexts for gracious melodies, beautiful singing, and elaborate scenic effects. The chorus, which had been used in Roman opera, gradually disappeared; and the recitative continued its evolution away from the ideals of the Camerata toward an almost nonmusical function in the presentation of dialogue. Only the aria flourished—with simple orchestral accompaniments and considerable vocal virtuosity—an important step toward the extraordinary solo singing technique of the eighteenth century.

In his latter years Monteverdi was associated with the Venetian school of opera. He had been appointed as *Maestro di cappella* at St. Mark's in 1613, a position he retained until his death in 1643, and as Venice began to dominate the field of opera he emerged as the greatest composer among the Venetian opera composers, the only one who managed to instill his great music with genuine dramatic qualities. The last and greatest of his operas is *The Coronation of Poppea,* produced in Venice in 1642. In it he uses *stile concitato* (agitated style), an orchestral stringed instrument effect utilizing pizzicato, tremolando, and other devices to depict strong emotions. He had developed the technique of stile concitato for an earlier work, a secular cantata called *The Battle of Tancred and Clorinda.* The libretto of Poppea is based on the story of the emperor Nero and his love for Poppea, wife of Ottone. It utilizes a wide variety of instrumental and vocal forms, all preceded by an allegorical prologue dealing with the great power of love over mankind.

Other important Venetian opera composers after Monteverdi include his pupil Pier Francesco Cavalli (1602–76) and Marc'Antonio Cesti (1623–69). Cavalli's *Giasone* and Cesti's *Il pomo d'oro* are the best-known works of these composers, but neither composer achieved the depth of dramatic insight and musical excellence of Monteverdi. The next important development in the evolution of opera began at Naples in the late seventeenth century and developed into a style known as Neapolitan opera, the dominant operatic style of the mature Baroque, which will be discussed in chapter 9.

Secular Vocal Music Other Than Opera

A number of nonoperatic vocal forms and styles evolved from the works of late Italian madrigalists such as Gesualdo and Monteverdi. An important aspect of this is seen in the fifth book of Monteverdi's madrigals, mentioned earlier as the point of departure from his prima prattica to the seconda prattica. The main innovation in the madrigals of Book Five was the use of continuo to accompany the voices, a device which predisposed the composer toward counterpoint based primarily on vertical considerations. One of the problems confronting the early seventeenth-century composer who utilized the modern style or stile moderno was how to achieve a full polyphonic texture, with its attractive richness of sound, while still utilizing the skeletal framework of the basso continuo. (*Stile moderno* and *seconda prattica* are synonyms, the former being more frequently applied to sacred music.) The Florentine composers such as Caccini and Peri had avoided this issue by composing exclusively in the new monodic style, completely turning their backs on the polyphonic textures that had been so beautifully utilized in the sixteenth century. At the other extreme were the ultraconservatives who continued to delight in the ample sonorities of Renaissance polyphony, perhaps with an occasional continuo thrown in for the sake of being up to date. The course of the continuing fruitful development of Baroque vocal forms, however, lay between these two extremes. Many means were employed to strike a balance between pure monody and counterpoint, the most important of which was to use a bass along with a multivoiced harmonic structure, textural variety being achieved by means of the concertato style.

Continuo madrigals utilizing concertato style are first seen in Book Six (1614) of Monteverdi's madrigals, published the year after the composer's appointment as choirmaster of St. Mark's in Venice. St. Mark's, the fountainhead of concertato style, undoubtedly exerted a strong influence upon Monteverdi, for he continued to use concertato devices with both instruments and voices in many varied combinations through the eighth and final book of his madrigals. In Book Seven (1619), entitled "Concerto," instruments are used to accompany the voices as well as for interludes by themselves. Book Eight (1638) is entitled "Madrigals of Love and War" and includes the *Battle of Tancred and Clorinda,* a work for two soloists, chorus, and orchestra which represents a formative stage in the development of the secular cantata. The *stile concitato* used in Book Eight, particularly in *Tancred and Clorinda,* illustrates Monteverdi's highly innovative use of instruments. It consists of pizzicato, tremolo, and other unique string devices to evoke the excitement of the drama, and represents an important contribution to the development of expressive idiomatic instrumental writing.

The term *cantata* was first used by Alessandro Grandi (d. 1630) in a publication of 1620, but another embryonic stage of the cantata may be seen in a collection of monodies entitled *Cantade ed arie* (1624) by Giovanni Berti. One of the compositions in the latter work is constructed as a set of strophic variations over a repetitive bass pattern moving predominantly in quarter notes with a ritornello for continuo alone interposed between variations. The use of repetitive bass patterns or grounds was very common in the seventeenth century, and out of this technique grew the concept of the Baroque ostinato variation as exemplified in works called *chaconnes* or *passacaglias,* to be discussed later.

The early traditional bass grounds were short patterns, many of them inherited from popular songs and sixteenth-century dance tunes such as the folia, passamezzo, and bergamask. They were used in both instrumental and vocal works of the seventeenth century. Among the most frequently used tunes for these bass lines are the Romanesca, and the Ruggiero shown in figure 54, both of which were well known as songs. Many composers also invented basses of their own, as the bass line became one of the most important unifying forces in seventeenth-century music.

Figure 54.

It is readily seen that the complex musical styles of the Baroque period evolved from a variety of influences inherited from the Renaissance and from the many innovative efforts of the earlier Baroque composers. Monody and madrigal were fused and bent to the dominating influence of the basso continuo; textural contrast was achieved through the concertato style; and repetitive bass figures and the ritornello furnished unity. Through these devices vocal music was endowed with increased pictorial powers. Indeed, the efforts to depict the text in the most highly representational manner reached such intensity that around 1630 the tide began to turn against viewing the text as the all-important point of departure for all elements of the music. One manifestation of this is seen in the gradual separation of the aria and the recitative. The recitative retained its function as the servant of the text, while the aria took on a new dimension as the handmaiden of melody and of purely musical expression. Aria melodies began to be written without strictly following the rhythm of the words, thus enabling the composer to concentrate on beauty of line, often setting a single vowel sound to a gracefully moving stepwise line of many tones. Out of this grew the style of composition for solo voice known as *bel canto,* a term that has come to evoke the spirit of Italian song, even though it was widely imitated throughout Europe and was influential upon both vocal and instrumental music throughout the eighteenth century.

Aside from opera, the vocal form that began to emerge most significantly among Italian composers was the cantata. Cantatas were written by Luigi Rossi, Marc' Antonio Cesti, and Giacomo Carissimi (1605–74). The words "cantata" and "sonata" were at first nothing more than parallel terms used to indicate whether a piece was to be sung, or "sounded" upon instruments. Thus no particular formal pattern was consistently followed in cantatas until the middle of the seventeenth century when the term began to indicate a composition for solo voice or voices accompanied by continuo, and in several sections which often formed a series of recitatives and arias. Some of Rossi's cantatas were of this type, although he also composed some which were much simpler in form utilizing strophic songs, strophic variations, or ostinato variations.

Although many German, French, and English composers followed the Italian models, by the middle of the seventeenth century they were also beginning to develop vocal styles which bore traces of nationalistic styles. In Germany, Andreas Hammerschmidt (1612–75) and Heinrich Albert (1604–51) composed solo songs of considerable originality, while in the courtly circles of France, the *air de cour* appeared in various forms, often as incidental music to the *ballet de cour* (court ballet). Similar efforts were made by English composers, often in connection with masques of the nobility (the English counterpart of the ballet de cour), although no significant English Baroque composers emerged until Purcell.

Sacred Vocal Music

Early Baroque innovations such as monody, continuo, and the concertato style, so common in secular music, were also used in the composition of early seventeenth-century church music, and, as in secular music, the old and new styles existed concurrently. The terms *stile antico* and *stile moderno* were perhaps more conventionally applied to sacred music than to secular, although their meanings are essentially the same as *prima prattica* and *seconda prattica.* Certainly the duality expressed by these terms is manifest in both sacred and secular music of the early Baroque. But in church music, because it was by nature more conservative than secular music, the older style lasted longer and was more influential than in secular music. Indeed, in the Roman Catholic Church there was enough opposition to the use of the new styles that a type of counterpoint originating in Rome and derived from the Palestrina style was practiced throughout the Baroque period. At mid-century many conservative composers still aspired to perfection in this so-called Palestrinian counterpoint. In his treatise entitled *Gradus ad Parnassum* (1725), Johann Fux attempted to codify this type of polyphony with a technique called "species counterpoint," an artificial system that has been used, until recently, for the teaching of sixteenth-century counterpoint, even though it was seldom practiced strictly in actual composition and certainly is not an acceptable technique for imitating the style of Palestrina. Many early Baroque composers utilized monody, concertato, and continuo as readily as the older polyphony, in some instances using the old and the new styles in the same composition.

But of greater importance than the pseudo-Palestrina technique was a style stemming from the polychoric works of the Venetian school known today as the "colossal" style. The style utilized vast groups of singers and players; of its many practitioners, the most outstanding is Orazio Benevoli (1605–1672), whose *Festival Mass* calls for two orchestras, two eight-part choruses, soloists, smaller groups of instruments, and a continuo for two organs, harpsichords, lutes and harps. Scored on fifty-three staves, the *Festival Mass* was written for the consecration of the Salzburg cathedral in 1628. Benevoli's later sacred works, most of them written for St. Peter's in Rome, demonstrate more fully (though a bit more conservatively) this composer's gifts for combining several performing units.

As the stile moderno gained ground in the early seventeenth century, the monodic and concertato styles became quite common in church music. One of the first to utilize the stile moderno in sacred music was Ludovico Viadana (1564–1645), who in 1602 published a collection of works for solo voice or voices with continuo. As implied by the title, *Cento concerti ecclesiastici* (One Hundred Church Concertos), these compositions made considerable use of concertato style and, because of the presence of the continuo, had the added advantage of being performable by small groups of singers, since a full harmony could exist in the continuo even if some voice parts were missing. This collection bridges the gap between the Renaissance motet and the new Baroque form of the same name. Of great significance in seventeenth-century works of this type is the fact that the presence of instruments and the use of concertato style caused many composers to write vocal lines which were quite instrumental in character, a practice that led to the Baroque instrumental style of vocal writing so vividly illustrated in the choral works of J. S. Bach.

The term *cantata* was applied to sets of religious monodies as well as to secular. Indeed, the earliest use of the term was applied by Grandi to a set of religious monodies under the title *Cantate ed Arie* (1620). As one might expect, Monteverdi, in his position as choirmaster at St. Mark's, composed numerous works which, though not called cantatas, utilized the new vehicles of recitative and aria in combination with instruments and choirs. Most of the works composed while he was in Venice use a free concertato style and also borrow from the world of opera. In fact, the dramatic methods of opera were turned increasingly to the service of sacred music at the same time that a religious influence began to be seen in opera. The most famous example of this is a work which falls ambiguously between opera and sacred music, entitled *La rappresentazione di anima e di corpo* by Emilio de' Cavalieri (c. 1550–1602). This work was first performed in 1600 as a part of an informal religious service in Vallicella under the sponsorship of S. Filippo Neri, one of the greatest spiritual leaders of the Renaissance. At St. Mary's church in Vallicella, Neri led prayer services under the aegis of a newly recognized order called the Congregation of the Oratory, whose headquarters had been transferred from Rome after its official recognition by Pope Gregory XIII in 1575. From it we have the word *oratorio.* The most direct ancestor of the Baroque oratorio, however is not Cavalieri's *Rappresentazione* but Anerio's *Teatro Armonico spirituali di madrigali* (1619), a collection of settings of the Bible and biblical stories in five to eight voices. It was not until 1635–40 that the term "oratorio" began to be conventionally applied to the musical works which were performed at the oratory.

The outstanding master of the oratorio in the mid-seventeenth century was Giacomo Carissimi (1605–74), whose works in the new medium were distinguished from opera by their religious subject matter, by the use of a *testo* (solo narrator—called the "evangelist" in later oratorio), by the frequent use of chorus for many dramatic and narrative devices, and by the fact that they were not intended to be staged as theater pieces, but rather to be presented in a semi-dramatic concert version. In general, these traits characterized the oratorio throughout the seventeenth and eighteenth centuries. A typical example of this type of semi-dramatic sacred work is Carissimi's *Jephtha,* to a Latin libretto based on the book of Judges. The testo introduces the story and narrates at various points throughout; Jephtha is played by a tenor; and the work includes arias, duets and choruses, concluding with a six-part chorus of lamentation by Jephtha's daughter and her companions. Continuo is used throughout along with concertato effects; and stile concitato is used at one point in the orchestra to depict Jephtha's victory over the Ammonites. Solo oratorios, some of which are almost indistinguishable from cantatas, were also written by Italian composers of Carissimi's generation.

In seventeenth-century Germany, church composers were strongly influenced by Italian practices. Although many Lutheran composers clung to the concept of the Renaissance motet well into the seventeenth century, the new monodic and concertato techniques were used as well, sometimes with chorale tunes furnishing the melodic material. Early seventeenth-century German composers such as Hassler and Praetorius were particularly fond of the Venetian polychoric style, further evidence of Venice's dominating position in European music of that time. Several terms have come to be applied to seventeenth-century sacred choral works based on Lutheran chorale tunes. These include the "chorale motet," a conservative polyphonic piece with or without continuo; and the "chorale concertato," a concertato setting of a choral tune, sometimes with cantus firmus techniques, and with continuo.

The German cantata based on a single chorale tune developed from the chorale concertato through expansion into separate arias, recitatives, and choruses. But much sacred music was written in seventeenth-century Germany without using chorale tunes for thematic basis. Such works include oratorios as well as compositions similar to oratorios under other titles such as settings of the "Passions."

Among the significant early seventeenth-century German composers are Johann Schein (1586–1630) and Samuel Scheidt (1587–1654). In addition to composing as many as thirty motets in the conservative polyphonic style, Schein used monody, concertato, and Baroque instrumental styles in his sacred music, often with elaborate treatment of the chorale tunes. His collection entitled *Geistliche Konzerte* (Sacred Concertos) consists of sixty-two short pieces with Latin or German texts designed for easy performance by one to five voices and continuo. Although Scheidt's vocal works are similar to those of Schein, he is best known as an organ composer. His chorale tunes in instrumental textures, particularly for organ, are among the earliest examples of the chorale variation technique.

But the greatest German composer of this period is Heinrich Schütz (1585–1672), who, although he is presumed to have written secular instrumental and vocal works which are now lost, is known today almost exclusively for his sacred vocal music. A student of Giovanni Gabrieli and Monteverdi, Schütz was well acquainted with all European musical styles, particularly those of the Venetian School. From 1617 until his death in 1672 he was Kappelmeister to the Elector of Saxony at Dresden, although during this period he spent a short time as Court Conductor at Copenhagen and once visited Monteverdi in Venice. His sacred music dates from 1619, and for variety and richness rivals the work of any composer in the history of music.

His first published work was a short collection of five part Italian madrigals written in Venice while he was a student of Monteverdi during the first decade of the seventeenth century, the only extant example of secular music in his entire output. The influence of the polychoric works of Gabrieli is vividly illustrated in the *Psalms of David* (1619) which are in the Venetian style with two, three, or four choruses and with groups of instruments. These colorful works are in direct contrast to his homophonic four-voice settings of a German translation of the Psalter (1628) which are almost Calvinistic in their austerity. The *Cantiones Sacrae* (1625), a set of polyphonic motets in the conservative church style, contain interesting and colorful harmonies as well as a number of examples of text painting clearly influenced by the madrigal.

The Thirty Years War badly depleted the musical forces of the Electoral Chapel, particularly from 1636 to 1639, and it was during this period that Schütz published his *Kleine Geistliche Konzerte* (Little Sacred Concertos), pieces of one to five voices with continuo (organ) accompaniment designed for easy performance by small groups. Although these fall into the category of the Baroque motet, a better example of the conservative contrapuntal motet style is found in *Geistliche Chormusik* (1648), a set of motets dedicated to the city of Leipzig and the choir of the *Thomaskirke.* In the preface to his work, Schütz deplores the decline in technical proficiency among younger composers and admonishes them to master counterpoint before going on to the newer concertato style.

Although many mid-seventeenth century conservative composers shared the sentiments expressed by Schütz in the preface to the *Geistliche Chormusik,* it must be added that Schütz himself was often startlingly advanced in his use of concertato style, as is vividly seen in the *Symphonia Sacrae,* a set of concertato motets published in three sections in the years 1629, 1647, and 1650. The first two are scored for small combinations of voices and instruments with as many as six parts plus continuo. The third part, completed after the Thirty Years War when the full resources of the Electoral Chapel could once again be utilized, makes dramatic use of the polychoric and concertato styles. A good example is seen in the motet *Saul, Saul,* excerpted in figure 55. The six solo voices, two full choirs, two sections of violins, and continuo are used to produce echo effects (as in the excerpt) as well as dramatic climaxes perhaps unequaled in all of Schütz' work. The influence of Monteverdi can be seen in both the second and third parts of the *Symphoniae Sacrae.* Indeed, some of the motets are revisions of Monteverdi's compositions, but the Monteverdian influence is even more apparent in his use of the stile concitato.

It is interesting to note that Schütz rarely, if ever, made use of Lutheran chorale tunes as thematic basis for his church music, although he frequently made his own settings of chorale texts. No chorale melodies are found in any of his compositions of the oratorio type which include *The Seven Last Words* (c. 1645), the *Christmas Oratorio* (1664), and three Passions composed toward the end of his life. The *Seven Last Words,* perhaps his most famous work, is similar to the *Christmas Oratorio* in that the choral movements make use of instruments at the beginning and end, although the *Christmas Oratorio* is on a larger scale. Both works use recitatives and vocal ensembles to tell the story, and both are in the typical semi-dramatic style of the oratorio. In the *Seven Last Words,* the words of Christ are accompanied by strings alone to lend added significance to these passages, a practice that was later adopted by J. S. Bach.

The three passions are settings from the Gospel according to St. Matthew, St. Luke, and St. John. The texts are followed quite strictly, with some use of word painting. The solo passages are set to lines which sound very much like Gregorian chant, while the words of the people (*Turba*) and the words of the disciples are in four-part choral settings in dramatic style. Schütz's compositions in the oratorio genre set a standard for Lutheran works of this type that was unequaled until the time of J. S. Bach.

Growth of Instrumental Styles

Again it is in Venice where the seeds of instrumental music were sown during the Renaissance, but its germination and flowering in the seventeenth century occurred also in other centers of Italy, as well as in Germany, France, and England. One reason for the remarkable growth of instrumental music in the Baroque period is that the major innovations in musical style at the beginning of the seventeenth century were readily adaptable to instruments. Some of them, in fact, such

Figure 55. Schütz, Saul, Saul.

as the continuo concept and the concertato style, were intrinsically instrumental in nature. The monodic style, which began as a vocal phenomenon, lent itself naturally to use by instruments, for the absence of a text in purely instrumental textures removed one of the major complications found in vocal monody. By mid-seventeenth century, instrumental music was comparable in quantity and quality to vocal music. Moreover, there soon appeared a variety of characteristic Baroque instrumental forms, textures, and techniques to add to the richness of this first great period of instrumental music.

This variety of instrumental activity can be rather arbitrarily placed in five general categories—arbitrarily, because it is impossible to categorize everything and because there was much cross-influence among the categories. They are: (1) ricercar-type pieces which had originated as vocal transcriptions of Renaissance motets, and which by the early seventeenth century took the form of imitative pieces in more or less continuous texture. They went by various other names such as *fancy, fantasia, capriccio, verset,* and *fuga,* the last of which gives a clue to the important type of composition that developed from the ricercar, the fugue. (2) Canzona-type pieces, which had also originated as vocal transcriptions and which were imitative, but which were sectional in form. Their sectional character was an important factor in the evolution of the four-movement *sonata da chiesa.* (3) Variation forms, particularly of the cantus firmus type which were of two basic kinds: (a) the ostinato variation such as the passacaglia, the ground, and the chaconne, in which a figure of several measures, usually in the bass, was repeated many times while variation figures occurred in the surrounding texture, and (b) pieces such as the chorale variation and chorale partita in which a complete melody is presented phrase by phrase with variation figures occurring in the surrounding texture. (4) Pieces derived from dances, or actual dances with stylized dance rhythms, some of which were linked together to form the dance suite or *sonata da camera.* (5) Improvisatory pieces for solo keyboard instruments and for the lute.

Ricercar Types

The sixteenth-century ricercar, derived as it was from the motet, took the form of a series of points of imitation, usually with a different melodic theme for each imitative section. The most important characteristic distinguishing the seventeenth-century ricercar from its Renaissance counterpart is the fact that its continuous imitative texture is based upon only one theme. The *Ricercar il dopo Credo* by

Girolamo Frescobaldi (1583–1643) is a typical example. This short organ piece, the opening of which is shown in figure 56 was published in 1635 in a distinguished collection of organ pieces by Frescobaldi under the title *Fiori Musicali* ("Musical Flowers"). The work is divided into two sections, the first consisting of the presentation and development of the theme in its original form in all the voices, the second being an exposition of the theme in augmentation, each of the four voices presenting the augmented theme once while the other voices develop the countersubject, followed by a statement of the theme in its original form in the top voice. Terms which we are using here such as *countersubject, augmentation,* and *exposition*—all closely associated with the fugue—reveal this piece to be an important stage in the evolution of the fugue from the ricercar. Indeed, except for the tonal relationships of the entrances of the subject, it could very well pass as a fugue. The concept of "answering" with the tonic and dominant relationship between entrances marks a later stage in the development of the baroque fugue, and thus does not characterize the early seventeenth-century ricercar.

Figure 56. Opening of an Organ Piece from Fiori Musicali, *Frescobaldi.*

Another type of keyboard composition similar to the ricercar but on a larger scale is the *fantasia* which appeared particularly in Holland and Germany. The great organist-composer of Amsterdam, Jan Sweelinck (1562–1621), as well as Samuel Scheidt and Heinrich Scheidemann (c. 1596–1663) composed many works in this form, most of them for organ. These organ fantasias, like other ricercar types, manifest many traits which would subsequently appear in the fugue, particularly those techniques which later were known as "fugal devices," such as augmentation, diminution, and stretto. But the main distinguishing feature of the fantasia is that it is a kind of variation form in which each section uses the same subject varied by means of different countersubjects, different contrapuntal techniques, or contrasting textures.

In England the term "fancy" (probably a corruption of "fantasia") was applied to ricercars as well as canzonas composed for ensembles or consorts of instruments. John Jenkins (1592–1678) composed numerous compositions called fancies, most of which fall into the category of the early polythematic ricercar, although he sometimes used the term to describe an introductory movement in imitative style which was followed by a group of dances. Later English composers, chiefly Matthew Locke (c. 1630–77) and Henry Purcell (c. 1659–95), composed imitative fantasias without continuo, mostly for stringed instruments. Thus, the fantasia can be viewed as the leading form of seventeenth-century English chamber music.

Canzonas and Sonatas

Just as the fugue evolved from the monothematic ricercar, so the sonata evolved from the multisectional canzona. Actually the term *sonata* as used in the early seventeenth century meant nothing more than to designate a piece of music as being intended for instruments —to be "sounded" rather than sung. It is just this distinction that the terms *cantata* and *sonata* dealt with at their inception, for they disclose little or nothing about the nature of a piece other than whether it was vocal or instrumental. Figure 57 presents three excerpts from an anonymous early seventeenth-century canzona entitled *Canzona per l'epistola* (possibly by Pasquini).

Each of the excerpts is the beginning of a section, and a different subject is used in each. Very little textural contrast can be heard in this piece except for a toccata-like ending with sweeping scale passages which, along with the title, indicates that the piece was intended for performance on the organ. The repeated note opening with its dactyllic rhythm is a vestige of the French polyphonic chanson from which the canzona developed.

Canzonas in which there was much greater contrast between sections gradually became typical. Some of these, such as one by G. M.

Figure 57. Excerpts from an Anonymous Early Seventeenth Century Canzona.

Trabaci (c. 1580–1647), are very similar to the fantasias of Sweelinck and his contemporaries and are sometimes called *variation canzonas.* Frescobaldi composed canzonas like these for keyboard, as did also his greatest pupil Johann Froberger (1616–67). Most canzonas, however, whether for keyboard or for instrumental ensemble, were constructed as a series of sections, each section with a different theme. Some contained many short sections (sometimes called "patchwork" or "quilt" canzonas), while others contained fewer sections of greater length. One of the more important composers of canzonas is Tarquinio Merula (b. c. 1600), who composed a number of ensemble canzonas of the latter type.

During the early seventeenth century the term "sonata" gradually acquired a more specific meaning and began to be used as a title for pieces in which the form was like the canzona but with certain special features. Sonatas were often scored for one or two violins or other melodic instruments with continuo accompaniment, as opposed to four-part ensemble pieces called canzonas which, because of the full harmonic texture, could be played with or without continuo. Also, the instrumentation was more frequently specified for sonatas than for canzonas, which enabled the composer to write more freely, expressively, and above all, more idiomatically. Thus, the ensemble canzona, even when a continuo was provided, can be thought of as a vestige of the Renaissance, while the sonata, with its idiomatic and imaginative use of the instruments is a child of the Baroque era. This is manifest in the fact that ensemble canzonas rarely were scored for specified instruments and were frequently performed by groups of Renaissance instruments such as viols or recorders. Sonatas, on the other hand, were often scored idiomatically for the newer violin-type instruments which evolved around the end of the sixteenth century.

Shortly after the middle of the seventeenth century the term "canzona" all but disappeared in favor of the word "sonata." The sectional character of the canzona (sonata) led toward the establishment (particularly by G. B. Vitali) of a clear-cut three-movement form in a fast-slow-fast pattern. The addition of a slow movement at the beginning was all that was necessary to transform this pattern into the standard four-movement *sonata da chiesa* with its slow-fast-slow-fast pattern. At the same time the form of the individual movements was crystalizing into the binary form which was used in almost all movements of Baroque sonatas from the time of Arcangelo Corelli (1653–1713), and was certainly the most frequently used single movement instrumental form of the Baroque.

As the ensemble of two violins with continuo accompaniment became increasingly common, it began to be known as the *trio sonata.* The term is entirely appropriate, for trio sonatas were usually scored in three parts on three staves—a staff for each of the solo instruments plus one for the continuo notated in figured bass. However, since the continuo required a bass instrument and a keyboard instrument, four players were usually used in performance. The most popular trio sonata combination consisted of two violins, harpsichord, and cello, although recorders, flutes, or oboes often substituted for violins.

Variation Forms

Most variation forms were of the type known as the cantus firmus variation, and within this category there are two basic types: (1) those in which a melody of several measures, usually in the bass, is repeated many times while variation figures occur in the surrounding texture, and (2) those in which a complete melody such as a chorale tune is presented phrase by phrase with variation figures occurring in the surrounding texture. The first type, also known as the *baroque ostinato variation,* includes the ground, the passacaglia and the chaconne.

Variations on short ground bass themes were composed since the late Renaissance. The English composer Christopher Simpson (c. 1610–69) in 1659 produced a volume entitled *The Division Violist* which, in addition to being one of the first gamba method books, furnished instructions for playing improvisations or "divisions" on a ground.

Chaconne and *passacaglia* are terms which, even today, do not have any clearly established distinction. They appeared around 1600, inheriting their characteristic triple meter from the earlier dance tunes from which they evolved. At first these ostinato basses were four bars in length, but the standard length—as seen, for example, in the Passacaglia in C Minor of Bach—was later established as eight bars of triple meter. One manner of distinguishing between the passacaglia and the chaconne is to include in the first category those works which utilize a bass tune throughout, while the latter category would include those which are based on a reiterated harmonic pattern in which a bass tune was not always apparent. This distinction, though it holds up for Bach's Violin Chaconne and Passacaglia in C Minor, was not consistently observed by Baroque composers and is not universally accepted today because of so many contradictory usages.

The second type of cantus firmus variation is represented by numerous works for organ in which each phrase of a chorale tune (or hymn or secular tune) is used as the basis around which figurations are woven. The German composers who wrote chorale variations were all influenced by Sweelinck and included his student Samuel Scheidt (who in turn influenced later German composers), Scheidemann, Franz Tunder (1614–67), and Nicholas Hanff (1630–1706). Scheidt's *Tablatura Nova* (1624), a large collection of organ pieces written in open score rather than the old tablature system, contains numerous examples of works based upon chorale tunes, as well as fugues, toccatas, and fantasias.

A third type of variation form, very popular during the Baroque, led more or less directly toward the late eighteenth-century theme and variations. This is the most flexible of all the Baroque variation forms, since it is based not upon a cantus firmus but upon the fixed harmonic pattern of a phrase or group phrases. Texture and figuration were easily varied from variation to variation, while remaining always within the fixed harmonic structure. The early strophic variations are examples of this type (i.e., songs with different accompaniments for the various verses), as is a set of Frescobaldi partitas based on the Romanesca theme (see fig. 54).

Dance Music

Stylized dances were important sources for the development of instrumental music in the Baroque, for the characteristic rhythms were found in both vocal and instrumental music. The dance pairs of the late Renaissance, such as the pavane and galiard, and the basse dance and tourdion, led to the Baroque dance suite or *sonata da camera.* In Schein's collection of twenty suites for viols in five parts entitled *Banchetto Musicale* (1617), each suite consists of a *padouana* (pavane) a *gagliarda,* a *courante,* and an *Allemande.* This is one of the first attempts at the unification of several movements into a single entity. Some of the suites, in fact, could be called variation suites in that the same melodic material is used in each of the movements of a single suite. In other suites the technique is not so obvious but the feeling of unity among the movements is present, nevertheless.

Johann Froberger (1616–67), the most distinguished student of Frescobaldi, composed suites of dances for harpsichord, assembling dances such as the sarabande, Allemande, and courante in various orders. On just one occasion the arrangement of dances which he arrived at coincided exactly with the pattern of movements in the sonata da camera of the late Baroque, that is, Allemande, courante, sarabande, and an added gigue. The Allemande, as its name implies, is a German dance, rather stately in quadruple meter. The courante is a fast "running" dance in triple meter, with frequent use of hemiola which adds occasional flashes of a 6/8 feeling within the framework of the triple meter. The sarabande is a slow stately dance with an agogic accent (length accent) on the second beat, while the gigue (English: jig) is a fast brilliant dance, often in 6/8 or another compound duple meter. These stylistic characteristics of the individual dances come from the French, while the concept of the dance suite as a single entity of several movements must be viewed as a contribution of the German composers.

Improvisatory Pieces

Most of the French dance suites (*sonata da camera*) discussed in the preceding section were written for solo instruments—many for harpsichord or lute. During the seventeenth century the lute was the all-important solo instrument, and its foremost exponent was the lutenist-composer Denis Gaultier (1600–72). It was he who developed the so-called "broken style," the characteristic lute texture which was later to be an important feature of the unaccompanied solo sonatas for violin and for cello by Bach. In broken style the illusion of several continuous voice lines is created by sounding tones first in one register, then in another to maintain the feeling of simultaneous activity in all of the implied voices. The technique was necessitated in lute music by the fact that a tone could be sustained only for a short time after the string was plucked. It was quite natural that broken style would be taken over by the bowed stringed instruments since they too, because of the bow technique, were incapable of sustaining more than two tones for any appreciable length of time. There is evidence that a certain kind of loosely strung Baroque bow could keep three or more strings vibrating simultaneously, a fact that is significant to the interpretation of slow movements such as the sarabandes in the unaccompanied Bach suites, although it still does not alter the significance of the broken style in music for bowed stringed instruments.

The French lute style was also important to the development of the French harpsichord (clavecin) idiom of the late seventeenth century as seen first in the music of Jacques Champion de Chambonnieres (c. 1602–72). The French clavecin style incorporated the ornamentations (*agrements*) and the broken style of French lute music, as well as the English penchant for fanciful titles. (The use of *Tombeau* as a title of a piece in memory of the departed, however, was a creation of Gaultier.) Among Chambonniere's pupils were Louis Couperin (c. 1626–61), the earliest composer of the famous family of French musicians, Jean d'Anglebert (c. 1628–91), and Nicolas le Begue (1630–1702). The initial development of the French clavecin style can be seen in the work of these composers. Widely imitated outside of France in the late seventeenth century, the style was characterized by a variety of textures including canonic and fugal passages, clear four-part writing, and improvisatory passages.

Through Froberger's suites the French keyboard style was carried to Germany. But the improvisatory style of his toccatas is of Italian origin—inherited from Frescobaldi, although he seldom matched the exuberance of his teacher's works. Froberger often followed a toccata-like passage with a section in the style of a ricercar or fantasia, thus providing the model for the later Baroque coupling of an improvisatory movement with a fugue, as in the organ works of Buxtehude and Bach.

It must, of course, be understood that keyboard improvisation was widely practiced in the sixteenth, seventeenth, and eighteenth centuries. And even though we have no accurate documentation of its exact nature, it is assumed to be similar in style to notated works in improvisatory style by composers who were famous for their improvisations, such as Frescobaldi, Sweelinck, Buxtehude, and, in the eighteenth century, Bach and Handel. The organ was a frequently used instrument for improvisation, and as early as the sixteenth century the ability to improvise in fugal or ricercar style was an important criterion for appointment to important organ posts in many of the churches of Europe. Improvisation exists today, of course, but in the Baroque era it was much more closely linked to the contemporary instrumental style in written compositions, simply because the composers themselves were the outstanding improvisers of the time.

8. The Mature Baroque

Opera—Secular Cantatas and Songs—Sacred Vocal Music—Ensemble Music—Organ Music— Solo Clavier Music

Opera

The discussion of opera in chapter 7 led through Venetian opera up to the most influential operatic style of the mature Baroque, the movement known as *opera seria* or Neapolitan opera. The latter name comes from the fact that many of the composers of the school were born in or near Naples and received their early musical training in one or another of the famous conservatories of the city. But the Neapolitan school of opera was by no means restricted to the city of Naples, for many of its practitioners were active in the musical centers of Spain, Italy, France and Germany much more than in Naples itself, and there is no real evidence to suggest that Neapolitan opera was peculiar to Naples. It was rather a general type, a late seventeenth-century Italian development which soon spread all over Europe and remained the dominating operatic style well into the Classical period.

At its height it was a rigidly stylized form, usually in three acts, consisting almost entirely of the alternation of short (usually secco) recitatives with arias, mostly of the *da capo* variety. Choruses were rarely used, and except for overtures, ritornelli, and occasional aria accompaniments, the orchestra played a minor role. The overture in Neopolitan opera, called the sinfonia, evolved ultimately to the classical symphony.

The aria became the all-important vehicle of Neapolitan opera, with several stylized types to be performed in a traditionally established order. Because of the emphasis on the aria, the bel-canto style of singing developed to such heights that virtuoso vocal technique in many instances become more important than musical expression. Undoubtedly the powerful and versatile castrato voices (adult male sopranos) contributed much to this development. In Neapolitan opera the coloratura aspects of the bel-canto style are emphasized—brilliance of performance and beauty of sound—but it should be remembered that the term *bel-canto* is also associated with beauty of sound and phrasing in a simpler song-like style, as in the chamber cantatas of Luigi Rossi and Carissimi.

The *opera seria* originated through the reforms of the Italian librettist Zeno (d. 1750) and his successor Metastasio (1698–1782). The major changes consisted of the removal of all comic scenes (which were reestablished later in *opera buffa,* with its emphasis on comic scenes) and the rigid separation of passages which were intended for setting as recitatives from those intended as arias. The subjects of the libretti were frequently drawn from legend and classical history. The aria passages in Metastasio's librettos were particularly remarkable for their melodious verse and musical rhythm, which accounts for the fact that of his thirty-five opera librettos, some were set to music as many as sixty or more times.

The various traditional types of arias in Neapolitan opera include *aria parlante, aria bravura,* and *aria cantabile,* and by the start of the eighteenth century, recitatives also began to appear in distinct types. These are the secco (dry) recitative consisting of continuo accompaniment (usually harpsichord and cello) plus the solo voice, and the *recitativo accompagnato* (accompanied recitative), which used additional instruments for greater dramatic effect. There was also a type of solo melody known as the *arioso* which was not formally organized to the point that it could be called an aria, and yet was not free enough rhythmically to be called a recitative.

One of the major differences between Neapolitan opera and the various early seventeenth-century operatic styles based to varying degrees on the philosophies of the Camerata was that the Neapolitan opera composers were not so intimately concerned with expressing the moods, passions, and poetic images of the text. They used the text as the starting point, of course, but with the new supremacy of the aria they were most concerned with writing an appealing piece of music, whether or not it happened to capture the characterization of the role or the dramatic import of the text. This is vividly seen in the operas of one of the great masters of the Neapolitan style, Alessandro Scarlatti (1660–1725). Surprisingly enough for an opera composer, his dramatic talent appeared to be slight. But because the emphasis was on the musical appeal of the arias rather than upon characterization and true drama, his considerable musical talents carried him through, for there are many great melodic passages in his arias even though the operas themselves do not stand up as dramatic entities. Although Francesco

Provenzale (1627–1704) is generally credited with being the founder of Neapolitan opera, Scarlatti stands out as the first truly significant composer in the Neapolitan style, Other Italian opera composers of the late seventeenth century include Giovanni Legrenzi (1626–90), Allesandro Stradella (1644–82), Carlo Pallavicini (1630–88), and Agostino Steffani (1654–1728).

Opera buffa (comic opera) developed as a spin-off from opera seria, in the form of comic scenes performed as intermezzi between the acts of opera seria in the late seventeenth century. Since there were three acts in the serious opera, opera buffa developed as a two-act form evolving from the two comic intermezzi inserted between the acts of the opera seria. The typical opera buffa of the early eighteenth century consisted of only two or three characters, no chorus, and was limited almost entirely to the alternation of recitatives with delightfully melodious arias. Probably the favorite subject was the love triangle, with mistaken identity used frequently as a comic device. Certainly the most famous, and perhaps the greatest *opera buffa* prior to those of Mozart is *La Serva Padrona* of Giovanni Battista Pergolesi (1710–36).

Of all the European countries, France most strongly resisted the influence of Neapolitan opera in the late seventeenth and early eighteenth centuries. With her long tradition of the *ballet de cour* (court ballet), and with drama raised to new heights by the classical tragedy of Corneille and Racine, it seemed pointless to ally theatre with song. Nevertheless, opera did develop in France. Although Italian opera was not totally unknown, it was the French ballet de cour, rather than a foreign import, which served as the matrix for the aristocratic French opera of the eighteenth century. In about the middle of the seventeenth century the ballet had begun to acquire some of the attributes of drama, including a coherent plot, and since *airs de cours* (strophic songs) had been used as incidental music with the ballet for some time, it was only a short step to the establishment of a real music drama.

For the ballet de cour in his household, Louis XIII had organized an instrumental ensemble known as the "Twenty-four Violins of the King," the first permanently established orchestra to use multiple players on a part. An important feature of the ballet was the overture performed by this orchestra. Later known as the French overture, it consisted of two parts—a slow introduction, often in a minor key with portentous dotted rhythms and rich harmonies ending on the dominant, followed by a fast fugal movement. In the eighteenth century a slow section was sometimes added after the fast fugal part, although this was not essential to the form.

The French overture form was developed most of all by Jean Baptiste Lully (1632–87). Although Lully produced a number of comedy ballets in cooperation with Moliere including the famous *Bourgeois Gentilhomme* (1670), the first genuine French opera was *Pomone* (1671) by the composer Robert Cambert (c. 1628–77) and the poet Robert Perin who in 1669 had become co-directors of the new French Royal Academy of Music. Seeing the great promise of the new form, Lully virtually abandoned ballet in favor of opera, and by political means took control of the new academy and remained the most powerful and influential composer in France for the rest of his life. During this time he produced fifteen operas in which the indigenous traits of French opera were well defined. Of these, *Alceste* (1674) and *Armide* (1688) are perhaps the best known.

Aside from the overture, one of the chief distinguishing characteristics of the new French opera was the recitative style which, unlike that of Italian opera, utilized frequent meter changes (from duple to triple or the reverse) in order to better serve the accents and inflections of the French language as spoken by the great actors of the French classical tragedy of that time. The flowing declamation that resulted from this was in keeping with the French tradition of the theater, another manifestation of which was the practice of avoiding the set piece by means of a smooth transition from recitative to aria, quite unlike the characteristic deemphasis of the recitative in favor of the all-important aria types of Neapolitan opera. In fact, the arias of French opera were considerably less pretentious than those of Italian opera— shorter, without extravagant ornamentation, and often in a simple binary form (aabb). Choruses figured importantly in French opera, and, as a vestige of the ballet de cour, were sometimes danced as well as sung. The French tradition of a ballet in the second act of an opera persisted in Paris throughout the nineteenth century.

The most important French Baroque opera composer after Lully was Jean Phillipe Rameau (1683–1764), mentioned earlier for his *Trea-tise on Harmony* of 1722 which articulated the fundamental bass principle and the theory of chordal inversion. His operas, although they followed the formal patterns of the Lullyian models, were more progressive harmonically and utilized a better quality of instrumental writing. The result was that for his earliest operas, dating from 1733 with *Hippolyte et Aricie,* he was accused of betraying French music by following Italian fashions. There ensued a verbal battle between the Ramists and the Lullists. However, in his master work *Castor and Pollux* (1737) and others among his later operas, the Lully adherents recognized the French dramatic touch, and he is today recognized as one of the great French masters of musical drama.

If anything, the theatrical tradition of England was stronger even than that of France—so strong, in fact, that a genuine native operatic tradition was not established in England until the twentieth century in the person of Benjamin Britten (1913). This is not to say that good operas were not composed by Englishmen, for they were, as early as the Commonwealth period (1649–60). But this was not because of any great delight that the English had in opera, but because theatrical presentations of any kind were prohibited during this period—until the time of the Restoration; and since it was possible for an opera to masquerade as a concert, the English were thus provided with something close to theater. Most such presentations were thinly disguised dramas in which music played only an incidental part, but in about 1682 John Blow composed the first real English opera, *Venus and Adonis.* (There may have been earlier ones which did not survive.) Henry Purcell (1659–95), the greatest English composer after Dunstable, was soon to follow with a work unique in the annals of operatic history, *Dido and Aeneas,* written some time before 1689.

Dido and Aeneas was written for a girl's school near London to a libretto by Nahum Tate, one of the least distinguished poet laureates of England. Derived from Virgil's *Aeneid,* its libretto is based on the love story of Dido, Queen of Carthage and the prince Aeneas. The influence of Lully is seen in the use of an orchestra similar to the "Twenty-four Violins of the King," as well as in the use of the French overture. Chorus is also used, playing much the same part that it does in the later Handelian oratorio, commenting on the action and occasionally taking a part in the plot, frequently in crowd scenes. The opera consists of three short acts made up of binary, rondo, and da capo forms; canons, ground bass movements, recitatives, and motet style. Its most famous aria occurs in the final act. Known as "Dido's Lament," it is based on five-measure chromatic ground bass melody strikingly similar to the one used later by Bach in the *Crucifixus* of the B Minor Mass (see fig. 58).

The influence of Neapolitan opera was carried to Germany by a number of Italian composers, chiefly Pallavicini, who produced operas in Dresden, and Steffani, who worked at Munich and Hanover. Steffani particularly influenced Reinhard Keiser (1674–1739) who produced over a hundred operas for Hamburg, (of which only twenty-five have survived), and George Friedrich Handel (1685–1759) who, although he did the bulk of his opera composing in England, was a native German. Handel's operas will be discussed in the next chapter.

Keiser's operas, composed during his forty-five years in Hamburg, the chief operatic center of the German Baroque, combine influences

Figure 58. Opening of "Dido's Lament" from Purcell's Dido and Aeneas.

of both French and Italian opera. The French elements include the French overture and dance numbers, while the Italian influence can be seen in the style of the arias and recitatives. Unlike the Neapolitan opera composers, however, he strove for significant dramatic expression in both his orchestration and his melodies, and also made some use of *singspiel* melodies (popular tunes used with dramatic presentations), characteristics which mark the beginning establishment of a native German opera. Keiser may have been the first German composer to try his hand at comic opera, a number of examples of which were written toward the end of his career, apparently in an effort to satisfy public taste. Georg Philipp Telemann (1681–1767), one of the last Baroque composers of German opera, also worked at Hamburg, and, like Keiser, also tried his hand at comic opera, the most famous example of which is *Pimpinone,* a short opera buffa composed in 1725. Toward the end of the Baroque period German composers turned their dramatic efforts much more toward sacred works such as passions and oratorios, while native German opera declined.

Secular Cantatas and Songs

As in the early Baroque, cantata developed concurrently with Italian opera during the late seventeenth and early eighteenth centuries, for most of the Neapolitan opera composers were also prolific composers of cantatas. The term *cantata* had originated in the early seventeenth century simply for the purpose of distinguishing vocal from instrumental works, but in the second half of the seventeenth century Italian cantatas began to have an identifiable shape of their own. From its monodic beginnings with strophic variations it finally evolved to a clearly defined pattern of alternating recitatives and arias for solo voice accompanied by continuo. The texts were usually on the subject of love and, although they often told a story, were not intended to be staged with costumes and scenery like opera. Designed for smaller more discriminating audiences, these ten- to fifteen-minute works maintained an elegance of detail and workmanship more characteristic of chamber music than of opera, and, indeed, are often called "chamber cantatas."

The best-known composers of these secular Italian cantatas of the later Baroque were Legrenzi, Stradella, and Alessandro Scarlatti. Scarlatti, the greatest of the three, excelled in his cantatas even more than in his operas, perhaps because the cantata did not require the dramatic and theatrical skills in which he was a bit deficient, and also because the more intimate medium allowed him greater opportunity for experimental effects. His cantata *Lascia, deh lascia* ("Cease, Oh Cease"), for example, contains distant modulations, a vocal line containing unusual leaps, considerable chromaticism, and a number of other remarkable devices for evoking the meaning of the text.

Although a single soprano voice with continuo accompaniment was by far the favorite medium for the chamber cantata, some utilized more than one voice, and instruments in addition to the continuo. A vocal medium not unlike the instrumental trio sonata with two equal high voices over a continuo accompaniment became a favorite of Steffani—one which was widely imitated by later composers. These and other modifications of the typical solo cantata set the stage for the sacred cantatas of J. S. Bach, many of which utilize several solo voices, instrumental sections, and chorus.

In France, Marc-Antoine Charpentier (1634–1704), a student of Carissimi, and Louis Clerambault (1676–1749) composed secular cantatas in the Italian style. Clerambault's cantatas contain recitatives in the Italian style (some in the Italian language) as well as French recitatives in the Lullyian manner. In Germany, Keiser and Teleman composed cantatas in both the Italian and German languages.

Only the English remained relatively untouched by the Italian influence in the late seventeenth century and, although there were a few attempts at imitating Italian vocal models, the best English vocal music owed little to foreign influences. Many English songs of this time were written for the theater as incidental music but there was also a vestige of the English madrigal known as the "catch," a part song intended for amateur performance which made clever use of humorous or off-color allusions. Presaging Handel's English oratorios were works such as Purcell's *Ode for Saint Cecilia's Day,* which uses soloists chorus, and orchestra.

In both France and Germany the solo song maintained a modest existence separate from the cantata. In France "airs" continued to be composed in the courtly tradition of the air de cour, while in Germany the most notable composer of solo songs was Adam Krieger (1634–66). His *Neue Arien* ("New Airs"), published in two collections in the decade after his death, are excellent examples of strophic songs with instrumental ritornelli. The use of orchestral accompaniments to songs was quite common in Germany at this time and became a characteristic of composite forms such as the Lutheran cantata and the oratorio.

Sacred Vocal Music

The center for the oratorio and Catholic church music moved from Italy to Vienna during the latter part of the seventeenth century. The four emperors who reigned in the court there from 1637 to 1740 were personally interested in the art of music, and through their influence and financial support Vienna became one of the foremost musical centers of the Western world, a position which it has retained to the present day. Although many composers such as Fux and Alessandro Scarlatti wrote voluminously in the ultraconservative pseudo-Palestrinian style discussed in chapter 7, many also composed Masses and other sacred vocal works utilizing Baroque techniques such as concertato and bel canto styles, continuo, multiple choirs, and idiomatic instrumental writing. Indeed, some Masses, such as those by Antonio Caldara (1670–1736), began to take on the appearance of a series of separate musical numbers, like an opera, with duets and arias interspersed with choral movements and instrumental ritornelli, although the recitative was not used in church music.

The Catholic church composers in Vienna in addition to Fux and Caldara include the Germans Johann Heinrich Schmelzer (c. 1623–80) and Johann Kerll (1627–93), and the Italians Antonio Draghi (1635–1700) and Marco Antonio Ziani (c. 1653–1715). All of them except Schmelzer and Fux were also noted opera composers, and the influence of this activity can be seen in their work. The ornate magnificence of the liturgical works composed by the Viennese composers of this time was in keeping with the elaborately beautiful Baroque cathedrals in which they were performed. The Karlskirche in Vienna (1715) designed by Fischer von Erlach, is one of the great manifestations of the

Baroque spirit—the zeitgeist which left its mark upon all European art of the early eighteenth century.

The fusion of north Italian and south German characteristics which produced the Viennese church music of the late Baroque can also be seen in the works of Johann Adolf Hasse (1699–1783) who, though best known for his operas which number over a hundred, also composed many oratorios, Masses, and other liturgical works, The Italians Legrenzi, Lotti, A. Scarlatti, and Pergolesi also composed sacred music, much of which is marked by a peculiarly mournful kind of chromaticism which can also be seen in the church music of Caldara. A good example of this is found in the opening of Caldara's *Stabat Mater* (fig. 59). This example contains an augmented sixth chord (E flat, G, B Flat, C Sharp), several diminished sevenths, and, at the very beginning, the melodic outline of an augmented triad.

The oratorios in both Italy and southern Germany at this time were, for the most part, modeled after Italian opera. That is, they used Italian rather than the Latin texts used by Carissimi and his contemporaries, and they consisted of an overture followed by recitatives alternated with solo or duet arias in bel canto style. Chorus was used sparingly and did not take on the importance that it acquired in the oratorios of Handel and the great choral works of J. S. Bach. Hasse's oratorio *The Conversion of St. Augustine,* composed at Dresden in 1750, is a good example of this type of oratorio, as are those of Benedetto Marcello (1686–1739).

In France, Charpentier was virtually the only composer to write oratorios, and these, like French Baroque opera, utilized French elements in order to depart from the Italian models. A number of accompanied motets, similar in style to the chamber cantata, were composed by late seventeenth-century French composers such as Lully, Charpentier, Michel-Richard Delalande (1657–1726) and Francois Couperin (1668–1733). Delalande, known for little else than his church music, was the most popular church composer in Paris during the early eighteenth century.

The Anglican Church of the seventeenth century was graced by the great choral works of Henry Purcell as well as the works of lesser composers such as Pelham Humphrey (1647–74) and John Blow. Relatively unswayed by the influence of the Italian Baroque, England's principal liturgical form was the verse anthem which had developed from the Latin motet during the late Renaissance. In the late seventeenth century it was a sectional form which achieved contrast by alternating solo with chorus. During the early seventeenth century the voices were usually accompanied only by organ, but during the Resto-

Figure 59. Caldara, Stabat Mater.

ration period and later the accompaniment consisted of continuo and often other instruments as well. An older type of anthem, known as the "full anthem," was also composed during the late seventeenth century, although it was not nearly as popular as the verse anthem. The full anthem was in the older motet style and, in a sense, was the English counterpart of the pseudo-Palestrinian style practiced by the conservative Roman Catholic composers of Italy. A good example is Purcell's *Thou Knowest Lord the Secrets of our Hearts.*

In 1677 Purcell succeeded Matthew Locke as "Composer in Ordinary for the Violins" and in 1679 also took over the position of organist and choirmaster of Westminster Abbey which had been held by his teacher, John Blow. He composed about sixty anthems, mostly verse anthems for Westminster Abbey. These works, more than any others, demonstrate his remarkable abilities to express the meaning of the words through musical means, to find the ideal rhythms for the setting of the English language, and withal to produce great music. A famous example is an anthem known as the "Bell Anthem" to the text "Rejoice in the Lord Alway." It opens with an extended instrumental section in French overture style and continues with verse sections for three solo voices alternated with choral sections. Aside from Handel, the most significant composer of church music in England after Purcell was William Croft (1678–1727), although no Englishman of that time reached the musical heights achieved by Purcell.

But the greatest achievements in Baroque liturgical music occurred in the German Lutheran Church, In the middle of the seventeenth century following the Thirty Years War, the churches of the Lutheran countries which had been under strictures of economy or had been damaged during the wars were reestablished and the period of 1650 to 1750 which followed became the Golden Age of Lutheran music. Theologically there were two opposing trends within the Lutheran church of this time—Orthodoxy and Pietism. The Orthodox beliefs held to the old established forms of worship including the use of elaborate vocal and instrumental resources in the musical services, while Pietism, the Lutheran manifestation of a growing movement in all Protestant religions, advocated freedom of religious beliefs, had little use for high art in worship, and preferred music of a simple, austere, and sometimes sentimental character. The Lutheran chorales, most of which dated from the earliest days of the Reformation fit well with these Pietist tendencies, and were the common musical heritage of all Lutheran composers of the Baroque era. At the same time the use of instruments, concertato style, solo voices, and continuo practiced by earlier seventeenth-century Lutheran composers such as Schein, Scheidt, and Schütz continued its development in the Orthodox centers; and after 1700 a mutually beneficial union of Orthodox and Pietist tendencies was embodied in the Lutheran choral cantata.

The growing practice of congregational chorale singing resulted in a smoothing out of the rhythmic irregularities in the chorale tunes, and

by the eighteenth century, chorales had acquired the rhythmic qualities familiar in the choral settings of Bach—near symmetrical phrases
of equal note values and a fermata at the end of each phrase. Schütz
had found no use for chorale tunes, but Franz Tunder (1614–67), a
student of Frescobaldi and organist at Lübeck, wrote a number of
chorale variations and settings of chorale tunes in monodic style for
solo voices. His contemporary, Andreas Hammerschmidt (c. 1611–75),
represents the Orthodox element in the mid-seventeenth century Lutheran church, for he composed elaborate instrumental accompaniments to his polyphonic choral works with little or no use of the
chorale.

Perhaps the greatest Lutheran composer between Schütz and Bach
is Dietrich Buxtehude (c. 1637–1707). He was successor to Tunder at the
Marienkirche of Lübeck (also his son-in-law), and is the master whom
Bach travelled from Arnstadt to Lübeck on foot to hear in 1705 (a
distance of about 200 miles), and with whom Bach studied for a period
of several months. Buxtehude established Sunday evening musical
services called *Abendmusiken* at the Marienkirche which were presented each year on several Sundays preceding the Christmas season,
and it was for these occasions that he composed much of his church
music. The typical *Abendmusik* service lasted about an hour, usually
included two cantatas and a chorale, and required the services of as
many as forty singers and instrumentalists.

Most of Buxtehude's cantatas are of the older Italian style. They do
not use recitatives and da capo arias, but do contain ariosos and instrumental ritornellos with much use of concertato style in both voices and
instruments. Not all of them are in German, nor do they all contain
chorale tunes. An excellent example of an Italian-style cantata with
Latin text is *Jubilate Domino,* a work for countertenor or alto solo, solo
viol da gamba, and continuo. It opens with an instrumental sinfonia
followed by contrasting sections which, though uninterrupted, are
long enough to be called movements, and which achieve their contrast
primarily by means of tempo and meter changes. As to the relationship
between voice and instruments, the virtuoso viol da gamba part in this
work predominates over the solo voice in a concertato texture that
sometimes finds the solo instrument in an accompanying role, but also
contains extended sections for the viol da gamba and continuo alone.
Others among his cantatas are like chorale variations in which each
stanza of the chorale serves as the basis for varied elaborations by both
voices and instruments.

An outstanding contemporary of Buxtehude is Johann Pachelbel
(1653–1706) who, though best known for his organ music, also composed sacred vocal music in the Italian style and frequently made use

of double chorus. Like Buxtehude, he also used Latin texts as well as German, for in many churches portions of the Lutheran service were still sung in Latin. Indeed, the Mass—in its shortened Lutheran form which included only the Kyrie and the Gloria—was usually sung in Latin, while other musical settings of the liturgy used either Latin or German.

The Lutheran cantata in the German language, however, was established as a direct result of a new type of sacred poetry for musical setting first developed by Erdmann Neumeister (1671–1756) in the year 1700. An Orthodox Lutheran clergyman with Pietistic tendencies, Neumeister produced texts which, because of their free rhyme schemes and irregular meters combined with their devotional and didactic intent, were admirably suited to musical settings which fused the best musical elements of both the Orthodox and Pietist persuasions. Added to the biblical passages and chorale texts were poetic texts intended to enhance the experience of worship by expanding upon the prescribed texts. These were often intended for setting as recitatives and arias, or as ariosos, and with their free madrigal-like quality, allowed the composers considerable freedom of musical expression. Bach used many such texts in his cantatas and Passions and, with the aid of the Leipzig poet Picander, developed the essential form for his chorale cantatas. Although the term *cantata* was applied rather indiscriminately to nearly any type of Lutheran church music for voices with instruments before and after Neumeister, the true Lutheran church cantata, in the strictest sense, was the result of his poetic innovations.

The most important forerunners of Bach in the production of chorale cantatas were Phillipp Krieger (1649–1725), Johann Kuhnau (1670–1722), whom Bach succeeded at Leipzig, and Friedrich Zachow (1663–1712), teacher of Handel. In the cantatas of these composers, particularly those of Zachow, can be found a variety of forms and styles including secco and accompanied recitatives, da capo arias, concertato style, choruses, and chorale settings. The hard-core Pietists objected to such elaborate music for the church, even though chorale tunes were used, but fortunately for the art of music, this did not prevent Bach from producing a monumental body of works in this form—perhaps as many as 300 cantatas for the various occasions of the church year, of which nearly 200 have survived. Other composers of cantatas in the eighteenth century include Christoph Graupner (1683–1760), Johann Mattheson (1681–1764), and Telemann. Some of the cantatas of these composers, particularly those of Telemann, began to show traits of the Rococo period (1725–50) as music evolved toward Classicism.

Settings of the *Passion,* the accounts of Christ's suffering and death in the first several books of the New Testament, were of particular importance to German church music. The Reformation composer Johann Walter (1496–1570) had in 1550 adapted the St. Matthew Passion to the German language and produced a musical setting, and, in the Catholic church, musical dramatizations of the story go back to the twelfth century. The Passion settings of the mature Baroque utilized all the musical resources of the time and, except for much greater use of chorus, are not unlike the Italian oratorios from which, in a sense, they are descended. That is, like oratorios, they are dramatic presentations of a story in music, unstaged and without costumes. Although numerous composers wrote Passions, the finest settings are those of Schütz, and the two complete surviving Passions of Bach (his obituary states that he wrote five), which will be discussed in the next chapter.

Ensemble Music

Among the most important instrumental composers of the late seventeenth and early eighteenth centuries are the Italian violinist-composers. They not only composed a vast body of literature for solo and ensemble stringed instruments, but also established a school of violin playing that has wielded a strong influence upon the technique of bowed stringed instruments even to the present time. It is no coincidence that the greatest makers of violin-type instruments lived at the same time that the first great music for these instruments was written.

The first true violins, as distinguished from the viol-type instruments, are attributed to Gasparo da Salo (1540–1609) who worked in Brescia, but the great Italian center for violin making in the seventeenth and eighteenth centuries was Cremona, where Niccolo Amati (1596–1684), Antonio Stradivari (1644–1737), Giuseppe Guarneri "del Gesu," (1698–1744), and many other great craftsman produced a tremendous quantity of fine violins, violas, cellos, basses, and other stringed instruments. Many of these superb instruments have survived two or three centuries of use and continue to be played and treasured by present-day performers. The presence of the finest violins went hand in hand with the development of orchestral and chamber music, and the most accomplished violinists of the seventeenth and eighteenth centuries were also distinguished composers.

In the last half of the seventeenth century, the most important developments in chamber music occurred in Bologna, where Maurizio Cazzati (c. 1620–77), G. B. Vitali (c. 1644–92), and his son Tomasso Vitali (c. 1665–c.1747) produced a large number of trio sonatas and solo violin sonatas with continuo accompaniment. The movements of these sonatas were in many instances influenced by dance rhythms. Some movements were slow and serene, often with canonic imitation, but seldom did these early Bolognese composers indulge in brilliant technical effects for the violin. Around 1667 G. B. Vitali, a student of Cazzati, established a standard fast-slow-fast pattern for the arrangement of the sonata movements which by 1680 was expanded into the standard slow-fast-slow-fast pattern of the church sonata or sonata da chiesa through the addition of a slow movement at the beginning.

The dance suite or sonata da camera also became established in the four- to six-movement pattern discussed in chapter 8—basically Allemande, courante, sarabande, and gigue, plus an optional da capo dance form inserted between the sarabande and gigue (called the galanterie), and often with a prelude. Neither the church sonatas nor the dance suites were invariably cast in the exact patterns described above, although the practice became increasingly consistent toward the end of the Baroque period.

By the late seventeenth century most of the movements of both the sonata da chiesa and sonata da camera were (except for the galanteries, which were in da capo form, and the preludes) in the standard Baroque binary form—the most important single movement chamber music form of the Baroque period. Until pre-classical times binary forms were predominantly monothematic with the standard tonal pattern shown in figure 60. It is important to note that a form of this type, its formal logic relying upon the fifth relation and upon the tonal center defined by the relationship of dominant to tonic, was not possible until the seventeenth century, and was the direct result of the evolution of the concept of tonality. We shall see later how, in the pre-classical period, sonata-allegro form evolved from this simple pattern.

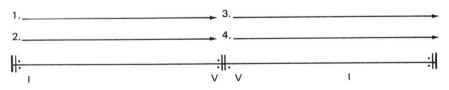

Figure 60. Binary Form. The Numbers and Arrows Indicate the Sequence of Repeats.

Although many solo violin sonatas with continuo accompaniment were written by the Italian composers of the late seventeenth century, the trio sonata was considerably more popular. As mentioned earlier, the term *trio sonata* does not indicate a form (they were written in all of the standard sonata patterns of the Baroque) but denotes a particular medium—two solo instruments plus continuo, requiring four players for performance. It was a highly flexible medium, for the two high, singing instruments could be used in a variety of ways, such as canonic imitation and other polyphonic devices, against the chordal undergirding of the cello and harpsichord. The cello occasionally joined the upper parts to furnish one voice of an imitative texture. The solo parts were most frequently written for violins, but flutes, oboes, or other instruments of soprano register were often substituted.

One of the greatest contributions of the Italian composers of the mature Baroque was the development of the concerto. The term had been in use since the sixteenth century, applied to both vocal and instrumental pieces, but in the late Baroque it came to denote a particular kind of orchestral medium developed first in Bologna around the end of the seventeenth century. The composer who contributed most to its early development was Giuseppe Torelli (1658–1709). There are three basic types of baroque concerti: (1) the concerto grosso which consists of two contrasting groups of instruments—a small group of solo instruments called the *concertino* against the larger group of orchestral players called the *ripieno;* (2) the orchestral concerto, which used much concertato style but without a solo group as in the concerto grosso; and (3) the solo concerto, which used only one solo player, usually a violinist, against the *ripieno* instead of the *concertino* group of solo instruments.

The environment of the church of San Petronio in Bologna where Torelli and other Bolognese musicians worked was undoubtedly a shaping influence upon the beginning development of the Baroque concerto. As was the case in many churches of the time, San Petronio maintained a small orchestra of accomplished professional musicians, but for special occasions additional less expert outsiders were added to the smaller group to form a larger orchestra. The presence of the small group of expert solo players as well as the larger group created a natural situation for the creation of musical works which utilized the soloists to good advantage in solo groups as well as the more numerous but less accomplished performers to form the *ripieno.*

The solo group or *concertino* of the concerto grosso frequently was a group identical to the trio sonata medium—two solo violins plus a continuo of cello and harpsichord. Although "concerto grosso" denotes a particular medium rather than a form, the term also implies a more or less standard formal pattern, particularly in the first movements. The typical first movement is in an allegro tempo beginning with the concertino and ripieno playing together in a tutti passage which is used later as the ritornello, and which modulates to a contrasting but related key such as the relative major or minor (depending upon the mode of the piece), the dominant, or the subdominant. Next comes a passage for the concertino in the contrasting key followed by the ritornello (played by the ripieno) based upon the material of the opening tutti. This ritornello is typically in a key other than the home tonality and is followed by a concertino passage in which the soloists modulate back to the tonic in preparation for a final ritornello which remains in the tonic for the final cadence of the movement. The essence of the pattern, then, is the alternation of a number of solo sections with tutti sections, beginning and ending with a tutti and with key contrast achieved by departure to closely related keys during the course of the movement. Although the number of solo sections and ritornelli varied, the final solo section would invariably modulate back to the tonic in preparation for the final ritornello played by soloists and orchestra together.

The element of dynamic contrast between a large and a small group exerted a strong influence on virtually all music of the Baroque, and from it we have the term *terrace dynamics.* It can be seen not only in concerto forms of the Baroque, but also in the contrast between manuals of the harpsichord and organ, and wherever concertato style is utilized in vocal as well as instrumental music.

Torelli's later concertos were mostly in a three-movement fast-slow-fast pattern which became the general rule for concertos of the eighteenth century. An accompanied fugal style was often used in the allegro movements, while the slow movements were in a conservative lyrical style with the ripieno used very sparingly. Most concerto grosso composers were quite conservative in their treatment of the solo instruments, often writing concertino parts which were only slightly more difficult than the ripieno parts. Torelli's solo concertos, however, were among the first to utilize the solo violin in a manner approaching the virtuoso style of the classical concerto. The form of the solo concerto was essentially the same as that of the concerto grosso. The orchestral concerto developed by Torelli used the concerto style and the ever-present continuo, but without the contrasting sections for soloists and tutti which were so typical of the concerto grosso and the solo concerto.

The greatest of the late seventeenth-century violinist-composers was Arcangelo Corelli (1653–1713), who fully assimilated the style of the Bolognese composers, laid the foundations of modern violin technique, and through his students, passed on a concept of violin pedagogy that has been important to the development of string playing even to the present day. Most of his life was spent quietly in the city of Rome, although he studied for four years in Bologna and lived for a short time in Germany. He composed forty-eight trio sonatas, of which twenty-four are of the sonata da chiesa type and twenty-four follow the pattern of the sonata de camera. In the Baroque fashion, he composed them in groups of twelve. Op. 1 and 3 are church sonatas, Op. 2 and 4, dance suites. Although the two types are clearly distinguishable, they are sometimes mixed, with non-dance movements occurring as first movements in the chamber sonatas, and some dance movements being found in the church sonatas.

His twelve solo violin sonatas (Op. 5) are standard fare for all students of the violin and consist of six chamber sonatas and five church sonatas plus the famous *La Folia* variations, a good example of the Baroque ostinato variation based on the famous *Folia* theme—an eight-bar, triple-meter melody used by a number of seventeenth-century composers as the basis for chaconnes or passacaglias.

Corelli's beautifully polished and finely balanced sonatas exemplify seventeenth-century chamber music at its best. The keyboard parts were originally written in figured bass without realization, as in figure 51 (the first page of the first sonata of Opus 5 as published in an eighteenth-century edition). His imitative textures sometimes include the cello playing thematic material but, for the most part, the bass line is of an accompaniment nature. The serenely contemplative slow movements probably did not sound as serene in Baroque performances as they do today. It seems that these melodic lines were deliberately left in a state of unadorned simplicity in order to allow the performers to demonstrate their skill and ingenuity in improvisation. Present-day performers, however, seldom attempt to embellish the music in this way, with the result that the performances, although they follow the notation, are probably not historically correct.

There are no extant compositions by Corelli other than instrumental works, and it is possible that he made no significant attempts in other directions. The only works other than the five works mentioned so far are the twelve concerti grossi of Op. 6, published in 1712 but perhaps composed as early as 1682. The first eight are in the form of the church concerto (concerto da chiesa), which does not necessarily indicate that they are in the four-movement pattern of the sonata da chiesa, but that they are serious in intent, designed for church performance. The last four fall into the da camera category, and many of the movements utilize dance rhythms. All twelve use a concertino consisting of the trio sonata medium—two violins, cello, and keyboard—and a string orchestra consisting of two sections of violins, a section of violas, and cellos and basses on the bass line. Probably the best known is the popular "Christmas Concerto," Op. 6, No. 8. Intended for a Christmas Eve performance, it contains a delightful, Christmas-like pastorale movement.

The Baroque "doctrine of affections" is particularly apparent in Corelli's music, for with few exceptions each of his movements maintains a single mood throughout—the slow movements with their beautifully limpid melodic style, and the fast movements with their vigorous unflagging rhythms. The device of the sequence, particularly in patterns of progressions of fourths or fifths, is found throughout Correlli's music—a direct result of the new concept of tonality with its dependence on the fifth relation.

One of Corelli's greatest achievements was his contribution to the development of the concerto grosso style, which led ultimately to the great Classical and Romantic works in the concerto genre. Other Italian composers who contributed to the development of the concerto include Tomaso Albinoni (1671–1750), Evaristo dall'Abaco (1675–1742), Francesco Geminiani (1687–1762), a student of Corelli who enjoyed a long and distinguished career as a violinist-composer in London and who published one of the first violin methods, and Pietro Locatelli (1695–1764), another Corelli student.

The violin-type instruments which came into prominence in the seventeenth century include the violin, viola, and cello, but it should not be presumed that other stringed instruments such as the lute and the viols were eclipsed. The lute maintained its importance well into the eighteenth century; and among stringed instruments of lower registers, the viol da gamba was the preeminent virtuoso instrument throughout the Baroque era. The cello did not become an important solo instrument until the Classical period, even though Bach, Vivaldi, and other composers contributed to its repertory.

English composers of the mature Baroque were influenced by both French and Italian chamber music, although the only really significant British chamber music produced at this time are two sets of trio sonatas by Purcell published in 1683 and 1697. In France the most important chamber music composers after Lully (other than Couperin, who will be discussed later) are J. B. Loeillet (1680–1738) who wrote sonatas and trio sonatas for various instruments, particularly for flute, and Jean-Marie Leclair (1697–1764), the most important violinist-composer of the French Baroque.

A great deal of chamber and orchestral music was written in Germany during the late seventeenth and early eighteenth centuries. Trio sonatas and other forms of chamber music were composed by George Muffat (1653–1704), Buxtehude, Telemann, Fux, Christoph

Graupner (1683–1760), Graupner's student Johann Fasch (1688–1758), and a number of others. In addition to the strong Italian influence, a number of students of Lully such as Muffat and Johann Kusser (1660–1727), carried the French style to Germany. Kusser (or Cousser) modified the French overture form by extending the fugal section and adding a third section in a slow tempo similar to the slow introduction. German orchestral dance suites often used the French overture as a prelude and as this practice increased the entire suite began to be called an "overture," as in the orchestral suites of Bach.

German chamber music, in addition to the strong influence of Corelli, was marked by an emphasis upon serious contrapuntal writing and fugal style. This can be seen in the sonatas of composers such as Fux and Graupner, and also in the solo violin music of Johann Jakob Welther (1650–1717) and Heinrich Biber (1644–1704), both of whom composed passacaglias in broken style for solo violin—precursors of Bach's great *Chaconne* in D Minor. Walther's twelve violin sonates published in 1676 were the first significant German works of this type, while Biber, although he composed operas and sacred choral music, is remembered chiefly for his contributions to the literature and technique of the violin. His *Biblische Sonaten* ("Biblical Sonatas") for violin, programmatic works describing the life of Christ, contain some of the earliest examples of *Scordatura* (altered tuning of the instrument to facilitate the playing of certain double stops) a technique which was used by Bach, by nineteenth-century composers including Schumann and Saint-Saens, and in this century by Kodaly and others. Another early German composer of instrumental music is Johann Rosenmüller (c. 1620–84), who in 1670 published a collection of eleven dance suites for five instruments with continuo.

Ensemble playing thrived in Germany during the Baroque era, as it did in England, because of a great interest in both countries in communal music-making. Not only the nobility, but also large numbers of the middle classes, met frequently in groups such as the *collegium musicum* for the purpose of playing and singing for their own amusement. Every city or town prided itself on its town band *(stadtpfeifer)*; and in many communities "tower music" (chorales or sonata movements played by wind instruments from a tower—*Turmsonaten*) was played from the church or *Rathaus* steeple—a vestige of the times when alarms were given by brass instruments playing from a tower.

Organ Music

German composers dominated organ music in the late seventeenth and eighteenth centuries due to the strong influence of the Netherlander Sweelinck and, to a lesser degree, of Frescobaldi. The instrument itself was more fully developed in Germany than in any other country, and many Baroque organs in Germany had three or more manuals and a complete pedal board. In the seventeenth century the chief organ builder was Arp Schnitger (1648–1718), a north German whose instruments were characterized by distinctive and contrasting tone colors and great brilliance of sound. In the eighteenth century the outstanding builder was Gottfried Silbermann (1683–1753), whose organs were generally more mild than Schnitger's, although still maintaining great brilliance in the mixtures. Replicas of Baroque organs are quite common today, their chief virtue being their ability to delineate several voices of a contrapuntal texture rather than fuse them into a block of homogenous sound as nineteenth century organs tend to do.

The outstanding organ composers before Bach were Buxtehude, Pachelbel, and Georg Böhm (1667–1733). Buxtehude and Böhm were of the north German school, while Pachelbel was the chief representative of the central German organ composers. South German and Austrian organ music, composed for the Catholic church, did not use the chorale and did not achieve the freedom and scope of organ music in northern and central Germany.

The north German composers wrote in a free style and in larger forms including the prelude, fugue, toccata, and chorale fantasia. Pachelbel and his central German contemporaries developed the chorale prelude and chorale variation, but did not work a great deal in the larger forms. Buxtehude, more than any other, exerted a strong influence upon the organ music of Bach. He succeeded Franz Tunder as organist of the Marienkirche in Lübeck, and it was there that Bach studied with him for a period of several months in 1705 and 1706. Buxtehude's organ music is bold and imaginative in style and includes numerous fugues with preludes or toccatas, variation forms using the titles chaconne and passacaglia, and numerous works based upon chorale tunes. His fugal works, whether entitled prelude and fugue or toccata and fugue, are unique for their freedom of form. Often the fugues are in two or three parts separated by free toccata-like sections, the subjects of the second or third sections derived from that of the first. His Prelude and Fugue in E Minor is a work of this type. Following the toccata-like opening, the first fugue section is presented without break followed by a free section similar to the opening, and another fugue section based on a subject clearly derived from the first. Figure 61 shows the two fugal subjects of this work.

Buxtehude's organ chorales are of various types from the extended chorale fantasia, of which *Nun Freut Euch* is a good example, to short chorale preludes, or motet-style organ works with thematic material

Figure 61. Fugal Subjects of Buxtehude's Prelude and Fugue in E Minor.

derived from a chorale tune. Pachelbel, unlike Buxtehude, often used
only a motive or perhaps only the first phrase of a chorale tune for his
organ chorales. He wrote works which can be described as chorale
fugues, with the fugal subject based on a chorale tune, short chorale
preludes using motives from a chorale tune, and free organ works
which are combinations of both of these types. Georg Böhm, who also
wrote in styles similar to those of Buxtehude, exerted a strong influence upon Bach, chiefly through his use of agrements (French ornaments).

By the late seventeenth century the fugue had been clearly established as a basic procedure made possible by the development of the
concept of tonality. Although it cannot be called a form, there are
certain aspects of fugal procedure which are common to most fugues,
and which can be seen in many of the great fugal works of J. S. Bach.
These traits are: (1) A fugue is based primarily upon one short thematic
idea called the subject, although the counterpoint used against the
subject, if it is used consistently enough to be called a countersubject,

may also become an important thematic element. (2) The number of voices (two or more) remains constant throughout the work, all of them first being presented in the course of the opening imitative exposition, usually alternating between the tonic and dominant keys in their entrances. In the progress of the fugue all of the voices need not always be present in the texture. (3) Fugal devices such as augmentation, diminution, and inversion may be used to develop the exposition material in various ways, are used in the sections following the exposition, and may occur throughout the fugue. (4) In addition to incidental entries of the subject in various keys to define the tonal architecture of the work, a final statement or final exposition of the subject in the tonic is found at or near the end of the work.

Figure 62 shows in synoptic form the fugal pattern described above. It is a short, concise four-voice fugue by Pachelbel, the subject based on a Gregorian chant tune, and with the final statement occurring in the lowest voice in measures 22 to 24. The full potential of this pattern or procedure was not revealed until the next generation in the great fugues of Bach.

Other German organ composers include Johann Gottfried Walther (1684–1748), a cousin of J. S. Bach, and George Muffat. Organ music did not develop in England and in the southern European countries as it did in Germany, but the French Baroque organ school is worthy of mention for its gracefully attractive settings of popular airs and for the French organ "Masses" of Francois Couperin—incidental pieces to be played in the course of the Mass. French organ music, in addition to its ornamentation, made particularly interesting use of tone color, and in many instances the stops to be used in a particular passage were specified by the composer.

Solo Clavier Music

The beginning history of solo music for harpsichord and clavichord was discussed in chapter 8. After Chambonnieres in France, and Froberger in Germany, the chief composers were Couperin and Rameau in France, who will be discussed in the next chapter, and Pachelbel, Buxtehude, Johann Krieger (1651–1735), J. K. F. Fischer (d. 1746), Kuhnau, Böhm, and Gottlieb Muffat (1690–1770) in Germany.

The most important type of keyboard music was the dance suite which continued in its various national forms—the *Ordre* in France, and, toward the end of the seventeenth century, the *partita* in Germany, both essentially the same as the sonata da camera which had originated in Italy.

Figure 62. Fughetta for the Magnificat *(complete) Pachelbel.*

The rhythmic characteristics of the four standard dance movements established in Germany in the seventeenth century were discussed in chapter 8. It is interesting to note the strikingly international
nature of the origins of these movements. The Allemande is probably
German (*Allemande* is the French word for German); the courante,
French; the sarabande, Spanish (although it was a much more passionate kind of dance in its original form); and the gigue (jig), English.

Other types of dances and movements with fanciful titles, continued to be found in dance suites, although the four- to six-movement suite became quite standard. Some examples of the sonata (i.e., sonata da chiesa) were written for solo keyboard instruments, although this was primarily a type of composition for instrumental ensemble. The binary form was used more than any other form in keyboard dance suites and sonatas, even though a variety of other forms were used, including free forms such as the toccata and prelude, fugal movements, and da capo forms for the galanteries.

9. The Culminating Figures of the Baroque
Couperin—Rameau—Vivaldi—Scarlatti— Handel—Bach

In France after Lully the more serious aspects of Baroque musical thought gave way to a characteristically French lightness and grace as a pre-Classical development known as the *style galant* ("gallant style") appeared. Lully's style continued to be revered by French musicians, but the style galant brought with it a new wit, intimacy, and artificiality very much in keeping with the Parisian spirit. Concurrent with the style galant is the movement in painting called the Rococo, of which the painter Watteau is the chief representative. Musically, the word "rococo" should not be viewed as a pejorative term, for it includes some of the finest examples of Baroque and pre-Classical music.

The style galant flourished during the regency period (1715–23) and the reign of Louis XV, which lasted until 1774. The movement caused a strong rivalry between the French and Italian styles and, although attempts were made to fuse the two, the French style dominated Paris. Italian concerto forms and trio sonatas, for example, were attempted by only a few French composers and a consciousness of French musical tradition became very strong. The true French taste was seen in operas in a light vein, ornate chamber music, and, above all, highly ornamented solo clavecin music, of which Francois Couperin was the most distinguished composer.

Francois Couperin

Couperin (1668–1733), called *"le Grand"* because of his excellence as an organist and to distinguish him from an uncle of the same name, is the earliest of the Rococo or style galant composers and the most illustrious member of a distinguished family that was active in France from the mid-seventeenth century for a period of two hundred years.

Employed by Louis XIV and XV, he taught music in the royal household, was organist of the Royal Chapel as well as in the Church of St. Gervais, and was clavecinist (harpsichordist) to the King. His religious music, written during the first half of his life, includes a considerable number of choral works in motet style, and the organ Masses mentioned earlier (*Livre d'Orgue,* 1690), consisting of forty-two pieces to be played during the course of the Mass. Replete with the typical French ornamentation of the time, these are the finest examples of French organ music in the mature Baroque.

A great admirer of Corelli's music, Couperin was strongly influenced by the Italian instrumental style. He used continuo in most of his ensemble music and introduced the trio sonata in France. His *Concerts Royaux* (1714–15), written for Sunday concerts of Louis XIV, are suites for continuo and solo instruments consisting of preludes, echoes, airs, and a variety of dance movements. They may have been written originally for harpsichord, but written records of the Sunday concerts show that they were performed by a variety of instruments, including strings, flute, oboe, and bassoon. Evidence of Couperin's partiality to Corelli is found in a collection of trio "concerts" entitled *Les Gouts-Reunis* (*"The Reunited Tastes";* 1724) scored for "all kinds of instruments" and continuo, concluding with a trio sonata entitled *Le Parnasse ou l'Apothéose de Corelli.* The collection purports to unite the Italian and French styles and in several of the seven movements of the concluding trio sonata Couperin successfully imitates the style of Corelli, but the rhythmic variety, facility, and ornamentation are nevertheless typical of Couperin's own unique style.

Not to neglect Lully, Couperin in 1725 composed the *Apothéose de Lully,* an instrumental work in thirteen movements in which Lully is musically depicted in the Elysian fields in the company of Apollo being entertained by Corelli and the muses. Apollo persuades the two composers that the ideal music would be a union of the two national tastes. The work concludes with a trio sonata which opens with a French overture in the Lullyian style followed by three movements in the Italian style, thus uniting the two styles. *Les Nations* (1726), a collection of four trio sonatas for strings and harpsichord, again demonstrates Couperin's international tastes, for each sonata opens with a movement bearing a nationalistic title: *La Francoise, L'Espagnole L'Imperiale,* and *La Pièmontoise.* The two suites for solo viol da gamba and continuo of 1728 are also worthy of mention. The first of these is in the established pattern of the sonata da camera with typical additions: prelude, Allemande, courante, sarabande, gavotte, and gigue, plus a seventh movement which is entitled *Passacaille or Chaconne—*

further evidence of the ambiguity and lack of distinction between these two terms.

Couperin's most famous works are his four books of suites *(ordres)* for harpsichord, published from 1713 to 1730. The movements of these suites, although they utilize the standard dance rhythms of the sonata da camera, are, for the most part, furnished with fanciful titles rather than dance names. Many of these have tenuous or unexplainable connections to the music. Titles such as *Baricades Misterieuses, Les Tic-Toc-Choc ou les Maillitons, Les Petits Moulins a Vent, La Nanette,* or *La Chemise Blanche* (the last found in the second viol da gamba suite) defy specific explanation, although they undoubtedly meant something quite definite to the composer (many of them seem to be character portraits) and perhaps to his audiences. The *ordres* vary from a few movements to as many as twenty, and many of the movements are extremely short. The pieces demand the use of both manuals of the harpsichord, and ornamentation *(agrements)* is an integral part of the music. Traits of the Rococo style are seen in Couperin's short repetitive phrases, intimate and often artificial elaboration of detail, tone-color contrasts by variation of the harpsichord registration, and movements of tenderly gracious sentiment. Among the more lengthy movements are a vigorous passacaglia and a number of movements in rondo form.

One of the most important characteristics in all of Couperin's music, but particularly of his clavecin music, is his imaginative use of decoration, seen most of all in his carefully indicated ornamentations. In his *L'Art de toucher le clavecin* (1716), the most authoritative early treatise on keyboard playing, Couperin put great emphasis upon the correct realization of the symbols used for notating the agrements. Present-day performers are often hard-pressed to preserve both the letter and the spirit of the rules set down by Couperin in this treatise, for, although much of it is quite explicit, there were obviously many things which were understood by his contemporaries as common practice and which are, therefore, not completely spelled out. The book also advocates a new rational method of fingering for the keyboard. Bach was known to be familiar with Couperin's clavecin music as well as the treatise on harpsichord playing, both of which influenced his music.

Jean Phillipe Rameau

Although Rameau (1683–1764) was about 50 years old at the time of Couperin's death, he had composed relatively little as a contemporary of Couperin, for the bulk of the works for which he is best known were written after Couperin's death. Trained for the law, he showed a precocious interest and talent in music and soon gave up a career as a magistrate to become an organist. He held various positions as a church organist, but wrote little music until around 1723, when he made some modest attempts at music for the stage. With the help of an extremely wealthy aristocrat and courtier named La Poupliniere (who also lent his patronage to Voltaire, Rousseau, Casanova, and other distinguished personalities), he ventured into a career as an opera composer and in 1733 produced his first opera, *Hippolite et Aricie.* The controversy that this work aroused (mentioned in chap. 8) set the pattern for the rest of his life, for through no fault of his own, in 1752 Rameau was again caught up in a pseudo-musical, but really political battle known as "the war of the buffoons" between the followers of Rousseau, who argued that Italian was the only suitable language for opera, and those who set Rameau up as the champion of opera in the French language. Unlike the earlier controversy between the Lullists and the Ramists, Rameau's group did not win this one and Italian opera came into fashion for a time.

Rameau's operas are similar to Lully's in many ways. The French overture form was practiced by both; both took great care with the declamation of the French language in the recitatives; the recitatives tended to be fused with the more formal pieces such as arias, choruses, and instrumental pieces; and both favored the traditional ballet and divertissement scenes. But these are in actuality only superficial similarities, for in matters of melodic and harmonic style Rameau is quite dissimilar to Lully. As he had stated in his *Treatise on Harmony* of 1722, Rameau believed that all melody was rooted in harmony, and, although he sometimes used chromatic harmony and even enharmonic modulation, his melodies were always strongly linked to the triad and to the harmonic progression. Moreover, his style of harmonic progression is of the eighteenth century—rooted firmly in the concepts articulated in his theoretical writings, with a clear awareness of the primary chords of dominant, subdominant and tonic in a diatonic framework.

Although primarily an opera composer, Rameau's contributions to the literature of instrumental music are also important, particularly the overtures, dances, and other instrumental sections of his operas. His clavecin pieces and his trio sonatas of 1741 are also worthy of mention. In the solo clavecin music he experimented with virtuoso effects somewhat in the manner of Domenico Scarlatti; and in the trio sonatas the harpsichord no longer plays exclusively the role of an accompaniment instrument but begins to share in the musical action along with the solo instruments. But in the history of musical thought,

Rameau's greatest contributions are found in his theoretical writings, for he was the first to articulate the theoretical concepts that were to shape the progress of music for two centuries to come. Just as the contrapuntal works of J. S. Bach represent the culmination of a period of polyphonic music extending back to the Middle Ages, so Rameau's theories, and their realization in his music, set the stage for the period of tonal homophony yet to come.

Antonio Vivaldi

The culminating figure among the baroque Italian violinist composers is Antonio Vivaldi (c. 1678–1741) who brought the concerto grosso to its height, continued the development of the solo concerto, and established the three-movement concerto form (fast-slow-fast) imitated by Bach and many subsequent composers. Like Bach, he fell into relative obscurity after his death, for his works were not brought to light and fully appreciated until nearly a century and a half later. Even then it was only a happy accident that his music was unearthed, for the initial interest in Vivaldi came about when some of his music was found among Bach's possessions, and by Bach's transcriptions of some of his concertos.

Born and musically trained in Venice, he became a priest in 1703, but because of his health he was relieved of normal priestly duties at an early age. In 1704 he was employed by the Ospedale della Pieta of Venice, an orphanage and foundling home for girls, and was appointed musical director of the institution in 1716, a position which he held almost until his death. The Ospedale maintained an excellent conservatory, and the young ladies of the institution were famous for their musical accomplishments. Thus Vivaldi had ample opportunity for composing and directing music in all instrumental and vocal media. Judging by Vivaldi's orchestration and the fact that his orchestra was known throughout Europe, the instrumentalists of the Ospedale must have been truly excellent performers.

Nicknamed "the Red Priest" because of the color of his beard, Vivaldi was a familiar name in the musical centers of Europe, for he traveled extensively and was one of the most productive composers of his time. No doubt many of his compositions are permanently lost, but his surviving works include over four hundred concertos for various solo instruments and orchestra, about fifty concertos of the concerto grosso type, dozens of trio and solo sonatas, a sizable quantity of religious choral music, and nearly fifty operas. In spite of his vast output, his works are uniformly of high quality, and, although at times there is a repetitive sameness in his writing, his music contains considerable variety of content and media.

Vivaldi's musical style is strongly influenced by that of Corelli, although his progressiveness is seen in the fact that the fast movements seem to dominate the form and are not broken up with frequent short slow sections as in the concertos of Corelli; nor does he use fugal writing as frequently as Corelli. The solo violin parts are virtuosic to an unprecedented degree, far more brilliant than those of the earlier Bolognese composers or Corelli. About two-thirds of his concertos are for a solo instrument, usually violin. These works manifest his remarkable abilities as a performer and mark an important step toward the development of the classical concerto. In comparison to earlier concertos, the solo passages are more extended and virtuosic, and the number of exchanges between ritornello and solo are increased. An oft-used device of Vivaldi and a hallmark of the mature three-movement concerto grosso form is the placement of three heavy chords like hammer strokes at the beginning of the first movement. The Baroque "doctrine of affections" is apparent in his use of strong unflagging rhythms remaining consistent throughout a movement; and frequent unison and rapid scale passages also characterize his concerto style.

Among his sonatas for various instruments with continuo are many that follow the strict pattern of the sonata da chiesa, with binary form used invariably for each of the four movements. A good example is found in the six sonatas for solo cello with continuo accompaniment, the most famous of which is number five, in E minor. Among the earliest examples of solo works for the instrument, all six of these cello sonatas follow the standard slow-fast-slow-fast pattern, and all of the movements are cast in the Baroque binary form—a manifestation of the crystallization of the Baroque sonata da chiesa in the eighteenth century.

Although Vivaldi is today known chiefly for his instrumental music, it would be a mistake to ignore his achievements in opera, cantata, motet, and oratorio. His operas are virtually unknown today, but in his time he was one of the most successful and frequently performed composers for the operatic stages of Venice. His religious music deserves to be better known, for although his Christmas Oratorio is frequently performed, there are numerous other works—many unpublished—which are known to be of excellent quality.

Among his most famous works are the twelve concertos entitled L'Estro armonico ("Harmonic Whim"), Op. 3 (1715) which are for one, two, or four solo violins. These concertos were well known to Bach, for he transcribed six of them for other instrumental combinations—three as harpsichord concertos, two as organ concertos, and one as a concerto for four harpsichords. A penchant for programmatic music is seen in Vivaldi's *Il Cimento de'armonia e dell 'Invenzione* ("The trial of Harmony and Invention"), op. 8 (c. 1725), a set of twelve concertos with titles such as "The Tempest," "The Hunt," and "The Pleasure." The first four of these are the famous *Seasons,* concertos for solo violin and orchestra based upon four seasonal sonnets presumably written by Vivaldi himself. Each of the concertos depicts its sonnet in a charmingly literal manner, manifesting the typically Baroque delight in programmatic devices. All are three-movement concertos in the fast-slow-fast pattern which by this time had become standard, with a solo violin part that begins to approach the scope and brilliance of the classical violin concerto.

Domenico Scarlatti

Son of Alessandro Scarlatti, Domenico Scarlatti (1685–1757) is the outstanding Italian harpsichord composer of the eighteenth century and one of the most innovative composers in music history. As a virtuoso he was unrivaled for technical fluency and brilliance—what Bach was to the organ, Paganini to the violin, and Liszt to the piano, so Scarlatti was to the harpsichord. So idiomatic is his harpsichord writing that every nuance of the instrument's sonority and every technical resource of the eighteenth-century virtuoso may be found in his 550 sonatas.

Most of his life was spent in the service of royalty. In 1720 or 1721 Scarlatti left Italy to enter the court of the King of Portugal, where one of his primary services was to give harpsichord lessons to the Infanta, princess of Portugal. In 1729 when the Infanta left Portugal to marry Prince Ferdinand of Spain, Scarlatti went with her to remain for the rest of his life in the service of the Spanish courts. Nearly all of his music was written in Spain, and in his later sonatas the influence of Spanish folk music is clearly apparent. The ominous sounds of muffled drums, the click of castanets, the strumming of guitars, the gaiety of folk gatherings with their village bands, the heart-rending lament of gypsy song, and above all the tense rhythms of the Spanish dances— all can be heard in his harpsichord sonatas; yet nearly all are cast in the standard Baroque binary pattern.

Scarlatti called his single-movement binary form pieces "exercises." Most of them written after 1745 are arranged in pairs in the same key intended to be performed together, so that, in effect, they are sonatas of two movements. There is little or no precedent for this practice, although some Italian composers including Alberti (c. 1710–40), for whom the *Alberti bass* technique is named, did compose two-movement sonatas consisting of a slow movement followed by a fast movement. Scarlatti's unique keyboard idiom appears to be entirely his own invention, for he had no predecessors in either Italy or Spain and, except for a few Spanish and Portugese imitators, no later composers adopted his style. His keyboard idiom is marked by large leaps, passages in thirds and sixths, broken style, repeated note, crossings of hands, the acciaccatura (a grace note played simultaneously with the principal tone but immediately released; also called a "crushed note"), and many other daring keyboard devices, most of which did not come into common use until the emergence of Romantic piano styles. As one of the chief composers of the pre-Classical period, his sonatas are an important stage in the evolution of the Classical sonata form. His greatness, however, lies not in the influence he had upon the course of music history, but upon the intrinsic value of his music itself. Couperin in the middle Baroque, and Scarlatti at its height, together produced a body of solo harpsichord music for which performers on the instrument must be forever indebted.

George Frideric Handel

Although German born, Handel (1685–1759) enjoyed a musical reputation of international scope. His greatest achievements lie in the field of vocal music, primarily in the fields of opera and oratorio, where his theatrical gifts were used to the best advantage. From the early chamber cantatas written in Italy to the English oratorios of his maturity, his style is marked by beautiful melodic lines and tremendous dramatic powers. His lyrically virtuosic writing for the solo voice was influenced by the Italian bel canto style as well as by the vocal music of Purcell, but there is also much in his choral writing that shows the influence of the church cantatas of his native Germany. Although the operas and oratorios are his most numerous works, he also composed a number of shorter vocal works—church music and several incidental choral works such as the *Ode for St. Cecilia's Day* and *Zadock the Priest,* an anthem written for the coronation of George II in 1727 which has been used for every English coronation since then.

Handel's instrumental output consists of keyboard, chamber, and orchestral music, but is not as impressive a body of literature as his vocal music. He was quite famous as an organ virtuoso and his best keyboard music is found among his eighteen organ concertos, many of which are rearrangements of his concerti grossi and trio sonatas which were, in turn, strongly influenced by the instrumental style of Corelli with whose music Handel was well acquainted. He also composed several incidental orchestral works for various occasions such as the famous *Water Music* and the *Fireworks Music* as well as a number of solo sonatas.

Born into a well-to-do bourgeois family, Handel had the means to travel quite freely, and as a young man spent three years in Italy absorbing the Neapolitan opera style and beginning to develop his tremendous melodic gift. Before he reached the age of twenty-five he acquired a considerable reputation as an opera composer, primarily through the success of *Agrippina,* premiered in Venice in 1709. The following year he traveled to London, which remained his home for the rest of his life, and where even today he is viewed almost as a national hero.

His London career was not without its ups and downs, however. Over a period of thirty years he produced forty operas sponsored, for the most part, by the Royal Academy of Music, which was founded in 1720 and of which he became a musical director. But toward the end of the first half of the eighteenth century the English middle-class audiences began to be increasingly disenchanted with the aristocratic Italian opera seria written by Handel. Although fluency in Italian was a fashionable affectation among the English aristocracy, the language barrier was still quite formidable, even as it is today. Also, Handel's allegorical or prototype characters—similar to those of Greek drama—did not satisfy the audiences' desire for realism. They preferred life-like, realistic figures to the mythical or historical heroes of classical drama; and found them, not in Handel's operas, but in the ballad opera, the eighteenth-century counterpart of modern musical comedy. Earthy, humorous, direct, and sung in English, the ballad opera strongly appealed to the middle-class London audiences. The most famous of these, *The Beggar's Opera* of Gay and Pepusch, dealt the death blow to Handel's efforts in the opera seria style.

Reluctantly, and after a struggle in which both his health and his solvency were threatened, Handel increasingly turned his attention to the composition of English oratorios. His oratorios were designed more as entertainments than as religious works, and because they were presented in concert form rather than acted out like opera, it was possible for Handel to use much more chorus than in his operas—an important factor for the later success of his oratorios, for the British have always held choral singing in great affection. The chorus, like the *Turba* of the Italian oratorios, represented crowd scenes. It became the center of the drama and functioned in a manner similar to the chorus of Greek drama, commenting or reflecting on the action and occasionally playing a part in the drama. In all other ways Handel's oratorios are very much like his operas, for they are in three acts like the opera seria, and they use the aria and the recitative in much the same way.

There is little or no difference in style between Handel's secular and sacred oratorios, with the exception of the *Messiah* (1742), which is unique among all of Handel's dramatic works. The choice of a New Testament subject, the life of Christ, is in itself unusual (a few parts are from the Old Testament), and the philosophical and contemplative mood of the work is unlike the other oratorios with their powerful dramatic conflicts. Handel's reputation rests in large part upon this renowned composition, and, for the English-speaking peoples, there is no choral work that is more popular. Yet it remains only a tiny portion of his total output, and probably not the most outstanding example of his artistry.

The sacred oratorio, with towering figures drawn from the Old Testament, provided the ideal vehicle for Handel's unique dramatic gift. One of the reasons for their success was that, because they were not so elaborately staged as opera seria with foreign singers and lavish scenery, they were less expensive to produce. One of the best known of these works is the oratorio *Judas Maccabaeus* (1746). Dealing with the exploits of a great Jewish military leader who lived around 160 B.C., it is a representative example of his finest and most mature oratorios. The three acts contain virtually all of the musical forms and styles found in his oratorios and operas. The fugal section of the French overture with which this oratorio opens illustrates Handel's typical contrapuntal style. Unlike Bach's fugal style, in which the voices give the effect of great melodic freedom and create a texture that appears to be the incidental result of the linear motion, Handel's fugal technique is inclined toward a homophonic style with measured changes of harmony, the motion of each voice being rather strictly controlled by the prevailing sonority. Also, Handel did not always maintain the polyphonic and linear consistency typical of Bach. Often, in a movement which is ostensibly contrapuntal, he would abandon a fugal or canonic texture for the sake of a dramatic device appropriate to the text at that point.

The first chorus of *Judas Maccabaeus,* opening with the words "Mourn ye afflicted children," illustrates the predominantly diatonic and homophonic harmonic idiom typical of Handel. The mood is one of sorrow and lament, but unlike Bach, who inclined toward highly colored chromatic sonorities for expressive purposes (as in the Crucifixus of the B Minor Mass), Handel portrays the mood by melodic inflection and superb treatment of the text in a relatively simple harmonic fabric. The bel canto style is evident in many of Handel's arias, and in both choral and solo music he often finds unique means for illustration of the text. A delightful example of his text painting is found in No. 24, a da capo aria sung by Judas Maccabaeus. The text begins with "How vain is man who boasts in fight the valour of gigantic might," and on each repetition of the phrase the second syllable of the word "gigantic" is set to a truly gigantic embellishment. The longest of these is shown in figure 63.

Figure 63. Vocal Embellishment from Handel's Judas Maccabeus.

Handel's most significant contributions to the instrumental repertory are found in his highly varied concerti grossi. In addition to the eighteen organ concertos mentioned earlier, he composed a set of twelve concertos for strings alone (Op. 6) which, in the Italian tradition, use the trio sonata medium as the concertino group. In addition, he composed a number of concertos using wind instruments in combination with the strings. A set of six concertos, Op. 3, called the oboe concertos, were composed at various times over a period of nearly twenty years and were collected for publication in 1734. With the pressures of producing large numbers of concertos, operas, and oratorios for various occasions as the need arose, Handel, like other Baroque composers, borrowed quite freely, not only from himself, but also from the music of other composers. The oboe concertos illustrate this practice, for many of the movements appear in different form in other compositions. The first movement of the sixth concerto of the set, for example, is a version of a movement from the opera *Ottone* (1723), while the second movement is from the overture of the opera *Il Pastor Fido*, appears also in the third suite for harpsichord, and later in the organ concerto, Op. 7, No. 4. In these instances he borrowed only from himself, but in the operas he was quite free in using whatever he could adapt to his purposes, even from the operas of other composers. This was quite customary, for the Baroque period knew no copyright laws, and it must be added that in most cases Handel's apparent plagiarism improved on the borrowed material—transformed, revised, and elevated it for its new environment.

In both instrumental and vocal music, Handel used textural and dynamic contrasts in striking ways. His sense of the dramatic was unsurpassed and for this reason his greatest strengths lay in theatrical media such as the opera and oratorio. His oratorios established a standard of choral writing in large works that has influenced composers ever since. Like Milton, whose writings he admired, and like Bach, Handel became blind in his last years, but he continued to compose, and enjoyed a distinction afforded to few composers—that of being renowned and honored in the musical world before his death as well as after.

Johann Sebastian Bach

It is a remarkable coincidence to find two composers of the stature of Handel and Bach (1685–1750), born in the same country, spanning almost identical periods in music history, and each with an almost equal right to be considered the greatest composer of his time. Their activities complement each other, but they are also strongly contrasting in many ways. Handel had a musical reputation of international scope, while Bach lived his entire life in relative obscurity in a small area of Germany. Handel is best known for his dramatic works, Bach for his religious and instrumental music. Handel's writing was predominantly vocal in style, while Bach's style, even in vocal music, is oriented to instrumental idioms. Handel painted on a vast canvas, more concerned with immediate and direct communication than with intricate detail. Bach devoted great attention to detail, communicating profound emotions through highly wrought musical structures. Although Handel was far better known in the eighteenth century, present-day tastes would choose Bach as the greatest composer of the Baroque era.

No composer in our musical heritage stands in a position of greater distinction, for Bach's sheer mastery of musical craft, applied to all media and forms, has never been equalled. His music represents both the culmination and the fusion of the many instrumental and vocal styles of the Baroque. He welded the characteristics of many different national styles of the seventeenth and eighteenth centuries into a musical expression that was uniquely his own. Suprisingly enough, his music was not well known until the nineteenth century. He composed for the needs of his various professional positions, for his students and colleagues, and for himself. Consequently, although known in musical circles, he led a life of relative obscurity—well acquainted with musical styles throughout the Western world, but not courting an international career.

He was most outstanding as a composer of instrumental music and religious choral music. So great was his attention to detail that every vocal and instrumental part became a work of art, and he reached emotional heights that transcend even the remarkable polyphonic intricacies of his music. His vast body of instrumental music includes solo works for harpsichord, organ, violin, cello, and viol da gamba, while his trio sonatas, concertos, and other ensemble works contain a remarkably varied array of instrumentation. But he is best known for his religious choral music, including the Passions, The *Christmas Oratorio*, the *B Minor Mass*, the *Magnificat*, the six motets, and his nearly two hundred extant church cantatas.

He was born in the small town of Eisenach in East Germany where he lived until his twentieth year when, after his parents' death, he moved to Ohrdruf to live with his elder brother Johann Christoph Bach, a student of Pachelbel. He moved to Luneberg to continue his musical training in 1700, and in 1703 took his first professional position as organist in a church in Arnstadt. It was during this period that he made his famous pilgrimage to Lübeck to study with Buxtehude, whose works became an important point of departure for both his choral music and organ works. From that time on he held positions successively at Mülhausen (1707–08), Weimar (1708–17), Cöthen (1717–23), and Leipzig (1723–50), all within a relatively small geographical area of Germany. As was typical of many German composers of that time, his career was closely associated with appointments to churches or courts, and during the Leipzig period, the height of his career, he was music director of several churches as well as cantor of the school of the Thomaskirche. His musical training was acquired principally by copying and studying the music of his forerunners and contemporaries. In the course of an outwardly uneventful life he became acquainted with the music of composers from all European countries except England, including Palestrina, Frescobaldi, Vivaldi, Couperin, Froberger, Corelli, Schütz, Sweelinck, Buxtehude, Pachelbel, Telemann, and many others, including Handel whom he never met.

The development of the Lutheran church cantata was discussed in chapter 9, and in Bach's works for this medium virtually every style and technique of the Baroque era can be found. His typical practice was to base a cantata upon a chorale tune and to conclude the cantata with a four-part harmonization of that tune. We will discuss in some detail the Cantata No. 140 *"Wachet Auf,"* known in English as "Sleepers Awake." It is scored for two oboes, English horn (called *Taille* in the original), French Horn, strings, continuo, soloists, and chorus. Like all of his church cantatas, it was composed for a specific service of the church year, in this case the twenty-seventh Sunday in the period of Trinity. It is believed to have been written in Leipzig around 1742. The beginning of the opening chorus presents the double reeds against the strings in a passage in concertato style followed by a section dominated by the violins up to the point where the chorus enters. At this point the sopranos present the first phrase of the chorale tune, while the orchestra continues in an uninterrupted flow of instrumental sound which continues to the end of the movement. Against the cantus firmus in the sopranos, the altos enter with the first statement of a fugato subject answered by the tenors and then by the basses, the three lower voices weaving a contrapuntal texture against the firm steady march of the chorale melody intoned by the sopranos. The subject of this fugal passage is derived from the first notes of the chorale tune which is heard above it, shortened and with added tones as in figure 64, which shows the first three notes of the soprano line and the fugato entrance of the tenors for comparison.

Figure 64. Excerpts from the Opening Chorus of the Bach Cantata Wachet Auf.

This fugato is only long enough to allow the sopranos to complete the first phrase of the chorale tune, after which the chorus drops out, leaving the orchestra to emerge in the manner of a ritornello prior to the second entrance of the chorus. The second choral entrance is like the first, the sopranos entering this time with the second phrase of the chorale tune with a fugato in the lower voices, again based on the first notes of the chorale phrase occurring above it. The second phrase completed, the orchestral ritornello again emerges and so it continues throughout the movement. There are eleven phrases in the chorale (including at the end a repeat of the first three phrases), and each of them is used as a cantus firmus over a fugato in the lower voices. The movement concludes with an exact repetition of the opening instrumental passage. This simple formal plan creates great unity in the movement, and illustrates a typical usage of the Lutheran chorale in a movement for chorus.

The second movement is a secco recitative for tenor, while the third is an aria in the form of a duet for the soprano and bass soloists. Typifying Bach's imaginative use of instruments in the cantatas, a solo obbligato is added to this aria, scored originally for *violino piccolo,* an obsolete violin pitched higher than the ordinary violin, which in modern performances is replaced by a normal violin. The first verse of the chorale text was used in the first movement, and in the fourth movement, following the duet aria, the second verse of text is sung by the tenors of the chorus accompanied by strings and continuo.

The fifth movement is an accompanied recitative, the strings being used, as was bach's custom, as accompaniment in a recitative representing the voice of Christ—adding meaning and distinguishing it from the ordinary secco recitative. This recitative is followed by another duet for soprano and bass, this time with an obbligato played by the solo oboe. The cantata then concludes with a typical four-part harmonization of the chorale tune, undoubtedly intended for congregational singing. In this work, as in many of Bach's cantatas, can be seen the fusion of many Baroque styles and techniques, including recitative and aria, concertato style, ritornello, da capo form, and the characteristic Baroque instrumental style which is apparent in the vocal lines as well as in the instrumental passages.

The cantatas of Bach varied a great deal as to form and content. Some are for solo voices without chorus, some use only a few instruments, some use a highly colored ensemble of voices and instruments; and they vary greatly as to length and number of movements. *"Wachet Auf,"* one of his best-known works, illustrates many of the technical features to be found in his cantatas, although it only begins to tap the musical riches to be found in this remarkable body of religious music.

His other sacred choral works include six unaccompanied motets, one for four voices *(Lobet den Herrn),* one for five voices *(Jesu, meine Freude),* and four for double chorus. All except *Lobet den Herrn* make use of chorale tunes. Bach used double chorus also in his famous *St. Matthew Passion,* a work which is perhaps the greatest expression of profound religious emotion in all the literature of music. The text is from the Gospel of St. Matthew, with poetic commentary added by Picander, a Leipziger who contributed other texts for Bach's religious music. The evangelist (counterpart of the *testo* in Italian oratorio) is a tenor, all of whose passages are cast in secco recitatives. In addition to the two choruses, the work requires an orchestra of flutes, double reeds, strings, organ and continuo, plus a children's choir which is conventionally used to sing the chorale tune in the first chorus, although this is not specified in the score. The work consists of 78 numbers in all. For lyrical beauty some of the arias of the work are unsurpassed, and for depth of emotion there is no music to equal certain of the choruses. After Bach's death it was not performed until 1829, when it was revived by Mendelssohn.

Bach's obituary states that he wrote five Passions, but only two have survived—the St. Matthew and the St. John, in addition to portions of a St. Mark Passion. His great *Christmas Oratorio* (1734) is a set of six cantatas which were written for performance at specific times during the Festival of Christmas. The *B Minor Mass,* a work of prodigious proportions, was composed during 1737 and 1738 for Frederick Augustus II at the Catholic court of Dresden. Although it is a setting of the complete text of the Mass (rather than the "Lutheran Mass," which consisted of only the *Kyrie* and *Gloria*), strictly speaking it is neither a Catholic nor a Lutheran Mass, for its extreme length makes it awkward for use in a liturgical service. The text is divided into 24 movements, and the music for a number of them was borrowed from cantatas written earlier. Instrumental obbligatos are found in a number of the arias, and the orchestra is one of the largest used by Bach, consisting of thirteen different wind parts, timpani, strings and continuo. The *Magnificat* (1723, rev. 1730), a festive work for five-part chorus and soloists, also uses a large orchestra with particularly brilliant use of the brass. It is in twelve short movements, concluding with a setting of the *Gloria Patri.* Most of his sacred choral works make extensive use of Lutheran chorale tunes (exceptions are the motets, the *Magnificat* and the *B Minor Mass*). His four-part harmonizations of these melodies are frequently used in present-day hymnals. For some of the more famous tunes, such as the Passion chorale ("O Sacred Head"), Bach composed a number of contrasting settings for use in various choral works. In keeping with the custom of Baroque religious composers, musical symbolism and programmatic devices can be found throughout his choral works. In the *St. Matthew Passion,* for example, there are eleven entries of the chorus on the words "Lord, is it I?" representing the eleven Apostles who asked this question—frequently the symbolism is not so explicit as in this instance.

The instrumental writing in all of his choral works is wonderfully imaginative in its striking use of tone color, and for its inventive melodic character in contrapuntal textures. These qualities are even more apparent in his purely instrumental works, one of the greatest examples of which is his set of six concerti grossi "for several instruments" known as the *Brandenburg Concertos* because of their dedication to the Margrave of Brandenburg. They were composed in 1721 when Bach was employed as Kapellmeister in the court of Prince Leopold at Cöthen. The Prince maintained a group of excellent instrumental performers and the concertos were composed with these players in mind, a fact that may account for the highly varied instrumentation among the six concertos. The varied use of wind instruments hardly typifies the standard instrumentation of the Baroque concerto grosso, but from the standpoint of form they are quite typical, with the standard three-movement form of Vivaldi used in four of the six concertos. The period at Cöthen was particularly productive of instrumental music because Bach was not required to compose church music or to perform on the organ during this time. The two solo violin concertos (in E major and A minor) were composed during this period, as well as the concerto for two violins and orchestra in D minor. The final movement of the E Major violin concerto is an excellent and very clear example of the rondo form which was to be used so frequently for final movements in concertos of the classical period. Of the four orchestral suites (called overtures because the first movements are French overtures), two were composed in Cöthen and two in Leipzig. His concertos for harpsichord and orchestra, however, were composed entirely in Leipzig for the *Collegium Musicum* of that city during the latter part of his life. There are thirteen of them, most of them arrangements either of Bach's earlier concertos or Vivaldi concertos, and they are scored for from one to four harpsichords with strings.

Cöthen was also the source of much of his solo harpsichord music. There he wrote the first volume of the *Well Tempered Clavier*, the *Two and Three Part Inventions*, the six *French Suites*, the six *English Suites*, the *Chromatic Fantasy and Fugue*, and a number of other harpsichord works. The second volume of the *Well Tempered Clavier*, and the *Clavierübung*—a large collection of harpsichord music including the *Goldberg Variations*, the *Italian Concerto* (a work without orchestra), and a number of partitas—were all composed later in Leipzig.

Bach's chamber music, most of which was composed in Cöthen, includes a number of sonatas for harpsichord and solo instruments. In most of these works (except for three sonatas for violin and three for flute) Bach did not use figured bass in the harpsichord part, so that the harpsichord is often on an equal footing with the solo instrument, with a polyphonic texture written out in full, usually two voices in the harpsichord and one in the solo instrument. Among the sonatas of this type are six for violin, three for flute, and three for viol da gamba. Bach wrote only a few trio sonatas, the most famous of which is the trio sonata from the *Musical Offering*—a famous set of five instrumental pieces (sixteen movements in all) composed in 1747 and based on a theme of Frederick the Great. The trio sonata from this work is scored for violin, flute, and continuo. The six sonatas for violin alone and the six for cello alone—excellent works and standard fare for every student of these instruments—were also composed during the Cöthen period.

In his various positions as director of music in church or court, Bach was expected not only to write music especially for many different occasions, but also to prepare it in rehearsal and to perform it. Consequently he, like most musicians holding such positions at that time, was thoroughly versed in all aspects of the art of music. The idea of specialization, with musicians being trained for performance, conducting, or composition did not become common until the nineteenth century. Thus, within the relatively small area in which he was well known, Bach's reputation as a performer was as great as his reputation as a composer. His ability to improvise at the organ or harpsichord was legendary, and many of his compositions for these instruments are brilliantly improvisatory in style.

Bach's organ music, the very center of the organ repertory, comprises only about 7 percent of his total output. It can be divided into four general areas: (1) teaching pieces such as the *Six Trio Sonatas* for organ (not trio sonatas in the conventional sense); (2) virtuoso concert pieces such as the *Toccata and Fugue in D Minor* and the *Toccata, Adagio and Fugue in C Major;* (3) deeply religious pieces such as the *Eighteen Chorale Preludes;* and (4) mature polyphonic works including the *Passacaglia and Fugue in C Minor,* the *Variations on Von Himmel Hoch,* and the later preludes and fugues.

The *Six Trio Sonatas* were written at Leipzig and, like the *Two and Three Part Inventions,* were written for a student, in this case his eldest son Friedemann. Bach wrote organ fugues in combination with preludes, toccatas, or fantasias throughout his life, most of them during the Weimar period, a few in Cöthen, and a few mature ones in Leipzig. His largest body of organ works based on Lutheran chorales is the *Orgelbüchlein* ("Little Organ Book"), which was intended to include 164 organ chorales for the entire church year, although only 45 were completed. Like the *Six Trio Sonatas* they fall into the category of instructional pieces, but they nevertheless constitute a deep expression of Bach's religious faith and are excellent pieces of music. On a larger scale are the *Eighteen Chorale Preludes* composed during Bach's last years and containing chorale fugues, fantasias and preludes, and illustrating every manner of treating the chorale known to the Lutheran organ composers of the Baroque.

It was Bach's custom in all of his music to explore every conceivable musical possibility in a given medium, form, technique, or religious subject. This characteristic can be seen in his cantatas spanning every occasion of the entire church year and utilizing a vast array of instrumental and vocal combinations; in the *Brandenburg Concertos,* which exhaust the instrumental possibilities available in the orchestra of Prince Leopold's household at Cöthen; in the *Well Tempered Clavier,* which demonstrate the feasibility of composing in every major and minor key when using tempered tuning; in the *Orgelbüchlein,* which was intended to span the church year with the appropriate organ chorales; and in virtually any major work that he composed. From the standpoint of fugal technique this exhaustive, sweeping approach to his craft is best seen in a volume of contrapuntal works called *The Art of Fugue.*

Figure 65. Main Fugal Subject of Bach's The Art of Fugue.

The Art of Fugue consists of fourteen fugues and four canons all in the key of D Minor and based, for the most part upon the fugal subject shown in figure 65. It is Bach's last great work and he died leaving it uncompleted, for it breaks off abruptly at the point where he first introduces the theme based on the four letters of his last name. In German B represents B Flat and H indicates B Natural, so that the pitches of the B-A-C-H theme are as shown in figure 66.

B A C H

Figure 66. B-A-C-H Theme from The Art of Fugue.

The instrumentation that Bach intended for *The Art of Fugue* is not known. The work was written in open score, and although some of the fugues have as many as eight parts, it may be that the work was intended for keyboard instruments. There have, however, been some successful present-day transcriptions of the work for strings and other instruments. It may very well be that Bach had no specific instrumentation in mind, and that, in keeping with the tradition of interchangeability of instruments or voices which still persisted in the Baroque, many different instrumentations might have been acceptable. In the course of the work every Baroque fugal device is utilized, including double, triple, and quadruple fugues in addition to much use augmentation, diminution, stretto, and inversion. The work stands as a compendium of the contrapuntal and fugal technique of the eighteenth century as well as a superb collection of polyphonic music.

In examining the fugal subjects composed by Bach, one quickly sees that they are predominantly triadic and that they are tonally conceived. And yet the seemingly incidental harmonies in his polyphonic textures are, to all appearances, completely the result of the linear-horizontal motion of the voice lines. Herein lies part of his greatness, for he more than any other composer was able to successfully resolve the age-old conflict between the vertical and horizontal aspects of music.

In his music can be found the fusion and the culmination of all the national elements of the Baroque—but his unparalleled technical skill and artistry is nevertheless outweighed by the human elements of his musical expression. For within his music, all somehow conceived within a deeply spiritual framework, exists a profundity of understanding and a beauty of thought that is without equal in the history of music.

IV. CLASSICISM

10. The Beginnings of Classical Style

Instrumental Media—Sonata Form—Classical Opera

Even while Bach in Leipzig was producing great music in a style that was emphatically and definitively Baroque, other composers, including his own sons, were writing music incorporating elements of a new style. The Rococo or style galant, as seen in the brief keyboard movements of Couperin, Rameau, and Domenico Scarlatti, emphasized the decorative elements of music—ornamentation of melodic lines, arpeggiation, and broken style. The aristocratic ease and decorative elegance of the Rococo were important to the development of the new Classical style, but of equal significance is a German movement of the mid-eighteenth century known as the *empfindsamer Stil* ("expressive style"), which strove for natural expression of feeling and emotion. Unlike the Rococo, it belonged spiritually not to the aristocracy, but to the middle class, and was characterized by a bourgeois simplicity and austerity that was at odds with the style galant. Seen particularly in instrumental music, *empfindsamer Stil* was realized primarily through two devices: (1) the melodic sigh figure which often took the form of a descending half step from the strong to the weak part of the beat with a diminuendo, and (2) considerable use of chromaticism applied to both harmony and melody. One of its chief practitioners was the most famous son of J. S. Bach, Carl Philipp Emanuel Bach (1714–88), who is today sometimes called the founder of Classical style.

The aristocratic Rococo and the bourgeois *empfindsamer Stil,* as two complementary elements of Classicism, symbolize the conflict and the social and intellectual changes that were occurring in the mid-eighteenth century. It was an era that saw the beginning of new philosophies and attitudes in the political world as well as in the cultural. In the world of letters men such as the English philosopher John Locke (1632–1704), Sir Isaac Newton (1642–1727), Voltaire (1694–

1778), the encyclopedist Diderot (1713–84), and above all Jean Jacques Rousseau (1712–78) were spokesmen for the complex movement known as the "Enlightenment." Generated by a spirit of intellectual revolt, the movement reached into all areas of human activity and laid all preexisting ideals and standards open to question. Out of it came such significant developments as the increased consciousness of human brotherhood and social need, empiricism, public education, the political revolutions at the end of the century, and the industrial revolution. The cult of naturalness espoused by Rousseau was manifest in much of the music of the time, for it was felt during the Classical period, which we can arbitrarily date as extending from 1750 to 1810, that music should be free of needless technical complication and capable of being easily understood by the average listener—entertaining, and at the same time, nobly expressive. Certainly not all music written during this time followed these precepts, but, at the same time, no composer was completely untouched by them. In addition, the musical world felt an increased concern for communicating with mass audiences, and public concerts came into vogue along with larger and less sophisticated audiences.

In Germany the Enlightenment movement (German equivalent: *Aufklärung*) was led by the philosopher Moses Mendelssohn (1729–86), grandfather of Felix Mendelssohn, but the greatest German philosopher of the late eighteenth century was Immanuel Kant (1724–1804), whose controversial *Critique of Pure Reason* (1781) added a new dimension to the Enlightenment and established its author as one of the great modern philosophers. The dramatist and critic Gotthold Lessing (1729–81) was also important in the German Enlightenment as German literature strove to throw off the domination of the French. Indeed, the seeds of Romanticism can be seen in both English and German literature of the late eighteenth century. In Germany the last quarter of the eighteenth century was known as the *Sturm und Drang* ("Storm and Stress"), after a drama by Friedrich Klinger (1752–1831). The term aptly catches the spirit of late eighteenth-century Germany, for it was a time of intellectual turbulence, and its art was characterized by greater subjectivity and intensity of feeling and expression. Although England produced no great composers of the Classical period, the characteristic realism of the time was captured in works such as the novel *Tom Jones* by Henry Fielding (1707–54), while the questioning of existing social, moral, and religious standards is beautifully expressed in the poetry of William Blake (1757–1827).

How much of this literary and intellectual activity can be heard in the music of the Classical period? Wagner and Richard Strauss notwithstanding, we must acknowledge that music cannot actually communicate specific concepts and philosophies to the listener. Yet something of Rousseau's naturalness can be heard in the beautiful simplicity of Gluck's melodic lines; the composers of the *empfindsamer Stil* strove for some of the same depth of expression as the German literary men of the *Sturm und Drang;* aural and pictorial realism can be heard in Haydn's *Creation;* and Mozart's *Magic Flute,* through its Masonic symbolism, deals with the subject of brotherhood. Yet the real link between music of the classical period and the spirit of the late eighteenth century cannot be articulated. It can be heard and felt only in a purely musical way, above all in the works of Haydn, Mozart, and the young Beethoven.

Because a greater homogeneity of style existed during the Classical period than in some other periods of music history, it is possible to make several valid generalizations about the technical features of Classical music. The harmonic vocabulary remained much the same as that of the Baroque, except that in the Classical period it was characterized by a slower harmonic rhythm. That is, the sonorities of Classical music change or progress at a slower rate so that a single sonority is heard for a longer period of time. Within the framework of a single sonority there is often a great deal of rhythmic motion, and the textures are clear and decorative rather than contrapuntal and weighty as in the Baroque. Much Baroque music, particularly that of J. S. Bach, is characterized by a polarity between the bass and the soprano voices, creating the impression of melodies at the top and the bottom of the texture with harmonic voices in between. In the Classical period the bass line frequently lost its melodic character and often did nothing more than furnish the bottom notes of the harmony to accompany the all-important melodic line. In music for the piano, the instrument which began to replace the harpsichord, the unimportance of the bass line was seen in the use of a texture consisting of an *Alberti bass* in the left hand and a single melodic line in the right, as in the Haydn example in figure 67. By means of keyboard devices such as this one, a single sonority could be retained for a longer time, maintaining interest by means of the motion among the various tones of the chord. Similar techniques were found in the Baroque period, but were not used in so simple and obvious a manner. Although most typical of piano music, such devices were used in orchestral and chamber music as well. In general, textures became increasingly homophonic and there was a trend away from complex polyphony. Baroque contrapuntal technique, however, was not forgotten, for there are many excellent fugues among the instrumental music of Haydn, Mozart, and Beethoven.

Figure 67. Excerpt from a Haydn Sonata.

One of the most striking differences between Baroque and Classical music is found in the phrase structure. Phrases of Classical music were much more likely to end with clear-cut cadences than those of the Baroque. Simple structures such as the double period became standard building blocks for new forms, the lengths of the phrases and their cadences creating a new kind of symmetry in the music. The most important form that developed was the sonata allegro form, while the rondo, minuet, and theme and variations, although not new, took on increased importance.

Instrumental Media

The most important new instrumental media to develop during the classical period were the symphony orchestra and the string quartet. The orchestra had existed in Baroque opera and in the concerto grosso, but in the Classical period it acquired a standard instrumentation consisting of two flutes, two oboes, two bassoons, two trumpets, two horns, two timpani tuned to the tonic and dominant, and strings consisting of sections of first and of second violins, violas, cellos, and basses. The cellos and basses usually played the same part (the bass sounding an octave lower), although in some late classical works, such as Mozart's Symphony No. 41, the "Jupiter," there are a number of passages in which the two lower string sections have independent parts. The finest classical symphony orchestra was the Mannheim orchestra founded by Johann Stamitz (1717–57). Famous for its precision and ability to produce remarkable dynamic effects, it employed about forty-five players, including four hornists. This, however, was an exceptionally large ensemble—most of the symphonies of Haydn and Mozart were written for an orchestra of around thirty-five players, with only two horns.

The clarinet had been invented in the early eighteenth century and a few Baroque composers including Handel and Vivaldi had written for it. It did not gain access to the symphony orchestra until the late eighteenth century, although, like the trombone, it was not uncommon in opera. Mozart used the clarinet occasionally, most notably in the Symphony No. 40 in G Minor, and stunningly in the Clarinet Concerto and the Clarinet Quintet. Mozart's solo works for the instrument were written for the clarinetist Anton Stadler. Another distinguished wind player of the time was the flutist-composer Johann Quantz (1697–1773), whose famous flute method also contains valuable information on performance practices of the eighteenth century.

The brass writing for the classical symphony orchestra invariably linked the handful of trumpets and horns to the timpani to furnish harmonic and rhythmic punctuation in forte passages. Rarely were the brass used melodically except in unusual works such as the horn concertos of Mozart and the Haydn trumpet concerto. The high trumpet playing art of the Baroque was lost to the Classical and Romantic periods, although many solo horn and trumpet parts demand virtuoso skills of the player. The trombone, an instrument of ancient ancestry, did not find its place in the symphony orchestra until the Fifth Symphony of Beethoven (1817).

Chamber music media of the classical period included the piano trio (violin, cello, and piano) and sonatas for violin and piano. In both of these media the piano predominated. It was not until the early nineteenth century that the violin and piano began to function on an equal basis in the sonata duo; and in most of the piano trios of Haydn and Mozart the cello functions as little more than a continuo bass—a vestige of the Baroque; and the violin is only slightly more important. The piano trio emerged as a chamber medium of three more or less equal parts in the early nineteenth century in the trios of Beethoven.

The most important chamber medium of the Classical period is the string quartet. It developed around 1745 from the trio sonata by the substitution of a viola for the harpsichord. In the earliest classical string quartets, the cello plays an unimportant and less interesting role than the continuo bass parts of many Baroque trio sonatas, and the inner parts, too, are often dull. In the mature string quartets of Haydn and Mozart, the four instruments begin to function with near equality, although the first violin still tends to dominate as the virtuoso voice of the ensemble. In these works, and later in those of Beethoven, the idiomatic writing for four instruments in a variety of textures ranging from complex polyphony to unison and simple homophony resulted in a medium that has remained the most important chamber music vehicle from that day to this.

The use of figured bass and basso-continuo gradually disappeared from all instrumental media of the classical period, although vestiges of these practices continued even into the nineteenth century. Haydn, for example, persisted in conducting his symphonies from the harpsichord, presumably filling in the harmonies in the manner of a continuo player, even though, except for his early symphonies, no continuo parts were written. The removal of the continuo particularly affected chamber music media, for it necessitated the writing of more interesting inner voices in order to fill in the harmony satisfactorily, and it was partly because of this that the string quartet developed as it did. Chamber music media which retained a keyboard instrument were slower in developing, since a piano could fill in the harmony as well as a harpsichord. Continuo persisted longer in opera than in any other medium because of its traditional use in secco recitatives.

Sonata Form

An examination of some of the movements of late Baroque and Rococo sonatas will reveal that the binary form, which had become firmly established as the most widely used form for sonata movements in the late Baroque, was evolving toward a new Classical form which would become known as the *sonata allegro form* or *sonata form.* The classical sonata as seen in the instrumental works of Haydn, Mozart, and Beethoven is a composition in three or four movements of contrasting tempo of which the first usually follows the pattern of the sonata allegro form. The derivation of this form from the Baroque binary form can best be seen in transitional pieces written during the late Baroque and Rococo in which the basic elements of the sonata pattern can be seen in incipient form. A good example is the first movement of Pergolesi's Trio Sonata No. 3 in G Major (1730), made famous by Stravinsky in his ballet *Pulcinella.* The basic binary pattern, like the diagram in figure 60, is clearly apparent in this movement although the repeat sign, which would normally be found at the end of measure fourteen, has been omitted. The sprightly main theme appears at the beginning in the tonic and in the second section (measure 15) is restated in the dominant. The features which mark it as an incipient sonata form are (1) the presence of a second tonal group or second theme appearing in the first section in the dominant key at measure 7 and returning in the tonic key in the second section at measure 35, (2) the developmental character of the material at the beginning of the second section of the binary pattern, measure 15 through measure 30, and (3) the clear-cut return of the main theme in the key of the tonic at measure 31. An examination of this movement or movements similar to it by many

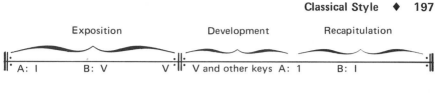

Figure 68. Sonata Form.

composers of the pre-Classical period such as Somis, Monn, and Stam-itz will reveal them to be similar to the pattern shown in figure 68.

Clearly derived from the binary form, sonata allegro form, because of the expansion of the section from the repeat sign to the return in the tonic, in the Classical period became a three-part pattern of exposition, development, and recapitulation. Sonata form remained the most important single movement instrumental form throughout the Classical and Romantic periods, and continued to be used, though often very freely, by many twentieth-century composers. Its essence is the presentation of the thematic material in the exposition, the elaboration of this material in the development, and its return in the recapitulation in almost the same way (except for key relationships) as presented in the exposition. The one element of the form which remained constant throughout the Classical and Romantic periods is the pattern of key relationships. That is, (1) an exposition which presents two main tonal areas of tonic and dominant—or tonic and relative major if the movement is in a minor key—with a cadence on the dominant—or relative major if the movement is in a minor key, (2) a development section which opens in the dominant—or relative major if the movement is in a minor key—and goes through various keys in the elaboration of the thematic material, concluding with a sizable section dwelling upon the dominant in preparation for (3) a recapitulation in which the two main tonal areas are both presented in the tonic key. As sonata movements became longer, additional tonal areas were often presented in the exposition, the slow introductions became more important, developments expanded greatly, and codas, often of considerable length, were added. Yet the basic tonal pattern as presented above remained clearly discernible in many symphonies of the nineteenth century, such as those of Brahms. In the twentieth century the basic principle of tonal contrast and return to a tonal center was applied to many sonata movements, even though functional triadic tonality with its tonic and dominant relationships was often replaced by new harmonic idioms.

In the Classical period the term "sonata" was used in the modern sense as a generic term denoting an instrumental composition of three or four movements. The three-movement pattern was most frequently found in piano trios, violin sonatas, and solo piano sonatas such as those of Haydn, and Mozart, while the four-movement pattern was characteristic of ensemble forms such as the string quartet and symphony. This multimovement form had developed in the early eighteenth century from the Italian opera overture (sinfonia) which around 1700 had evolved from a tri-sectional movement into a three-movement fast-slow-fast pattern consisting of an allegro, a short lyrical andante, and a finale using a dance rhythm such as a minuet or gigue. One of the first to use sinfonias separately as concert pieces was G. B. Sammartini (1701–75) who in Milan began to write concert symphonies in the pattern of the sinfonia. Baldassare Galuppi (1706–85), and Niccolo Jomelli (1714–74) composed similar concert versions of the Italian overture and the practice was soon adopted by composers in France, Germany, and Austria. Some of Mozart's early symphonies also follow this pattern.

One of the first to use the four movement pattern found in the symphonies and quartets of Haydn, Mozart, and Beethoven was Johann Stamitz. Essentially, this occurred simply by adding a fourth movement to the sinfonia, but at the height of the classical period the four-movement pattern crystallized into a standard form which is illustrated in the following table:

First Movement: Sonata allegro form, frequently with a slow introduction cadencing on the dominant. (The introduction is a vestige of the French overture.)

Second Movement: Slow and lyrical, with various possible formal plans such as sonatina (a diminutive sonata form), theme and variations, or rondo. Usually in a key contrasting to that of the first movement such as the subdominant or relative major.

Third Movement: Minuet and trio, often replaced by the scherzo in the Romantic period. Usually in the same key as the first movement.

Fourth Movement: Rondo, sonata form, or theme and variations. Same key as the first movement.

Stamitz' four-movement symphonies were essentially Rococo in style, but the Viennese composers Georg Monn (1717–50), Georg Wagenseil (1715–77), and Michael Haydn (1737–1806), brother of Franz Joseph, developed a Classical style which contains many of the Viennese characteristics which were to be found later in the symphonies of Mozart. Their sonata forms are characterized by considerable thematic contrast between tonal groups. North German composers such as Johann Graun (1703–71) and C. P. E. Bach for the most part wrote symphonies in the older three-movement pattern, but their development sections showed considerable progress toward the type of unified and imaginative thematic development that became an important feature of Haydn's style. (One of C. P. E. Bach's greatest contributions was his *Essay on the True Art of Playing Keyboard Instruments,* the most important treatise on ornamentation and musical interpretation of the mid-eighteenth century.)

Two other sons of J. S. Bach were active during the developmental years of the Classical period. Wilhelm Friedemann Bach (1710–84), the eldest son, was a remarkable organist and composer who wrote in the style of his father as well as in the newer fashions of the style galant. The youngest son, Johann Christian Bach (1735–82), after study in many musical centers of Europe, established himself in London where he became known as the "London Bach" and enjoyed a long career as an opera composer, performer, and teacher. Contemporary with him in London was the Englishman William Boyce (1710–79), whose conservative symphonies are virtually the only Classical instrumental music of distinction by an English-born composer.

A number of foreign composers were working in Paris during the early Classical period, including the German Johann Schobert (c. 1720–67), who is believed to be the first to introduce orchestral effects into keyboard writing, and the Belgian Francois Gossec (1734–1829), who wrote symphonies, string quartets, and comic operas, and became one of the first directors of the Paris Conservatory. In Paris after 1770 a form known as the *symphonie concertante* developed which was like the symphony except that it used two or more solo instruments in concerto-like effects. The Italian Giovanni Cambini (1746–1825) and a number of French composers were active in the development of this type of composition. The classical concerto form, to which the symphonie concertante is related, began to use a modified sonata form in the first movement, some of the earliest examples of which were composed by C. P. E. Bach and Johann Christian Bach.

Classical Opera

The state of opera in the early eighteenth century is vividly illustrated in Benedetto Marcello's *Il Teatro alla Moda* (1720), a volume of twenty-four chapters satirizing the operatic abuses of the time. Its complete title reads: "Theatre a la mode, or a sure and easy method for effectively composing and performing Italian operas in the modern manner, in which is given useful and necessary advice to poets, composers, musicians of either sex, impresarios, instrumentalists, engineers, painters, decorators, comedians, tailors, pages, extras, prompters, copyists, the protectors and mothers of female virtuosos, and other persons belonging to the theatre." In its ironic way it presents a clear and living picture of the operatic practices of the time, for it advises librettists to ignore the conventions of good poetry and drama, tells composers to write in such a way as to satisfy the singers need for meaningless virtuoso display by placing inappropriate embellishments on the wrong words, tells singers to have their ornamentations and cadenzas written by someone other than the composer with no regard for the drama itself, advises the director (who is both deaf and dumb) to cut entire scenes rather than take one good aria away from the *prima donna,* recommends plagiarism to all, and emphasizes the extreme importance of elaborate stage effects, stage animals, etc.

There is no doubt that Neapolitan opera had in many instances degenerated into a kind of fashionable circus in the early eighteenth century. The conventional aria da capo, for example was often performed with its recapitulation elaborately ornamented by the singer with little or no regard for the drama; and it was not unusual for a singer to have a favorite successful aria transplanted from one opera to another in order to delight his or her devoted followers in the audience. The recitatives, in which the plot was unfolded, were disposed of as quickly as possible (always secco) in order to get on with the real show which centered around the ridiculous virtuoso performances of the singers. The vanity and arrogance of these popular virtuosi apparently knew no bounds, for they treated poets, composers, and directors with equal discourtesy and set the style for prima donna behavior for many years to come.

These widely recognized operatic abuses occurred, for the most part in opera seria, and one effect was that opera buffa with its direct appeal, simple staging, and clever drama, became increasingly popular and called attention to the defects of opera seria. Pergolesi's *La Serva Padrona* (1733) was eminently more successful than his efforts in serious opera and, indeed, has outlasted in popularity virtually every opera written before Gluck. Other successful composers of Neapolitan opera were Handel, Nicola Porpora (1686–1768), and Johann Adolph Hasse (1699–1783). Hasse was one of the most successful opera seria composers of the pre-Classical period, and enjoyed a long career in which he composed around eighty operas, most of which were based on librettos of Metastasio.

As composers began to bring musical drama in line with the changing ideals of the time, their efforts were directed toward making Italian opera more natural, and two of the earliest composers in this reform were Jomelli and Tommaso Traetta (1727–79). Both were influenced by the French taste, which led them toward a more cosmopolitan type of opera. The increased naturalness that they espoused was in line with Rousseau's ideas, but the most striking reforms were triggered in Paris in 1753 by the *Guerre des Bouffons* ("War of the Buffoons"), so called because it was occasioned most directly by the presence of a visiting Italian opera company in Paris which performed opera buffa (hence *Bouffons*). On this occasion they performed *La Serva Padrona,* and nearly every Parisian with intellectual or cultural pretensions took part in the ensuing controversy, which centered around the relative merits of Italian and French opera. Rousseau, the chief spokesman for the partisans of Italian opera, argued that French was a language unsuitable for singing and that the French were in fact an unmusical people who had no real music of their own. On the other side were the champions of Rameau, Lully, and French opera. In the heat of debate, extreme and sometimes foolish statements were made by both sides. Rameau an unwitting protagonist who took no active part in the argument, ended up on the losing side, for Rousseau and his followers were in the majority and the fashion shifted from French to Italian opera.

Twenty years later Gluck wrote a letter to Rousseau in which he professed to be interested in enlisting Rouseau's help in creating a type of opera which would be "noble, sensitive, and natural," and international in style in order to abolish foolish national distinctions in music. Contrary to a popular notion, the "war of the buffoons" did not spark Gluck's operatic reforms, except perhaps very indirectly. Reforms had begun long before, for virtually every opera composer had been aware of the need for revitalizing the Neapolitan opera tradition or doing away with it, and Jomelli and Traetta had begun to compose operas which, although in the Italian language, contained enough French and German elements, to be called international in style. Although their operas were singers' operas, they reintroduced choruses and ensembles in their later works, thus achieving greater dramatic unity and minimizing the importance of virtuoso singing.

The composer upon whom the full realization of these operatic reforms fell, Christoph Willibald Gluck (1714–87), was born in

Bohemia, studied music in Prague, and then in Milan with Sammartini, traveled extensively as an opera conductor, and became an official court composer in Vienna in 1754 where he composed a number of comic operas in the opera buffa style. During this time French *operas comiques* (light operas in French, with spoken dialogue) were performed frequently in Vienna and it was from these that Gluck learned the French operatic style with its syllabic settings, melodic restraint, and freedom of phrase structure. He was greatly influenced by the operatic reform movement in the late '50s and his acquaintance at this time with the poet Raniero Calzabigi (1714–95) was most opportune, for in 1762 the two artists produced their first collaborative work, *Orfeo ed Euridice,* the masterpiece which is known as Gluck's first reform opera. Calzabigi also wrote the libretto for Gluck's *Alceste* (1767) and in its preface the composer articulated his operatic philosophies. His purpose was to end the deterioration of Italian opera, and to let the music benefit the poetry, all in the service of the plot without extraneous elements, in a unified dramatic work that achieved a beautiful simplicity by whatever means necessary. To this end the overture became an integral part of the drama, virtuoso singing for its own sake was completely eliminated, the recitatives became more important and were supported by orchestral expression of the dramatic situation, the da capo aria lost its importance, and the contrast between recitative and aria was minimized. The "beautiful simplicity" of which Gluck spoke in the preface to Alceste is apparent in many parts of both *Orfeo and Alceste.* Perhaps the most famous example is the aria *"Che faro senza Euridice"* in which the Italian melodic grace is combined with German depth of expression and French elegance in a manner that characterizes the composer's mature style.

Gluck's letter to Rousseau of 1773, mentioned earlier in connection with the "war of the buffoons," prepared the way for Gluck's operas in the French language which were produced in the '70s in Paris at the height of his career. His desire to produce French opera appealed to the patriotism of the French public, and by representing himself to Rousseau as a composer desirous of abolishing foolish national distinctions in music and as a champion of "naturalness," he did much to assure the success of *Iphegenie en Aulide,* which was produced in Paris in 1774. The libretto is French in every way, for it is an adaptation of Racine's tragedy *Iphegenie.* After the premiere Rousseau acknowledged Gluck's success in using the French language and admitted that he had been wrong in the stand taken twenty years earlier in the "war of the buffoons."

Gluck followed this success with French translations of both *Orfeo* and *Alceste;* and in 1777 he produced *Armide,* based on a libretto which had been used almost a hundred years earlier by Lully. The composer Niccolo Piccini (1728–1800) rather innocently became involved in a famous rivalry with Gluck at this time which virtually split the Parisian opera going public into two camps, the "Piccinists" and "Gluckists." The details are unimportant but, like Rameau in 1752, Piccini was the unwitting victim of a controversy which stirred up enough excitement in Parisian journals and salons to assure a successful premiere for *Armide,* and Gluck now rivaled Louis XV as the talk of Paris. The culmination of his career came in 1779 with the production of *Iphegenie en Tauride,* a classical tragedy in the grand tradition which utilized all the operatic resources at Gluck's command.

Gluck's philosophy of subordinating the music to the drama had some influence for a generation or so after his death. Piccini, his erstwhile rival and the defeated champion of Italian opera in Paris, adopted many of the stylistic elements of French opera, and Gluck's ideals were also kept alive in the operas of Etienne-Nicolas Mehul (1763–1817), Luigi Cherubini (1760–1842), and Gasparo Spontini (1774–1851). But the effect of Gluck's reforms was not lasting, and his greatness lies in the operas themselves rather than in his innovations.

Spontini and Cherubini, both Italians working in Paris after the French Revolution, brought grandeur, excitement and suspense to their operas. A favorite vehicle was the "rescue plot" or "rescue opera" in which the hero was saved from harm at the last minute, a situation which appealed to a public who vividly remembered the terrors of the Revolution. The use of daring rescues, stage effects, grand choruses and ensembles, turbulent crowd scenes and all the other operatic and theatrical resources of Spontini and Cherubini led to the "grand opera" period of the early romantic era.

Pergolesi had been the most successful opera buffa composer of the pre-Classical period, but the famous Italian poet Carlo Goldoni (1707–93) added a new dimension to this operatic medium in the Classical period by writing comic librettos which were less farcical and more realistic than the absurd plots used earlier. His excellent poetry was set in opera buffa style by many composers, including Galuppi, Piccini, and Florian Gassmann (1729–74). Another significant development in the opera buffa medium was seen in the works of Giovanni Paisiello (1740–1816) and Domenico Cimarosa (1749–1801). Paisiello, who also composed instrumental and sacred music, wrote about one hundred operas, of which his *Barber of Seville* (1782) is the most famous. Cimarosa also composed in other media, but is today remembered most of all for his *Secret Marriage* (1792). A distinguishing trait of the classical opera buffa is the ensemble finale which, in the hands of Piccini, reached a high level of organization using a rondo form. The opera buffa reached its height in the works of Mozart, to be discussed in the next chapter.

National styles of light opera other than the Italian opera buffa all had one trait in common—the use of spoken dialogue. The French opera comique was usually in a simple style with strophic songs, duets, trios, and a simple song type called the *ariette.* The form had little of the sophistication of opera buffa. Rousseau, a self-trained musician, composed one of the earliest examples in 1752, shortly before he took a stand against opera in the French language in the "war of the buffoons." Entitled *Le Devin du village* ("The Village Soothsayer"), the work was unusual in that it contained recitatives rather than spoken dialogue, although it was in the French language. Operas comiques were composed by many French composers during the Classical period, reaching a high point in the operas of Andre Gretry (1741–1813), a Belgian who worked in Paris. His operas contain both serious and comic plots but fall into the opera comique category because they contain spoken dialogue. Indeed, it was this distinction primarily which determined whether an opera should be performed at the Opera Comique or at the Paris Opera. The latter institution, properly called the *Academie Nationale de Musique,* accepted for performance only operas which contained no spoken dialogue. Gretry's masterpiece is *Richard the Lion Hearted* (1784), which falls into the category of "rescue opera."

The English counterpart of the opera comique was the ballad opera. *The Beggar's Opera* of Gay and Pepusch, mentioned earlier in connection with Handel, is one of the few to survive, although many others were written. In Germany a more important national opera type developed in the form of the *Singspiel.* It originated around mid-century as a comic drama in German with folk songs and popular tunes added, and soon it was popular throughout Germany and Austria. In north Germany, the chief composer of *Singspiel* was Johann Adam Hiller (1728–1804) whose works were marked by considerable Italian influence with da capo arias in coloratura style and ensembles in buffa style; but his use of traditional strophic arias in folk-like style became a permanent trademark of the Singspiel. In 1778 Vienna established an opera house for Singspiele called the Burgtheatre, comparable to the Opera Comique in Paris. A large repertoire of German operas were composed for the Burgtheatre and it became the national center for the Singspiel. Singspiele composed in the eighteenth century by composers such as Umlauf and Dittersdorf continued to show the Italian influence in certain arias, but always contained simple, strophic, folk-like airs, interspersed with spoken dialogue. The form reached its height in the Classical period in the Singspiele of Mozart, which will be discussed in the next chapter.

Sacred music declined in quality and quantity during the Classical period, for the Enlightenment was a secular age. In the Catholic southern countries, a few composers continued to compose church music in the pseudo-Palestrinian style popular in the Baroque, but the trend was to apply the techniques of Italian opera to sacred music. Lutheran music also declined in quality, as did English church music, although the semi-secular oratorio continued to maintain popularity in both countries. Haydn's efforts in this form are the best of the Classical period, while his Masses, along with those of Mozart, represent a high point in eighteenth-century Catholic church music even though they are today not considered appropriate for liturgical use.

Secular song, however, began to be revitalized in Germany as composers such as Graun, C. P. E. Bach, and Quantz composed solo songs which led to the great period of romantic Lieder in the nineteenth century. The texts began to be taken from the works of the great German poets such as Goethe, while the song style possessed some of the same folk-like traits as Singspiel. Thousands of songs in hundreds of collections were published in the last half of the eighteenth century in Germany, most of them strophic, in simple but expressive syllabic settings with chordal piano accompaniments. Mozart, Haydn, and Beethoven wrote songs of this type, but the true romantic lied did not come into being until the early nineteenth century in the songs of Schubert.

11. Haydn and Mozart

Haydn's Symphonies—Haydn's String Quartets—
Haydn's Vocal works—Mozart's Operas—Mozart's
Concertos

Franz Josef Haydn (1732–1809), lived a large part of his life in the relative security and seclusion of a wealthy aristocratic household, and thus was somewhat removed from the mainstream of the Enlightenment. Yet he more than any other single composer represents the spirit of the Classical period in music. Born before Mozart during the height of the Baroque and living after him well into the nineteenth century, he fused the diverse elements inherited from the Baroque into a unified style that not only epitomized the best of the Classical period but led forcefully into the Romantic.

Born to a working-class family in the small town of Rohrau in southern Austria, Haydn came to Vienna as a child to become a choirboy in St. Stephen's Cathedral. Although invited to become a castrato and remain an employed singer in the Cathedral, he left the Cathedral choir school at the age of seventeen to partake of the rich musical environment of the city of Vienna. The city's musical community was at that time controlled by the aristocracy who soon became aware of Haydn's talents, and he was employed in various capacities in several Viennese households until 1761 when he entered the service of the Esterhazys, fabulously wealthy patrons of the arts, where he remained for a period of nearly thirty years.

As director of music in a wealthy and aristocratic household, his role was that of a servant, but he seems to have accepted this position with good grace. Indeed, the situation was ideal in many ways, for the Esterhazys employed a professional orchestra at Haydn's disposal, and he had the time and seclusion necessary to produce the musical works that were expected of him. During this time he established a reputation throughout Europe and England that rivals and in some ways parallels that of Handel. In 1790, when he was retired and pensioned by the

Esterhazys at the age of fifty-eight, he was engaged by the English impresario Salomon, to compose and conduct in London. His success on his first visit resulted in a return engagement in 1794–95 and he returned to retirement in Europe as the most distinguished composer of his time.

Haydn's achievements are centered in his 104 symphonies and in his 83 string quartets. These works were composed throughout his life and show the evolution of Classical style as well as the development of his personal style. His works in these media influenced both Mozart and Beethoven, particularly for the technique of thematic development —the use of motives and fragments rather than complete themes in a polyphonic developmental texture. Haydn was also a prolific composer of sacred music, producing 14 Masses for chorus, orchestra, and soloists and a number of shorter works for the church. Perhaps in an effort to emulate Handel's success with the oratorio, Haydn also composed two monumental works in this medium, *The Creation,* and *The Seasons.*

The works mentioned above comprise the bulk of the works for which he is well known, but he also composed over 50 piano sonatas and a vast amount of chamber music in media such as the piano trio, sonatas for violin and piano, and various other instrumental combinations including nearly 200 chamber works involving the baryton, an obsolete stringed instrument played by his patron, Prince Nicholas Esterhazy. Although he did not equal Mozart as a composer of concertos or operas, he composed two cello concertos (D Major and C Major) which are among the earliest distinguished works in the concerto repertory for that instrument, and also wrote concertos for both piano and violin. He felt that his operas were best heard in the environment for which they were written—that is, the Esterhazy theatre—and he made no effort to compete with Mozart in this medium. He spent his last years in the seclusion of semi-retirement, during which time he was not as productive as earlier, although he continued to produce works of the finest quality, including the two oratorios which were composed around the turn of the century.

Haydn's Symphonies

Of the 104 symphonies composed throughout Haydn's life, the last twelve, composed in London and called the "London Symphonies," are justifiably the most famous. Most of the earlier ones were composed for the orchestra at the Esterhazy estate except for the six symphonies (nos. 82-87) known as the "Paris Symphonies" (1785–86) because they were commissioned for a concert series in Paris, and numbers 88 to 92, which were commissioned by private individuals. Most of the later ones are in the standard four-movement pattern discussed in the previous chapter, but within this framework there is great diversity of form, wealth of thematic material, and variety of orchestration. All of them show a remarkably inventive and resourceful technique, and, viewing them as a whole, they show a gradual evolution of developmental craft which culminated in a developmental technique that was equaled only by Beethoven.

The minuets all follow the standard pattern of two binary forms in triple meter, the second one called the Trio, with the first one played after the Trio by means of the da capo device to form an overall ABA form. But no composer of the Classical period was able to infuse the minuet with greater variety and interest than Haydn. By virtue of irregular phrase lengths, surprising rhythms, imaginative orchestration, and resourceful key contrast, nearly all of his minuets transcend the stereotyped pattern. Some of the later ones, because of their greater length, faster tempos, and developmental character, lead toward the Romantic scherzo form which was first used by Beethoven and which replaced the minuet in many symphonies of the Romantic period.

The evolution of the Classical style from the Baroque is seen in the fact that the harpsichord is essential as a continuo instrument in the first forty symphonies—up to about 1770. These earlier symphonies are marked by Baroque traits such as the use of solo instruments in concertante style (as in a concerto grosso), unison passages, sequences, chain suspensions in slow movements, and a tendency to spin ideas out in the Baroque instrumental fashion rather than to use frequent clear-cut cadences to create a periodic phrase structure. The finales tended to be light-weight movements in moderately fast 3/8 or 6/8 meters; it was not until his later symphonies and quartets that Haydn realized that a finale of greater impact was necessary to successfully round out the four-movement pattern.

The period after 1770 can be called Haydn's mature period, and the symphonies of this time, such as numbers 44, 47, 56, and all of those numbered above 80, are marked by a new kind of developmental technique which first appeared in the six string quartets of Op. 17 (1771) and reached maturity in the six quartets of Op. 33 (1781), which Haydn said were "composed in a new and special manner." The new technique has been called "motivic development" but this does not sufficiently describe it for it involves idiomatic instrumental writing and greater equality among the parts, as well as a new kind of organic unity achieved by extracting short motives from longer themes and using them, often exclusively, in developmental passages in which homophonic and polyphonic elements are successfully combined. Motivic development is the most important element that Beethoven inherited from Haydn's style. It is a hallmark of the music of both composers and is also seen to a lesser degree in the instrumental works of Mozart. Apparent most of all in the first and last movements of Haydn's symphonies, it is by no means restricted to the development sections, for there are many passages in the expositions which are highly developmental in character. Indeed, very often the thematic material of the second tonal group is motivically derived from if not the same as the theme of the first tonal group to lend great organic unity to the exposition. Thus, the terms "first theme" and "second theme" are often inappropriate in describing the sections of a mature sonata exposition of Haydn, for frequently the same theme is used in both tonal groups.

The finales of his later symphonies, in general, have much greater impact than the finales of his earlier works. They are often in duple meter, longer, and much more developmental than earlier finales. Many of them are in rondo form, often modified with the tonal plan of sonata form to create a pattern which has been called the sonata-rondo, a form which was later used frequently by Beethoven.

Haydn's slow movements in both the early and late instrumental works are characterized by great warmth, lyricism, and depth of expression. He frequently used a spacious sonata form or a theme and variations in slow movements; and many of them, particularly after 1770 during the *Sturm und Drang* period, contain much chromaticism along with daring modulations to create effects that presage the harmonic style of the Romantic period.

Haydn's Symphony No. 104 in D Major, the "London" Symphony, illustrates many of the traits of Haydn's mature symphonic style. It opens with a slow introduction in D minor which, in its use of spacious dotted rhythms, the minor key, and the cadence on the dominant, shows the influence of the Baroque French overture. Then the sonata movement proper begins with a sprightly theme in the parallel major, a choice example of the double period (fig. 69). The six-note motive, shown by a bracket in figure 69, illustrates one aspect of the technique of motivic development, for the development section which follows is built exclusively out of this terse thematic germ, and it is used a great deal in the exposition and recapitulation as well. By passing it among the instruments of the orchestra in polyphonic development in many harmonic contexts, Haydn reveals the fragment to possess a potential only hinted at in the opening of the exposition—here indeed is a prodigious developmental technique. Note also that the main theme of the movement is used in both the first and second tonal groups.

Figure 69. Opening Theme of the Allegro First Movement of Haydn's Symphony No. 104.

The second movement of the "London" Symphony is a free variation form containing a theme and three variations. The movement is in G major, the key of the subdominant, but the first variation introduces the key of G minor, which permits the composer to indulge in some characteristically colorful chromaticism. The minuet which follows is typical of Haydn's great achievements in this form. Shortly after the first repeat sign (the repeat of the first section of the minuet is written out) the upper woodwinds and violins interject a heavily accented chord on the third beat of the measure which, because of the regular rhythm of the minuet meter, sounds as if it should be followed by a downbeat on the next bar. This unrealized upbeat is followed by two measures of total silence, an excellent example of Haydn's imaginative use of rhythm and surprise. The Trio is surprising in its key of B Flat major, quite distant from the home tonality of D Major, an example of the third relation which was to become an important trait of the harmonic style of the early Romantic period.

The technique of fragmentation and motivic development is apparent also in the Finale, an exuberant movement which demonstrates the increased importance of the finale in Haydn's later works. The main theme, presented in figure 70, is organized motivically as shown by the brackets. The excerpt from the development shown below illustrates the use of diminution as a developmental technique.

Also among the twelve London Symphonies are the famous "Clock" Symphony (No. 101), the "Surprise" (No. 94), and the "Military" (No. 100). The "Oxford" Symphony (No. 92), not among the twelve London Symphonies, is so named because it was performed on the occasion of Haydn receiving an honorary doctorate from Oxford University in 1791. The impresario Salomon represented Haydn to the

Figure 70. Excerpts from the Last Movement of Haydn's Symphony No. 104.

English as "the greatest composer in the world." Undoubtedly he was —after Mozart's death and before Beethoven had reached his height— and this must have spurred Haydn to his greatest efforts, for the symphonies of the London period are among the most distinguished achievements in all the symphonic repertory.

Haydn's String Quartets

Like the symphonies, Haydn's quartets span the full length of his productive career, and in them can be seen the same evolution of technique that is apparent in the course of his symphonic writing. Most of the quartets are composed in sets of six, and the earliest of these, the sets of Op. 1, 2, and 3 (1755–65) are little more than Rococo trio sonatas arranged for four stringed instruments. Works of this type, which often went by such titles as divertimento, serenade, or cassation, were composed by many mid-eighteenth-century composers. Many of them are in five movements with two minuets, and they show the young Haydn in an effort to compose instrumental works which do not rely on the continuo for support. It is possible, since he was called upon to produce music for outdoor entertainments such as garden parties during this period, that the need to eliminate the harpsichord was a condition imposed upon him by his patrons. In any case, these works illustrate the manner in which the string quartet medium originated —by the substitution of the viola for the harpsichord in the trio sonata group.

The influence of the Rococo trio sonata is seen in the character of the lower parts in these early works, for they are relegated almost completely to a supportive role, leaving the first violin to emerge as the virtuoso soloist. Gradually in the course of his career Haydn developed a texture unique to the medium of the string quartet in which the four instruments function almost equally, beautifully fused into a fabric in which homophonic and polyphonic elements are combined, and the idiomatic resources of the instruments are exploited to the fullest. Because of his tremendous innovative achievements in this medium, and because he established a standard of quartet writing to which all later quartet composers aspired, Haydn has been called the "Father of the string quartet."

His characteristic quartet style begins to be seen in the quartets of Op. 9 (1769), although the first violin still dominates. The importance of Op. 17 and Op. 33 to the technique of motivic development has already been mentioned, but the quartets of Op. 20 added a new element in that the four parts are, for the first time, treated almost equally. The final movements in the second, fifth, and sixth quartets of this set are four-voice fugues, a logical solution to the problem of achieving equality among the parts. The minuet in each of the quartets of Op. 33 is called a *scherzo*, presumably the first use of this word as the title of the third movement of the classical four-movement pattern. But these are not scherzos in the true Romantic sense—Beethoven must receive the credit for that development. Haydn did not use the term in any later works, but many of his minuets from Op. 33 on have something of the mood and speed of the Romantic scherzo.

Haydn wrote string quartets over a period of fifty years, continually experimenting with daring harmonic relationships, contrapuntal devices, and developmental techniques. Perhaps his greatest quartets are the six of Op. 76 (1797–98), which contain some of his most famous movements—the "Witches' Minuet," a strict two-voice canon from the second quartet of the set, the "Fantasia" from the sixth which contains some of the most daring modulations in all of his music, and Number Three, the famous "Emperor" quartet which gets its name from the slow movement a theme and variations based on a Hymn written by Haydn for the Emperor which later became the Austrian national anthem. An illustration of one important aspect of his overall style is found in the first movement of the "Emperor" quartet where at one point in the development Haydn sets up a drone bass pedal point on E in the viola and cello over which the violins play a sturdy rustic tune suggestive of a peasant dance. This melody is motivically derived from a five-note motive heard near the beginning of the movement, but its folk-like character illustrates an important stylistic trait, for Haydn, perhaps because of his peasant ancestry, frequently made use of tunes which seem to spring from Bohemian or German soil. His use of such melodies is always fully integrated in his style so that seldom do they produce an incongruous effect, except when done intentionally for a humorous effect.

Haydn's Vocal Works

In addition to many solo songs written throughout his career, Haydn was at various times occupied with small forms of sacred vocal music, single-movement works designed for incidental use in religious services. His Masses, particularly the six composed between 1796 and 1802, are works of more significant proportions. They contain orchestral writing similar to that of his later symphonies, the quartet of soprano, alto, tenor, and bass soloists, and an overall form that departs from the opera-inspired alternation of recitative and aria toward a structure of vocal-symphonic movements in which chorus, orchestra and soloists are integrated. Perhaps the most famous of these late Masses is the "Mass in Time of War" (1796), also called the *Paukenmesse* (Timpani Mass).

The sacred choral work entitled *The Seven Last Words of the Redeemer on the Cross* has an interesting history. It was originally composed as a set of programmatic orchestral movements, all in relatively slow tempos, as a commission from the Cathedral of Cadiz in 1785. Subsequently it was arranged as a seven-movement string quartet (Op. 51), and still later Haydn arranged it with added choral parts. This work, however, is overshadowed by the two great oratorios, *The Creation* (1797–98) and *The Seasons* (1798–1801). Haydn had become acquainted with Handel's oratorios during his visits to London and was particularly moved by a performance of the *Messiah* in 1791 at Westminster Abbey. The influence of Handel, transformed and elevated by Haydn's mature symphonic style, is apparent in the choral writing as well as in the breadth, power, and grandeur of these two works. Both oratorios are religious in nature, but much of their charm lies in their simple depiction of man's great joy in nature and the simple life. Written by a man nearing seventy years, they are nevertheless imbued with a youthful outlook and real spiritual vigor.

The development of the late eighteenth-century Classical style owes more to Haydn than to any other single composer. In his music can be heard the naive simplicity suggested by the nickname "Papa Haydn" given him by his devoted musicians at Esterhaza, but in addition to the folk-like humanity of his music there is found a nobility of expression, a superbly polished style, and a sophistication that certainly matches and perhaps excels that of Mozart and Beethoven. Although he did not storm the heavens in the manner of Beethoven, nor achieve the lyrical spontaneity and psychological depth of Mozart, he was nevertheless an innovator of remarkable genius who opened paths for Beethoven and the beginnings of the Romantic era.

Wolfgang Amadeus Mozart (1756–1791) played almost as important a part as Haydn in perfecting the characteristic instrumental style of the late Classical period, for the music of these two composers together represents every significant aspect of the Classical style. Although Mozart certainly excelled Haydn in the opera and the concerto, he perhaps did not equal him as a composer of symphonies and string quartets.

One of the chief distinctions in style between the two composers is found in the nature of their thematic material. Whereas Mozart's works overflow with a wealth of flowing and spontaneous melody, Haydn tended toward melodies which were motivically organized, and from which, in his mature works, he drew short motives to build complete movements which were organized and unified with great developmental skill. Mozart might use as many as four or more well rounded singing melodies in an exposition, while Haydn might base an entire exposition on material from a single eight-bar theme. Haydn's short motives lend themselves better to extended development than do the self-contained, well-rounded lyrical expressions of Mozart, and perhaps for this reason Mozart's development sections tend to be shorter than those of Haydn. Also Mozart's phrase structures tend to be more symmetrical than those of Haydn—Mozart more frequently composed in four- or eight-bar phrases, while Haydn quite often arrived at phrase lengths of five or seven bars.

Another difference can be found in the quality of their harmonic expression. The harmonic style in works such as Mozart's G Minor Quintet (K. 516) for string quartet plus a second viola, or the C Major String Quartet (K. 465, "The Dissonance"), demonstrates his dramatic and expressive use of dissonance and chromaticism. Haydn's harmonic daring was seen much more in the use of remarkable tonal contrasts between sections of considerable length than in Mozart's brand of chromaticism and dissonance. There is a richness of harmony in Mozart's music which evokes the spirit of the Romantic era to follow, and it may partly be accounted for by the great melodic and contrapuntal activity of the inner voices of his instrumental textures. These are generalizations to which there are many exceptions, however, for during the period of relatively close acquaintance between the two composers (Vienna, 1781–83) and after, Haydn's music is marked by increased chromaticism, and Mozart's later symphonies and string quartets contain considerable use of motivic development. It has often been said that their styles are almost indistinguishable, and for certain works this may be true—attesting to the homogeneity of style in the Classical period. But in addition to the subtle distinctions mentioned above, there is a difference of spirit and mood that cannot be easily described in words but which is apparent in the sound of the music. This may be attributed to the fact that Mozart was not endowed with Haydn's apparent inner repose and equanimity—that, as a child of the Enlightenment, Mozart was not content to accept things as they were, but rebelled—usually unsuccessfully, it must be added—against his assigned station in society. In this, and in the nature of his life style, he was a precursor of Beethoven and the Romantic ideal of the artist.

It is generally acknowledged that no musician in Western history was endowed with greater artistic gifts than Mozart. His inventive musicality, his dramatic and psychological instinct, his musical memory, his performance ability, and his sheer creative genius form an aggregation of talents that is surely unparalleled in the history of music. He demonstrated these remarkable gifts at an early age, composing at the age of five and presenting piano concerts at six. His father Leopold Mozart, a composer and violinist of some distinction, was in a position to make the most and these talents, and took the child prodigy at the age of seven on a concert tour that covered all of the principal musical centers of Europe. One of the chief influences absorbed during these years of youth was that of the music of Italy, and Mozart's later style was marked by an ideal fusion of Italian and Germanic elements.

Saturated in all aspects of music-making throughout his childhood, Mozart arrived at young manhood with an assurance and mastery of his art that is unrivaled. He was perhaps the only composer in history who was able to hear in his mind a complete composition prior to beginning work on it, and was also able to work out mentally in advance nearly every technical detail. The act of notating the music, according to his own testimony, was often nothing more than setting down on paper what was already complete in his mind.

He began his adult career as a musical employee in the household of the Prince-Archbishop of Salzburg, but his spirited nature could not readily accept the role of servant, and at the age of twenty-five he left Salzburg to pursue his career in Vienna. Hoping that he would find greater artistic freedom in that musical city, Mozart spent the remaining ten years of his life tormented by a constant futile struggle against poverty. Yet in spite of the shortness of his career, he composed about a dozen operas, over 41 symphonies, close to 40 concertos, of which about half are for piano, over 20 string quartets, a vast amount of chamber music for various combinations, including 37 violin sonatas, a quantity of sacred music for chorus and orchestra, and many incidental compositions including divertimenti, piano sonatas, etc.

Of his forty-one numbered symphonies (there are several unnumbered ones) the most famous are among the last ten, including the

Haffner (No. 35), the *Prague* (No. 38), the E Flat Major (No. 39), the G Minor (No. 40), and the *Jupiter* (No. 41). At about the same time that Haydn began to depart from the strong Baroque and Rococo influence apparent in his early symphonies (the early '70s), Mozart, yet under twenty, produced his first mature works in this form. It was the beginning of the *Sturm und Drang* period and this influence can be heard in the Symphony No. 25 (K. 183). Cast in G minor, a key Mozart habitually used to evoke a mood of somber poignancy, the work is notable for its intense seriousness and for its formal unity. His earlier symphonies, composed between the age of eight and seventeen, are generally shorter and in a lighter mood, many of them in the nature of the divertimento. Interestingly, the twenty-fifth is the first of his symphonies in a minor key; and a similar mood can be heard in the fortieth which is also in the key of G minor. His later symphonies are generally in the standard four-movement pattern used by Haydn and many of them, particularly the last three composed in 1788, are distinguished by considerable use of the technique of motivic development. Yet this developmental technique, perhaps partially learned from the music of Haydn, in no way inhibited his magical gift for melody, for in spite of the increased thematic unity of these last symphonies they are filled with melodies of surpassing beauty.

Over the twenty-year period of Mozart's mature productivity (approximately 1770 to 1791) he composed about two dozen string quartets in which the development of his style can be clearly seen. The first thirteen, written before 1774, are rather light works, many of which could well be performed by string orchestra as by string quartet. Some of them, however, have fugal finales which show Mozart's growing interest in the possibilities of the string quartet as a chamber medium of four equal parts. His best known quartets are a set of six composed between 1782 and 1785. In their use of motivic development, idiomatic writing, and near equality of the parts, these works show a strong influence of Haydn, and because they are dedicated to him, they are often called the "Haydn" Quartets. The last three quartets (1789–90) were written for the King of Prussia, who was an accomplished cellist, and these more than any of his quartets are marked by equality among the four parts. Because of his efforts to produce an interesting part for the King to play, the cello part is so soloistic that these three quartets have been nicknamed the "Cello" Quartets, even though the other parts are equally interesting. The six quartets dedicated to Haydn and these last three are his greatest works for the medium.

Mozart's Operas

Mozart's amazing versatility is nowhere more striking than in the area of music drama. It was the ideal vehicle for a composer of Mozart's varied talents, and his operas benefited greatly from his ability to coordinate many diverse musical factors in the service of the libretto. His skill in writing for orchestra, solo voices, and for chorus, when directed toward the task of dramatic characterization, produced a beautifully unified musical as well as dramatic effect. Not the least of his talents was his ability to penetrate the depths of each individual character. Because of his unerring psychological instinct, his characters come alive in a manner unequaled in pre-nineteenth-century opera. Unsatisfied with the prototype characters of earlier opera composers, Mozart achieved musical characterizations of unique, individual personalities—a new kind of realism in tune with the Enlightenment, and a precursor of realism in opera of the Romantic period. It is seen partly in the expressive orchestral accompaniments and partly in the vocal lines themselves. One of his great achievements is to produce this kind of characterization in ensembles of several voices. This is seen particularly in his finales of his operas where a clear impression of each individual character is produced by using distinctly different melodic styles for each.

Except for *Don Giovanni* (1787), his mature operas fall into the three general categories of opera seria, opera buffa, and Singspiel. *Don Giovanni* has been classified as a tragicomedy, for in spite of its opera buffa traits, it possesses a tragic grimness that is at odds with the lightness of Italian comic opera. More properly in the buffa category are *Cosi fan tutte* (1790), and *The Marriage of Figaro* (1786), both with libretti by Lorenzo da Ponte (1749–1838), who also wrote the libretto for *Don Giovanni.* These along with the Singspiel, *Die Zauberflöte (The Magic Flute,* 1791) and the hastily composed and rather undistinguished opera seria, *La clemenza di Tito* (1791), comprise the operatic achievements of his later years. His earlier opera seria, *Idomeneo* (1781), is remarkable for its fine orchestration, particularly in the brass and woodwinds. Experimentation with orchestral timbre is more prevalent in Mozart's dramatic works than in the symphonies, undoubtedly because of the restrictive stylistic requirements of the Classical symphony orchestra, but also because of the expressive needs of musical theater.

Although *The Abduction from the Seraglio* (1782) falls into the category of the Singspiel, his greatest achievement in this form is *The Magic Flute,* a unique and epoch-making work which has been called the first great German opera. Its libretto was written by the enterprising Viennese theatrical manager Emanuel Schikaneder (1751–1812), whom Mozart had met in Salzburg in 1780. The complex and fantastic plot is cast in two acts, with allegorical references to current politics in Austria, and to Freemasonry. Both composer and librettist belonged to the influential Masonic organization which had developed as a product of the Enlightenment, and which included in its ranks such distinguished figures as Voltaire, Goethe, Haydn, and Frederick the Great.

The music of *The Magic Flute* is marked by great diversity of musical styles and forms. The overture is a sonata form with a slow introduction and a development section containing a fugal elaboration of the principal theme. At the very opening are heard three fortissimo chords representing knocks which are symbols of Freemasonry, as is also the central tonality of E Flat major. The folk element characteristic of Singspiel is represented throughout *The Magic Flute* by the arias of the character Papageno. His opening number, *"Der Vogelfänger bin ich ja,"* is a good example, in the form of a simple strophic song in German folk style. The arias sung by the Queen of Night, on the other hand, with their elaborate coloratura passages are typical of Mozart's opera seria style. Much of the music in the opera, however, lies between these two extremes of sophisticated Italian opera and German folk song, a typical example of this kind of fusion being the first act duet between Papageno and Pamina, *"Bei Männern welche liebe fühlen."*

An unusual device for Mozart is his use of motives and even entire phrases that occur throughout the course of the *Magic Flute.* Devices such as the three Masonic chords and Papageno's whistle anticipate Wagner's *leitmotif* technique, one of several ways in which this opera contributed to the establishment of a native German opera. The Finale of *The Magic Flute* exemplifies Mozart's skill in achieving an effective curtain scene. In this as in many of his operas, the ultimate unraveling of the plot takes place in the finale, lending a dramatic significance to a section that, in the hands of a lesser composer, could have been little more than a musical set-piece.

Mozart's Concertos

As mentioned earlier, the first movement of the classical concerto consisted of a sonata form with a number of modifications appropriate to a musical medium employing a virtuoso soloist in concert with a symphony orchestra. The main modifications are (1) the double exposition, (2) the use of frequent trills in the solo part, and (3) the cadenza. The double exposition consists of a complete exposition for the orchestra alone, followed by a second exposition for the solo instrument accompanied by the orchestra. In Mozart's concertos the second exposition often presents new thematic material in the solo part, but the basic pattern of tonal groups remains quite consistent between the two parts of the exposition. The stylized trills played by the soloist in the classical concerto serve to delineate the form and are typically heard at the end of each main section played by the solo instrument. The trill invariably occurs on one of the tones of the dominant chord followed by a tutti entrance of the orchestra on the tonic. The cadenza originated as an improvised embellishment of the final cadence of the movement and usually occurs at the end of the recapitulation just preceding the coda. It is usually prepared by a crescendo to a tonic triad in second inversion played by the orchestra, and the improvisatory part which the soloist then plays is, historically at least, an elaboration of the resolution of the I 6/4 to the dominant. Although a solo performer of the eighteenth century might conceivably have prepared his cadenza beforehand, it was not normally written out by the composer, although most modern editions of classical concertos include cadenzas which have been used by prominent performers. Figure 71 is a diagram of a typical first movement concerto form of the Classical period, a pattern which was used with modifications in many of Mozart's concertos.

The second movement of the classical concerto is invariably a lyrical slow movement with various possibilities of form such as the rondo or sonata patterns, while the finale might be either a rondo or sonata form in a fast brilliant tempo. Each of these movements might also contain a cadenza, although its presence in the first movement is obligatory.

Although Mozart wrote several horn concertos, violin concertos, and a clarinet concerto, all of which are standard repertory works for these instruments, the center of his achievements for this form are the seventeen piano concertos composed in Vienna from 1782 to 1791. Unlike the Baroque concerto, the orchestra in these works functions on a symphonic level and the relationship between orchestra and soloists is that of two major protagonists in a drama. It is this concept of the concerto that Mozart passed on to the nineteenth century and which is seen so vividly in the concertos of Beethoven. Indeed, a few of Mozart's piano concertos are quite "Beethovenesque" in style, particularly the tragic C Minor Concerto (K. 491), and to a lesser degree, the famous

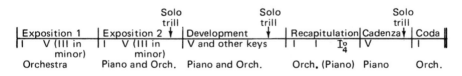

Figure 71. Sonata Form in the Classical Concerto.

D Minor (K. 466). Others are more lyrically poetic, such as the G Major (K. 453) and, above all, his last concerto, K. 595, in B. Flat major.

Mozart wrote a quantity of church music including a number of Masses, some of which are relatively undistinguished. But his greatest sacred choral work is without doubt the monumental *Requiem,* which was mysteriously commissioned during the final year of his life. In poor health and poverty-stricken, he was obsessed with the idea that this funeral Mass was to be his own. Although he worked feverishly to complete it, he died with a small portion yet to be done. It was completed after his death by his pupil Sussmayer. Mozart's *Requiem* stands as the final expression of an artist who failed to achieve the personal recognition that should have been his, but who left to the world a legacy of musical works containing some of the most deeply dramatic and lyrical music in all of Western history.

V. THE ROMANTIC CENTURY

12. Beethoven and the Beginning of the Romantic Era

*The Piano—Chamber Music—The Nine
Symphonies—Vocal Works—Romanticism*

Placing the end of the Classical period and the beginning of the Romantic rather arbitrarily around 1810 or 1815, large portions of Beethoven's productive life fall into both periods. Indeed, the works of his first period, up to about 1804, are firmly grounded in the traditions of the eighteenth century, at the same time containing elements suggestive of the later Beethoven. But during his second period, approximately 1804 to 1816, Beethoven increasingly infused his music with evocative qualities, musical innovations, and new concepts of form that transcended the frameworks of the Classical style and set precedents for the art of the Romantic era. During his third and final period, from 1816, Beethoven was beset by increasing deafness, almost totally losing his hearing around 1820. The works of these last years in some instances went beyond the understanding even of his progressive younger contemporaries in the early Romantic period, for the meditative and visionary qualities of his late works are the unique expressions of an artist whose music stretches far beyond the limitations of historical periods. Here is the genius who stands titanically with one foot in the eighteenth century, the other in the nineteenth, but whose music addresses itself timelessly to all of mankind.

Born in Bonn at the height of the Enlightenment, he entered a world bristling with new ideas. The seeds of Romanticism were already germinating and in many instances were coming to early fruition, for the era was teeming with activity and thought. New worlds of philosophy, science, and art were being explored, and the late eighteenth century was a time of conflicts—scientific thought against religious faith, freedom of the individual against absolutism, emerging socialism against flourishing capitalism. Much of what seemed new to the nineteenth century was the clear result of ideas, concepts and attitudes that were formulated earlier. The political, social, and philosophical upheavals of the last years of the eighteenth century could not conceal the fact that the seeds of revolution were planted long before the onset of the Romantic era. In music, Haydn and Mozart had used techniques which later became stylistic traits of the Romantic period, and the same was true of artists in other fields. For example, the paintings of Jacques Louis David (1748–1825), the poetry of William Blake (1757–1827), and the writings of Goethe (1749–1832) contain much prophecy of artistic as well as philosophical trends of the later nineteenth century. In all areas of human endeavor the nineteenth century should be viewed as the child of the eighteenth.

Of great significance to the artist in the early nineteenth century was the decline of patronage of the church, the state, and the aristocracy. It was the beginning of the artist's emergence as a free individual and Beethoven, more than any other, provided the nineteenth century with its model for the Romantic artist. Throughout his life he played a role in society quite different from that of his predecessors. Haydn, to all appearances, had been content with his role as servant; and Mozart, though rebelling against patronage and dying in poverty, failed to successfully establish himself as an independent artist. But even as a boy Beethoven showed a spirit of independent self-reliance that could accept no part of the role of servant, and as a mature artist he yielded no precedence to mere noblemen. When necessary, he accepted their patronage, but demanded that he be treated not as an equal but as the superior person that he was. The growth of the music-publishing industry and the increasing middle-class audience gradually freed him from complete dependence upon the patronage system and, though never affluent, he was able to establish financial as well as artistic independence.

With the successes of the child prodigy Mozart fresh in his mind, Johann Beethoven, a second-rate professional musician, had similar aspirations for his five-year-old son Ludwig. There was no doubt of the young Beethoven's precocity, but his was not the fresh and flexible personality of the young Mozart, and his father's attempts to exploit him as a child prodigy were failures. In spite of lessons on the violin from his father, and guidance from his father's rather mediocre musical colleagues in Bonn, he was largely self-taught until his tenth year, when he began to receive lessons from Christian Gottlob Neefe, an excellent musician who introduced the boy to Bach's *Well Tempered Clavier.* But the Mannheim school and the music of Haydn and Mozart had already begun to influence Beethoven, and Bach's contrapuntal textures had no immediately apparent effect. By 1784 he was a competent enough musician to hold a court position as assistant organist and in 1787 on a visit to Vienna he met Mozart, improvised for him, and received a few lessons. It was on this occasion that Mozart was quoted as saying enthusiastically of Beethoven, "Watch that lad, some day he'll make a noise in the world." During this same period Beethoven's mother died and the sixteen-year-old musician was left with the care of his two brothers and a rather dissolute father. Luckily, he was able to secure additional work in the form of teaching and made some important friends among the nobility, particularly the Von Breunings, and Count Ferdinand Waldstein, whom Beethoven later immortalized by dedicating his Opus 53 piano sonata to him.

Beethoven had met Haydn in 1790 when the distinguished composer had visited Bonn, and in 1792, on a second visit, he took the time to examine Beethoven's music in some detail and encouraged him to come to Vienna to study with him. With Waldstein's help, this came to pass, and Beethoven's career as a composer was launched. The Viennese aristocracy were kind to this slight, unkempt, crude provincial from Bonn and it was not long before his successes at improvisation gained him entry to the most distinguished palaces of the city. The inhabitants of these households were the same who treated Haydn and Mozart as servants, and it was during this time that Beethoven, accustomed to mingling with the Von Breunings and Waldstein on equal terms, established a reputation as one who could be treated only with deference. The fashion of the times helped him to be able to do this, but the force and perhaps the charm of his personality were more important factors in his early successes.

He had published a few early compositions in Bonn, the most notable of which are three piano sonatas (not included among the thirty-two with opus numbers). In 1795 his first mature compositions appeared, the three piano trios of Op. 1. In the meantime, not totally satisfied with his work with Haydn, Beethoven studied with several other teachers, of whom the most influential was Albrechtsberger (1736–1908), a well-known pedagogue who filled in the empty places in his sketchy training and gave him the technical discipline that he needed.

The first signs of deafness appeared in 1798, and by 1801 he realized that his career as a performer would soon be over. During this first period of mature productivity he used all the forms and techniques inherited from the eighteenth century in composing works such as the six string quartets of Op. 18 and the First and Second symphonies, compositions which represent an ideal culmination of the Classical period at the same time that they are unmistakably marked by Beethoven's unique musical personality. The strongest influences during this period were the Mannheim composers and the music of Haydn and Mozart. The technique of motivic development, inherited most of all from Haydn, is apparent in all of the works of this period. An examination of practically any of the mature sonata allegro forms of this time will reveal a motivic structure more tightly knit even than that of Haydn.

In the middle period he began to stretch the classical forms to the breaking point. It was a time of mature and determined self-expression, of impassioned externalization. To contain his sweeping and tumultuous ideas of this time, it was necessary for him to expand the traditional matrix of the Classical symphony. He lengthened development sections, expanded codas to the point that they became substantial architectural components, endowed his slow introductions with a new breadth, and increased the number and kind of instruments in the symphony orchestra. This expansion reached a peak during the first part of his third period in the Ninth Symphony (1817–23) which, in addition to the usual instruments of the classical orchestra, calls for piccolo, contrabassoon, four horns, three trombones, a number of percussion instruments, plus a full chorus and four vocal soloists. At the same time, there are works of the middle period such as the Op. 95 string quartet, which show an increased tightening of form, manifest in shorter movements of great organic unity.

Although Beethoven accepted commissions, and in some instances obliged his patrons with requested musical effects, such as the inclusion of Russian themes in the "Rasoumovsky" Quartets of Op. 59, he was completely his own master in regard to the type of music he composed. He did not cater to a limited public and was the first to practice the principle of "Art for Art's sake." At times he seemed to be addressing a vast audience of the future, one that was not limited by social levels and political boundaries, but at other times, such as in the last string quartets, he seemed to be writing for himself and for the select few capable of understanding him.

Although it is putting it too strongly to say that Beethoven is "the man who freed music," he did establish many important precedents for the music of the Romantic period. Among these is the sheer vastness of symphonic expression as seen in the increased length of his symphonies and the greater number of musicians needed to perform them. The romantic concept of the symphonic tone poem owes much to the *Coriolanus* and *Egmont* Overtures, and to the Sixth or *Pastorale* Symphony —all symphonic works which are more or less programmatic in nature. In evolving the scherzo form from the Classical minuet, Beethoven opened the way for unique scherzo movements in the works of Brahms, Chopin, Mendelssohn, Berlioz and other nineteenth-century composers.

Freer use of variation technique—an important feature of Romanticism—is seen in a number of Beethoven's variation forms, but particularly in the *Diabelli Variations,* op. 120, a set of thirty-three variations for piano solo based on a theme by the publisher Diabelli. In this work many of the variations are more distantly related to the theme than in the classical theme-and-variations, and each variation has its own particular mood or character, producing great contrast within the total work. The term "character variation" aptly describes this free and typically romantic concept of the variation form.

Another innovation is seen in his set of songs, *An die ferne Geliebte* ("To the Distant Beloved"), a work that can be called the first Romantic song cycle in that it is a self-contained "set" or "cycle" of solo songs with piano accompaniment bound together by a central theme, with the piano playing a part in the expression of the images of the poetry. The solo song with piano accompaniment is the medium through which Romanticism was most purely and freely expressed, and lieder occupied a central position in the works of such important Romantic composers as Schubert, Schumann, Brahms, and Wolf. The epitome of Romantic lieder is the ideal fusion of poetry and music representing an important feature of Romanticism in general—the synthesis of the arts. Another less important but related innovation is found in his short piano solos called "Bagatelles," which set the precedent for the romantic "character piece" for piano solo exemplified by the *Songs Without Words* of Mendelssohn and the *Preludes* of Chopin.

The use of dynamic change, whether subtle or extreme, is another important feature of romanticism found in the music of Beethoven. Although expressive dynamics were first notated in the late sixteenth century (see chap. 5), dynamic markings were still relatively new, even in the eighteenth century. There are many works of J. S. Bach which contain no dynamic markings at all in the autograph editions, and Haydn and Mozart, although they invariably used them, kept them within a traditionally prescribed framework, with relatively few extremes. In Beethoven's music, particularly in the middle and late periods, dynamics become an important expressive element of the music and are quite carefully notated. A profusion of *sforzandi* and sharp dynamic contrasts are among the most striking features of his music, adding greatly to the character of intense and boundless energy that characterizes many of his works.

Beethoven's vast range of expression required new and expanded concepts of musical form. As a scion of the Classical period, his musical structures are models of balance and cohesiveness; yet in their scope and grandeur some of them are supremely Romantic. With great economy of means, he built movements of epic length from a few terse motives woven into a fabric of great dramatic and expressive impact. Something of his painstaking work habits can be deduced from his sketchbooks, many of which have been preserved. They stand as vivid testimony to the assiduously self-critical manner in which he approached the craft of musical composition.

Whether expressed by dynamic outbursts as in the Fifth Symphony or by moments of hymn-like lyricism as in the slow movement of the "Archduke Trio," Op. 97, the music of the middle period is pervaded by a quality of impassioned humanity. During the third period, from about 1816 until his death, Beethoven's music took on a new quality of calm affirmation and reflective assurance. Many of his contemporaries could not understand some of the music of this period and attributed certain enigmatic effects to his deafness, saying that the ideal conceptions heard in his inner ear were not musically practicable when realized in actual sound. This attitude is understandable in terms of works such as the string quartet, Op. 133 (the Great Fugue), or in parts of the Ninth Symphony, yet perhaps Beethoven would have explored the same obscure worlds of sound had he not been deaf, for the abstract qualities of the music of this period are the result of his concern with purely musical matters—thematic variation, textures, the development of motives, and contrapuntal devices. The most significant and most representative works of this time are the late quartets, in which, with few exceptions the Classical forms of Haydn and Mozart are heard only as vestiges.

The changing relationship between the artist and society in the early nineteenth century is manifest in the disparity in musical output between Beethoven and classical composers such as Haydn and Mozart. Beethoven composed nine symphonies against Haydn's one-hundred-and-four and Mozart's forty-one; seventeen string quartets against Haydn's eighty-three; and only a few concertos against over forty by Mozart. This is partly explained by the fact that Beethoven's compositions are often lengthier than those of his Classical predecessors, and partly by his slow, painstaking work habits. But Beethoven's position in society was different from that of earlier composers. He was neither *Kapellmeister* nor court composer. Unlike Haydn and Bach, he was not obliged to compose, rehearse, and perform music for any occasion that might arise. Although he accepted commissions and from 1800 on accepted a guaranteed income from several Viennese noblemen, his works were the products of his own musical inclinations and his desire for personal self-expression. He hoped for public response and perhaps for immortality, but he maintained a social status quite different from that of earlier composers—a new relationship of artist to society that continues even to the present.

The Piano

The piano began its development in the mid-eighteenth century and reached a form similar to that of the modern piano about a century later. The chief distinction from the harpsichord, its Baroque counterpart, is the fact that the volume of sound produced by the piano is controlled by the weight or pressure of the attack on the key. It was thus much more capable of producing crescendos, diminuendos, and subtle as well as extreme dynamic contrasts than the harpsichord, in which dynamics as well as timbre were controlled by a system of stops. Muzio Clementi (1752–1832) was one of the earliest composers to devote a great deal of attention to the piano, and both Haydn and Mozart contributed much to its literature. But the piano for which these classical composers wrote was a facile instrument with a shallow key action and no damper pedal—not the instrument of Beethoven's nineteenth-century piano compositions. The invention of the double-escapement and the damper pedal added new dimensions to piano literature—vividly seen in the piano sonatas and concertos of Beethoven. The nineteenth-century piano had a deeper key action and was therefore more percussive and produced a larger sound than the piano of the Classical period, and in works such as the *Hammerklavier* Sonata, Op. 106 and in the Op. 109, 110, and 111 sonatas, Beethoven made much of the possibilities of the new instrument.

Outstanding among the piano sonatas of his first period is the famous *Pathetique* Sonata, Op. 13, in which hints of the new piano technique can already be seen. Its final movement is a superb example of the Classical sonata-rondo form. Perhaps the greatest of the middle-period piano sonatas are the *Waldstein,* Op. 53, and the *Appassionata,* Op. 57, in both of which can be seen the expansion of Classical forms typical of his middle-period works, even though the traditional key relationships of the Classical patterns are still present. Beethoven wrote variation forms throughout his life, but one of the traits of his third period works is a preoccupation with variation technique, not only in the formal theme-and-variation plan, but in the use of techniques such as varying the repetition of a theme in the recapitulation of a sonata form, or in varying the repetitions of a rondo theme (which had occurred as early as the middle movement of the Op. 13 sonata). Experimentation with variation technique can be seen in the *Diabelli Variations* mentioned earlier, and also in works such as the Op. 109 piano sonata, which contains a remarkable set of variations as the final movement.

Beethoven was an excellent performer on the piano and in addition to the thirty-two piano sonatas, wrote five piano concertos of which at least the first three (Op. 15 in C, Op. 19 in B Flat, and Op. 37 in C Minor) were for his own use. His concertos are related to those of Mozart in their use of the orchestra as a symphonic instrument to contrast with the virtuoso soloist, as two protagonists in a drama. He retained the classical three-movement pattern but intensified the content and expanded the form. The G Major Piano Concerto, Op. 58, and the *Emperor,* Op. 73, are the two largest works in this form. Between these two comes the unique Violin Concerto in D Major, Op. 61, which he also arranged as a piano concerto. This, his only concerto for the violin, is one of the great standard works for the instrument. The Triple Concerto for piano, violin, and cello (Op. 56) is a less distinguished work.

Chamber Music

Beethoven's outstanding achievements in chamber media are his seventeen string quartets, which fall clearly into the three periods of his career. The most famous of the Op. 18 Quartets of the first period is number four in C minor which, in addition to exemplifying the culmination of the Classical style, shows the unique mood that Beethoven typically evoked when writing in the key of C minor. The three "Rasoumovsky" quartets of Op. 59 are perhaps the most virtuosic of his works for this medium, although the late quartets may be more demanding from a purely musical standpoint. Commissioned by Count Rasoumovksy, they were composed in 1807 and are unprecedented from the standpoint of quartet texture, for they achieve an equality among the four parts that was unparalleled even in the greatest quartets of Haydn. His growing interest in polyphonic textures and contrapuntal devices is heard in these middle-period quartets, particularly in the final movement of Op. 59, No. 3 in C Major, which is an extended fugue with a remarkably long subject in a very fast tempo first presented by the viola. Op. 74 and 95 also fall into the middle period, although the *Serioso,* Op. 95, has a terse and highly unified quality suggestive of the third period.

His late quartets (Op. 127, 130, 131, 132, 133, and 135) include those works which most puzzled his contemporaries, who felt that his deafness created a barrier of understanding between the composer and his audience. Op. 135 (F Major) is an exception, however, for it is cast in the standard four-movement pattern and is clearly in the Classical tradition. Op. 127 is also in four movements, but the others depart radically from Classical form. Op. 131 (C Sharp Minor) is in seven movements played without pauses between movements and its fourth movement is a unique set of variations. The original Finale of Op. 130 is the complex and esoteric fugue which became the *Grosse Fuge* (Op. 133) when Beethoven substituted an Allegro Finale in sonata form as the Finale of Op. 131. Op. 132 (A minor) is in five movements, of which the third is a profoundly lyrical slow movement utilizing the Lydian mode. Along with Haydn and Mozart, Beethoven raised the medium of the string quartet to a level that could be approached in the nineteenth century only by Brahms, and in the twentieth century only by Bartok and perhaps a few others.

His other chamber works include several early string trios (violin, viola, and cello), two quintets for string quartet with a second viola, ten sonatas for piano and violin, five sonatas for piano and cello, eight piano trios, a trio for clarinet, cello, and piano, the unique Septet for winds and strings, and number of other works for various instrumental combinations. The most frequently performed of these are the piano trios, the violin sonatas, and the cello sonatas, all of which are standard repertory pieces. In these works the piano functions as an instrument of equal or more importance in comparison to the violin and cello, a characteristic which is in part inherited from the Classical period—as in the piano trios and violin sonatas of Haydn and Mozart—but which is also a manifestation of Beethoven's interest in creating chamber music textures of more or less equal parts in which all of the instruments participate in a texture of both homophonic and polyphonic elements.

The Nine Symphonies

The First and Second Symphonies have been mentioned as examples of Beethoven's first period—typifying the culmination of the Classical style. But all except the Sixth fall more or less into the Classical pattern of four movements, and only the Ninth can be said to be a third-period work. The Third Symphony, Op. 55 (The *Eroica*), is notable for its addition of a third horn to the usual pair found in the Classical orchestra, and for the use of the scherzo in place of the minuet for the first time in a symphony. The word "scherzo" is simply the Italian word for joke and had been used as a musical title long before its evolution as a form. Haydn used the term in his Op. 33 Quartets as a descriptive title for minuets which were lighter and more whimsical than usual, but which were certainly not in a new pattern. This probably set the precedent for Beethoven's use of the term, but in his hands it became a new form. The minuets of both his First and Second Symphonies were in much faster tempos than usual for that form, anticipating the very fast tempos characteristic of the scherzo. Although usually in triple meter, the scherzo often incorporates elements of humor and surprise which are not essential to the minuet, but the chief distinguishing traits are the increased developmental character and the formal pattern. Often a scherzo will incorporate a second statement of the trio or even a second trio based on new material to form a pattern of ABABA or ABACA, and a few of Beethoven's scherzos are in sonata form. Occasionally the scherzo veers away from its typical mood of lightness and whimsy toward a more serious or ominous kind of humor, as in the scherzos of the Fifth and Ninth Symphonies. The internal structure of the scherzo is clearly derived from the minuet, but its evocative qualities are of the Romantic period.

The title *Eroica* (Heroic) for the Third Symphony originated, according to legend, from Beethoven's intention to dedicate the work to Napoleon whom the composer presumably idolized because of his humanitarian and egalitarian leadership. When Napoleon was declared Emperor, so the story goes, Beethoven tore up the title page and removed the dedication in anger and disappointment with his erstwhile hero. It is a work of unprecedented length, truly a symphony of heroic proportions and expressive qualities appropriate to such a dedication, and it is also revolutionary from the standpoint of form. The tightly knit first movement is in sonata form, with much development of motives from the simple triadic first theme, but the exposition presents a number of additional themes which are also used in the course of the movement. The second movement is a funeral march in C minor with a heroic shift to C major in the middle section. The trio of the remarkable scherzo which follows makes good use of the three horns in a fanfare-like section of true nobility. The Finale is a unique set of variations based on two themes which are presented separately, the first of which is the bass line to the second, a device which allowed the composer to create a double set of variations of great inner logic. The second of these themes introduces a cyclical element, for it begins with the same three tones (E flat, G, E flat) as the very first theme of the opening movement. Thematic linkages of this type occur frequently in Beethoven's later works, as, for example, among the movements of the Fifth Symphony, which are tied together with the famous four-note motive.

The Fourth, Fifth, and Sixth Symphonies were composed in close proximity between the years 1806 and 1808. The Fourth is not particularly innovative, for it follows the standard four-movement pattern, reverting to the use of the minuet for the third movement, and evokes a light-hearted mood of classical spirit. The famous Fifth Symphony is notable for its use of trombones for the first time in a symphony, which the composer reserves (along with the piccolo and contrabasson) for maximum effect in the Finale, linking the added sonority to the striking shift from C minor to C major, which is said to be a symbol of triumph over fate. The Sixth Symphony, The *Pastorale,* is in five movements, each depicting a scene from the country. Its form is derived from the four-movement pattern, with the "Merrymaking of the Peasants" turned into a scherzo and the "Storm" added as an extra movement before the Finale. Although it contains some literal depictive devices, such as the imitation of bird calls by the woodwinds in the second movement, it is a prime example of a symphonic work existing at both the programmatic and purely musical levels. Beethoven himself warned the listener not to take the descriptive titles too literally, calling them "expressions of feeling rather than depiction."

The Seventh Symphony, completed in 1812, is remarkable for its long introduction and for its famous A minor slow movement, an allegretto in rondo form which, like the slow movement of the Third, introduces the key of the parallel major in a lyrical middle section. The Eighth Symphony, also completed in 1812, is relatively short, intense, and conservative in form, but its mercurial humor and its impelling vigor create an expressive quality unique among Beethoven's symphonies.

The innovations in the performing forces of the Ninth Symphony have already been mentioned, but the work is unique from other standpoints as well. As in the Fifth Symphony, the full complement of musicians is reserved for the Finale, and the chorus and vocal soloists do not enter until well into the final movement. The text is drawn from Schiller's "Ode to Joy," and the stanzas selected by Beethoven reflect his belief in the brotherhood of man. The first three movements bear vestiges of Classical patterns, and the scherzo is notable for its use of a single rhythmic motive built into an entire movement in sonata form. But the Finale is in a formal pattern all its own. Themes from the previous movements are introduced in a long tumultuous introduction followed by a baritone recitative, based on a theme presented earlier by the basses and cellos. The soloist rejects the themes from the previous movements by singing, "O friends, not these tones, but let us rather sing more pleasant and joyful ones," followed by the theme of the "Ode to Joy," which had been presented earlier by the orchestra.

Beethoven's reverence for the music of J. S. Bach is seen in his preoccupation with contrapuntal devices in the music of his third period. The *Grosse Fuge* is one example of this, but it is seen also in his use of a double fugue in the Finale of the Ninth Symphony. Beethoven himself conducted the premiere performance of the Ninth in 1824. He had become so deaf by this time that at its conclusion he had to be turned around to be made aware of the audience's applause. As his crowning achievement in the symphonic form, the work stands as the supreme expression of his ethical beliefs, and reflects the romantic concept of music as an intensely personal means of self-expression.

Vocal Works

On a par with the Ninth Symphony among Beethoven's third-period works is the Mass in D, The *Missa Solemnis,* Op. 123. It was intended for the coronation of Archduke Rudolph in 1820 but was not completed until 1822, and was neither published nor performed in its entirety during the composer's life time. Like Bach's B Minor Mass, it is inappropriate for liturgical use, although it has been performed in the church service. Its orchestral scoring includes four horns and three trombones in addition to the organ, soloists, and chorus. The choral writing shows the influence of Handel, whom Beethoven particularly admired, but unlike Handel's oratorios, there are no separate solo numbers. Instead, it is like a vast choral symphony in five movements with the chorus and soloist alternating within each movement to preserve the five sections of the Ordinary of the Mass. Thematic linkage among the movements is heard in the use of a descending third motive which first appears in the first movement on the word *Christe.*

Although Beethoven's musical output centers in his instrumental music, there are a number of additional works which are worthy of mention. As mentioned earlier, the song cycle *An die ferne Geliebte* is notable as an early example of a form that was to have great importance to the Romantic period, and he wrote many other songs throughout his life for various occasions. The *Fantasia* in C minor, Op. 80, is scored for the unique combination of piano solo, orchestra, and chorus. He also wrote an earlier Mass in C Major, Op. 86 and a number of incidental cantatas and oratorios, the best known of which is the oratorio *The Mount of Olives.*

A unique place among Beethoven's vocal works must go to his only opera *Fidelio,* op. 72. Although it is a rescue opera of the type that was popular around the turn of the century, it rises above the conventions of the plot. In the course of several revisions of the work between 1805 and 1814, he composed four different overtures. The final one is known today as the *Fidelio Overture* while the first three are known as the *Leonore* overtures after a character in the plot for whom the opera was originally named. The third of the *Leonore* overtures is particularly popular today as a concert overture.

In 1802 Beethoven wrote a letter now known as the "Heiligenstadt Testament" which was intended to be read by his brothers after his death. In it he describes his growing deafness in moving terms, expressing an agony that is almost unbelievable when viewed alongside the joyful and exuberant Second Symphony which he was writing at the same time. Obviously the inner life of the artist and his day-to-day grapplings with the realities of his existence were on two completely different planes. But the deeply personal outpourings of his musical expression are apparent throughout his life. Written testimony to this is found on the first page of the original score of the *Missa Solemnis* where he wrote, "From the heart—May it go to the heart," expressing one of the most important traits of the Romantic artist—the desire for direct and uniquely personal self-expression.

That the Romantics claimed Beethoven as their own is readily understandable, for they believed that he had broken the restrictive bonds of the Classical styles—freed music from the tyranny of prescribed formal patterns. But they went too far in assuming that his music was completely free of restriction, for his sense of musical and formal logic was as precise and well-developed as that of Haydn. It is true that new methods of formal organization were necessary after Beethoven, but not simply because he had "broken form asunder." He brought Classical forms to the height of their development, proceeding along the same paths trod by Mozart and Haydn, but in works such as the first movement of the Op. 132 String Quartet he carries the Classical sonata pattern so far that it is exquisitely shattered in his hands. The fact that throughout his life he was inspired by the philosophies of a new era marks him as the first true Romantic in music; but there is boldness, magnificence, and depth of spirit in his art that is timeless, transcending his great historical importance and marking him as one of the two or three giants of all musical art.

Romanticism

In the course of this chapter a number of specific aspects of Beethoven's music were mentioned as precedents for important musical trends of the Romantic period. These included the expansion of sonata form and the symphonic pattern, the enlargement of the orchestra, freer use of the variation form, the beginning development of the song cycle and the character piece, harmonic innovations, and programmatic tendencies. These specifically musical phenomena will be seen developing throughout the music of the Romantic era, but the Romantic movement extended into all areas of nineteenth-century culture and can perhaps better be viewed in poetry and literature than in any of the other arts. Although it is difficult to relate the inherently nonverbal concepts of music to the literary arts, some aspects of Romantic thought as presented in nineteenth-century literature and poetry can, at least outwardly, be linked with musical trends of the time.

The Romantic attitude of "boundless yearning" is in reality nothing more than a symptom of a more essential trait of nineteenth-century thought, the response of the individual to his new role in society. Surface aspects of this are seen in the idealization of the past in the novels of Scott and Dumas; the exotic and erotic elements of Shelley, Keats, Coleridge, and Poe; the themes of social injustice that pervade the works of Hugo and Dickens; and the grappling with ethics and morals in the poetry of Blake. These reflect a general dissatisfaction with the world as it is—a yearning for an ineffable ideal or the desire to escape to the past or the distant. But these are also the exteriorizations of deep conflicts rising within the spirit of man, for there were elements of the new free society that made him very uncomfortable. In the past men had viewed themselves typically as being small but integral parts of a complex hierarchy—a highly organized society at the very top of which were the church, the state, and the aristocracy —not necessarily in that order. Musicians such as Bach and Haydn moved rather comfortably within prescribed limits in this society. Their greatness is not diminished by this, for their music not only fulfilled its immediate purpose but also spoke across the centuries in a more universal language.

But Beethoven, more than any other nineteenth-century figure, typified the new Romantic artist who stood not on one rung of a long and carefully built ladder but in a position accessible to all of society with the power to exert his influence where he willed. This presented conflicts to the artist, for he could no longer accept society's solutions to his problems, but felt inwardly obliged to come to grips with problems that earlier artists had accepted as unchangeable. This is vividly apparent in the impassioned musical outbursts in works such as Beethoven's Third, Fifth, and Ninth Symphonies. In all of these works we hear the conflict resulting from the dramatic working out of an inner problem—coming to grips with fate—the titanic struggle to resolve opposites. Conflict is one of the elements essential to the unique quality of Beethoven's music, and it was the compelling wish to express intense inward feelings that produced such contrast and diversity in nineteenth-century art.

The following passage is found in Blake's *Marriage of Heaven and Hell* (1793):

Without Contraries is no progression. Attraction and Repulsion, Reason and Energy, Love and Hate, are necessary to Human existence.

The implied philosophy in this passage deals with man's new view of himself as a unique individual capable of dealing with the problems and conflicts of human existence in his own way. Its essence is found in the idea of opposites, a concept man has contemplated in various ways throughout the ages. In music of the Romantic period, contraries or antitheses are not mutually exclusive like up and down, hot and cold, lightness and darkness. Instead, they complement each other like the positive and negative poles of an electric battery, with a constant state of flux from one pole to the other.

One of the manifestations of this romantic "polarity" is found in the relationship of the composer to his audience. The romantic composer tended to believe that he was, at least in part, writing for audiences of the future. This attitude seems at first glance to be incompatible with the fact that in the early nineteenth century a mass bourgeois audience was becoming a reality, an audience larger and less knowledgable than those of Bach, Haydn, and Mozart. The idea of immortality inherent in the concept of composing for the future had to be accommodated to the reality of a mass contemporary audience, and if composers were writing for the future, they themselves must be the audiences for whom "immortal" composers of the past had written. There are some interesting conflicts in these ideas, and along with them went the fact that the composer's new-found freedom, although it enabled him to be more idealistic toward his art, also made it necessary to him to bear the full responsibility of his survival as an artist.

An important side effect of the composer's new view of himself was the development of the science of musicology, and it was during the early nineteenth century that the music of J. S. Bach was rediscovered. Mendelssohn, Schumann, and Brahms, along with many other distinguished musicians, were members of the great *Bach Gesellschaft* which, around mid-century, undertook to publish his complete works, much of which had fallen into obscurity after his death. The universality of Bach's music, along with its expressive quality and its chromaticism, appealed greatly to nineteenth-century musicians, and he soon was viewed by many as the greatest composer of the past.

The diversity of Bach's music represented a parallel with the great contrast and diversity of Romantic music. This nineteenth-century diversity was the direct or indirect result of the composer's changed view of himself, and in listing a few composers of the era the greatest of contrasts can be seen: Carl Maria Von Weber, who is best known as an opera composer; Schubert, who failed in his operatic attempts but made great contributions to romantic lieder; Berlioz, the great orchestrator; Chopin, who wrote almost exclusively for solo piano; and Wagner, who strove for an impossible fusion of the arts. But with such varying and diverse achievements among nineteenth-century composers, what are their unifying stylistic traits? Why do we group them together and call them Romantic composers? What are their affinities?

One of the first and most important areas of common ground is their relationship to sound itself. If we examine practically any composition written prior to the nineteenth-century, we find that control of timbre is not a primary element of the craft of musical composition at that time. Obviously tone color exists whenever a tone is played, and no musician of any period could have been unaware of significant differences in timbre among the various instruments and voices. But even as late a composer as J. S. Bach did not bother to indicate the instrumentation of some of his most significant compositions, for example, *The Well Tempered Clavier, The Art of Fugue,* and sections of *The Musical Offering.* His music is certainly not abstract, yet the specific use of certain timbres for their expressive qualities was not yet an important facet of the art. Thus, even in the Baroque period when instrumental music was flourishing, idiomatic and expressive orchestration was a relatively new concept. The strings and continuo of the concerto grosso had a more or less standardized role to play and this was true even of the somewhat more colorful instrumentation of the classical orchestra. In the symphonies of Haydn and Mozart, the brass and timpani are traditionally linked together for rhythmic and harmonic punctuation in forte passages, the basses and cellos invariably play the same part, and the woodwinds have a standardized role in an orchestra that rarely varied in instrumentation from one composition to another.

But in the orchestra of the Romantic period things were beginning to change. New instruments were added and they began to be combined in new and different ways. Schubert and Von Weber were among the first to do this and, as a side effect, the first textbooks on orchestration began to appear. Berlioz' *Treatise on Instrumentation* and Rimsky-Korsakov's *Principles of Orchestration* are both still used today as standard orchestration textbooks. It is significant that books of this sort had not been written prior to the nineteenth century.

The artistic treatment of tone quality was important not only in the orchestra but in other media as well. Composers such as Chopin, Schumann, and Liszt, with the larger nineteenth-century piano at their disposal, produced such coloristic and dynamic effects in their piano music that the instrument began to rival the diversity of tone color and sonority available in the symphony orchestra. Thus, sheer sound, with its varying timbres and dynamics, became a very significant factor in the expressive qualities of Romantic music, a role that it had perhaps played in ancient music but not to a great extent in music since the Middle Ages.

There is a great "contrary" in this, for the expressive use of tone color is both old and new. New because it was revitalized and treated with great imagination and refinement by the Romantics, and old because it returned to early man's relationship to musical sound—to the mysterious and magical excitement of a single tone. One result of this preoccupation with timbre and sonority was that the symphony orchestra became considerably enlarged in the nineteenth century. This expansion had begun with the symphonies of Beethoven, was carried further by composers such as Berlioz and Wagner, and culminated in the prodigious orchestra of Richard Strauss. Berlioz, Strauss and other composers even included instructions in their scores regarding the number of instruments that should be present in each of the string sections in order to be sure that the sound of the strings balanced the increased sonority of the winds and percussion.

At the opposite extreme of the vast Romantic orchestra is the typically romantic interest in the miniature. Schumann, Chopin, Mendelssohn and the other composers wrote numerous short, often simple piano pieces, many of them less than a page in length, following the precedent set by Beethoven with his *Bagatelles* for piano. These "character pieces" were often published as collections, such as the Chopin *Preludes,* the Mendelssohn *Songs Without Words,* and the Schumann *Scenes of Childhood.* More significant among small-scale works was the development of romantic lieder and the song cycle which reached great heights of musical expression in the music of Schubert, Schumann, Brahms, and Wolf. One reason why miniature song-like structures became so important in the Romantic period is that the motivic development, organic unity, and economy of means characteristic of the Classical style was believed to have been carried to its ultimate development by Beethoven; and, aside from the fact that it was going out of fashion, few Romantic composers had the technical skill possessed by the giants of the Classical period. Thus, long flights of spontaneous, flowing, lyrical melody were preferred to tightly organized elaborations of motives; and even in symphonic forms the influence of folk song and lieder was very strong. Certain composers such as Schubert, Schumann, Mendelssohn, and Brahms managed in some of their large-scale works to combine Romantic lyricism with the technique of motivic structure, but more often long flights of expressive melody or extravagant display took the place of organic unity.

The late eighteenth century had seen the beginning development of a new kind of nationalistic spirit—a Romantic attachment to the homeland and its natural environment. It became common for the artist to express strong nationalistic feelings in his work. This was seen in the use of folk tunes or folk-like melodies, and in the use of programmatic devices to depict nationalistic subjects, particularly elements of the beautiful natural surroundings of the artist's homeland. A river, a landscape, or a tree became appropriate material for artistic interpretations, particularly when it was clearly a part of the artist's national heritage. The use of folk music or folk-like music reached its highest development in the Romantic period in the works of the Bohemian composer Antonin Dvorak, but nationalism is also seen in the music of Smetana, Grieg, Sibelius, and a group of late Romantic composers called "The Five." Nationalism found a natural means of expression in the symphonic tone poem, a free orchestral form developed by Berlioz and Liszt which culminated in the symphonic works of Richard Strauss.

The nationalistic and programmatic tendencies of romantic composers reflects a general nineteenth-century interest in areas outside of the artist's craft. This proceeded in the direction of erasing clear-cut boundaries between the arts, and as a side effect musicians and artists of all kinds became more verbally communicative in regard to their work. Wagner, Liszt, Schumann, Berlioz, and many others wrote profusely, not only on the arts and the position of music among them, but on other subjects as well. Dozens of esthetic philosophies were propounded and dissected and there were significant efforts to combine the arts. A popular attitude expressed by Walter Pater was that "music" was the art to which all others aspired" and even poetry took a second place to the subjective and emotional expression of Romantic music. Fusion of the arts found its ideal form in the art song, particularly in lieder, and usually neither the poetry nor the music suffered in this alliance. But other more pretentious attempts at fusion of the arts were less successful. Great as Wagner's music is, his music dramas, following the precepts of his *Gesamtkunstwerk* theories, excessively emphasized orchestral sonority with a proportionate loss to the arts of drama, poetry, dance, and scenic design.

Of equal importance with tone color and sonority in Romantic music are the harmonic innovations of the nineteenth century. New tonal relationships appeared, such as the increased use of the relationship of two triads with roots separated by a third or a tritone in place of the eighteenth-century fifth relationship. Most important of all was the use of dissonance and chromaticism to express great emotional intensity. Chopin, Liszt, and Wagner were among the most important composers who contributed to the vocabulary of dissonant harmony. Throughout the nineteenth century there can be seen a gradually decreasing emphasis on the traditional tonic-dominant concept, a process that led ultimately to the shifting triadic harmony of the impressionists and to the twelve-tone technique. Indeed, Wagner is considered by many theorists to be the progenitor of the twelve-tone system, for in some of his more extreme passages his chromaticism reached such a point that nearly all of the twelve tones of the chromatic scale are heard in close proximity.

Striking contrasts continued to be seen throughout the Romantic era—simple character pieces beside imposing symphonies and the intimate melodies of lieder beside the grandiloquent gestures of opera. But, as the true Romantic knows, the Romantic spirit is a universal state of mind, common to mankind in every era; and this may be why nineteenth-century music is so popular today. We are drawn to its human idealism, its boundless yearning, its great diversity, and its emphasis upon deeply personal self-expression.

13. The Early Romantic Period

Schubert—Schumann—Chopin—Mendelssohn—Berlioz—Liszt—Early Romantic Opera

Franz Schubert

The popular image of the Romantic composer as an unhappy and improvident garret artist is epitomized in the short life of Franz Schubert (1797–1828). He was born near Vienna and throughout his life was conscious of living in the shadow of Ludwig Van Beethoven. Like Beethoven, he has a strong link with the Classical tradition, particularly in his instrumental music. But unlike his great contemporary, Schubert was endowed with a melodic gift that was intensely Romantic in nature. This is seen most of all in his many lieder composed throughout his productive life, and is a saving feature of his instrumental music, much of which suffers from a developmental technique which tends to be long-winded and not as tightly-knit as that of the classical masters. In only a few of his instrumental works, such as the "Great" C Major Symphony, the Quintet in C Major (Op. 163), the piano trios (op. 99 and 100), and certain string quartets can he be said to have mastered the Classical forms. But this deficiency is more than compensated for by the magical melodic passages which are heard throughout his music—finely wrought moments of surpassing beauty. The nature of these melodies renders them generally unfit for motivic development—their meaning is found in their self-contained beauty rather than in their potential for elaboration. In his instrumental works, such melodies often occur as the theme of the second tonal group in a sonata form.

The melodic gift is perhaps the most important stylistic trait marking him as a true Romanticist, but another important feature is his harmonic style. In addition to using chromatic chords such as the Neapolitan sixth, in his longer works he makes use of striking key relationships—sudden shifts to distantly related keys, particularly between major keys separated by a major third. This device, which has been called the "third relation," was anticipated in the music of Beethoven, notably in the *Missa Solemnis* where it is an important aspect of the overall structure. A good example is found in the first movement of Schubert's B Flat Major piano trio, Op. 99. The movement is a sonata form with the tonic key for the first tonal group and dominant for the second tonal group, but in the course of the first tonal group he passes from B Flat major to D major and concludes the section just before the second tonal group with a cadence on the dominant triad of the key of D major. This in itself is a good example of the third relation, but even more striking is the manner of introducing the lyrical melody of the second tonal group. The shift is effected by means of the tone A, common to the A major triad with which the first tonal group had ended, and the F major triad which follows. The cello sustains the common A with some undulating repeated notes and then proceeds with a breathtaking melody in F major, a magically simple device which makes the new key sound incredibly fresh.

Another Romantic trait of Schubert is found in the extremes in size among his compositions. The "Great" C Major Symphony, and the C Major Quintet are works of epic proportions, demonstrating mastery of Classical forms in a Romantic language. But at the other extreme are numerous very short songs and piano pieces, many of which are assembled in cycles, but which nevertheless demonstrate the Romantic interest in the miniature. Another Romantic characteristic is found in his interest in instrumental tone color as seen, for example, in the use of the clarinets and horns in the "Unfinished" Symphony.

During the seventeen or so years of his productive life Schubert composed about a thousand compositions, including several unsuccessful operas and other stage works, nine symphonies, the famous "Trout" Quintet, op. 114, with a variation movement based on the song of the same title, the C Major Quintet, about fifteen string quartets, several of which make use of melodies from his songs, the Octet, op. 166, for winds and strings, inspired by the Beethoven Septet, numerous miscellaneous chamber works, several choral works, an impressive array of piano compositions, and over six hundred songs. Schubert's gift for short lyrical forms is most striking in his lieder, for here the musical poet is in his natural element. He wrote them quickly and spontaneously, as many as a dozen in a single day. Much of the poetry is of the first order, as is generally true of romantic lieder, and Schubert's talent for evoking poetic images by means of the piano as well as the voice is at times almost miraculous. Verses which have been set by Schubert somehow never again seem complete without his music. Some of his lieder are sophisticated art songs, while others have the simple appeal of folk song. The vast majority of them are strophic in form, occasionally with modifications from verse to verse. A few, however, are through-composed *(durchkomponiert)*, using new material for each verse of the text.

Hundreds of his songs, such as the very early *Gretchen am Spinnrad* (1814), *Erlkönig*, and *Der Doppelgänger*, were written as isolated single songs; but he also composed three great song cycles, *Die Schöne Müllerin*, (1823) *Winterreise* (1823) (both to the poetry of Wilhelm Müller), and *Schwanengesang* (1828), to verses of Heine. *Winterreise* was written during a period of poverty and illness, at a time when the mournful images of Müller's rather mediocre poetry must have appealed strongly to the composer. One of his most deeply expressive works, it was composed almost concurrently with the sunny and tender B Flat Major Trio, Op. 99.

It is in his instrumental music that we see Schubert's strong link with Haydn, Mozart, and Beethoven. So strong is this relationship, particularly with Beethoven, that Schubert is often called the last of the Viennese Classicists. This is particularly apparent in his symphonies, most of which possess all the basic traits of the Classical symphonic pattern even though there are many passages in which the key relationships, orchestration, and melodic style are distinctly Romantic in flavor. As a composer of string quartets, he is in the lineage that began with Haydn. Although he did not often achieve the idiomatic quartet texture found in the best quartets of Haydn, Mozart, and Beethoven, his "Death and the Maiden" Quartet (with a set of variations based on the song "Death and the Maiden" as the slow movement) and the A Minor Quartet, both composed in 1824, are among the great works for the medium.

Robert Schumann

Schumann (1810–56) was the first important successor to Schubert as a composer of lieder. As an author, poet, and music critic, he personifies the multifaceted character of the Romantic era. Perhaps because he was a man of letters as well as a musician, he had a natural affinity for the combining of words with music. He selected the poetry for his songs with unerring good taste from the works of Byron, Goethe, Heine, and other outstanding poets of the time. He did not become vitally interested in composing lieder until 1840, the year of his marriage to Clara Wieck, daughter of his former piano teacher, Friedrich Wieck. His two great song cycles *Frauen-Liebe und Leben* and *Dichter-*

liebe, both written in that year, are on a par with the best of Schubert's lieder. Schumann's lieder style differs from that of Schubert in his more prominent use of the piano. In Schubert's songs, although the piano is a skillful partner in the evocation of poetic images, it still seems to be playing the role of an accompanying instrument. But in Schumann's lieder, the instrument and voice are treated almost equally, and there are many extended sections for the piano alone. When it does function as an accompanying instrument, the piano lends great strength to the poetic images of the text by means of Schumann's truly romantic treatment of harmony and texture. The piano textures are akin to those of Chopin in their use of the damper pedal to sustain widely spread tones of a chord and in their frequent use of chromaticism.

 Frauen-Liebe und Leben typifies the Romantic song cycle at its best. Its text, from the poetry of Adelbert von Chamisso (1781–1838), depicts a woman's thoughts from when she first sees her lover through their courtship, marriage, and birth of a child; it closes with her meditations on the death of her beloved. The typically Romantic imagery of the poetry undoubtedly attracted the composer because of his state of mind during his courtship and marriage to Clara Wieck. The eight songs of the cycle show remarkable variety of mood and texture, ranging from the chorale-like effect of I, to the repeated chords against a triadic melody in II, the quasi-martial effect of III, the fluid inner-voice line of IV, the unison piano figure at the start of V, the recitative effect of VI, the arpeggiated piano figure in VII, and the tragic declamatory style of VIII. With all of this rich contrast, Schumann produced a highly unified work bound together with a number of cyclical devices, the most prominent of which is the return of the piano motive of the first song at the end of the final movement as an epilogue for the piano alone. Following the woman's bitter expression of emptiness and denial of the exterior world, this epilogue dramatically reinforces her silent withdrawal into the world of her memories as it recalls their first meeting at the beginning of the cycle.

 Schumann's song forms are freer than those of Schubert. He preferred through-composed forms, and when he used a strophic pattern, as in the opening song of *Frauen-Liebe und Leben,* he modified the strophic repetitions to fit the varying rhythms and moods of the stanzas. Although most romantic composers wrote lieder, the most important successor to Schumann in this medium is Brahms, followed by Hugo Wolf, who is known primarily for his songs.

 Schumann's earlier efforts at composition were almost entirely for piano solo. He studied piano as a child and made his first attempts to write music at an early age, but did not seriously turn to a musical career until nearly twenty. Then in his eagerness to become a fine concert pianist, he invented a mechanical practice gadget with which he permanently injured his right hand. With his pianistic aspirations thus ended, he eagerly turned his attention to composing. Prior to 1840 he composed almost exclusively for piano solo, and the foremost interpreter of the works of this time was Clara Wieck, who was later to become Clara Schumann. The works of this period include numerous short character pieces, many of them grouped in collections such as *Kinderscenen, Kreisleriana, Novelleten, Intermezzi,* and *Papillons.* Many features of the Romantic piano idiom are found in these works —rhythmic patterns and accents that conflict with the meter, abrupt and surprising shifts of harmony, chromatic chords, ninths and sevenths, etc., and widely spaced arpeggiations fused by means of the damper pedal. There is also a strong programmatic tendency apparent in his use of fanciful titles for his piano music, most of which were added after the music was composed. Only occasionally did he relate specific "programs" to his instrumental music in the form of stories or poems. One such instance is his orchestral music to Byron's *Manfred,* Op. 115.

In his other instrumental music, consisting primarily of symphonies, concertos, and chamber works, Schumann is often criticized for the inadequacy of his orchestration, his ineptness in idiomatic instrumental writing, and for a conception of form unsuited to large-scale instrumental works. Although there is some truth in these generalizations, there are nevertheless some outstanding works in his instrumental output, including the Piano Quintet (piano and string quartet), Op. 44, the Piano Quartet (violin, viola, cello, and piano), Op. 47 (both composed in 1842), the Cello Concerto, Op. 129, and the Piano Concerto, Op. 54. His three string quartets contain moments of great lyrical beauty in their slow movements, but in general sound as if they were conceived for the piano rather than for the unique medium of the string quartet. His best chamber works are those which include the piano, such as the two mentioned above, a reflection of the increased use of the piano as a chamber music instrument in the nineteenth century.

Schumann's essentially lyrical way of thinking inhibited his efforts in the symphony. In spite of his admiration of Bach and Beethoven, he could not quite manage to combine Romantic lyricism with Classical structural techniques—Schubert, Mendelssohn, and Brahms all outdid him at this. Nevertheless, in spite of their structural flaws, Schumann's four symphonies have maintained lasting places in the symphonic repertory. In particular, the First and Fourth Symphonies are attractive for their fresh Romantic lyricism.

In addition to some rather unsuccessful efforts in conducting and teaching, Schumann was one of the finest music critics of his time. Always genuinely interested in the work of other composers, it was he who first publicized the promising talents of the young Johannes Brahms. His penetrating and incisive criticism did much to raise the low musical standards of his time, and he was one of the founders of the famous *Neue Zeitschrift für Musik,* one of the earliest critical journals in the field of music. One of the few truly humane and likeable composers in music history, his last years were beset by physical and mental illness and his life ended tragically in a private asylum near Bonn.

Frederic Chopin

In 1839 Schumann wrote in a review in the *Neue Zeitschrift* that Frederic Chopin (1810–49) was "indeed the boldest and proudest poetic spirit of the time." He was reviewing the *Preludes,* Op. 28, the *Mazurkas,* Op. 33, and the *Waltzes,* Op. 34, all works for piano solo; and in the pianistic world, then as now, Chopin was incomparable. At the height of his career the Paris critics called him "the Ariel of the Piano," and musical encyclopedists and biographers since that time have described him in only the most superlative terms. His art is closely linked with the technique and mechanical development of his instrument, for by Chopin's time the piano had acquired the double escapement, the damper pedal, and the compass of the present-day piano. The damper pedal and the double escapement had been in use earlier, but the increased length of the keyboard, longer strings, and bigger sound boards were important to the dynamic range and coloristic requirements of Chopin's music.

Chopin capitalized on these structural developments of the piano in many ways, but perhaps the most striking is his left-hand accompaniment figures, most of which span a much larger range than can be played in one hand position, a trait that was made possible by the sustaining effect of the damper pedal. The damper pedal was also important to some of his harmonic innovations, for in many of his accompaniment passages one arpeggiated sonority shifts to another within a single figuration so that, because of the fusing effect of the damper pedal, a momentary overlapping of two sonorities occurs. This, combined with a marked tendency toward chromaticism, resulted in a unique harmonic idiom. His melodic style is marked by great rhythmic freedom, singing lyrical passages, chromaticism, and wide ranges. Frequent rapid melodic flourishes create an improvisatory feeling in which a seemingly unmeasured number of notes are set against a

strictly metered left-hand accompaniment figure. In his own performances of his music and in his piano teaching, Chopin advocated a
strict metrical approach to piano playing, in which the left-hand figurations would establish a firm rhythm against which the right-hand
melody might hold back or push forward slightly for expressive purposes. This use of rubato in the right hand led to frequent abuses in
later interpretations of his music, in spite of the fact that the composer
himself set the style for a reasoned metrical approach to expressive
performance.

Chopin was at his best in shorter forms, and in his hands the
Romantic character piece reached a pinnacle of perfection. In addition
to the *Preludes, Mazurkas,* and *Waltzes* the collections of these short
piano pieces include the *Nocturnes, Etudes, Polonaises,* and *Impromptus.* The *Polonaises, Mazurkas,* and *Waltzes* reflect the Polish influence in Chopin's music, for he was one of the earliest composers to
manifest Romantic nationalism in his music. Born in Poland of a
French father and Polish mother, his childhood was spent in Warsaw
in the households of the Polish nobility where his father was employed as a teacher of French. Undoubtedly the composer's recollec-
tions of the courtly Polish social events is reflected in many of his
dance pieces. These are not dances per se in Chopin's interpretations,
but rather artistic idealizations of certain characteristic dance rhythms
and forms of Poland. In spite of his great love for his birthland, the
Polish influence should not be overemphasized, for the strongest force
in his art comes from the music of German composers, particularly
those who combined German technique with Italian styles—notably
Mozart and J. S. Bach. Chopin revered the *Well Tempered Clavier,* was
said to play it every day, and undoubtedly modeled the key scheme of
his twenty-four preludes after it.

But the French can lay an equal claim to Chopin, for most of his
career was spent in the Parisian salon society where the intimate
melodic charm of his *Nocturnes* and *Impromptus,* and the introspective poetry of his highly refined and reserved performance style
opened many doors for him. Chopin's use of the title "Nocturne" came
from the *Nocturnes* of the popular Irish pianist, John Field. Chopin
also received some of the influence of Clementi's keyboard style from
Field, who had been a student of Clementi. Another influence, particularly on his melodic style, comes from the music of Vincenzo Bellini
(1801–35), an Italian opera composer whose romantic bel canto style is
of the first order.

Although Chopin's gifts are not shown to the best advantage in the
larger forms, his two piano concertos (E Minor, Op. 11 and F Minor,

Op. 21), in spite of their deficiencies of orchestration, are worthy of note for their brilliant piano writing. The four Ballades and the *Scherzos* are exceptional examples of his ability to compose more extended compositions, as are also his two piano sonatas (Op. 35 in B Flat Minor and Op. 58 in B Minor) and the Sonata, Op. 65, for cello and piano. Many of these longer works show a remarkable formal freedom, and demonstrate a unique potential for free extension of ideas which Chopin was not able to fully realize during his relatively short life.

Felix Mendelssohn

Unlike the Romantic composers discussed so far, the life and career of Mendelssohn (1809–47) were attended throughout by favorable circumstances. Grandson of the distinguished eighteenth-century philosopher, Moses Mendelssohn, the environment of his well-to-do and cultured family was well suited to intellectual and artistic pursuits. Hegel and Goethe were among the family associates during Mendelssohn's childhood, and his early efforts both as composer and performer received the critical attention and guidance of some of the most distinguished musicians of the time. With these advantages and his native musical talent, he became a thoroughly mature performer and composer at remarkably early age. When he was only seventeen a household orchestra performed his *Midsummer Night's Dream* Overture to an audience of enraptured guests. This auspicious beginning led to a distinguished career as a composer, but Mendelssohn did not quite accomplish as much as one might have expected of so gifted an individual. It has been said that the achievements of his earliest years of maturity were never surpassed in his later career. One reason for this is that he excelled in a number of different roles, and although he wrote an incredible quantity of music, much of his time was taken up with activities such as conducting, teaching, promoting performances of other composers, and concertizing on both the piano and the organ. Active in virtually all musical fields, he was unable to devote the unstinting effort necessary to transcend the limitations of his own fluency. To have achieved the passionate expressiveness of Berlioz, or the profoundly poetic lyricism of Schubert or Schumann would have been foreign to his glib, cosmopolitan, and highly polished musical personality.

Mendelssohn's orderly and conservative mind was linked strongly to the Classical tradition. He was an enthusiastic organizer of programs of the music of Bach, Mozart, and Beethoven, and in 1829 he presented the first nineteenth-century performance of the *St. Matthew Passion,* an event which marked the beginning of the Bach revival and led to the establishment of the Bach *Gesellschaft.* He strove to preserve the Classical ideals against the ravages of Romanticism, and in so doing, achieved technical mastery of all the Classical forms and media. But there are, nevertheless, distinctly Romantic traits in his music, particularly in his orchestration. His famous *Fingal's Cave Overture* (1830, also called the *Hebrides Overture*) evokes a typical nineteenth-century image of a subject in nature by means of an orchestral expression that is truly Romantic. The scoring is marked by the use of the French horn and the clarinet as melodic instruments, by subtle new blends of woodwind colors, by expansion of the role of the brass beyond simply giving rhythmic and dynamic support in tutti passages, and by using the strings in many new ways, particularly to create harmonic accompaniment textures by means of arpeggiated passages, repeated notes, etc. Although he did not expand the orchestra in the flamboyant manner of Berlioz, he built upon the Classical tradition to create new orchestral colors and textures. The *Fingal's Cave Overture* is one of the earliest examples of the programmatic concert overture, of which Beethoven's *Egmont* and *Coriolanus* overtures were precursors.

Although Mendelssohn composed a large number of lieder and choral works, the center and most distinguished portion of his output is his instrumental music, In addition to several programmatic concert overtures such as *Ruy Blas* and *Calm Sea and Prosperous Voyage,* he composed five symphonies of which the *Scotch* (No. 3), the *Italian* (No. 4), and the *Reformation* (No. 5) are the most famous. (These are in addition to twelve symphonies for strings written in his youth.) His chamber music shows a strong influence of Beethoven, particularly apparent in the six string quartets. Included among his various chamber works are two excellent piano trios, two sonatas for cello and piano, one for violin and piano, and a unique octet for two string quartets (Op. 20). A striking feature of his instrumental music is his magical ability to create moods of sparkling lightness, an effervescence particularly characteristic of his scherzos and passages in scherzando style. Good examples are found in the Scherzo of his String Quartet in E Minor, Op. 44, No. 4, in the incidental music to *A Midsummer Night's Dream,* and in the scherzos of his symphonies.

One of his finest orchestral works is the *Concerto for Violin and Orchestra* in E Minor, Op. 64. Although it is cast in the traditional three-movement pattern and has most of the traits of the Classical concerto, it also contains several Romantic innovations, such as the linkage of the first and second movements to eliminate the intermovement pause, a cadenza in the first movement completely written out by the composer, the use of orchestral trills in the first movement in place of trills in the solo instrument, and, at the outset, the elimination of the double exposition, with the soloist beginning immediately with the main theme.

Well known as a conductor, Mendelssohn was particularly popular in England, which he visited several times, often conducting works for chorus and orchestra. The British love of choral singing which made Handel's oratorios so successful also contributed to Mendelssohn's popularity, and his two oratorios, *Elijah* and *St. Paul* were performed frequently in England. Mendelssohn is one of the few romantic composers to produce distinguished choral works—he was equaled or surpassed in this medium only by Brahms and perhaps Bruckner. One reason for the paucity of great nineteenth-century choral works is that after the Enlightenment the few serious artistic efforts directed toward sacred music seemed not to be inspired by the deep religious feelings that motivated composers such as Bach and Palestrina. Mozart's *Requiem,* some of Schubert's Masses, Brahms' *German Requiem,* the unique unaccompanied choral works written for the Russian church by Dmitri Bortniansky (1751–1825), the anthems of Samuel Wesley (1810–76), and several of Bruckner's works stand out as exceptions. Berlioz' extravagant combinations of chorus and orchestra will be discussed later. Other efforts, such as those of Charles Gounod (1818–93), suffered from Romantic sentimentality and a musical style that could not begin to emulate the profoundly religious expressions of the great sacred works of the Baroque and Renaissance.

Mendelssohn's *Elijah* is perhaps the last great sacred oratorio in the tradition of Handel, but a new secular vocal form called the Romantic part song began to gain popularity. The typical Romantic part song is in four or more parts, often for men's voices, may be accompanied or unaccompanied, and is in a predominantly homophonic texture, with much of the spirit of the folk song. Many of the texts were on nationalistic or folk subjects, often by distinguished Romantic poets. The part song began in the late eighteenth century along with the rise of nationalistic feeling, and Schubert, Schumann, Mendelssohn, Brahms, and many other Romantic composers contributed to its literature. Largely neglected in this century, there is nevertheless some excellent music to be found in these secular vocal works, particularly among the part songs of Schubert and Brahms.

Perhaps the best known of all Mendelssohn's compositions are the many short character pieces for piano called *Songs Without Words.* Standard fare for all students of the piano, these attractively lyrical pieces represent his best melodic style. Mendelssohn's highly refined

sensibility preferred not to be strongly associated with the revolutionary trends of the Romantic period. He was sometimes pictorial, even
programmatic, but the conflict and struggle associated with Romantic
expression is missing from his music—or appears only in a highly
refined form, somewhat lacking in emotional impact. The true Romantic spirit is seen much more vividly in the flamboyant outbursts of an
earlier nineteenth-century composer of another nationality—the
Frenchman Hector Berlioz.

Hector Berlioz

Berlioz (1803–69) is perhaps the most enigmatic composer of his
time. His contemporaries as well as succeeding generations seemed to
view him in various ways. Some early Romantic musicians saw
him as a crude and incurable radical and his talents were only partially
recognized. To Wagner and others of the later nineteenth century he
must have seemed in some ways quite old-fashioned. But today he is
recognized as a truly great artist whose music embodies the spirit of
Romanticism while it speaks to the twentieth century in a way that
few composers of the past have done. At the same time—and here is
an instance of Romantic polarity—his music also evokes images of
antiquity, for there is something almost primitive in some of his melodic and harmonic passages.

The most striking feature of his music is the audacious brilliance
of its orchestration. First of all, he was uniquely talented in writing
idiomatically for the instruments in their most rewarding registers,
while making unprecedented demands on the players' technical skills.
But more importantly, he dared to combine the instruments to produce
sounds that had never before been heard from the orchestra. Instances
of this are heard throughout his music—the mixture of strings with
low flutes at the beginning of the "Love Scene" in the *Romeo and Juliet
Symphony,* the brilliant opening flourish of the *Roman Carnival Overture,* the double basses divisi in four-part pizzicato at the beginning of
the "March to the Gallows" and the chordal passage for four tympani
at the close of the "Scene in the Country," both from *Symphonie Fantastique,* and the colorful use of percussion in virtually all of his works.

Early nineteenth-century music was dominated by German and
Austrian composers, and Berlioz as a French musician, held a unique
place in the Romantic world, for his stature was unequaled by any
other French composer of his time. Apparently well aware of his
singular position, he wrote a great deal about himself and his music,
and about the music of his contemporaries. For the better part of thirty

years his living came primarily from his work as a music critic. He had little formal musical training as a child, for his father, a well-to-do physician, was determined that the boy should study medicine. In spite of his musical talent and interest, which was apparent at an early age, he was obliged to comply with his father's wishes, but when he went to the medical school in Paris in 1821 he found ample opportunity to satisfy his musical inclinations. Although he reluctantly completed a Bachelor of Science degree in medicine in 1824, he had already undertaken several ambitious projects as a composer, and finally in 1826 secured his father's permission to enter the Conservatoire, where he remained as a rather intractable student for a period of two years. His *Memoirs,* published the year after his death, reveal much about the man and his life, but are not completely reliable as autobiography.

The concept of the symphonic poem begins with Berlioz and culminates in the works of Strauss, although the term itself was invented by Liszt. Nearly everything that Berlioz wrote is in some way programmatic, bearing descriptive titles or supplied with a "program" to furnish the audience with a key to the extra-musical associations of the music. But his sheer musicality and sense of formal logic enabled him to infuse virtually all of his works with a musical meaning that transcends these programmatic elements. He devised a technique known as the *idée fixe,* a unifying melody that recurs with modifications throughout an extended work to pull many diverse ideas together and add formal logic. Often it carries symbolical or dramatic significance in the program of the work. In his best-known work, *Symphonie Fantastique,* composed in 1830, the idée fixe is the melody shown in figure 72. Representing the artist's beloved, it is heard in various forms in each of the five movements of the work.

Figure 72. Idée Fixe *from Berlioz'* Symphonie Fantastique.

The concept of the idée fixe led to similar unifying devices in the works of other programmatic composers such as Liszt and Richard Strauss, and to the development of Wagner's leitmotif principles.

Berlioz' expansion of the symphony orchestra has been mentioned earlier, but another outlet for his extravagant imagination is found in the combining of large forces of instruments and voices in new ways. This can be seen in the secular oratorio *Damnation of Faust* (which has been performed as an opera) and other works, but is most striking in his *Requiem,* a vast work which, in addition to soloists, chorus, and orchestra, uses four separate brass choirs and eight pairs of tympani deployed in the various corners of the performance hall. His fascination with these large combinations of vocal and instrumental forces and his literary bent inevitably led him to produce major works in the area of opera. Chief among these are *Beatrice and Benedict, Benvenuto Cellini,* and *The Trojans,* all of which deserve greater popularity in the operatic repertory. His *Roman Carnival Overture,* often performed on symphonic programs, is drawn from *Benvenuto Cellini,* where it functions as the overture to the second act.

Additional works in his instrumental output include a number of programmatic concert overtures such as *Rob Roy,* based on a story of Sir Walter Scott, and *The Corsair,* from Byron. Another work, also based on a theme of Byron, is the unique *Harold in Italy,* a kind of programmatic concerto for viola and orchestra, one of the first major works to use the instrument in extended solo passages. It was written for Paganini, but because of its lack of sufficient instrumental display, he never performed it. This work, indeed all of Berlioz' works, show him as the revolutionary who upset all previous notions of orchestral technique, exerting a profound influence upon such later composers as Richard Strauss and Rimsky-Korsakov. Because of the great influence of his Romantic innovations, and because he lived so far into the nineteenth century, he can be viewed as the culmination of French Romanticism; but there is also a strain of Classical purity in his spirit which begins to be seen only in such later works as *The Trojans* and *Beatrice and Benedict.* Everything that he wrote was essentially dramatic. Like Shakespeare, whom he admired above all writers, Berlioz truly believed that "All the world's a stage."

Franz Liszt

Berlioz' influence touched Franz Liszt (1811–86) more than any other early Romantic composer. Liszt composed in all instrumental and vocal media and was the most distinguished piano virtuoso of his time, but his most important contribution to music was the development of the symphonic poem. His technique of expressing extra-musical ideas through the medium of the symphony orchestra was essentially an extension of Berlioz' concept of the idée fixe. An important difference between the two is that Berlioz tended to use a well-rounded theme of substantial length as the primary thematic element in an extended composition, as in *Symphonie Fantastique,* while Liszt used a short motive which he transformed and modified according to the requirements of the program. This can be clearly seen in *Les Preludes,* the only one of his twelve symphonic poems that is standard in today's symphonic repertory.

Liszt was appointed music director of the Weimar court in 1848, and his fame and avowed support of "progressive music" soon established it as an important center for new music. Here he devoted himself almost exclusively to the symphonic poem and in 1856 composed *Les Preludes.* Programmatically it is loosely based upon *Meditations Poetiques* by Lamartine, a short poem which lends itself best to free interpretation rather than to detailed realism. The opening measures of the violin part (shown in fig. 73) present the three-note motive which formally binds the work together.

Figure 73. Liszt, Les Preludes, *Opening Measures.*

The single movement work is in six sections opening with an andante. Figure 74 shows the manner in which the basic motive is used in the course of the composition.

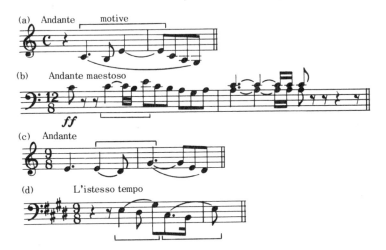

Figure 74. Use of the Basic Three Note Motive in Les Preludes.

Liszt's career began as a very successful child prodigy, and even in his youth he achieved international renown as a pianist. During his early years in Paris he came under the influence of such significant musical figures as Chopin, Berlioz, and Paganini. Chopin's influence can be seen in his imaginative piano textures and his harmonic experimentation. His interest in programmatic music was reinforced by his association with Berlioz, and he was inspired by Paganini to build a piano technique equal to that great violinist's command of his instrument.

As an internationally renowned virtuoso and composer, he lived a colorful life on a grand scale. His rather public love affairs, his sincere religious calling to a minor clerical order, and his various other adventures have been immortalized by his many biographers. Like Schumann, he was a friend of other composers, and as a conductor and teacher he did much to raise the musical standards of the time. Another contribution—one which it is difficult for us to fully appreciate in our era of recorded music—is found in the many piano transcriptions that he made of the music of Bach, Beethoven, and other great composers of the past, thus creating a wider audience for these composers, whose works in the larger media were not as well known as they are today.

Until the Weimar period he wrote a great deal for piano, and his remarkable piano virtuosity is clearly apparent in his many compositions for the instrument. The nationalistic element is apparent in his

Hungarian Rhapsodies, and his *Transcendental Etudes* and the two piano concertos have established lasting places in the concert repertory. Much of his music for piano solo seems to be straining toward the sonority of the symphony orchestra, and, paradoxically, his orchestral music seems to realize an imaginary ideal in piano sound. He had a natural gift for orchestration and this can be seen in the variety of textures that he achieved in his piano music. Chopin's influence is present, but there is also a luster and force that is uniquely Liszt's. The piano exerted a strong influence upon all compositions of the Romantic period, ranging from the microcosmic qualities of lieder and the character piece to the vast sonorities of the symphony orchestra.

Liszt's open and generous spirit proved itself in the support of many younger nineteenth-century composers including Dvorak, Grieg, Borodin, and Tschaikovsky. But the most important composer to come under his wing at Weimar was Wagner, who married Liszt's daugher Cosima, and who became the most influential figure of the late Romantic period.

Early Romantic Opera

In Paris, the operatic center of Europe during the early Romantic period, the influence of Gluck had remained alive in the operas of Mehul, Spontini, and Cherubini. As mentioned in chapter 10, their works led to the phenomenon known as "grand opera," of which the chief composer was Giacomo Meyerbeer (1791–1864). Grand opera, following the French operatic fashion, made as much use of grandiose spectacle as it did of musical effect. Eugene Scribe (1791–1861), the chief librettist for the school, wrote librettos designed to offer every opportunity for crowd scenes, ballets, and choruses. The style was established by two of Meyerbeer's best operas, *Robert le Diable* (1831) and *Les Huguenots* (1836). Although he was a skillful composer with a real gift for effective orchestration, Meyerbeer along with the librettists and other participants in the operatic enterprise, seemed willing to sacrifice dramatic and musical integrity for the sake of theatrical effect. Nevertheless he was not without influence upon later composers including Bellini, Wagner, and Verdi, particularly in regard to the handling of the operatic orchestra. Other composers of grand opera include D. F. E. Auber (1782–1871), Gioacchino Rossini (1792–1868), and Fromental Halevy (1799–1862). Halevy's *La Juive* ("The Jewess," 1835), and Rossini's *Guillaume Tell* (1829) are perhaps the best works in the genre of grand opera, a style which was marred most of all by its unabashed sensationalism.

The librettos of grand opera were based, for the most part, upon serious melodramatic or historical plots. On the lighter less pretentious side, however, was the French Opera Comique which, as in the eighteenth century, differed from serious opera in its use of spoken dialogue in place of recitative. Many of these were highly romantic and sentimental in plot, such as those of Ferdinand Herold (1791–1833) whose *Zampa* (1831) is fairly well known. Others were on the wittier and lighter side, such as Auber's *Fra Diavolo* (1830) and his many other light operas. Holding even greater popular appeal were the *Tales of Hoffman* and *Orpheus in the Underworld* of Jacques Offenbach (1819–80). Counterparts of these light operas in other countries included the operettas of Gilbert and Sullivan in England, and these of the younger Johann Strauss (composer of *Die Fledermaus*) in Vienna.

Of greater musical significance is an operatic style similar to opera comique which, because of its Romantic melodic style, has been called "lyric opera." On a larger scale than opera comique, but still not as pretentious as grand opera, it was generally based on a romantic drama or fantasy. Gounod's *Faust* (1859), based upon Part I of Goethe's great drama, is the finest example of this operatic style. Its original version utilized the spoken dialogue typical of opera comique, but Gounod later added recitatives. Its elegant lyricism, its dramatic unity, and its relative lack of Romantic excesses have made it one of the most popular operas of all time.

Perhaps equally famous is the opera *Carmen* by Georges Bizet (1838–75) which received its first performance in Paris in 1875. Its antimoral and rather sordid plot was unique for its time, and it set precedents for realism in opera which were significant to late nineteenth-century opera, particularly to the so-called *verismo* school. The work has a rhythmic vitality, a melodic beauty, and a spare but highly effective orchestration that is representative of the finest features of French Romanticism. Obviously, its tragic plot is not appropriate to the category of opera comique in spite of the fact that its original version contains spoken dialogue.

The operas of Berlioz were mentioned earlier, but it should be added that no French composer of his time equaled him as a composer of opera. *The Trojans,* a five-act work of prodigious length, has been called the romantic consummation of the French opera tradition of Rameau and Gluck. Superficially related to the grand operas of Meyerbeer, its dramatic and musical integrity, and its faithfulness to the intentions of Vergil's *Aeneid* mark it as one of the greatest of music dramas.

Italy was touched less by the spirit of Romanticism than either

France or Germany and, consequently, the development of its opera proceeded along rather orderly lines, with the traditional separation of opera seria and opera buffa continuing well into the nineteenth century. Opera was the chief musical medium for Italian composers of this time, and Rossini, Gaetano Donizetti (1791–1848), and Bellini were the chief composers before Verdi. Rossini was a master of opera buffa and his works in this medium such as *La Scala di seta* ("The Silken Ladder"), *La Gazza Ladra* ("The Thieving Magpie"), and *L'Italiana in Algeri* ("The Italian Woman in Algiers") are still fresh and effective today. His most famous opera buffa, *Il Barbiere di Siviglia* (1816), ranks with the best examples of Italian comic opera. Rossini's style is marked by typical Italian traits of lucid textures, bright effective rhythms, clear phrase structures, and a spontaneous and flowing melodic gift. His orchestration, while not daring, is remarkable for its assurance and clarity. A favorite device characteristic of many of the overtures to his operas is the long orchestral crescendo, accumulating instruments in an unflagging rhythm to arrive at an effective climax. His overtures, frequently heard on present-day symphonic programs, have become even more popular than the operas for which they were written.

Although Donizetti was one of the most prolific of the nineteenth-century Italian opera composers, he is remembered today for only a few works, chiefly *Lucia di Lammermoor* (1835), *L'elisir d'amore* (1832), and *Don Pasquale* (1843). The last two fall into the category of opera buffa, and *Don Pasquale* ranks with the best of Rossini's buffa operas. Not a remarkably inventive composer, much of his work is lacking in musical interest. Bellini is a composer of greater stature, and of his ten operas, *La Sonnambula* (1831), *Norma* (1831), and *I Puritani* (1835) have maintained lasting places in the repertory. His melodic style is marked by a deeply poetic elegance that is truly Romantic in spirit. Bellini's works were heard frequently in Paris and his melodic style influenced Chopin, particularly in the *Nocturnes.*

Germany, as the country where Romanticism flourished most intensely, found a natural outlet in the composite form of the opera. Singspiel was the chief progenitor of German Romantic opera, and Mozart's *Magic Flute* stands as the first work to overcome the pervading influence of French and Italian music in German operatic centers. The chief composer of Romantic opera in Germany before Wagner was Carl Maria von Weber (1786–1826). His teachers were Michael Haydn and Abt (Abbot) Vogler (1749–1814), the organ builder, composer, teacher, and theorist who is immortalized in one of Browning's poems. Weber's three major operas are *Der Freischütz* (1816), *Euryanthe* (1823), and *Oberon* (1826). *Freischütz* must be viewed as the first major

Romantic German opera, although there were two others also performed in 1816, E. T. A. Hoffman's *Undine* and Ludwig Spohr's *Faust.* A number of features of *Freishütz* represent important traits of German Romantic opera, including (1) plots drawn from legend or medieval history, (2) supernatural elements entwining with the fate of the characters, (3) scenes emphasizing the wildness and mystery of nature, and (4) folk elements as in Singspiel, frequently in the form of village or country scenes. In addition there is a strong quasi-religious moral tone often represented symbolically by the characters and events of the plot.

Musically these traits are realized through (1) the use of German folk tunes or folk-like melodies as in Singspiel, (2) an orchestral style which utilizes the darker colors of winds such as the clarinet and the French horn in various combinations and which uses the strings to weave evocative accompaniment textures by means of arpeggiation, tremolo, repeated notes, etc., and (3) a greater emphasis on counterpoint and harmony for expressive purposes than was found in either French or Italian opera of the time. Another feature of German opera which had been present as early as the *Magic Flute* is the use of recurring themes of motives for their symbolical significance in the drama, a feature which is found in *Freischütz* and which culminated in the leitmotif techniques of Wagner. Another feature of *Freischütz* which became an important aspect of Wagner's philosophies of music drama is that the overture is more than simply an aggregation of tunes from the opera arranged to precede the rising of the curtain; it is a thoroughly worked out symphonic composition in sonata form designed as an intrinsic part of the overall drama. Weber established a number of precedents for German opera in general and Wagner in particular, but he is also remembered for his music itself. His melodic gift, his sense of orchestral color, and his fine dramatic sensibility mark him as one of the outstanding composers in the history of opera.

14. The Late Romantic Period

Wagner and Verdi—Brahms—Russian Music—
Other Nationalists—Opera After Wagner—
The French Scene

Wagner and Verdi

The operas of Giuseppe Verdi (1813–1901) and the music dramas of Richard Wagner (1813–83) together represent the culmination of musical theatre in the Romantic period. One of the few similarities between the two is that each devoted himself almost exclusively to composing for the operatic stage. In virtually every other way they are at opposite extremes, yet their works complement each other in such a way as to illustrate nearly all of the many diverse aspects of nineteenth-century opera.

Verdi's operas embody the bel canto heritage and an emphasis on stage action—the essence of the Italian tradition of singer's opera. In Wagner's music dramas, on the other hand, the singer is often nearly eclipsed by the orchestra, for the dramatic continuity exists most of all in the action and interaction of his instrumental leitmotifs, woven into complex and highly expressive orchestral textures. Verdi often set lucid vocal solos against simple orchestral accompaniments, achieving the finest in musical simplicity, while Wagner's polyphonic musical fabrics represent the opposite extreme of well-organized musical complexity. Wagner usually portrayed allegorical, legendary, or even superhuman characters, while Verdi's characterizations, though often melodramatic, are realistic and human. Wagner's harmonic expression capitalized on chromaticism and dissonance, while Verdi was harmonically more conservative. The operas and music dramas of these two masters together represent the finest operatic achievements of the Romantic era.

Wagner, although not universally recognized as the greatest composer of the nineteenth century, is viewed today as the most influential nineteenth-century musician, the one whose ideas most influenced the musical thought of the twentieth century. His entire career was marked by an intense determination not only to succeed as a composer of opera, but to dominate the musical world of his time. In spite of limited formal training in music, he realized these aspirations to a remarkable degree. A man of tremendous ego—a self-styled superman —he believed himself to be the supreme composer of the nineteenth century as well as a significant poet and philosopher. Although the value of his achievements outside of music is open to question, his gifts were universal in nature, and his ability to teach himself whatever he needed was certainly not limited to music.

Within him was a strong urge for innovation, and early in his career he began to work toward a new kind of musical drama that would combine all of the arts into a magnificent and deeply significant entity which was to be called a *Gesamtkunstwerk* (universal art work). The principle points of the theories upon which he based the *Gesamtkunstwerk* concept were (1) that poetry should be restored to its rightful place as the primary stimulus of the music; (2) that, as Beethoven had demonstrated, instrumental music was capable of evoking strong emotions, and thus the orchestra should not be used simply as accompaniment but also for dramatic expression to reinforce word associations and express what words cannot; (3) that historical, allegorical, or legendary material was the proper subject for music drama rather than the melodramatic and realistic plots then in vogue; (4) that "feeling" was more important than "understanding"—to this end he developed new poetic devices; and (5) that the many operatic cliches, such as the stereotyped ensemble, the "set piece" aria, and the conventional overture, did not properly serve the dramatic purpose of opera and should be eliminated. To achieve this, continuity was essential, with no break between arias and recitatives as are found between the "numbers" of most earlier opera. Wagner's continuous unbroken orchestral texture has come to be known as his "endless melody." To merge recitative and aria, he developed a type of vocal line called *Sprechgesang* (speech-song) in which the voice half declaims, half sings the text in a manner that led toward the elimination of periodic phrase structure.

Wagner carried out these theories quite consistently in his cycle of four music dramas entitled *Der Ring des Nibelungen* (1. *Das Rheingold*, 2. *Die Walküre*, 3. *Siegfried*, 4. *Gotterdämmerung*). Characters, emotions, recurrent ideas, typical situations, and even a few stage props were depicted musically by means of leitmotifs, which are melodic fragments woven into a continuous symphonic texture recurring constantly throughout the drama in varying forms appropriate to the action. The progress of the drama can actually be followed through the interaction of these predominantly instrumental leitmotifs, so that the singers on the stage become merely the exteriorization of the real drama taking place in the orchestra. This association of words to music is reinforced by Wagner's orchestration, for his imaginatively expressive use of the instruments is a powerful force in evoking the moods and emotions represented on the stage. So important did the orchestra become in Wagner's music dramas that, in spite of his professed belief in an ideal fusion of all of the arts, music predominated. The *Gesamtkunstwerk* concept, logical as it may have seemed, might have had a limiting effect were it not for Wagner's melodic gift, his mastery of orchestration, and his harmonic daring.

Wagner's harmonic style wielded a strong influence upon the twentieth century. Using the chromaticism of Chopin and Liszt as a point of departure, he developed a harmonic idiom based upon chromatic dissonance, seventh and ninth chords, a continuous fusion of one sonority into another, and, above all, upon a deliberately vague and ambiguous tonal center. The gradual dissolution of the tonal concept occurring throughout the nineteenth century reached a point of near demise in certain of his later works such *Tristan and Isolde,* a music drama based upon Arthurian legend. Figure 75 presents an excerpt from the opening of the prelude to this work, a famous passage which serves well to demonstrate his revolutionary style. This and other passages set the stage for the twelve-tone technique and other harmonic developments of the early twentieth century.

Figure 75. Opening of the Prelude to Tristan and Isolde, *Wagner.*

Wagner's music dramas profoundly affected the course of late nineteenth-and twentieth-century opera. His theories and their realization in his music dramas resulted in an increased awareness of opera as an art form of significant content rather than merely as entertainment. His abandonment of the set piece—the separate arias, recitatives, choruses, and ensembles—led not only toward a continuous musical texture with the orchestra as a connective force, but also toward a de-emphasis on phrase and period structure. Classical balance and symmetry were replaced by what might be called a musical "stream of consciousness." Among his most significant operas and music dramas are *Rienzi, The Flying Dutchman, Tannhäuser, Lohengrin,* the four operas of *The Ring, Tristan and Isolde, Parsifal,* and *Die Meistersinger von Nürnberg.*

Meistersinger is perhaps the greatest of his operas. Begun in 1845 and completed in 1867, it is based historically upon the sixteenth-century guilds of Mastersingers. As in all of Wagner's operas, the libretto was written by the composer himself. Wagner used several names of real Mastersingers and paraphrased some of their poetry in a libretto which presents the age-old issue of the clash between tradition and the innovative creative spirit of art. The Mastersingers guild symbolizes tradition, with the character Beckmesser satrically representing the misuse of tradition through blind adherence to rules. Beckmesser is a not too thinly veiled representation of the excellent Viennese music critic, Eduard Hanslick who had written adverse criticism of Wagner's work. The character of Hans Sachs along with the hero Walther may have symbolized Wagner's view of himself as the wise, mature artist who was also endowed with the power of unbridled and revolutionary creativity.

In spite of their great length, each of Wagner's operas possesses a discernible overall musical shape—powerful dramas in symphonic form. Several of them are in arch form like a vast ABA, while others, including *Meistersinger,* are cast in a gigantic bar form (AAB). Bar form was particularly appropriate for *Meistersinger* because it was a song form used by the Mastersingers. Acts One and Two are the two *Stollen,* the action of Act Two being almost parallel to and a kind of parody of Act One, while Act Three is a gigantic *Abgesang,* with an additional unifying factor in the Finale which is an expanded and varied version of the Prelude. Wagner believed that the overture or prelude should be an intrinsic part of the drama, not simply an isolated instrumental piece preceding the opera. The beautiful Prelude to Act Three of Meistersinger exemplifies this philosophy, for it carries the inner action of the drama, particularly in relation to the noble character of Hans Sachs. *Meistersinger* was composed with a lighter touch than any of Wagner's other operas. It contains some folk-like melodies, perhaps suggested by the nationalistic subject matter, resulting in a simpler, less chromatic idiom, and it also has comic scenes, very rare in Wagner's works.

Inevitably a musician of Wagner's self-centered and dictatorial nature would succumb to the lure of the baton. Because of his keen perception of orchestral sound and the strength of his dominating personality, he was a highly successful conductor. As composer as well as conductor he made unprecedented demands upon the orchestra players' technical skill. To find an ideal environment for the production of his music dramas, he secured financial backing for the construction of a theater designed especially for him at Bayreuth, a center which still stages festival productions of his works.

Wagner wrote voluminously in prose, dabbling with varying degrees of significance in playwriting, philosophy, poetry, and even politics. During the Wagner cult which sprang up in the late nineteenth century his complete prose works were published in ten volumes and were subsequently translated into several languages. In addition, the literature about Wagner is unbelievably large. Among the many avid Wagnerites who wrote logically or illogically, pro or con, about Wagner and his art were such persons as Baudelaire, Galsworthy, Hardy, Mallarmé, Nietsche, Shaw, Swinburne, Valery, Whitman, and many others. His influence is still felt today, for he is one of the three or four most significant nineteenth-century figures in Western culture. In the world of artistic thought he has perhaps had as much impact as Darwin and Marx in their respective spheres. Only in recent years have we been able to view him subjectively. He embodies the synthesis of romantic mysticism, sensuality, spectacle, fantasy, idealism, individuality, nationalism—virtually all of the general traits associated with Romantic thought plus most of the specifically musical ones. Ruthless, tyrannical, egotistical, self indulgent—Wagner nevertheless takes his place in history not only for the indelible mark he left upon the stream of musical thought, but also for the value of his music dramas themselves.

Verdi was not the influential figure that Wagner was, but his operas equal and perhaps surpass those of Wagner for their great dramatic qualities and for their intrinsic musicality. It took a man of Verdi's stature to maintain the Italian tradition of "singer's opera" against the overpowering Wagnerian influence in the second half of the nineteenth century. That he was able to do so is partly because of his strong nationalistic feelings and his deep consciousness of the Italian operatic tradition. Not only was he reared in this musical tradition, he was also involved with the Italian nationalists who were working for a united Italian government in the mid-nineteenth century. His political commitments resulted in his election to the first Italian Parliament in 1860. His involvements with life, people, and his country mark him—in sharp contrast to Wagner—as one of the most humane of the many great figures in music history.

Verdi's orchestra always played a role subservient to the voices.

He treated the orchestra masterfully, was well in touch with new orchestral developments, and was quite willing to experiment for the sake of the right dramatic effect. Yet the singing characters on the stage were always the center of the action. He emphasized the separate colors of solo instruments and often used the brass section as a group. In general, his orchestration sounds clear and brilliant like that of Berlioz rather than thick and diffuse as in the scores of Wagner.

The characters of Verdi's operas were represented as living creatures, not as mythical or allegorical figures. His relatively short librettos contain no extraneous material and are filled with human passion and emotion. His masterful dramatic characterization is realized through his use of orchestral color, harmony, rhythm, strongly contrasting dynamics, but above all through his vocal lines. His melodies strikingly depict the dramatic characters as well as the particular mood or emotion of the moment. So individualized is each singer's melodic line that in ensemble scenes, such as the famous quartet from *Rigoletto,* each character's unique qualities stand out distinctly while contributing to the overall musical and dramatic effect. Verdi's attractive tunes are often combined with rhythmically clever orchestral accompaniments. Many of his melodies might be called "catchy," but they are also supremely expressive, especially in his later works where wide ranges and large leaps contribute much to their evocative qualities and characterization.

With the exception of *Falstaff,* all of Verdi's librettos are essentially serious, with intense dramatic contrast at a very fast pace. He wrote none of the Librettos himself, although he frequently worked with the librettist in the final polishing. The literary sources include Shakespeare, Hugo, Dumas, Byron, and Schiller, and emphasize violence, passion, and pathos in the typical melodramatic manner of the Romantic period. His best known librettist was the Italian poet and composer Arrigo Boito (1842–1918), who wrote the librettos of his last two operas, *Otello* and *Falstaff,* both based upon Shakespeare. Perhaps because of Boito's skill as an opera composer, both of these librettos are well suited to Verdi's gifts and contributed significantly to the success of the operas.

In contrast to Wagner's lush polyphonic textures, Verdi favored direct and relatively simple musical communication. Except in a few instances, he avoided the continuous texture adopted by Wagner, maintaining the separation of self-contained arias, recitatives, and ensembles. Each act is a separate unit built out of these set pieces and only rarely do themes recur from one act to another. Because of this his works do not have the symphonic breadth and the scope of development found in Wagner's best works, but this was done consciously, for

Verdi viewed opera as theatre, not as a symphonic form. There are no leitmotifs, *Gesamtkunstwerk* ideas, or theories about art apparent in his operas, and the orchestra functions simply to support the action on the stage. His overtures, when they exist, do not call attention to themselves but are designed to set the stage for the dramatic action. Verdi used a relatively large orchestra, and he used it well but he never allowed it to become the primarily element of the total work as in Wagnerian music drama.

Of Verdi's twenty-six operas, the best known of his early career are *La Traviata, Il Trovatore,* and *Rigoletto.* His middle-period works include *Don Carlos, Un Ballo in Maschera,* and *La Forza del Destino,* culminating in *Aida,* premiered in Cairo in 1871. His last two operas, *Otello* and *Falstaff,* both written in the decade following his seventieth year, are unquestionably the best. *Falstaff,* based on *Henry IV* and *The Merry Wives of Windsor,* is his only comic opera. Written by a composer of nearly eighty years, its wit and human warmth have made it one of the most popular works in the repertory. Among Verdi's few non-operatic works is his *Requiem,* written between *Aida* and the last two operas in memory of Italian patriot and writer, Alessandro Manzoni. Although it has many operatic elements and is in some ways indebted to the *Requiem* of Berlioz, it is a deeply moving work of true religious feeling.

Otello is unique among his operas for its continuous texture, suggesting that in his last years even Verdi may have been touched by the influence of Wagner. Nevertheless, the texture is quite unlike that of Wagner, for separation of numbers is often implied by the orchestra playing a few measures of an accompaniment figure prior to the entrance of the voice. To satisfy Verdi's demands for extremely fast pacing in *Otello,* Boito cut the original Shakespearean play from 3500 lines to fewer than 800. Obviously, what is left is not Shakespeare's *Othello* but a fast-paced drama with the same story, using many of Shakespeare's lines in almost literal poetic translation.

The value of Verdi's musical contribution lies not so much in his influence upon later composers as in the intrinsic beauty of his operas themselves. However, he was not without influence upon later opera, for the "verismo" movement, with its stark realism and sordid detail, owes much to Verdi's kind of realism. At the other extreme is Wagner, whose influence upon the twentieth century came not so much because of his operas and music dramas per se, as for his musical and esthetic philosophies and for his innovative approach to harmony and texture.

Johannes Brahms

In contrast to Wagner and to other innovators such as Liszt and

Berlioz, Johannes Brahms (1833–97) stands out as a unique figure in the late nineteenth century for his concentration upon the established instrumental forms and for his classical reserve. Because his music is almost entirely nonprogrammatic, it can be called abstract, but it is nevertheless warm and expressive in a purely musical way. Brahms' works represent the continuation of the Classical trend within Romanticism at the same time that they evoke the true Romantic spirit and reveal their composer as a man of intelligence, strength, and idealism.

The Classical elements in his music fall almost entirely in the area of form. Many of his sonatas, chamber works, and symphonies use the Classical four-movement pattern, usually with the first movement in sonata form. Scherzos, rondos, and variation forms abound in his instrumental works and there are even isolated examples of minuets. In his sonata forms it is apparent that he was operating on Classical principles, basing the form upon the conflict and interplay of contrasting ideas and upon the architectural relationship of tonal areas. His characteristic technique was marked by the development of short fragmentary ideas in the Classical manner, but his melodic style and harmonic idiom are distinctly Romantic.

He venerated not only the music of the recent past—Haydn, Mozart, and Beethoven—but also that of the Renaissance and Baroque. This can be seen in his use of techniques such as the passacaglia, fugue, and fugal devices. The ending of his *Variations on a Theme of Joseph Haydn* (Op. 56) and the Finale of the Fourth Symphony are both examples of the passacaglia, the first being particularly remarkable because it is based upon a five-bar passacaglia theme derived from the main theme of the set of variations. Fugues and fugatos are found throughout his works, often showing the strong influence of J. S. Bach. The Finale of the E Minor Cello Sonata (Op. 38), for example, is a fugue with a subject almost identical to the theme of the *rectus* of Contrapuncti XVI and XVII in the *Art of Fugue*, and Brahms treated it with some of the same devices Bach used. Also there is an occasional archaic quality in Brahms' melodies as well as in his harmonies that resulted from his use of modes, an indication of the influence of Renaissance vocal music. One of the most famous examples of this is the second movement of the Fourth Symphony which opens with a Phrygian melody played by woodwinds and horns.

His treatment of rhythm is one of the most important aspects of his style. Many of his phrase lengths create unsymmetrical patterns, and at times, the rhythm of the melody is at odds with the rhythm of the meter, creating interesting cross-rhythms or syncopations. Recurrences of a melody are often cast in a changed relationship to the bar line, adding new rhythmic interest to a theme heard earlier. His orchestration is in the Romantic style, but conservatively so. Many of his works contain a type of orchestration that can be called the "German nature sound," emphasizing the more darkly colored instruments of the orchestra such as horns, clarinets, violas, and cellos, as in Mendelssohn's *Hebrides Overture.* Although he wrote for a large symphony orchestra, he did not aspire to the flamboyant and highly colored world of sound explored by the programmatic composers of his time. Unlike composers such as Berlioz and Liszt, Brahms used orchestral color primarily to serve the other elements of the music.

The Romantic side of Brahms is found in its purest form in his many songs. He composed more than two hundred lieder, and in them the piano plays an even more important role than in the songs of Schumann. Brahms' songs, along with those of Hugo Wolf (1860–1903), constitute the most significant contribution to art song literature in the late Romantic period. The influence of folk song, seen in so many of Brahms' melodies, is particularly apparent in his lieder. Many of the lieder melodies are simple and triadic but profoundly beautiful, as in the *Sapphische Ode* and *Immer Leiser,* while others are rhythmically and harmonically more complex. The piano parts are always appropriate to the text, but rarely can they be called simply accompaniments, for the piano is always equal to if not more important than the voice in the expression of the moods and images of the poetry. He composed lieder throughout his life, culminating in the *Four Serious Songs* (1896, Op. 121) with biblical texts, also arranged for orchestra.

The use of folk-like melodies throughout Brahms' music shows the nationalistic side of his character, but his is not a narrow nationalism, for coupled with a certain elemental quality heard in much of his music, his works have a universal kind of attraction that appeals to all social and intellectual levels. Perhaps this is partly accounted for by his humble origins, for he was born into a family of very moderate means and as a boy was required to work as a tavern pianist. When he was twenty his talents were discovered by Schumann, who wrote in the *Neue Zeitschrift* of Brahms, the "young eagle," as the most significant young composer on the horizon. This was an important event to Brahms' early career and he became a fast friend of the Schumanns, and after Robert's death in 1856 he maintained a devotion to Clara that nearly led to their marriage.

Because of his high standards and painstaking self-criticism, Brahms' total output is not remarkably large; but it is notable for its overall excellence. He discarded many compositions and suppressed many of his early works, leaving a body of music that is predominantly instrumental, including four symphonies, two piano concertos, one violin concerto, the unique *Double Concerto* for violin and cello, two concert overtures (the *Academic Festival* and the *Tragic*), and a large and uniformly good body of chamber music. Indeed, it is safe to say that Brahms was the most successful chamber music composer of the late Romantic period. In a medium as abstract and characteristically nonprogrammatic as chamber music, it is necessary to rely on a purely musical means of expression of the type in which Haydn, Mozart, and Beethoven excelled. So great were the problems of accommodating Romantic concepts of melody and harmony to the Classical ideals of form and development that very few late nineteenth-century composers wrote fine chamber music. In fact, composers such as Berlioz, Liszt, and Wagner hardly attempted it. Brahms alone, with his painstakingly acquired technical craft, produced a body of chamber music in the best tradition of the Classical masters.

About two-thirds of Brahms' chamber works include the piano, while in the works of Haydn, Mozart, and Beethoven, chamber music with piano is definitely in the minority. This not only shows Brahms inclination toward the piano, but is also indicative of the Romantic attitude toward the instrument. The piano was without doubt the most popular solo instrument of the Romantic era, and it also became important in chamber music. Brahms' chamber works with piano include three piano trios, the Op. 114 trio for clarinet, cello, and piano, the Op. 40 trio for violin, horn and piano, three piano quartets (Op. 25, 26, and 60 for piano and strings), the Piano Quintet (Op. 34 for piano and string quartet) and the sonatas for a solo instrument plus piano (three for violin, two for cello, one for viola, and two for clarinet). Some of his finest piano writing is found in these works, although he also composed a number of fine works for piano alone including the *Fantasies* (Op. 116), the *Intermezzi* (Op. 117), three sonatas, and a number of variations. He was himself a fine pianist and wrote extremely well for the instrument, making startling demands upon the technical skill and endurance of the pianist. His piano writing does not have the luminous, poetic quality of Chopin, partly because he preferred thicker textures, and partly because he seemed to be striving toward orchestral sonority. There seems to be little or no difference between his solo piano style and the style of piano writing in his chamber works. Indeed, in many of his chamber music textures, the piano emerges as a virtuoso solo instrument.

His chamber works without piano include three string quartets (Op. 51, Nos. 1 and 2, and Op. 67) which are as popular as those of Haydn, Mozart, and Beethoven. His fondness for the clarinet is seen in the several chamber works mentioned earlier as well as in the Clarinet Quintet (Op. 115 for clarinet and string quartet). All were written for the distinguished clarinetist Mühlfeld of the Meiningen orchestra. The Brahms and Mozart clarinet quintets are the two greatest works for this rather unusual instrumental combination. In addition to the string quartets, Brahms' works for strings alone include two string quintets and two string sextets.

All of his orchestral works are frequently heard in today's concert programs. Of his four concertos, two are for piano and orchestra. The Second Piano Concerto, Op. 83 in B Flat Major, is particularly notable for its symphonic character and for its departure from classical concerto form. A work of great lyrical and structural beauty, it seems to transfer the Classical concerto concept to symphonic form. The Violin Concerto, Op. 77, evokes a feeling of classical reserve similar to that of the Beethoven Violin Concerto with which it also has in common the key of D Major. The Double Concerto, Op. 102, perhaps inspired by the Baroque concerto grosso, is particularly popular with today's audiences.

The four symphonies stand as the greatest works in this form after Beethoven. The First (Op. 68), composed over a period of twenty years, was completed in 1876. The Second (Op. 73) was finished a year later, and the other two followed within a decade. All of them follow the Classical four-movement pattern, and in many ways represent the continuation of Classical trends within the nineteenth century. Brahms was a devout admirer of Beethoven and strove for the same kind of dramatic intensity and conflict characteristic of Beethoven's nine symphonies, a trait that is particularly apparent in the development sections, which often are the central, dominating sections of the movements. Many of the movements are outwardly conservative in form, manifesting all of the tonal and structural characteristics essential to the forms of the Classical period, but the melodic style, particularly in the themes of second tonal groups of sonata forms, are characteristically romantic, with a self-contained singing beauty that is rare in Beethoven's music. The harmony and orchestration are also characteristic of the nineteenth century, though not in the innovative and extroverted manner of Wagner. A favorite device is the use of parallel sixths at the top of the orchestral texture to intensify the lyrical lines in the upper instruments.

The Classical principle of organic unity is extended in Brahms' symphonies to include all four movements. This is well illustrated by the Second Symphony in which a three-note motive presented at the outset by the cellos and basses is used in various forms throughout all the movements. This motive, found in the first three notes of the excerpt in figure 76, has been shown by some analysts to be the basis for nearly all of the thematic material in the entire symphony. In addition to its many occurrences in the first movement, it occurs in significant places throughout the other three movements. Several notable instances of this thematic relationship are shown in figure 77. A careful analysis will show many other examples. Cyclical devices such as this became very prevalent in symphonic works of the late nineteenth century, of which the most famous example is perhaps the D Minor Symphony of Cesar Franck which draws virtually all of its material from a three-note motive heard at the beginning.

Figure 76. Opening of Brahms' Second Symphony.

In championing the young Brahms, Schumann hoped to have a new exponent of the Germanic "Music of the Future" movement—the cause so strongly supported by Liszt at Weimar and Wagner at Bayreuth. But in this he was wrong, for Brahms drew much more upon the past than upon the new ideas of the late nineteenth century in establishing his unique means of musical expression. After a few unpleasant encounters with the Liszt-Wagner camp, Brahms quietly withdrew from all controversies and continued to produce masterworks that breathe the true spirit of Romanticism at the same time that they reflect his veneration of the art of earlier times.

Russian Music

The strongest movement in late nineteenth-century nationalism occurred in Russia, a country which had remained relatively untouched by European Romanticism until mid-century. By that time two significant Russian composers had emerged, Michael Glinka (1804–57) and Alexander Dargomijsky (1813–69). They are known today chiefly for their operas, particularly Glinka's *Russlan and Ludmilla* and Dargomijsky's *The Stone Guest,* both based on subjects of

Figure 77. Use of the Basic Three Note Motive in Brahms' Second Symphony.

Pushkin (1799–1837), the first great Russian poet. The unmistakable Russian qualities in these two operas mark the beginning of the Russian nationalist movement in music.

Late nineteenth-century Russian composers actively resisted all European influences, particularly that of Wagner, in order to establish and maintain a truly Russian musical tradition. Five of them, who were informally drawn together by common musical philosophies, began to be viewed as a group and were dubbed "The Five" by the Russian critic, Stassov. The group consisted of Mily Balakirev (1837–1910) who was viewed as mentor, Cesar Cui (1835–1918), Alexander Borodin (1833–87), Modeste Mussorgsky (1839–81), and Nicholas Rimsky-Korsakov (1844–1908). They used Russian history and legend as the basis for their operas, which was their most characteristic medium, and filled their music with a uniquely Russian flavor by using folk songs and dance music of their country. The works of Balakirev and Cui are rarely heard outside of Russia today, but some of the music of the others has gained great popularity with Western audiences. Borodin's Second String Quartet, his Second Symphony, and the *Polevitsian Dances* contain many melodies of great beauty. Mussorgsky's *Pictures at an Exhibition,* particularly in its orchestral version by Ravel, and the opera *Boris Goudonov* are established masterworks. Rimsky-Korsakov, who orchestrated many of the works of the other members of the group, including *Boris Goudonov,* is perhaps the greatest nineteenth-century master of orchestration. Although primarily an opera composer, he is best known outside of Russia for orchestral works such as *Capriccio Espagnole* and the ballet *Scheherezade.* His orchestration is marked by imaginative and idiomatic treatment of the instruments, highly varied and colorful textures in which each instrument is used to the best advantage, and by much use of percussion instruments of many kinds. He was the only teacher of Igor Stravinsky, and his orchestral influence can be seen in the early works of that great twentieth-century master.

Peter Ilyich Tchaikovksy (1840–93), though not a member of "The Five," shared their nationalistic attitude. His nationalism, however, seemed to be a natural and intrinsic part of his style rather than a trait which needed to be self-consciously applied. The general mood of his music as well as the frequent use of certain characteristic melodic inflections gives it its Russian flavor. But, unlike "The Five," he was quite willing to be influenced by European Romanticism. His orchestration shows the influence of Berlioz and Liszt, and from the standpoint of sheer musical craft, he owes much to Brahms. The last three of his six symphonies are mature masterpieces marked by a Romantic expression of the most impassioned sort. Their ravishing melodies, spectacular climaxes, and intense contrasts have made them extremely popular with today's audiences. He used an orchestra larger than that of Brahms to achieve unprecedented extremes in dynamics, resorting to markings ranging from *ppppp* to *fffff*.

Of equal popularity with the symphonies are his works for solo instrument and orchestra—the Violin Concerto, the First Piano Concerto in B Flat Minor, and the *Rococo Variations* for cello and orchestra. The European tradition is seen in the influence of Classical form in his music, but he also made use of colorful and violent orchestral outbursts that are typically Romantic as well as Russian. His vital and inventive rhythmic style shows the influence of Brahms, with frequent cross-rhythms and reiterated syncopations. His strong programmatic tendencies can be seen in the Overture-Fantasy *Romeo and Juliet,* the Symphony-Fantasy *Francesca da Rimini,* and *Caprice Italien,* all of which fall into the category of the orchestral tone poem. The tuneful ballets *Swan Lake, Sleeping Beauty,* and *The Nutcracker* are extremely popular, and two of his eight operas, *Eugene Onegin* and *Pique Dame,* are frequently performed. Much has been made of Tchaikovky's tormented life, his neuroses, and his sexual maladjustment, although it has not been proven that these factors exerted much influence upon his art. His large output of music had considerable influence on certain later composers, and stands by itself as the product of a highly gifted and imaginative composer.

Other Nationalists

The area of Bohemia, which in the nineteenth century included part of Austria and most of Czechoslavakia, had a strong nationalistic movement centering musically in the works of Bedrich Smetana (1824–86) and Antonin Dvorak (1841–1904). The folk heritage of Bohemia was large and diverse, with folk songs and dance tunes marked by unique rhythms derived from the language and a pervasive melancholy offset at times by extreme contrasts. Bohemian dances such as the *dumka* and the *furiant* contain a wealth of striking rhythmic ideas.

Smetana's music is not as widely known as that of Dvorak, although a few of his works, such as the overture to his opera *The Bartered Bride* and the *Moldau* from the programmatic symphony *Ma Vlast,* are extremely popular. His works are often performed in Czechoslavakia, where he is considered the father of the Bohemian musical tradition. Dvorak, although he composed many songs and choral works, is known most of all for his orchestral and chamber music and is recognized as a late Romantic instrumental composer of the first rank. Only the last five of his nine symphonies are included in the usual numbering, with the result that the famous *New World Symphony,* actually the ninth, is usually called the Fifth. The Fourth Symphony, actually the Eighth, is also very popular, along with the Violin Concerto and the Cello Concerto, both staples of the repertory. He also composed many string quartets, piano trios, and other chamber works. The Bohemian folk influence can be heard in much of his instrumental music, and the influence of Brahms is apparent in his efforts to fuse the Classical forms with Romantic expression.

In his early career Dvorak worked as a violist and violinist while trying to further himself as a composer. Gradually, after much effort and some help from Brahms, who recognized his talent, he gained international recognition. In 1892 he came to the United States to become director of the newly established National Conservatory in New York. Here he encouraged American composers to draw upon elements of their own national heritage, such as work songs and Negro spirituals, rather than submit to the strong influences of European music. He composed some of his best music in America, including the "American" Quartet, Op. 96, the Cello Concerto, which was dedicated to the American cellist-composer Victor Herbert, and the "New World" Symphony.

Dvorak encouraged the younger composers of Bohemia to utilize the rich folk music of their country, and in his own music fused nationalism with Classical structural principles. He was undoubtedly influential in stimulating significant research in folk music and folk-lore during the early twentieth century. Never really happy outside the boundaries of his beloved Bohemia, he returned in 1895 and in 1901 became director of the Prague Conservatory, a position he held for the remaining years of his life.

Another distinguished Czech nationalist composer of a later generation is Leo Janacek (1854–1928), who was active well into the twentieth century and who might be appropriately discussed in connection with modern music. He was an avid collector of East European folk music and based his mature style upon the rhythms and inflections of Moravian folk music which, in turn, draws some of its unique rhythmic qualities from the nature of the language itself. He was one of the first to consciously turn away from the strong influence of Western European music, particularly that of Germany. In his research in folk music and in his successful efforts to absorb its influence into his own style he set precedents for later twentieth-century composers such as Bartok and Kodaly. A revival in the popularity of his music has been seen in recent years, and his Violin Sonata and two string quartets are becoming better known, along with his *Glagolitic Mass* (1926) and orchestral pieces such as the symphonic rhapsody *Taras Bulba* and the *Sinfonietta* (1926). His greatest works were written near the end of his life and, although they evoke the romantic tradition, they also speak meaningfully in a twentieth-century language of tremendous drama and emotional power. Indeed, works such as the *Sinfonietta* and the Second String Quartet in some ways outshine the music of Bartok and Kodaly. Janacek's greatness has not yet been fully recognized, for he deserves to rank among the great composers of the nineteenth and twentieth centuries.

In Norway the nationalistic movement was embodied in the music of Edvard Grieg (1843–1907). Steeped in the influence of German Romanticism during his youth, he became vitally interested around 1863 in promoting a Scandinavian musical tradition. In 1867 he opened a Norwegian Academy of Music, and was engaged as a conductor in

Oslo (then Christiana). International fame came soon after the premiere in 1869 of his celebrated Piano Concerto in A Minor, which he played in Copenhagen. Like Dvorak, the nationalistic aspects of his music are found in the use of folk-like melodies rather than in the exact quotation of folk melodies of his country. His best-known works other than the piano concerto are the two orchestral suites arranged from the incidental music that he composed for a performance of Ibsen's *Peer Gynt* in 1874. Of his numerous songs, *Ich Liebe Dich* has enjoyed tremendous popularity, and his Sonata for Cello and Piano and his String Quartet in G Minor are also frequently performed. His music, although melodically charming, is marred by excessive symmetry of phrase structure and a sense of form that is deficient in pieces of extended duration.

English nationalism is represented by Edward Elgar (1857–1934), the first really distinguished English composer since Henry Purcell. Elgar's nationalism is manifest in an ineffable British quality rather than through the use of folk elements. His orchestral and harmonic style is similar to that of Dvorak. His interest in composing large works for chorus and orchestra is characteristically British. He wrote many oratorios, some on subjects drawn from Arthurian legend, of which the most famous is *The Dream of Gerontius.* Among his orchestral works the Cello Concerto and the *Enigma Variations* are the best known.

No discussion of Romantic nationalism could be complete without mention of the great Finnish composer Jan Sibelius (1865–1957). His is the greatest musical achievement in any of the countries north of Germany, and the reverence held for him in his native land may be greater than that of any other country for its favorite native composer. Like Elgar, his nationalism was achieved without the use of folk elements per se, yet his musical expression is so strongly linked with Finland that it seems to sing of the brooding lakes, deep forests, and rugged countryside of that somber country. A number of his early orchestral works are symphonic poems based on the Kalevala, the Finnish national epic. These works held tremendous appeal for the Finnish people during their struggle for independence from Czarist Russia during the last years of the nineteenth century. So popular did his music become during this time of strong nationalistic feeling that he was raised to the eminence of a national hero, and the Finnish government granted him a lifelong stipend to allow him to devote himself exclusively to composition.

Sibelius' overtly nationalistic works include the four Legends based on the Kalevala (*Lemminkainen and the Maidens, Lemminkainen in Tuonela, The Swan of Tuonela,* and *The Return of Lemmin-*

kainen), *En Saga,* and *Finlandia,* all composed prior to 1900. His greatest achievements, however, are the seven symphonies written from 1899 to 1924 and the Violin Concerto (1905). He also composed for smaller media, including works for voices, piano and strings, but his greatest strength lies in his orchestral music. His orchestration, often very lush, is unique for its frequent exploitation of the somber colors of the lower instruments and for the use of the instruments in families —the strings alone, double reeds as a choir, or the brasses in massed effect. His striking contrasts, jagged syncopated rhythms, and his pulsating accompaniment figures show the influence of Tchaikovsky. Like Tchaikovsky, Sibelius used a large orchestra, occasionally dividing the strings into eight or more parts, and often with added wind instruments. His string writing frequently makes use of repeated notes, tremolando, and arpeggios in thick harmonic textures.

But his greatest originality lies in his concept of musical structure. He often seems to be utilizing a process that is the reverse of the classical technique of motivic development. That is, instead of extracting motives from themes stated early in the composition and developing a structure out of these fragments in the Classical manner, he often begins with fragmentary ideas, and only after they start to accumulate and take on new interrelationships do they begin to form longer themes. Often a singing Romantic theme is heard at the climax of a work, the product of motives and fragments presented earlier. A tendency toward cyclical techniques and the erasing of divisions between movements is seen in many of his symphonies, culminating in the Seventh, which is a one-movement work with a unique arch structure.

Opera After Wagner

There were no late nineteenth-century German composers capable of equaling Wagner's operatic achievements. Nevertheless, virtually all were affected by his dominating influence, particularly in regard to continuousness of texture, orchestration, harmony, and the leitmotif technique. Perhaps most important of all was the influence of Wagner's attitude toward opera—his view of the medium as a serious drama of significant content. *Hansel and Gretel* by Engelbert Humperdinck (1854–1921) is perhaps the best known German opera of this period, and is an example of the fairy tale opera (*Märchenoper*) popular in late nineteenth-century Germany. The greatest German Romantic opera composer after Wagner is Richard Strauss, who will be discussed later.

The Italian opera composers of the post-Wagnerian period should be considered more as successors to Verdi than to Wagner, although

Wagner's influence was felt in the southern European countries as well as in Germany. Even before Verdi's death there arose in Italian opera a new interest in realism which came to be known as the verismo movement. Bizet's *Carmen,* with its unhappy ending, amoral plot, and unheroic characters, is an earlier French manifestation of this trend, while in Italy the composers Pietro Mascagni (1863–1945) and Ruggiero Leoncavallo (1858–1919) are the chief representatives of the movement. Mascagni's *Cavalleria Rusticana* (1890), with its realistic plot of life among peasants, is one of the most famous examples, even though its tuneful sentimentality is a bit at odds with the seriousness of the plot. Leoncavallo more successfully combined realism with musical theatre in his *I Pagliacci* (1892). Its famous Prologue, outlines the essence of the verismo movement—the presentation of life as it is. Based on a tragic story of a traveling troupe of clowns, *Pagliacci* contains an opera within an opera in the form of a unique *commedia dell'arte* presentation by the operatic clowns themselves.

The chief successor to the verismo movement is Giacomo Puccini (1858–1924), the great Italian opera composer who is chiefly responsible for carrying the tradition of singer's opera into the twentieth century. The popularity of such works as *Manon Lescaut* (1893), *La Boheme* (1896), *Tosca* (1900), and *Madame Butterfly* (1904) vividly testifies to the great success Puccini's operas achieved, not only during his lifetime but even to the present day. Their melodiousness owes much to the influence of Verdi, but his melodic style is nevertheless uniquely and appealingly his own. Characterized by long high tones at many climactic points, "sobbing" motives, and orchestral doubling of the voice line (often by the cellos), his arias are skillfully and effectively set in predominantly homophonic textures. Puccini frequently strove to evoke the mood of the dramatic setting by means of his harmonic idiom—pseudo-Oriental harmonies in *Madame Butterfly,* dramatically expressive dissonances, and the like. His later works include the *Girl of the Golden West* (1910), a trilogy of short operas completed in 1912 which includes *Gianni Schicchi,* and the unfinished *Turandot* (1924), completed after his death by Franco Alfano.

French opera after Gounod is represented chiefly by Bizet, mentioned earlier, and by Jules Massenet (1842–1912). Massenet's *Manon* (1884) is based on the libretto that was later used for Puccini's *Manon Lescaut.* Massenet's typically French talent for suave sentimental melody has made many of his tunes more popular than the operas from which they were extracted. *Thais Meditation,* for example, famous as an instrumental solo, is much better known than the opera *Thais* (1894) from which it was taken. Another French opera composer of this period is Gustave Charpentier (1860–1956) whose best-known opera is *Louise* (1900).

The French Scene

But there were musical achievements in late nineteenth-century France that were considerably more significant than the operas of Massenet and Charpentier. Cesar Franck (1822–90) and Camille Saint-Saens (1835–1921) are the chief representatives of a new current in French music based upon the use of the harmonic vocabulary and formal innovations of the late nineteenth century cast in the established instrumental media. Saint-Saens, an extremely facile composer, is remembered today chiefly for his three piano concertos, his orchestral suite *The Carnival of the Animals,* and his fine *Cello Concerto in A Minor.*

Franck's works contain much chromaticism in a unique harmonic idiom that may be a side-effect of his having been a proficient improviser on his favorite performing instrument, the organ. The technique of the instrument may have led Franck into certain characteristic kinds of "creepy-fingered" modulations in which the tonal shifts result from moving one finger after another to adjacent keys while sustaining the other notes of the chord. He also applied the cyclical principle quite systematically, most notably in his famous D Minor Symphony, his only work in this form, in which much of the material of all of the movements is derived from the three-note motive played by the basses and cellos at the beginning of the work. Both the motive itself (which is almost identical to that of *Les Preludes*) and the technique of its elaboration throughout the work owes much to the influence of Liszt. The center of Franck's output is in instrumental works such as his symphonic poems, chamber music, and organ works, but as a church composer of considerable religious zeal, he also composed sacred choral music and oratorios.

Franck's harmonic style can be viewed as a point of departure for another excellent French composer, Gabriel Fauré (1845–1924). Fauré's music, like that of his teacher, Camille Saint-Saens, embodies the aristocratic elegance of the French musical tradition and for this reason neither can properly be called a post-Romantic composer. Romantic excesses seem tasteless and foreign to the French spirit. But Fauré is nevertheless a significant figure in late nineteenth-century French music, for his harmonic style in some ways led to the unique harmonic idiom of Impressionism. His melodic style, appealing as it is, is at times almost opressively stepwise and modal, perhaps a result of the influence of plain chant to which, as a church musician, he was exposed throughout his life. The elements in his style which presage Impressionistic harmony include freely moving seventh chords, enharmonic modulations, and considerable chromaticism, though not in the emotionally charged style of Wagner. Poise and Classic balance are apparent in all of Fauré's music—quite at odds with late German Romanticism. His best-known work is the *Requiem,* but he also composed a quantity of chamber music and solo piano works. He was one of the founders of the National Society for French Music, and through his pupil Nadia Boulanger (1887–   ) his influence was felt significantly upon twentieth-century composers both in and outside of France.

Franck's outstanding student, Vincent D'Indy (1851–1931), is another important French composer of this period. Primarily an instrumental composer, his best-known work is his First Symphony, "*On a French Mountain Air*." This symphony is remarkable for a French work because of its use of a folk tune as the principal thematic material, and, like many of D'Indy's works, it shows the influence of Franck in the cyclical technique of using the basic theme in various transformations throughout the course of the work. Wagner's influence—strong in France during the last quarter of the nineteenth century—is seen in D'Indy's *Fervaal,* an opera which deserves to be better known.

The music of Franck, Sibelius, and certain other late nineteenth- and early twentieth-century composers, in France and elsewhere, bears some of the traits of the phenomenon we are calling post-Romanticism. But the real center of Post-Romanticism was in Germany and, for the most part, French composers resisted the Germanic influences of the end of the century.

15. The Aftermath of Romanticism

Post-Romanticism—Impressionism—Debussy—Ravel

Post-Romanticism

Post-Romanticism, a rather imprecise term, refers to the extravagant expansion of musical and emotional expression during the late nineteenth and early twentieth centuries, particularly among German composers. As Romantic expressiveness began to burst the seams of the symphony orchestra, it seemed that the Romantic era was dying of its own excesses, and new esthetic ideals were soon to come. The activities of post-Romantic composers extended well into the twentieth century and were paralleled by events that ushered in the new musical philosophies of the modern era. The first violent reaction to these Romantic excesses was the Impressionistic movement, which will be discussed later in this chapter.

The most important German post-Romanticists are Anton Bruckner (1824–96), Hugo Wolf (1860–1903), Gustav Mahler (1860–1911), and Richard Strauss (1864–1949). Bruckner barely fits the category chronologically, but is included here because of the great influence he had upon Mahler, because of the nature of his music, and because, like the others, he was so strongly influenced by Wagner. He was primarily a symphonist, and in his nine works in this form (the Ninth was left unfinished) can be heard the same conflict of Classic and Romantic elements heard in the symphonies of Brahms. But their Wagnerian harmonic idiom, their great and sometimes deadly length, and the vast orchestra for which they are scored mark them as products of the post-Wagnerian era.

There is in Bruckner's music a feeling of pervading sorrow, a chronic despondence that is characteristic of much of the art of the time. Similar moods can be seen in the novels of Emile Zola, as well as in the works of Proust and Thomas Mann. Suicide, illness, guilt, a neurotic desire to comprehend infinity, and a yearning for the past are characteristic literary subjects of this period. The *Weltschmerz* (world-pain) of the early Romantic period, so poignantly expressed in the works of artists such as Goethe and Schumann, was intensified at the end of the century, and the term *fin de siécle* began to be used to describe the characteristic late nineteenth-century attitude. Implicit in this expression is nostalgia for the past, a revulsion for the present, and a vision of eternity. Sometimes the post-Romantic composers expressed these things in very beautiful ways, but more often than not the musical result was one of excessive sentimentality or overblown emotion. Sometimes, when the ponderous length of a work seems to be striving vainly for a glimpse of eternity, the result for some listeners is sheer boredom.

The length of some of Bruckner's compositions is emphasized and aggravated at times by his penchant for extremely slow harmonic rhythm, a Wagnerian harmonic conception so static that a single sonority may be heard for minutes at a time. The variation principle is seen in his symphonies on a gigantically expanded scale, so much so that it has been said that the last six symphonies are simply grandiose variations of the first three. Bruckner's deep and unquestioning religious spirit is beautifully expressed on a symphonic scale in his Masses and the famous *Te Deum,* works which are among the finest examples of nineteenth-century choral music.

Among the most musically successful products of the post-Romantic era are the songs of Hugo Wolf. Their success may be partly accounted for by the limitations of the song cycle medium in which the excesses characteristic of symphonic music were not so easily effected, but, to Wolf's credit, his piano parts are seldom symphonic in character and his vocal lines are always beautifully singable. As mentioned earlier, Wolf is in the direct line of succession to the greatest song composers of the earlier Romantic period—Schubert, Schumann, and Brahms. Most of Wolf's 250 songs were composed in the decade of 1887 to 1897, and are based on the poetry of Eduard Mörike, Eichendorff, Goethe, and upon Spanish and Italian poems in German translation (the *Spanisches Liederbuch* and the *Italienisches Liederbuch*). The Wagnerian influence is present in his songs, particularly in regard to the harmonic idiom, but it is applied with discrimination; and by taking the best of Wagner's methods, Wolf emerges with intensely exquisite miniatures which are in their way more expressive than works such as *Tristan* or *Parsifal.* In songs such as *"Das verlassene Mägdlein"* and *"Verborgenheit,"* Wolf goes to the very limits of tonality, and in some instances steps just beyond, in a harmonic expression that presages twentieth-century developments. His respect for the poetry is unprecedented among song composers, and in the titles of the song collections he placed the name of the poet above that of the composer. This attitude is realized by musical imagery which evokes the moods of the poetry without sacrificing abstract musical beauty. Wolf composed in other media, including choral and symphonic works, opera *(Der Corregidor)*, and two string quartets of which the most famous, the *Italienische Serenade,* was arranged from an earlier piece for small orchestra.

Gustav Mahler was strongly influenced by Bruckner, but, because of his adventurous treatment of instrumental combinations, his great melodic gift, his technical skill, and his remarkable imagination, he stands out as one of the great musical figures of the Romantic era. He enjoyed a busy and successful career as a conductor and, for the most part, devoted only his summers to the task of musical composition. He was director of the Vienna Opera from 1897 to 1907, principal conductor of the New York Metropolitan opera from 1907–09, and conductor of the New York Philharmonic from 1909 to 1911. Undoubtedly his experience and skill as an orchestral conductor contributed to the effectiveness of his imaginative orchestration, but in spite of the fact that he devoted a large portion of his career to opera conducting, he made no attempts to compose in the operatic medium.

Mahler's achievements as a composer center in his nine symphonies (he left a tenth uncompleted), and his four song cycles for solo voices and orchestra of which *Das Lied von der Erde ("The Song of the Earth")* is the most famous. The symphonies are typical of the post-Romantic era in their length, the immensity of the required performing forces, their formal complexity, and their programmatic content. His orchestration was on a par with that of Berlioz, and because of his constant professional contact with a rehearsing orchestra, he had the opportunity to make an incredible number of revisions in the orchestration of his scores. Indeed, few of the present published versions, even of his earlier works, include all of his revisions and corrections, and new editions of most of his scores are badly needed. The vast size of the orchestra for which he wrote is demonstrated by an examination of any of his scores. The Second Symphony (1895), for example, is scored for four flutes (two of them alternating on piccolos), four oboes, five clarinets, three bassoons, contrabassoon, six horns, six trumpets, four trombones, tuba, six tympani, a vast array of percussion, an additional percussion section which plays with its own section of four horns and four trumpets as a separate brass and percussion group, four harps, organ, alto and soprano soloists, chorus, and a huge string section. Voices are used in four of his symphonies, and the Eighth, because it uses an incredibly large assemblage of singers and players, has been subtitled the *Symphony of a Thousand.* He also used unusual devices when his musical ideas called for them, such as the mandolin in the Eighth Symphony and in the *Song of the Earth,* and the solo violin tuned a whole step sharp in the Fourth Symphony to represent the medieval vielle in his musical representation of a dance of death. The originality and scope of his orchestration is equaled by his skill in writing for the instruments, for he was one of the most accomplished orchestraters in music history.

Throughout the nineteenth century many symphonic composers had departed to varying degrees from the classical four-movement symphonic pattern. These departures included cyclical devices, erasing of movement divisions, extension and expansion of the forms, tremendous increases in thematic and tonal contrast, and expansion of the performing forces. In Mahler these tendencies reached a point of no return. His works are often marked by an amazing number of contrasting themes, cyclical devices, Wagnerian harmony fused at times with folk-like melodies, expansion of form and harmonic language, and the vast performing forces discussed earlier. His symphonies rang down the curtain on a century and a half of symphonic activity. In a very real sense he is the transitional figure between Wagner and the modern Viennese school of Schoenberg, Berg, and Webern, for after Mahler attempts to expand the harmonic and formal possibilities of the traditional symphonic scheme were pointless, and the evolution of a new harmonic language and formal rationale was inevitable. But in spite of the post-Romantic qualities in his music, which can be described as excessive, his musical style, in his symphonies as well as his songs, is essentially lyrical. As heir to the German lieder tradition, his song cycles manifest the deep beauty of poetically inspired music while they also evoke the turmoil and at times the despair of the late nineteenth century. The *Songs of Wayfarer* (1883) and the *Kindertotenlieder* (1908) represent the culmination of Romantic lieder in symphonic form, while *The Song of the Earth* with its seven movements for alto and tenor soloists with orchestra is an evocation of the full range of human emotions as well as the composer's musical farewell to life. In this work, as well as in the Ninth and Tenth Symphonies can be seen something of Mahler's own reaction to the excesses of post-Romanticism—an increased austerity and apparent renouncement of some of the lushness of the late nineteenth century, and greater use of contrapuntal textures.

In the music of Richard Strauss can be heard all of the traits of the other German post-Romanticists, but because he lived so far into the twentieth century (he died after the Second World War), his later works also show some influence of the new musical developments of the early twentieth century. He represents the culmination of the programmatic trend in Romanticism and is in the direct line of succession to Berlioz, Liszt, and Mahler. But, like all of the German post-Romanticists, the strongest influence apparent in his music is that of Wagner. Because of his excellent musical training as a child, he composed competently at a remarkably early age in a style that showed the influence of Brahms as well as a mastery of the Classical forms. With his first tone poem, *Aus Italien* (1887), he turned his attention to programmatic music, and there followed a series of masterful tone poems which, along with his operas, gained him international recognition as the most famous German composer of the early twentieth century.

Like Mahler, he was also well known as a conductor, and this activity paralleled his career as a composer. With his professional conductor's knowledge of the orchestra, his orchestrational talents were on a par with those of Berlioz, Rimsky-Korsakov, and Mahler. But Strauss demanded more of the instrumental performers than any of these composers, and expanded the orchestral resources to an unprecedented degree. His soaring melodic lines and difficult passages involving wide leaps and rapid arpeggios are so demanding that orchestra players often find it necessary to practice his instrumental parts as they would a concerto; and these parts are frequently used as audition material in employing new personnel in professional orchestras.

Strauss' skill in musical depiction of extra-musical phenomenon in his tone poems is without parallel. From the first notes of *Til Eulenspiegel* one feels the spirit of mischief and exuberance appropriate to a story of the follies and pranks of a young scapegrace; in *Don Juan* there are several frankly sexual symbols clearly apparent in the music, especially if one's mind is attuned to the sexual overtones of the story; and in *Don Quixote* the literal sound of baaing sheep and clanking bells is cleverly imitated by the orchestra. Essentially Strauss' programmatic devices fall into two categories: (1) the literal depiction or imitation of extra-musical phenomena, and (2) the more abstract evocation of an emotion or mood—linked to the situation but not depicting it specifically. The first category includes examples such as the flutter-tongue passages in *Don Quixote*, which imitate the sound of the baaing sheep, and the sporadic rhythm of the repeated chords at the opening of *Death and Transfiguration*, which depict the last respirations of a dying man. Examples in the second category are more numerous and include the heroic unison horn melody in *Don Juan*, which begins with an ascending octave to portray the Don's impassioned feelings toward Donna Anna. (Probably this passage was also intended to depict the more specific image of tumescence.) Another example in the second category is the mood of philosophical contemplation established at the opening of *Also Sprach Zarathustra.*

An important criterion for excellence in programmatic music is the degree to which the composer achieves purely musical beauty at the same time that he effectively portrays the extra-musical element —the story, poem, or whatever. With few exceptions Strauss was equal to the task of being both musically meaningful and depictive. The Wagnerian influence is apparent in his use of leitmotif techniques, but his lucidly complex multivoiced textures achieve a kind of polyphony that is quite different from that of the Bayreuth master. His rhythms are highly diverse and he often capitalized upon extremes of dynamics. For the most part his harmony is based upon nineteenth-century practices with extreme chromaticism and daring dissonances, but occasionally the twentieth-century influence is apparent in a passage that might be classed as polytonal or modal.

From the standpoint of form, Strauss was highly adaptable to the requirements of each individual libretto or program, which accounts for the great diversity of both style and structure in his operas and tone poems. Because of this, each tone poem has its own unique form. *Ein Heldenleben* ("A Hero's Life," Op. 40), for example, can be viewed as a large sonata form, parts I, II, and III forming the exposition; part IV, the development; part V, the recapitulation; and part VI, the coda. This work is also remarkable in that the recapitulation presents a number of themes from his earlier compositions, representing the hero's deeds of peace. Completed in 1898, the work is scored for an orchestra appropriate for the autobiography of a romantic hero, including eight horns, five trumpets, two harps, four bassoons, two tubas, seven percussion instruments, a large string section, etc. A similar example of programmatic elements shaping the form is *Don Quixote,* which is cast in the shape of a vast theme and variations.

His most remarkable general feature is his ability to invent appropriate motives, themes, harmonies, and orchestral sounds for the purpose of characterizing the events, persons, and ideas of his operas and tone poems. In addition to those mentioned earlier, his tone poems include *Macbeth, Sinfonia Domestica,* and the *Alpine Symphony.* Of his fifteen operas, the best known are *Salome, Elektra, Der Rosenkavalier, Die Frau Ohne Schatten,* and *Ariadne auf Naxos.* He composed several concertos for various instruments, some relatively undistinguished chamber music, and a few piano pieces during his early career, but the center of his output is in his tone poems and operas. He also was an excellent lieder composer, although only a few of his songs are well known outside of Germany. The bulk of his work was completed by 1912, which is the year of *Ariadne auf Naxos,* but he was not idle in his remaining years, for he wrote a number of operas in the twenties and thirties, and in 1945 produced an instrumental work entitled *Metamorphoses* for twenty-three solo string instruments, an illustration of the neo-classical tendencies in his later works.

As an international musical figure, Strauss traveled widely. He nevertheless remained spiritually rooted to his native Germany, which may have accounted for his unfortunate involvement and sympathy with the Nazi party prior to and during World War II. After the war, most of his royalties accumulated outside of Germany were confiscated as war reparations, and, although he continued to compose until 1948, he spent his last years in straitened circumstances. Like Sibelius, who lived even further into the twentieth century, Strauss was unable to assimilate the new ideas of his younger contemporaries. Although he was known as a fiery rebel during the first part of his career, the twentieth century viewed him as a conservative in contrast to composers such as Stravinsky, Bartok, Hindemith, and Schoenberg.

There are a number of other post-Romantic German composers worthy of mention, such as Max Reger (1873–1916), who is best known as a composer of rather austere, thick-textured and intellectual instrumental works, and Hans Pfitzner (1869–1949), whose opera *Palestrina,* based on the legend of Palestrina's association with the Council of Trent, has achieved considerable recognition. Of greater significance to this period of music history is Alexander Scriabin (1872–1915), an unclassifiable Russian composer who began by writing short piano pieces in the style of Chopin, but who in his maturity produced a number of works of a unique mystical, almost Oriental expression, which were based on highly innovative harmonic schemes. Using the chromaticism of Liszt and Wagner as a point of departure, Scriabin, in orchestral tone poems such as the *Poem of Ecstasy* (1907) and *Prometheus* (1910), and in several of his ten piano sonatas, utilized a harmonic scheme that strove to break the bonds of tonality by means of sonorities based on vertical projections of intervals other than the third. One of these sonorities, upon which Prometheus is based, (shown in fig. 78) has been called the "mystic chord." Although it appears to be a projection of augmented, diminished, and perfect fourths, in actuality it can be analyzed as an inverted projection of thirds, not unlike an eleventh chord.

Another innovation associated with *Prometheus*—suggestive of the multimedia endeavors of the late twentieth century—is his use of

Figure 78. Scriabin's "Mystic Chord."

a projection screen upon which colors are supposed to be projected during the performance of the music. Although his ideas were bound up with the esthetic aims of the twentieth century, Scriabin's musical language seems to have been too personal and rarified to have had a significant impact upon modern times. Nevertheless, a number of his innovations presaged twentieth-century developments, and his antitonal tendencies and his unique brand of mysticism may have indirectly influenced later composers.

It was to be expected that the extravagant expansion of musical and emotional resources of the late nineteenth and early twentieth centuries would be met by a growing reaction in the opposite direction, particularly in France. It became increasingly obvious that the Romantic period was dying of its own excesses. Although the activities of the post-Romantic composers extended well into the twentieth century, a strong reaction to Romanticism occurred in the last two decades of the nineteenth century in the form of the French Impressionistic movement.

Impressionism

The term *impressionism* comes originally from the movement in painting led by Monet, Renoir, Manet, Degas, Sisley, Pissaro, and a number of other French artists active during the last twenty years of the nineteenth century. The most striking feature of these Impressionist painters is their use of light and color in striking new ways. In their efforts to capture the lights, shadows, and colors of the world around them, they found new techniques to replace the outworn academic formulas of nineteenth-century art. The shimmering textures and hazy outlines of some of their paintings seem to be related to the music of some of the French composers of the time, for musicians and painters were motivated by the same desires to be freed from the oppressive traditions of the Romantic century and to find a valid and newly relevant artistic expression.

The same was true of the poets, and as an artistic counterpart of musical impressionism, the Symbolist movement in poetry was even more important than painting. Mallarmé, Rimbaud, Verlaine, and other French poets were striving to endow poetry with music's ability to express general truths rather than conceptual actualities—to hint and suggest rather than to make outright statements—to express the unutterable. Words became symbols, and the sounds and rhythms of spoken French were used to evoke emotions that could not be concretely portrayed. In Mallarmé's own words, the purpose of Symbolism was "to evoke in a deliberate shadow an unmentioned object through allusion." Indeed, he believed that "to name the object is to sacrifice three-fourths of the pleasure in it." The Symbolist poets believed strongly in the kinship of poetry and music, and they were swayed by Wagner's writings on the fusion of the two arts.

In spite of Wagner's strong influence in Paris and of Debussy's admiration for his music, musical Impressionism began in Paris as a reaction against the excesses of German post-Romanticism. Debussy's attraction to Wagner's music was tempered by a hearty distaste for his Romantic excesses; and yet in many ways Impressionism is an extension of Romanticism. Among other things, the orchestra of the Impressionistic composers is similar in size, instrumentation, and complexity to that of the post-Romanticists, and a preoccupation with programmatic expression is common to both periods. The blurring of phrase structure is as common in the music-dramas of Wagner as it is in the works of Debussy, and there are many characteristic harmonies common to French Impressionism and German post-Romanticism. The similarities are there, yet the musical language of Impressionism differs sharply from that of post-Romanticism.

These differences in musical style rather interestingly parallel the differences between the French and German temperaments—German system and methodology against French nonchalance, emotionalism against subtle French sensibility, lofty German idealism against matter-of-fact realism, and ponderous rhetoric against evocative understatement. Most of these comparisons are easier to comprehend in actual sound than in terms of specific technical features. The structure, thematic organization, and development that was so important to the German Romanticists are handled quite casually in many Impressionistic works; and it is usually quite pointless to try to fit the works of Debussy and Ravel into conventional preconceived formal patterns. Impressionistic music is almost always programmatic in one sense or another, but leitmotif or idée fixe devices are seldom employed, and the programmatic element is often no more than an allusion rather than a full-fledged story as in much Romantic program music. Many Impressionistic melodies are short and improvisatory in character, in artificial scales or in modal style. ("Modal" is used here in the twentieth-century sense as, for example, a melody in the Dorian mode with triadic harmony, but without benefit of tonic and dominant implications.) The rhythms are often free or obscure to create a sense of mystery or a feeling of nonchalance, a feature that is linked with the deliberate blurring of phrase outlines and clearly related to the objectives of Symbolist poetry and Impressionistic painting. On the other hand, there are moments of clear pulsating rhythms in Impressionistic music, some of which are almost primitive in their regularity.

Orchestration is of great importance to the Impressionistic style. The Impressionistic orchestra is large, with a full complement in all of the sections and with many percussion instruments, but seldom is it called upon to produce an extremely large volume of sound. Rather, the instruments are heard in unique and subtle combinations to produce magical effects of color and texture. Divisi in the strings is frequent, and the colors are often washed with the sound of two harps. The woodwinds are frequently used in their low registers, the brass often play pianissimo or with mutes, and the exotic percussion sounds add many more colors that create unreal images of distant places.

But the harmonic element is perhaps the most important single feature of the Impressionistic style. Most of the harmonies used by Debussy and Ravel were found in earlier nineteenth-century music, but it is the manner in which they are used that creates the Impressionistic harmonic style. Most Impressionistic music is tonal to the extent that the pieces begin and end in the same key, with a continuing relationship to a tonal center. But this key relationship is no longer achieved primarily by means of the tonic-dominant phenomenon. The fifth relation had slowly lost ground during the nineteenth century and in Impressionistic music begins to be superseded by (1) "planing" or chords moving in parallel motion (fig. 79), (2) passages using the whole-tone scale, though seldom strictly, (3) "modal" progressions with major and minor triads, but without the tonic-dominant progression (fig. 80), and (4) chords or passages separated by the third or tritone.

The basic sonority continued to be the triad, but frequently with added dissonant tones. Often such dissonances were neither prepared nor resolved in the traditional manner, but were simply placed in the chord to furnish additional harmonic color. Also, the triadic projection of thirds frequently extended beyond the seventh chord to form ninth, eleventh, or thirteenth chords (fig. 81). Fusion of harmonies, perhaps related historically to Chopin's piano music, is also found as one arpeggio shifts to another to achieve a momentary blend of two chords.

Figure 79. Debussy, Sarabande.

Figure 80. Debussy, Passepied.

This may have led to twentieth-century polychordal practices in which lengthy passages are built by superimposing one series of harmonies upon another. The textures themselves were also unique, not only in the orchestration, but also in the manner in which wide spacings and arpeggiations were utilized. In these and many other ways the Impressionists led toward the harmonic developments of the twentieth century.

Outside of France a few composers were moving in the same directions. Chief among these is the Italian Ottorini Respighi (1879–1936), whose two descriptive orchestral pieces *The Pines of Rome* and *The Fountains of Rome* show many Impressionistic-traits, particularly in orchestration. The Americans Charles Griffes (1884–1920) and Charles Martin Loeffler (1861–1935), and the Englishman Frederick

Figure 81. Ravel, Valses Nobles et Sentimentales.

Delius (1862–1934) all showed the influence of Impressionistic music, particularly that of Debussy. But the real spirit and center of the movement is in France, and is embodied in the works of Debussy and Ravel.

Claude Debussy

Often called the Father of Musical Impressionism, Debussy (1862–1918) was French to the core. Nevertheless, his musical style is the result of many varied influences, some of which are not French. Something of Debussy's harmonic style is anticipated in the music of Moussorgsky and other Russian Romantics. Debussy had visited Russia in 1882, and it is probable that his unique harmonic language was influenced by his knowledge of Russian music acquired on that visit and later. He was also interested in Japanese music and other Far Eastern art, and shared Gauguin's and other French painters' fascination with the exotic subjects of the South Seas. The French poets of the time also influenced him, and he wrote a number of songs to their poetry. His piano textures show the influence of Chopin, and, inevitably, the mark of Wagner is upon him too. Wagner's influence is seen not in esthetic ideals, for Debussy's French sensibility could not stomach his excesses, but the two composers have much in common in technical matters such as the use of certain kinds of ninth chords, orchestration, and in the blurring of phrase structures to achieve continuous texture and vagueness of outlines. As a youth Debussy admired Wagner's music, but a visit to Bayreuth in 1889 turned him into a vehement anti-Wagnerian, and he soon joined the cause supported by Fauré, Erik Satie (1866–1925), and other French composers who were bound together by the firmly held belief that French music should be truly French—unadulterated by other national influences. There are indeed certain innate Gallic traits in the music of French composers of preceding centuries. Composers such as Jannequin, Lully, Couperin, Rameau, and Gounod have in common a purity of style and a typically French kind of effervescent Classicism in which beauty of sound and intrinsic musicality are more important than impassioned emotional expression. Debussy's inclinations and temperament led him in the same direction, as expressed by the title which he proudly affixed to his name in the publications of many of his later works: Claude Debussy, *Musicien francais.*

Born near Paris, he entered the Paris Conservatory at the age of eleven and soon showed his teachers and fellow students that he was not to be bound by arbitrary rules and conventions. Progressing rapidly as a composer and pianist, at the age of twenty-two he won the Prix de Rome, highest honor for a composer at the Conservatory, with his cantata, *L'Enfant prodigue* ("The Prodigal Son"). The prize, which is still offered in France and other countries, provided for a period of study and work in Rome, and during his sojourn there he composed *La Damoiselle elue* ("The Blessed Damozel"), a secular cantata based on the poem by Dante Gabriel Rossetti.

In 1894 after his return to Paris his career was well launched with the first of his mature orchestral works, a rhapsodic single-movement work based on a poem of Mallarmé entitled *L'Apres-midi d'un faune.* His other major orchestral works are *Nocturnes* (1899), *La Mer* (1905), and *Images* (1912), all of them three-movement works of which *La Mer* is the longest and most impressive. In spite of their fanciful titles, these works are not musical narratives in the manner of the Romantic tone poem, but are free and evocative impressions of extra-musical phenomena achieved by means of subtle and fantastic orchestral colors and a concept of melody and form that creates its own kind of musical logic without the use of traditional forms.

In his chamber works Debussy used preconceived formal patterns somewhat more than in his orchestral music. This is particularly true of his single string quartet composed in 1893, a uniquely beautiful and very popular work. In 1915 he began work on a projected set of six sonatas for various combinations of instruments, of which three were completed. These are the *Sonata for Cello and Piano* (1915), *The Sonata for Flute, Harp and Viola* (1915), and the *Sonata for Violin and Piano* (1917). Although the titles of these works are conventional, they are quite unlike the so-called "absolute" or abstract musical expression characteristic of Classical chamber music. In fact, with their moments of ironic pathos, subtle satire, and magical imagery, they sound almost programmatic. Technically they are marked by great economy of means, short melodic ideas woven together with a minimum of formal thematic development, fluctuating tempos, and unique treatment of the instruments.

Debussy's personal style of composition in his piano music is important to the development of the technique of the instrument, for the proper performance of these works requires a technique and performance approach quite different from that of the Classical and Romantic piano literature. His style is well suited to the instrument, but his filigreed textures, fusion of sonorities, abundant use of pedal, and wide spacing demand a piano technique equal to the task of suggesting the subtle and varied colors of his orchestral works. Many of the works have become staples of the modern piano repetory, including several suites, the *Etudes,* two volumes of *Preludes,* and several miscellaneous works.

Throughout the nineteenth century the art song had centered in Germany in the lieder of Schubert, Schumann, Brahms, and Wolf. Debussy added a new and typically French flavor to the art song repertory in some fifty songs composed to the texts of Symbolist poets such as Baudelaire, Mallarmé, and Verlaine. The exquisite inflections of the French language and the subtle imagery of the poetry resulted in a style far different from that of German lieder. Debussy's songs, with their rarified and perfumed atmospheres, may lack the earthy emotion and expressive immediacy of the songs of Schumann, but their lyrical French elegance contrasted with moments of voluptuousness or moods of abandon create an artistic effect of great beauty. Perhaps his most popular work in the art song medium is the short cycle *Chansons de Bilitis* to the decadent poetry of Pierre Louys.

Debussy's only opera, *Pelleas and Melisande,* based on the play of Maurice Maeterlinck, stands as a unique work in the history of opera. With its dream-like atmosphere and musical understatement, its characters take on a mystical, symbolic significance; and never does an operatic set-piece intrude to break the spell. The texture is almost entirely continuous and the voices sing in a free declamatory style, for the most part at a low dynamic level. The orchestra achieves tremendous suggestive power, even though the instrumental textures are spare and the colors of somber hue. The recurrence of a few motives in varying forms throughout the opera results in a loose unity and a form as free and intangible as the play itself.

Debussy manifests the Gallic temperament and an instinctive approach to composition. His music, with its pleasing esthetic surface, can be thoroughly enjoyed at a superficial level, but is also marked by an admirable working out of ideas and a variety of structural plans that raise it to a sophisticated artistic level. His innovations, many of them achieved instinctively, had considerable influence upon the twentieth century. In his own words, "Rules are established *by* works of art, not *for* works of art."

Maurice Ravel

Although their musical styles are distinctly different, Debussy and Ravel (1875–1937) also had much in common. Both came under the spell of the Symbolist poets and Impressionist painters, both were repelled by the excesses of German post-Romanticism, both were attracted to exotic elements such as Spanish rhythms, and both used descriptive titles, although neither could be called a programmatic composer in the late Romantic sense. Above all, both were musicians of intensely Gallic temperament and sensibility who believed that the primary purpose of art was to delight the senses.

Ravel's music added elements of clarity and order to the Impressionistic movement, and by no means did he work in Debussy's shadow. While Debussy often relied upon intuition in his composition, Ravel, a student of Fauré, was one of the surest craftsmen among all of the composers in music history. His precise workmanship is seen in his lucid handling of phrase structure, harmonic motion, counterpoint, dissonance, and orchestration. His compositional skill manifests the Classical spirit to such a degree that he is viewed as one of the most important composers in the early twentieth-century movement known as Neo-classicism. Unlike Debussy, Ravel preferred functional diatonic harmonies to vague nebulous sonorities such as those based upon the whole-tone scale. Ravel's harmonies are also inclined to be less chromatic than those of Debussy, for there are many extended passages in Ravel's music which contain no accidentals beyond those in the key signature. Typical impressionistic sonorities such as ninth, eleventh, and thirteenth chords are found in his music but more often occur as the result of carefully conceived contrapuntal motion, rather than as diffuse masses of sound as in Debussy's music.

In regard to orchestration, Ravel was more consciously aware of what would work in the orchestra than was Debussy. Although the two used many of the same orchestral devices, Ravel's scores are more immediately rewarding to the performers and, because of his careful attention to detail, are easier to prepare in rehearsal. Ravel's music is at times more orchestrally complex than Debussy's, but his timbres are more clearly etched, and his knowledge of the idiomatic capabilities of the instruments was on par with that of Rimsky-Korsakov or Strauss. A number of his orchestral works were originally conceived as piano pieces, such as the *Alborado del Grazioso* (1912), *Le Tombeau de Couperin* (1919), and his orchestral version of Moussorgsky's *Pictures at an Exhibition.*

Ravel's piano works were as important as Debussy's in expanding pianistic techniques; indeed, there is evidence to suggest that Debussy's piano music owes much to that of Ravel. Among Ravel's best-known piano works are *Jeux d'eau* ("Fountains," 1901), the *Sonatina* (1905), and several collections such as the *Valses nobles et sentimentales* (1911) and *Gaspard de la nuit* (1908). He also contributed much to the vocal repertory with works such as the song cycle for voice and orchestra *Scheherezade* (1903), the operas *L'Heure Espagnol* (1907) and *L'Enfant et les sortiléges* (1925), and a number of art songs which, like Debussy's create musical atmospheres far different from those of Romantic German song.

Ravel's Classical spirit is most apparent in his chamber music, which includes a string quartet (1903), a piano trio (1915), a sonata for violin and piano (1927), and one for violin and cello (1922). He also wrote several chamber works which combine a solo voice with instruments, such as *Trois Poémes de Mallarmé* (1913) and the *Songs of Madagascar* (1926), which are freer in form than the purely instrumental chamber works. His major orchestral works are *Rapsodie Espagnol* (1907), the choreographic poem *La Valse* (1920), which somewhat bitterly evokes the moods of early nineteenth-century Vienna, the ballet *Daphnis and Chloe* from which he drew the material for two orchestral suites, the famous *Bolero* (1928), and the two piano concertos (one for left hand only), both completed in 1931.

Debussy and Ravel together represent one of the most important periods in the history of French music. Ravel, partly because of his consummate mastery of the craft of musical composition, was in the forefront of early twentieth-century composers. In addition to giving impetus to the Neoclassical movement, which will be discussed later, his handling of instrumental colors established an ideal that has inspired many younger composers. The music of both composers significantly affected the course of music in our time, and helped to effect a transition from the nineteenth century to the twentieth.

VI. THE TWENTIETH CENTURY

16. Musical Thought in the Twentieth Century

In examining the music of our century, we are met by tremendous diversity of musical style, media, and technique. So striking is this vast array of trends, movements, and techniques, and so varied are its manifestations, that one is tempted to think of the twentieth century quite differently from earlier periods in music history. The Classical period forms a kind of conceptual entity in which there is a degree of homogeneity of style, and for this reason it is possible to make a number of valid generalizations regarding the stylistic features of the Classical period as a whole. But it is difficult to generalize about the music of our century, partly because of its great diversity and partly because time has not yet winnowed the chaff from the wheat to clearly delineate the major trends of our time. For this reason our discussion of twentieth-century music begins with an attempted overview of the salient stylistic traits of the music of our time.

Our century began with a realization by many composers that the harmonic system which crystallized in the Baroque period, and which had been the basis for nearly all Western music up to 1900, had been stretched to the breaking point. Its possibilities for meaningful expression appeared to be exhausted. By 1750 the diatonic-triadic system with its tonal architecture controlled by the tonal center had been brought to the pinnacle of its development—culminating in the music of J. S. Bach. The gradual demise of this system began almost immediately with Bach's sons, particularly Carl Phillipp Emanuel Bach and continued into the twentieth century with composers such as Strauss and Debussy. Essentially, this metamorphosis took place through a gradual expansion of the use of chromaticism. J. S. Bach had used much chromaticism, and the use of all twelve tones in fairly close succession can be found in the music of Renaissance composers such as Gesualdo or Marenzio. But the eighteenth-century system of tonal architecture with its reliance on a tonal center defined by the diatonic scale created the possibility—indeed the necessity—of a new kind of chromaticism based on modulations to subsidiary tonal centers other than the home tonality. Musical architecture gained by the dominance of the tonal system, but expression lost. The diatonic scale was to music what the rule of the unities was to classical tragedy—a sure means of organization, but a restrictive one.

In the nineteenth century the need for greater expression in harmony led to more frequent and more distant modulations. This had begun in eighteenth-century works such as C. P. E. Bach's *Abschied von meinem Silbermannischen Klaviere,* continued in works such as the Fantasia of the Haydn String Quartet Op. 76, No. 6, and numerous works of Schumann, Liszt, and Chopin—finally arriving at a point of no return in late nineteenth-century works such as *Tristan and Isolde.*

In Wagner's music, particularly in *Tristan,* endless modulation and abundant chromatic dissonance made it impossible for the musical form to be controlled by the tonal center. This paved the way for new harmonic developments in the twentieth century, particularly the twelve-tone system used by Schoenberg, Berg, and Webern. It also gave rise to the term *atonal,* a word that is loosely, and for the most part, incorrectly applied to a great deal of twentieth-century music. Schoenberg and his Viennese followers disliked the term, and with good reason, for strictly speaking, music without tonality is impossible unless the term *tonality* is restricted to mean diatonic tonality. In any group of different pitches, even if randomly selected, one tone will stand out as having greater importance; this is the tonal center or tonality for that set of pitches. Schoenberg believed that in so-called atonal music there might be many different tonalities within a single piece. Thus, the term tonality need not be restricted to the concept of all pitches in a composition being related to a single tone.

With the excessive chromaticism developing during the late Romantic period, the ears of audiences were being prepared for the leap to a number of different kinds of twentieth-century harmony. Western man had been receiving cumulative aural conditioning through the music of several centuries past, and sonorities presumably unique to twentieth-century harmony had been heard generations earlier in other contexts. For example, the chords of seconds, fourths, and sevenths found in the quartal harmony of composers such as Hindemith and Bartok were common in medieval music and occurred as calculated dissonances in Renaissance polyphony.

The expanding use of modulation and dissonance had, by the end of the nineteenth century, made the ear receptive to virtually any combination of pitches, no matter how dissonant, provided that they were audibly derived from the diatonic tonal system in use for centuries. Given this fact, it still required a strong force to sever the tie that held harmony to a tradition that had outworn its usefulness.

Preparation for the leap into twentieth-century harmony came, most of all, from Richard Wagner, who carried diatonically-derived chromaticism (and along with it, Romanticism) to the very brink. The actual leap was made by a number of composers, including Charles Ives and Erik Satie, but the composer who contributed most to the concept of scale of twelve unfettered chromatic tones was Arnold Schoenberg, who implemented and codified a system of composing with twelve tones related only to one another.

The element of rhythm also underwent great changes in the twentieth century, particularly in regard to meter. What the diatonic scale was to harmony at the end of the Romantic era, so the bar-line was to rhythm. Bar lines began to be used sparingly in the fifteenth century, somewhat more frequently in the sixteenth (particularly for instrumental music), and then came into common use in the early Baroque. Significantly enough, bar lines and the diatonic scale came into their own at about the same point in music history.

The most important function of the bar line is, of course, to furnish the performer with a regularly recurring mark in time to which he can relate the rhythms of the music itself. Obviously, the bar line is indispensable in ensemble performance, for without it, the performers could only with great difficulty fit their individual parts into the total texture. By the end of the nineteenth century, however, it became clear that the bar line and the musical meter system had strongly shaped composers' attitudes toward rhythm. The insidious influence of the steady pulse of the meter dictated by the bar line tended to inhibit freedom of rhythmic thought. At the same time, musicians began to be aware of the beauty to be found in the untrammelled rhythmic flow of Gregorian chant and medieval and Renaissance choral music, and in the rhythmic subtleties of Oriental and African music, none of which were originally notated with bar lines.

Many nineteenth-century composers had sought to transcend the tyranny of the bar line. The cross-rhythms and unusual accents in Schumann and Brahms, Chopin's rhythmic freedom in melodic lines, and Tschaikowsky's and Sibelius' use of unsymmetrical meters and jagged accents are all cases in point. Interesting rhythms and music of lasting value were produced in many of these works, but the situation called for a more dramatic change. Rhythms that could not be accommodated to the conventional meter system needed to be written.

Gradually, in the late nineteenth and early twentieth centuries, composers began to use more frequent changes of meter and in some instances to omit bar lines altogether. This rhythmic freedom can be seen in the works of Ravel, Ives, and above all, in the music of Stravinsky. The scores of works such as *The Rite of Spring* or *The Story of a Soldier* (or practically any Stravinsky score) are sprinkled profusely with meter signatures such as 1/4, 5/16, 5/8, and 7/8, along with the conventional 3/4 and 4/4. Rather than eliminating the pulse or beat, frequent change in meter has the effect of giving it added life, of allowing it to soar in any direction without the strictures of imposed symmetry. The beat is there, but fluctuates constantly. And within these varied and unsymmetrical measures the rhythm of the music found a new source of vitality that led toward further rhythmic innovation later in the century.

Thus, dramatic changes began to take place in both the harmonic and rhythmic aspects of twentieth-century music. Yet a third musical element was being revitalized in the twentieth century as a result of developments which had begun much earlier. This was the element of timbre.

By the middle of the Romantic period a number of combinations of voices and/or instruments had been established as conventional musical media. These included the string quartet, the piano trio, the art song, the symphony orchestra, opera, etc. These highly varied and colorful media reflect an important feature of Romantic music—the composer's fascination with the colors and timbres of musical sound. Tone color has been equally exciting to the composers of our century. The expanded use of percussion, *musique concrete,* electronic music, the prepared piano, countless experiments with conventional instruments and new uses for the human voice are all examples of twentieth-century composers continuing to probe the possibilities of the fascinating element of timbre.

Although many twentieth-century composers continued to write for a symphony orchestra similar to that of the Romantic period, the early twentieth century also saw a reaction against nineteenth-century orchestration. Composers such as Stravinsky and Ravel favored orchestral clarity and vivid, well-defined colors to the lush, homogeneous, sometimes overblown sounds of nineteenth-century orchestrators such as Wagner, Brahms, Bruckner, and Mahler. On the other hand, Berlioz and Rimsky-Korsakov may have directly influenced twentieth-century orchestration through their imaginative use of the instruments in flamboyant orchestral textures of remarkable lucidity and color.

The reaction against the nineteenth century resulted in many composers writing for unique combinations of instruments and voices. Schoenberg's *Pierrot Lunaire* (1912), scored for contralto soloist and five players (flute [alternating with piccolo], clarinet [or bass clarinet], violin [or viola], cello, and piano) is an early example of a composer letting his musical imagination dictate the medium rather than to be satisfied with a preexisting combination. The classical media have nevertheless survived, and composers such as Bartok have proven that their coloristic limits have yet to be reached. Indeed, his six string quartets, composed between 1910 and 1939, stand even today as a compendium of unique timbres available to the stringed instruments.

Perhaps the most striking developments in the expansion of tone color are taking place in electronic media. The use of pure electronic sounds, electronically-mutated timbres, or combinations of these along with voices or conventional instruments are rich with possibilities for the future. Other new sources for the exploration of timbre are being uncovered by scholars working in the relatively new area of ethnomusicology. Just as early twentieth-century composers found an interest in the sounds of jazz and South American music, some of today's composers have found inspiration in the music of Africa, India, and the Orient.

Melody, the prime moving force in music through the ages, continues to be of utmost importance to twentieth-century composers. Vital to melody, regardless of style, is the contrast of forward motion to points of full or partial repose. Thus, the feeling of phrases and cadences continues to be as significant in twentieth-century music as in the music of the eighteenth and nineteenth centuries. Obviously, phrases and cadences in twentieth-century music are quite different from their eighteenth- and nineteenth-century counterparts. Terms such as *double period* and *authentic cadence* do not apply to much of the music of our century. But if we define the phrase as a more or less complete musical thought ending in a cadence, then the term applies to the music of Bartok and Dallapiccola as well as to that of Mozart and Schumann.

To illustrate one kind of forward thrust found in twentieth-century melody, let us examine the opening of the second movement of Bartok's Second String Quartet (fig. 82). At first glance, the eighth rest in bar 3 and the quarter rest in bar 5 suggest that the excerpt is perhaps divisible into three phrases. But the tempo and rhythm, and particularly the four sixteenth notes in bars two and four, lend to these rests a character of tense expectancy which links together the three fragments into one seven-bar phrase. All of the musical elements play a part in defining the cadence at bar 7. Since the diminished fifth has been the dominating melodic interval throughout the phrase, the arrival in bar seven at the harmonic interval of a perfect fifth (D and A, viewing the E flat as an appoggiatura) creates a feeling of harmonic repose at the same time that it establishes a tonal center of D. Rhythmically, the tension created by the two instances of four sixteenth notes being followed by a short rest is alleviated by the steady drive of eighth notes to the final chord. The feeling of crescendo created by the addition of two instruments in bar 3 and by the fortissimo final chord plus the overall melodic contour lends to this phrase the character of an emphatic introductory gesture.

Figure 82. String Quartet No. 2, Bela Bartok, Opening of Second Movement.

Another twentieth-century way of delineating phrase structure is found in figure 83, the complete final movement of Luigi Dallapiccola's *Quaderno Musicale di Annalibera* for piano (also arranged as *Variations for Orchestra*). The work was composed by strict use of the twelve-tone system, which will be discussed later in more detail. This brief movement is a good example of accompaniment and melody in a twelve-tone work. In fact, its texture is not unlike the accompanied monody of the early seventeenth century, except that the melody tones in this example are not derived from the harmonic accompaniment.

Quartina is a poetical term meaning a four-line verse, like a quatrain, and each of the four lines can be viewed as a musical phrase. There are two basic factors which contribute to this phrase structure. The first is found in the harmonic logic of the piece, for each line

QUARTINA

Figure 83. Quaderno Musicale di Annalibera, *Luigi Dallapicolla, Final Movement.*

contains two simultaneously presented forms of the tone row, one in the melodic line and one in the accompaniment. The composer's choice of the forms and transpositions of the row have an overall logic that affects the total movement. The fact that each line is a discrete harmonic and melodic unit helps to create the effect of each line of score existing as a separate musical gesture—a phrase.

The second major factor that contributes to the phrase structure is the individual contour of each line of the melody. When expressively played the cadence feeling at the end of each line is unmistakable. The melodic arch of the first phrase is a particularly good example of this.

Figure 83 serves also to demonstrate the departure from the melodic conventions that were generally accepted by composers of many generations prior to the twentieth century. One important concept of melody as practiced by most composers for centuries past was to make it as singable as possible, even in instrumental music, and one of the precepts was to use an abundance of stepwise motion. Note that stepwise motion is found at only a few points in this melody and that large intervals such as sevenths and ninths occur frequently. Note also that the rhythms are very free. Two consecutive notes of equal duration occur only rarely and there are a number of ties across the bar line. This demonstrates the twentieth-century composer's desire to avoid the kind of symmetry suggested by the presence of regularly recurring bar lines. There are, of course, many other melodic styles to be found in the twentieth century, but this serves well to introduce the general melodic trends of our time.

Twentieth-century contrapuntal writing owes much to the past. The concept of polyphony that developed during the Renaissance has influenced contrapuntal thinking even to the present. The fugue is the child of the ricercar, just as the passacaglia finds its forebears in the grounds and divisions of the seventeenth century. Fugues, canons, and ostinato variation forms have by no means disappeared from use in this century, and a basic philosophy of contrapuntal writing remains with us today. Indeed, the classical twelve-tone system of Schoenberg utilizes thought processes similar to those used by Bach in his fugal writing and by Machaut in his isorhythmic motets. The basic idea of a logical relationship between two or more seemingly independent voice lines remains as valid today as in the sixteenth century, even though the melodic freedom and striking sonorities characteristic of the twentieth century have opened up new possibilities in polyphonic writing. Also, today's contrapuntists find new means for musical expression in extremely wide spacing of voices, striking contrasts of timbres, fascinating new textures in which a voice line may consist of several pitch lines moving in parallel motion, and, above all, new manifestations of the rhythmic element.

The diversity of musical forms to be found in twentieth-century music is indeed remarkable. Erik Satie professed to invent a new form for each composition, and many twentieth-century composers find little or no use for the traditional matrices of the past. On the other hand, some composers of our time have found use for such a basic pattern as the sonata form, suggesting that there may be a timeless

logic to the concept of exposition, development, and recapitulation—
although the tonal implications of the Classical sonata-allegro form are
almost useless to the twentieth-century composer. Other forms of the
past have been used in new ways, often to parody a stereotyped pattern. Repetition of ideas still is found in twentieth-century music, but,
in general, there is greater emphasis on the evolution of one idea from
another—development through genuine mutation rather than
modified repetition.

Polytonality, modality, the use of new scales and pitch systems,
tone clusters, microtones, and many other manifestations of the expansion of harmonic language are found in the music of twentieth-century
composers. It has often been said that the extreme use of dissonance in
today's music reflects the heightened tension and swift pace of life in
our time. Whether or not this is true, we have reached a point in music
history where consonance and dissonance must be treated as relative
terms. In a sense, this started when we first began to have a repertory
of music spanning several centuries. We may have been asked to hear,
for example, an augmented sixth chord as being quite dissonant within
the context of the music of J. S. Bach, somewhat less so in Mozart
(though still supremely expressive), and in Schumann or Liszt, almost
consonant. In listening to many different kinds of music, we learn to
hear consonance and dissonance in relation to a style, an historical
period, or to the context of a specific composition. Audiences of earlier
times, since they did not have the vast repertory made available by
modern developments in scholarship, communications, and technology, probably did not listen to music quite as we do today. The ears
of twentieth-century audiences have had to readjust swiftly and frequently in order to cope with and enjoy the many different kinds of
music to be heard today. This may explain why in the '70s for the first
time in history, a sizable portion of our world audience is intelligently
appreciative and receptive toward new music.

Exciting music which seems to depart from the tradition of the
times has always been attacked by the more conservative members of
the musical community. Instances of writers assailing new works
which later became venerated classics can be found throughout music
history. Often enough, these same writers lauded compositions which
were subsequently forgotten simply because these works lacked the
all-important factor of originality. As recently as 1955, the music critic
Henry Pleasants in his book *The Agony of Modern Music* said, "Serious music is a dead art. The vein which for three hundred years offered
a seemingly inexhaustible yield of beautiful music has run out. What
we know as modern music is the noise made by deluded speculators
picking through the slagpile."

Undoubtedly, Mr. Pleasants was reflecting the attitude of a sizable portion of musical audiences in the '40s and '50s, but there are signs in the '70s that the situation is changing for the better. Charitable foundations and, indeed, our state and federal governments are initiating or increasing subsidies to composers, and are beginning to support performances of new music. New works are being commissioned by our symphony orchestras (often with the support of outside agencies) and our social and business organizations, schools, and places of worship are active in promoting new music. For the most part, our composers have found homes in our colleges and universities, where music departments are devoting increasing attention to performing and studying new music and where enlightened and receptive audiences are to be found.

It is important to remember that radical departure from tradition is by no means the sine qua non of fine contemporary music. There are many twentieth-century composers who have found fresh ways to utilize the musical material of the past. At the same time, there are twentieth-century compositions which are of worth, not so much as music, as for their innovations—works which have added something new to our musical language. Often these works are most demanding to the listener. But just as our minds have been stretched to apprehend the phenomenal advances in science and technology of recent decades, so do we increase our aural capacity in order to understand and enjoy the rich diversity in the new music of our time.

17. The Early Twentieth Century

*Satie—Les Six and Neoclassicism—Stravinsky—
Schoenberg, Berg, and Webern—Bartok—
Hindemith—Russian Music—Ives and the
American Scene—Other Composers*

Erik Satie

One may ask, why begin a discussion of twentieth-century music with Satie (1866–1925)? He achieved no great fame as a composer, none of his compositions stand as imposing monuments in the repertory of twentieth-century music, nor was he a remarkably prolific composer. Nevertheless, through his music as well as through his biting and witty commentary, he exerted a strong influence on the music of the early twentieth century, an influence that can be traced in the music of Debussy, Ravel, Schoenberg, Honegger, Poulenc, Milhaud, and others. Some of these composers were happy to acknowledge their debt to him, for Satie was in the forefront of the artists who strove during the early years of the twentieth century to break ties with the nineteenth. He is perhaps the earliest European composer who, properly speaking, can be called a modern composer. Born in 1866, he saw the arrival of musical Impressionism, but saw also that impressionism was not for him (although his friendship with Debussy lasted almost until Debussy's death in 1918). In works composed as early as 1887 he utilized techniques which transcended Impressionism and led toward striking developments in music of the twentieth century. There was an element of mysticism in his makeup, which led him to join the order of Rosicrucians around 1890, and this, combined with his innate clarity of musical thought, lends to some of his music a character of monastic simplicity that was at odds with the Impressionistic esthetic—much more in tune with the twelfth or twentieth centuries than with the nineteenth. A medieval quality can be heard in several of his numerous works for piano solo, particularly in the *Gymnopodies*, the *Sarabandes*, and the *Gothic Dances*.

In the visual arts, the early twentieth century was the time of

Fauvism, Cubism, and Expressionism, and the influence of all three can be heard in Satie's music. Artists such as Matisse, Picasso, and Kokoshka were breaking ties with the nineteenth century; and in literature and poetry, such figures as James Joyce, T. S. Eliot, Jean Cocteau, Kafka, and Gertrude Stein were gaining eminence for works of art which often seemed to deny the traditions of the past century. Satie fell in well with these new movements and, soon breaking with the Rosicrucians, found himself caught up in the Parisian society of artists, musicians, dancers, and literary men of whom Jean Cocteau was a chief figure. Indeed, Satie's most spectacular work, the ballet *Parade,* was the result of a collaboration of many artists, including Picasso, Diaghilev and Nijinsky. The story is by Cocteau and it was he who guided this innovative dance production to fruition in 1917. During this period Satie founded the *Nouveaux Jeunes* a group of young musicians, primarily French, which included the members of *Les Six.* This group strove to purge French art of German and Russian adulterants—to establish a music based solely on Gallic traditions and sources. The works of French composers such as Jannequin, Couperin, and Rameau became models for the *Nouveaux Jeunes* in their reaction against oppressive German Romanticism.

Throughout his life Satie was the champion of simplicity and the enemy of pretentiousness. This can be seen in the titles of some of his compositions—*Three Pieces in the Shape of a Pear, Disagreeable Impressions, Cold Pieces,* and *Dried-up Embryos.* Some of the musical directions in his scores parody Debussy's impressionistic markings with such tidbits as "sheepishly and coldly," "like a nightingale with a toothache," "with tenderness and fatality," and so on. Some of this seeming flippancy may have been designed to camouflage his seriousness as a composer—perhaps to forestall criticism of his music. Yet, it must be acknowledged that the Romantic and Impressionistic music against which he rebelled needed to be satirized in order to establish the esthetic ground rules of the twentieth century. His remarkable personality was a curious combination of loneliness, sensitivity, bitterness, keen intelligence, and mordant humor. These qualities can be heard in his music.

Among his best-known works are several sets of piano pieces, each in three movements, written between 1887 and 1890. Anticipations of twentieth-century harmonic techniques can be found in all of these works. Figure 84 is an excerpt from one of the three Sarabandes, composed in 1887. Note that the ninths and sevenths in some of the sonorities in this passage do not resolve normally (i.e., by step) but simply remain on the same note to become consonant in the next sonority, a

Sarabande for piano, Erik Satie

Figure 84. Satie, Sarabande.

technique which was also used by Debussy and other early twentieth-century composers. The free use of parallel fifths also anticipates twentieth-century practices, as does the modal flavor of the passage. The example in figure 85 from *Le Fils des Etoiles* anticipates the kind of quartal harmonies that were later used by a number of twentieth-century composers, including Milhaud, Hindemith, and Copland.

One of Satie's most distinguished works is the symphonic drama entitled *Socrate* (1919). The work, in three parts, is scored for female voice and chamber orchestra, while the text is based on parts of Plato's *Dialogues* in French translation. The music succeeds in creating an atmosphere of intellectual serenity worthy of Socrates.

En blanc et immobile

Figure 85. Satie, Les Fils des Etoiles.

Les Six and Neoclassicism

In January 1920 the French music critic Henri Collet published an article entitled "Les Six Francais" in the French journal *Comoedia*. The six composers who were the subject of his article had all been members of *Les Nouveaux Jeunes* formed in 1917 with Satie as their prophet and Cocteau as their literary spokesman. Les Six includes Darius Milhaud (1892–   ), Louis Durey (1888–   ), Georges Auric (1899–   ), Arthur Honegger (1892–1955), Francis Poulenc (1899–1963), and the only female member, Germaine Tailleferre (1892–   ). The group was held together for a few years by their common rejection of Romanticism, Impressionism, and all other "isms," and by their adoption of jazz and popular music as important elements of their musical styles. Although they were highly controversial in the twenties, each soon went his separate way, and only three members—Milhaud, Honegger, and Poulenc—established themselves as significant composers. These three, as well as Stravinsky, who was living in Paris at the same time, were chief among the many composers to subscribe to the philosophies of the new movement known as Neoclassicism.

Although it cannot properly be called a style because of the many directions it has taken, Neoclassicism in general rejects descriptive music, the large Romantic and Impressionistic orchestra, and excess in any form in favor of dispassionate formal clarity, precise but often unsymmetrical rhythms, polished contrapuntal textures, and harmonies with clean biting dissonances rather than lush chromatic sonorities. Baroque and Classical works were their models but they also injected elements of popular taste such as jazz and ragtime into their music. To some extent Neoclassical music manifests the eighteenth-century spirit, but it is realized in the dissonant harmonies, varied instrumental colors, and striking rhythms of this century.

Honegger was of Swiss parentage but was born in France and lived in Paris most of his life. His music, like that of Milhaud and Poulenc, is eclectic and derivative at the same time that it manifests the precepts of Neoclassicism and the French Six. He is, however, viewed by some as the most significant composer among the Six, and a number of his works have achieved considerable renown. One of his earliest and most successful mature works is his symphonic movement entitled *Pacific 231* in which he imitated both the sound and the physical impression of a speeding locomotive by means of striking orchestral and rhythmic effects. It created something of a sensation as a twentieth-century programmatic piece when it was premiered in 1923. Another work of the same year is the oratorio *King David*, which has achieved even greater popularity, partly because of its somewhat meretricious harmonic and orchestral style, and partly because the vocal parts are easy enough to be performed by amateur choirs. Written in a rather "Hollywoodish" style that has immediate appeal to unsophisticated audiences, it is scored for soprano, alto, and baritone soloists, chorus, orchestra, and a narrator who functions in a manner similar to the evangelist of eighteenth-century oratorio.

On a higher musical and dramatic level is Honegger's *Jeanne d'Arc au bucher* ("Joan of Arc at the Stake"), an elaborate dramatic oratorio to a text by Paul Claudel. Scored for five soloists, five speaking parts, chorus which speaks as well as sings, children's chorus, and orchestra, it utilizes ancient and modern folk tunes, Gregorian chant melodies, and dance tunes in a powerfully dissonant though conservative harmonic idiom. The part (speaking role) of Joan of Arc has been popular with a number of cinema actresses, including Ingrid Bergman. Honegger was also successful as a composer of film scores, and in the field of opera he is best known for *Antigone* (1927), based on Sophocles' drama with a libretto by Cocteau.

Milhaud was born in Aix-en-Provence and, though devoted to his homeland, spent considerable time in other parts of the world, including Brazil, the United States, and various European countries. He is one of the most prolific and facile composers of the twentieth century, having written a vast number of works in virtually all musical media, including works with electronic instruments and experiments combining cinema with music. Because he writes so quickly and so much, some of his music is marred by a lightness and frivolity that is highly superficial. At the same time, he has combined his melodic gift with folk and popular elements, and Neoclassical and other techniques to create a style that is uniquely and unmistakably his own. His output is uneven, but includes a large number of works of great beauty and musical value. Among his best-known works are the *Saudades do Brazil* ("Souvenirs of Brazil," 1921) based on Brazilian folk rhythms and melodies, *La Creation du Monde* ("The Creation of the World," 1924) with its jazz, blues, and ragtime elements, and the oratorio-opera *Columbus* (1928) which, for Milhaud, is a curiously earnest and profound work. Manifesting his Jewish lineage is the solemn *Sacred Service* (1947) and the opera *David* (1954), commissioned for a Jerusalem performance to celebrate the 3000th anniversary of that city as the capital of David's kingdom. His native region of Provence is celebrated in his *Suite Provencal* (1937), a work which evokes the folk spirit of southern France.

In his nonprogrammatic instrumental works such as the symphonies, string quartets, and concertos he demonstrates his mastery of form and classical techniques in a modern idiom with remarkable lucidity and facility. His fourteenth and fifteenth string quartets, written to be performed separately or simultaneously, demonstrate his contrapuntal skill. The Concerto No. One for Cello and Orchestra (1935) is a characteristic example of his unique way of combining trivial and profound materials in a Neoclassical style combined with popular and folk elements. It opens with a profoundly dramatic cadenza for the solo cello followed by a melody which, though charming, would not be out of place in a cabaret. These seemingly incompatible elements are successfully combined in a short and formally concise first movement. The second movement, a deeply beautiful and complex lyrical movement, is the longest of the three and the raison d'etre of the total work. But it is followed by a tarantelle finale—a favorite dance rhythm of Milhaud—that can only be described as garish.

This facile but seemingly nonchalant approach to structure and materials is very typical of Milhaud. His operas, however, are perhaps less marred by this approach because of the composite nature of music drama. In them can be seen the complete gamut of Milhaud's musical style—polytonality, catchy dance rhythms, moments of captivating lyrical beauty, and popular and folk elements, for the most part all successfully combined by his remarkably facile technique.

Poulenc, a Parisian through and through, is particularly noted as a composer for voices and was the most instinctive composer among the French Six. Among his best works are several works for the musical theatre including *La Voix humaine* (1959), a work like Menotti's *Telephone* in that the plot is borne entirely by a single character carrying on a satirically humorous telephone conversation, and *The Dialogue of the Carmelites,* a serious three-act opera. Among his choral works, the best known is perhaps the *Mass in G* for a cappella chorus (1937), and he also composed a number of songs which are frequently performed. Poulenc was strongly influenced by his friend Georges Auric, whose brilliance, general sophistication, and musical knowledge he greatly admired. Auric is the only other member of the French Six to have achieved anything approaching distinction in the musical world of the mid-twentieth century. He is known particularly as a composer of film scores.

Igor Stravinsky

The activity of Stravinsky (1882–1971) as a composer spanned nearly seventy years, and in his works can be seen most of the important musical trends of the century. Undoubtedly the most celebrated composer of the first half of the twentieth century, he was often several jumps ahead of contemporary musical thought. When he did adopt the practices of other composers, as in the instance of his turning to serial technique after 1952 and his use of jazz and ragtime after World War I, he endowed the borrowed elements with a new meaning and branded them with his own unique and powerful musical expression.

He was born in Leningrad (then St. Petersburg) and was raised in a good musical environment that afforded much opportunity to become well acquainted with Russian music, particularly the operatic repertory, since his father was leading bass of the Imperial Opera. The young Stravinsky, though not a child prodigy, was encouraged to study music but not with an eye to making a career of it. His parents preferred that he should study law and he was duly enrolled in the University of St. Petersburg Law School. His only period of formal musical study took place under the guidance of Rimsky-Korsakov during the period of 1903–06, shortly after he left law school. In his autobiography (1935) he describes Rimsky-Korsakov as a "great teacher," and the influence of that excellent composer can be seen in the music of Stravinsky's pre-World War I period in his use of melodies reminiscent of Russian folk tunes and in his skillful and flamboyant orchestration.

Although Stravinsky composed a number of student works during the first decade of the twentieth century, the three ballets mark the real beginning of his remarkable career, and were written from 1909 to 1913, all for Diaghilev and all produced by him in Paris. These works, *The Firebird* (1910), *Petrouchka* (1911), and *Le Sacre du Printemps* ("The Rite of Spring," 1913), all use a large orchestra not unlike that of the late Romantic period and all are still very popular with today's audiences, although they are more frequently performed as concert pieces than as ballets. All but *The Rite of Spring* had extraordinarily successful premieres. The premiere of that work was extraordinary too, but in a different way, for at its first performance it touched off an audience reaction that is unparalleled in the history of music. In his last years Stravinsky still spoke of that event as a "scandal." To that Parisian audience on that eventful spring evening in 1913 *The Rite of Spring* seemed to have severed all ties with musical tradition, and many of the listeners expressed their dismay and confusion at the barbaric orchestral sounds they were hearing by rioting.

The subtitle of *Le Sacre,* "Scenes of Pagan Russia," attests to the strong Russian influences found in Stravinsky's early works, such as an orchestra similar in size to that of Rimsky-Korsakov and the use of primitive folk-like melodies of Russian character. The dissonant and anti-Romantic harmonic language of the work is the result of his abundant use of polytonality, triads with both a major and a minor third, and non-triadic sonorities such as quartal chords (chords built of fourths and fifths rather than thirds). The new harmonic vocabulary was so different from that of previous periods in music history that it is not difficult to see why the work precipitated such a violent reaction. It turned the corner on a new era and many composers from that time to this have been strongly swayed by the musical language of this and other Stravinsky scores.

But the rhythm in *Le Sacre* is even more striking than the harmony. Unusual meter signatures such as 5/16, 1/4, and 11/4 create a constantly shifting rhythmic pulse, even though the beat is always present with its powerfully primitive impact. At times the insistent rhythms create an ostinato pattern of the type that was to become an important stylistic trait in Stravinsky's later works. His use of the instruments in *Le Sacre* is another way in which he set precedents for the new era. A favorite device was his use of the instruments in extreme or uncharacteristic registers to produce new varieties of tone color. Such an instance occurs at the very beginning of *Le Sacre* in the opening solo for bassoon in its very highest register. In addition to unique combinations of instruments, he also used instruments which are rarely found in the symphony orchestra, such as the guiro (a South American instrument made of a serrated gourd which is scraped with a stick), alto flute, and bass trumpet. The primitivism in the impelling rhythms, powerful harmonies and unusual timbres of *Le Sacre* find counterparts in the early twentieth-century paintings of Rouault, Matisse, and Picasso. Primitivism in various forms became an intrinsic part of Stravinsky's style in many later works.

Much has been made of the significance of the premiere of *Le Sacre* (from which Stravinsky escaped through a window) as an important turning point in all of twentieth-century art—as the beginning of the modern era. But as we have seen repeatedly throughout history, such changes are seldom as precipitous as they seem. In the visual arts Fauvism, Cubism, and Expressionism were already underway and painters had begun, like Stravinsky, to break ties with the nineteenth century. In literature and poetry, figures such as Joyce, T. S. Eliot, Kafka, Cocteau, and Gertrude Stein were already gaining eminence. It is true that all of these artists denied some parts of their heritage, but all of them also maintained certain strong ties with the artistic traditions of previous centuries, though not necessarily of the late nineteenth century.

In Stravinsky's case, although traditional elements may be found in all of his works, tradition is most vividly seen in works which were frankly based upon earlier styles or upon the actual compositions of earlier composers. Such works include the ballet *Pulcinella* (1919), which is based on Pergolesi's music, the *Symphony in C* (1940), which follows structural principles of the Classical period, *The Rake's Progress* (1951), after Mozart's operatic style, and the ballet *The Fairy's Kiss* (1928), after Tschaikovsky. An important stylistic trait is revealed in these works—Stravinsky's preoccupation with the contrast of the idioms of earlier periods with his own musical style. This is clearly apparent in the ballet *Pulcinella* (also arranged as an orchestral suite and as the *Suite Italienne* for cello and piano). A great deal of the music in this work is quoted more or less literally from the music of Pergolesi, but frequently the material is reworked to express something totally new. Stravinsky, like Haydn, Beethoven, and other great composers of the past, capitalized upon the expectations of his audience so that within the predictably captivating style of Pergolesi, Stravinsky's own interjections come as brilliant and lucid flashes, surprising and charming in their effect.

During the World War I period, Stravinsky was living with his wife and children in Switzerland, and it was at this time that he turned from the large-scale orchestral expressions of his three earlier ballets toward greater economy of means in compositions for smaller groups. Perhaps war-time austerity may have partly accounted for the new directions he took at this time, but he was also conditioned by a desire to leave the excess baggage of the large Romantic symphony orchestra behind. Out of it came the Neoclassical movement which colored the music of many other composers of various nationalities for several decades.

Among Stravinsky's earlier works which show the influence of Neoclassicism are *L'Histoire du soldat* ("The Story of a Soldier," 1918), *Ragtime* for eleven instruments (1918), and *Pulcinella*. He moved to Paris in 1920, and in the music of the period from 1920 to 1925 the Neoclassical spirit is more fully realized. These works include the *Symphonies of Wind Instruments* (1920), the *Concerto for Piano and Wind Orchestra* (1924), the *Concertino for String Quartet* (1920), and the *Octet for Winds* (1923). From this time until the early 1950s he continued in the Neoclassical vein, but in a variety of styles, only rarely accepting either a form or a medium as it was passed on to him. An extraordinary quality of his music in the period to 1952 is its fluctuation and evolution of style. Stravinsky seemed determined not to repeat himself or to slip into stylistic ruts, and the result is a body of music from this period that includes such distinguished works as the opera-oratorio *Oedipus Rex* (1927, rev. 1948), the ballet *Apollon Musagette* (1928), *Symphony of Psalms* (1930, rev. 1948), *Concerto in*

D for Violin and Orchestra (1931), *Symphony in C* (1940), *Symphony in Three Movements* (1945), and the opera *The Rake's Progress* (1951).

In retrospect a few general stylistic traits emerge from the music of this period, in spite of the fact that each work remains unique. One feature is a near addiction to melodic and rhythmic ostinato figures, although they are handled in such a way as to minimize the repetitive quality and to capitalize on varying rhythmic relationships to other aspects of the texture. But his most striking trait is his rhythm—vital, unsymmetrical, pulsating, vibrating, inventive rhythm. Many changes of meter, unusual meter signatures, unpredictable accents, phrases of uneven length, and rhythmic patterns that rarely turn out as expected—all of these abound in his music. From the standpoint of harmony and counterpoint, he steadfastly remained dissatisfied with outworn sonorities and textures. When using techniques of the past, such as the double fugue in the second movement of the *Symphony of Psalms*, he found ways to infuse the old device with new life and meaning. The harmonies of the pre-1952 period tend toward quartal sonorities, triads with added tones, pan-diatonicism (use of all the tones of the diatonic scale, but in clusters and new chord forms), and poly-tonality.

Stravinsky came to America in 1939 to deliver a series of lectures at Harvard, and with the outbreak of World War II decided to remain in this country, establishing U.S. citizenship in 1945. From 1952 until his death he made considerable use of tone rows, in spite of the fact that he had been opposed to the twelve-tone technique in the twenties and thirties. In his use of serialism he developed an intricate contrapuntal style which was less accessible and more abstract than that of his earlier works. His adoption of a twentieth-century technique which had been in common use for a generation pointed the way for younger composers who, guided by his example, had up to that time avoided serialism. The first work in which he made some use of serialism is the *Cantata 1952.* The works of this last period did not gain the popularity of his earlier music because of the austerely esoteric nature of his new musical language. They include *In Memoriam Dylan Thomas* (1954) for tenor and eight instruments, a large-scale choral work written for the Cathedral San Marco at Venice entitled *Canticum Sacrum* (1956), the ballet *Agon* (1957), *Threni* (1958) to a text from the Lamentations of Jeremiah, *Movements* for piano and orchestra (1959), and *The Flood* (1962), a television ballet. Among these, *Threni* is the first to fully incorporate the twelve-tone system by means of a complete row.

Stravinsky died in April 1971 in New York City, leaving a heritage of masterworks unsurpassed by any composer in our history. He believed that the composer's task was to sift the musical elements of his imagination and impose limits upon them in order to achieve greater artistic freedom. In his own words, "The more art is controlled, limited, worked over, the more it is free." Through his phenomenal imagination and technical craft he indeed freed himself to become one of the immortal creative spirits of music.

Schoenberg, Berg, and Webern

One reason for the great importance of the twelve-tone system during the early twentieth century is that it furnished a new means of organizing pitches at a time when it had become apparent that the tonal system in use for the past two and a half centuries had outlived its usefulness. The preceding chapter contained a discussion of the establishment in the Baroque period and the gradual demise during the eighteenth and nineteenth centuries of the diatonic tonal system with which most of the music of the past several centuries had been composed. In spite of the fact that a great many composers even today still find some use for the diatonic scale, and that it is still used in virtually all popular music, the twelve-tone system must be viewed as the single most important development in musical theory during this century. The composer who contributed most to its development and codification is Arnold Schoenberg (1874–1951).

Born in Vienna, Schoenberg was very conscious of his link with German post-Romanticism, particularly with Wagner, whose music he used to demonstrate the validity of the new system. His early-period works such as the string sextet *Transfigured Night* (Op. 4, 1899) and the cycle for chorus, soloists, and orchestra entitled *Gurrelieder* (1901) show the influence of the post-Wagner environment of his youth. To him it was most logical to move from the extreme chromaticism of this time toward the abandonment of the diatonic tonal system. The first step, which occurred in the works of the pre-World War I period, was to replace the diatonic key center with free chromaticism. Because these works lacked the form and unity furnished by a diatonic key center, they tended, for the most part, to be assemblages of brief movements such as the *Three Piano Pieces* (Op. 11), *Five Orchestral Pieces* (Op. 16), and *Pierrot Lunaire* (Op. 21). These works represent the early twentieth-century movement known as Expressionism which originated in the parallel movement in painting represented by the works of artists such as Kollwitz, Kokoschka, Kandinsky, Munch, and others, most of whom were German. The same spirit is found in the novels of Kafka and Herman Hesse, and in the poetry of Paul Stefan George.

Perhaps also the movement is marked by the influence of Freud, for in all of the arts, Expressionism is characterized by a preoccupation with the inward realities of the human mind. The Impressionist painters had been concerned with things outside of the self, such as still lifes, the play of light, and form in objects perceived, while the Expressionists were concerned with the inner conflicts and torments of the psyche—the troubled or psychotic mind. Expressionism, as the name implies, is a reaction against Impressionism at the same time that it is a kind of extension or aftermath of post-Romanticism.

Pierrot Lunaire (which can be translated as "Moonstruck Pierrot") is an excellent example of Schoenberg's kind of Expressionism. Composed in 1912 to twenty-one short poems by Albert Giraud (in Schoenberg's translation to German), it is not a twelve-tone work, but is an important step in the evolution of the system. In the style of his second period, it is freely atonal, with a rhythmic irregularity in keeping with the departure from traditional techniques. It is scored for contralto soloist and five players—flute (alternating with piccolo), clarinet (alternating with bass clarinet), violin (alternating with viola), cello, and piano. The free atonality of the work is emphasized by the use of *Sprechstimme,* a technique in which the voice intones its part in a half-singing, half-speaking manner, with inflections corresponding to the rhythms and emotions of the words. Approximate pitches are indicated in Sprechstimme but are not intended to be clearly defined, although the rhythm is notated quite strictly. The technique produces an effect of mystery, drama, and great emotional intensity.

Each song in *Pierrot Lunaire* is a miniature in which the voice is used with some combination of the eight instruments and five players; and each deals with a separate episode in Pierrot's psychotic reality. Formal unity relies on the text, with purely musical structures such as the complex canons of numbers seventeen and eighteen also contributing to the design of the work.

Gradually, during the years before and after World War I, Schoenberg began to evolve a new harmonic system with a new unifying concept which would allow composers to produce works of considerable duration without the aid of the diatonic tonal system. The technique, which he called "the method of composing with twelve tones," is well adapted to contrapuntal thinking, and makes use of an established order or series of the twelve tones of the chromatic scale—an arbitrary arrangement of twelve pitch names called the tone row. The idea of a movement or work being based upon and characterized by a particular tone row was fully revealed for the first time in the final movement of Schoenberg's *Five Piano Pieces* (Op. 23, 1923). Every note in the movement is based upon the row shown in figure 86.

Figure 86. Tone Row of the Final Movement of Schoenberg's Five Piano Pieces.

A basic principle of the system is that every one of the twelve tones of the row must be presented in the established order before any of them is repeated. (Immediate repetition is allowed as an extension of the original tone.) In a sense, this is a highly organized manifestation of a basic principle of composition in any style—that those tones which have been least used up to a given point in a composition will at that point have the greatest effect of freshness and harmonic impact. Within the system there are four basic forms of the row: (1) the original or basic form; (2) its melodic inversion; (3) its retrograde; and (4) its retrograde inversion (melodic inversion of the retrograde). These four forms may, in the course of the work, begin on any one of the twelve notes of the chromatic scale to furnish the composer with a total of forty-eight different forms and transpositions of the row. These forms may be used simultaneously or overlapping, in strict usage deriving all of the harmonic and melodic material from the presentations of the various forms of the row in their established order of pitches. Possibilities for textural variety are increased by permitting any of the notes to be played in any octave. Because the tones are used in series, the system is often called the *serial* technique, while in Europe the term *dodecaphonic* is often substituted. Rows of fewer than twelve pitches have been used by some composers, particularly in more recent times, and serial techniques have also been applied to elements of music other than melody and harmony to control every aspect of the music. For these more recent developments, the term *serial* technique is more appropriate since the other terms are limited to the pitch element handled in rows of twelve tones.

During Schoenberg's third period (1923–33) he applied the twelve-tone system to most of his compositions, including the *Suite for Piano* (Op. 25), *String Quartet No. Three* (Op. 30), and the *Variations for Orchestra* (Op. 31). In 1931–32 he composed two acts of a projected three-act opera entitled *Moses and Aaron,* a profound work which shows the deeply religious side of Schoenberg's nature. Because he was a Jew, he could not remain in Austria under the Nazi regime and in 1933 he came to live in the United States. The period from that time until his death in 1951 is known as his fourth period, and is characterized by use of the row with greater freedom and, on occasion, the return to a purely tonal style with key signatures. Some of the outstanding works of the fourth period are the Piano Concerto (Op. 42, 1942), *A Survivor of Warsaw* (Op. 46, 1947), for narrator, male chorus, and orchestra, and *Kol Nidrei* (1938, Op. 39), for speaker, chorus, and orchestra. Among the strict twelve-tone works of this time are several chamber works and the Violin Concerto (Op. 36, 1936). Schoenberg's uncompromising belief in the rightness of his musical philosophy sustained him through many years when his compositions were misunderstood. Today it is clear that his theories pointed to the future and led to significant developments in the technique of musical composition.

As a teacher in the musical community of Vienna, Schoenberg attracted many students, among the most gifted of whom were Alban Berg (1885–1935) and Anton Webern (1883–1945). These three—Schoenberg, Berg, and Webern—constitute the modern Viennese school of composition. Berg, a composer of keen dramatic sense, found the best outlet for his expressionism in the two operas *Wozzeck* (1922), and *Lulu,* left uncompleted at his death in 1935. He was freer in his use of the twelve-tone system than was Schoenberg, and often included conventional triads in his tone rows which lent a more traditional flavor to his harmonic language. His *Lyric Suite* (1926), for string quartet, and the Violin Concerto (1935) both use tone rows containing triads and, perhaps because of their relatively conservative harmonic effect, have achieved greater popularity then many other works of the modern Viennese school. Berg's opera *Wozzeck,* a non-twelve–tone work, is recognized today as a classic of great power and compassionate humanity.

Webern's music embodies the most extreme applications of the twelve-tone system and from him came the idea of extending the idea of serial composition to encompass the elements of rhythm, timbre, and dynamics as well as pitch. Schoenberg and Berg both showed an inclination toward short forms, but in Webern the urge for brevity is carried so far that some of his movements are shorter than a minute in duration. During the two decades after his death, no composer's influence was felt more strongly. Stravinsky based the style of his final period upon Webernian principles, and composers such as Karlheinz Stockhausen and Pierre Boulez have attempted to carry Webern's serial techniques so far as to control every aspect of musical composition by means of an approach that has come to be known as *total control* or *total serialism.*

One characteristic feature of Webern's technique is his use of two-, three-, and four-note fragments in a texture in which the fragments pass from one instrument to another in a constantly fluctuating fabric of subtle tone colors. A technique developed by Schoenberg known as *Klangfarbenmelodien* consisted of frequently changing the instrumentation during the course of a single melodic line. Webern carried this even further, in some cases assigning each tone of a melodic line to a different instrument, an aspect of his style that has strongly influenced composers of the fifties and sixties.

The dynamic element of Webern's subtle musical language is carefully notated with many small crescendos and diminuendos, usually at a low level of volume. His intricate rhythmic organization conveys a feeling of great clarity of design and freedom of thought. His light transparent textures are carefully worked out as to counterpoint, instrumental color, and the relationship of one instrument to another. Perhaps no composer in music history achieved such remarkable economy of means, for his total output of thirty-one works (not including student compositions) has been recorded in full on four discs. During his early pre-twelve–tone period he wrote a number of songs with instrumental ensemble or piano accompaniments. These demonstrate his lyrical gift, as do also the instrumental works of this period such as the *Five Movements for String Quartet* (Op. 6, 1909) and *Five Pieces for Orchestra* (Op. 10, 1913). His first twelve-tone work was the *Three Sacred Folk Songs* (Op. 17, 1924) for voice and three instruments, and in the ensuing years he continued to refine his style in such masterworks as the *Symphony* (Op. 21, 1928), *Concerto for Nine Instruments* (Op. 24, 1934), and *Variations for Orchestra* (Op. 30, 1940).

Also among his last works are the two cantatas, the first (Op. 29) composed in 1940; the second (Op. 31), in 1943. *Cantata No. 1* is scored for soprano, mixed chorus, and small orchestra and shows the composer's lyrical gift at its best. Based on a German text by Hildegarde Jone, the three movements of the work total about seven minutes in duration and are based on the row shown in figure 87. Note that this row divides equally into two hexachords and that the second hexachord is the retrograde inversion of the first—an illustration of the mathematical complexities of Webern's musical mind and of the possibilities of the use of hexachords in the twelve-tone system.

Webern endured his share of hardships under the Nazis in Austria and did not live to see his artistry fully appreciated. This quiet man

Figure 87. Tone Row of Webern's Cantata No. 1.

of genius was accidentally and tragically killed by an American soldier at the close of the Second World War in 1945. In the following years he soon achieved the recognition he deserved and is now recognized as one of the most influential figures among twentieth-century composers. Among the many twentieth-century composers who adopted serial techniques in varying degrees are Luigi Dallapiccola (1904–   ), Ernst Krenek (1900–   ), Wallingford Riegger (1885–1961), Rolf Liebermann (1910–   ), and many younger composers.

Bela Bartok

One of the strongest influences upon Bartok's music was the folk-lore of his native Hungary. Unlike Dvorak, Bartok (1881–1945) found a natural means of assimilating the rhythms and inflections of the music and language of his homeland into his music without artifice or incongruity. Thus, although his music is a twentieth-century manifestation of the nationalistic movement, it is quite different from that of the Romantic era. For one thing, because of his painstaking research methods in unearthing Hungarian folklore, the folk elements of his music are much more authentic than nationalistic works of the nineteenth century. He and his distinguished fellow composer Zoltan Kodaly (1892–1967) corrected many widespread misunderstandings about the true nature of Hungarian folk music. In the works of both can be seen the fresh and exciting rhythmic, melodic, and harmonic influences of the music of the Hungarian countryside.

Bartok began to study folklore in a scientific manner around 1907, the year he became a teacher of piano at the Royal Hungarian Music Academy in Budapest. He and Kodaly, who was also a member of the faculty, began in their music to make use of a harmonic concept peculiar to Hungarian folk music. Essentially, this concept is to view the intervals of the perfect fourth, perfect fifth, second, and seventh as being harmonic intervals usable as basic (consonant) sonorities, very much as in quartal harmony. Folk music also led Bartok to the use of unique modes or scales, particularly the pentatonic, which he occasionally cast in polytonal textures. Other harmonic devices such as the simultaneous or near-simultaneous use of major and minor triads on the same root, and whole-tone passages contributed much to his harmonic language. The natural pulse and cadence of the Hungarian language as seen in folk song had a direct influence upon his rhythmic style.

These folk influences helped free Bartok from the influences of the music of Liszt, Wagner, Strauss, and the entire European tradition which was his natural heritage. The result was a unique style that evokes the spirit of the twentieth century and also reaches back to the instrumental forms of the classical period. Yet Bartok did not count himself a Neoclassicist. He was influenced by Stravinsky and The Six as well as by Schoenberg, but he was able through the force of his musical personality to assimilate these influences without sacrificing his own identity. He was at opposite poles with the anti-emotionalism of the French Six and believed in the power of music to express strong states of emotion and experience. Like Stravinsky, Bartok had a penchant for ostinato figures, and also used irregular meters and terse asymmetrical rhythmic ideas. Perhaps because of his background as a virtuoso pianist, his rhythms often have a percussive and driving quality that is uniquely his.

His earliest piano works, composed between 1908 and 1910, are similar to nineteenth-century character pieces. These *Bagatelles, Elegies, Burlesques,* and *Sketches* show the influence of folk song as well as his love of the miniature, as do also his famous piano study pieces, the five volume *Mikrokosmos.* On a larger scale are the *Sonata for Piano* (1926), the *Concerto for Two Pianos and Percussion* (also with orchestra, 1941) and the three piano concertos (1926, 1931, 1945). The Third Piano Concerto, completed a few days before his death, is his crowning achievement for the instrument. Like many of his later works, including the Sixth String Quartet (1939), it is harmonically quite conservative.

Although he wrote two violin sonatas, a *Rhapsody* for clarinet, violin, and piano, and a set of forty-eight duos for two violins, his greatest chamber music achievement is his set of six string quartets. Composed throughout his life, they show the gradual evolution of his style and contain many innovative string techniques such as *col legno* (striking or bowing the string with the wood of the bow), snap pizzicato, fingernail pizzicato, new possibilities for harmonics and double stops, and glissandi. In addition to being a compendium of twentieth-century string sounds, the six string quartets reveal Bartok's phenomenal craft, deep imagination, and his sincere belief in the power of music to express universal human emotions. They place him in the direct line of the string quartet tradition established by Haydn and continued in the works of Mozart, Beethoven, Schubert, and Brahms.

His works for small orchestra include *Music for Strings, Percussion, and Celesta* (1935) and the *Divertimento for Strings.* He also composed many songs, the majority of them arrangements of Hungarian folk songs, and two large vocal works, the *Cantata Profana* (1930) and the opera *Bluebeard's Castle* (1911). His outstanding works for large orchestra include *Concerto for Orchestra* (1944), in which each of the instruments is cast in a virtuoso role, the Violin Concerto (1938), and the unique *Concerto for Viola and Orchestra,* which can be counted as his last work since it was completed after his death by his friend Tibor Serly. Bartok had come to the United States in 1940 because of the Nazi invasion of Austria and Hungary and, though he received considerable recognition as an artist, his last years were plagued by ill health and financial insecurity. In this century he stands as a lonely figure who attached himself to no particular school or system of composition, but whose works constitute a fusion of many twentieth-century styles into a unique and powerful means of expression.

Paul Hindemith

Hindemith (1895–1963), one of the outstanding German composers of this century, represents the best aspects of the German tradition. A versatile musician who achieved early distinction as a violist and conductor, he was also a fine teacher and the author of several textbooks on music theory and composition. He taught at the Prussian State Academy of Music from 1927 to 1935, subsequently at Yale University, and spent his last years in Switzerland.

He was an extremely prolific composer who wrote well in virtually every musical form or medium, and whose highly organized musical language bespeaks his belief in the power of music to communicate ethical and moral states of mind. In rare instances his music can be warm or whimsical as in his *Symphonic Metamorphoses on Themes of Weber* (1944), but in general his music evokes moods of seriousness or austerity. His large output of chamber music includes seven string quartets, several chamber concertos, and many sonatas for nearly every type of solo instrument with piano. Many of these sonatas are the result of his interest and support in the cause of *Gebrauchsmusik* ("music for use"), a movement active during the third and fourth decades of this century which was based on the belief that music should be as much the domain of amateurs as of professional musicians, and that music should serve a purpose. Hindemith, in his support of this philosophy, wrote many pieces for amateur and student performers as well as for mechanical media such as the player piano.

In his early works composed during the twenties, he experimented boldly with form and harmony in an austere and highly dissonant style with a contrapuntal approach that seemed to allow accidental dissonances without regard for harmonic considerations. He wrote several operas during this period including *Cardillac* (1926) and *News of the Day* (1929), the latter being a bizarre Expressionistic work based on news stories. In the thirties, in line with his support of *Gebrauchsmusik*, he seemed more interested in communicating with a large mass of listeners, and his style began to have an almost romantic warmth, with less dissonance, well-defined tonal structures, and expressive melodic lines. The important works of this period include the ballet *Nobilissime Visione* (1938), *The Four Temperaments* (1940), the opera *Mathis der Maler* (1934), from which he also extracted a symphony, three piano sonatas, and the *Symphony in E Flat* (1940). Gradually during this period he developed a style akin to Neoclassicism, but which, with its fugal and passacaglia techniques and its use of the concerto grosso concept, is more properly called Neobaroque.

Hindemith's most significant works composed after 1940 include the opera *Die Harmonie der Welt* ("The Harmony of the World," also made into a symphony), the song cycle *Marienleben* (revised in 1948 from an earlier version), *Ludus Tonalis,* a work for solo piano that explores the world of Hindemith's contrapuntal technique, and a choral work to Whitman's *When Lilacs Last in the Dooryard Bloom'd* (1946). Like Milhaud, Hindemith was so prolific that some of his works fall short of his usual standard of excellence, but his style has been highly influential upon many composers during the thirties and forties, and his better works more than suffice to establish him as a significant twentieth-century composer.

Russian Music

Perhaps because of the strong influence of the Soviet state, music in Russia is generally more conservative than that of most other European countries. The U.S.S.R. asserts that its art should serve to strengthen the character of the people and instill national pride. Clear and direct communication is most desirable, and the artist is warned against obscurity, abstraction, and excessive experimentation—this in a nation whose very government is founded upon political philosophies that are new and unique to the twentieth century. In spite of rather strong enforcement of these Soviet artistic ideals, some excellent music has been composed in twentieth-century Russia. After midcentury there seemed to be some loosening of artistic strictures, to the extent that there was considerable exchange of composers and performers between East and West. Shostakovich visited the United States in the late fifties. Stravinsky was allowed to visit his native land in 1962, and there has been some exchange of artistic ideas. Nevertheless, in the seventies there are signs that the restrictions are as severe as ever, as the news media carry frequent stories of outstanding Soviet artists who from time to time fall into official disfavor. Perhaps Russia's greatest contribution to twentieth-century music is found in its performing artists. Performers such as the cellist Rostropovich, the violinist Oistrakh, and the pianist Richter represent some of the greatest achievements in instrumental artistry in all of music history.

Sergei Prokoviev (1891–1953) and Dmitri Shostakovich (1906–   ) are the outstanding composers of twentieth-century Russia. During the early part of Prokoviev's career, up to 1934, he traveled widely in Western Europe and the United States, coming under the same general influences as his contemporaries such as Stravinsky and the French Six. Among his best-known works of this period are the *Scythian Suite* (1914) the *Classical Symphony* (1917), a kind of satirical parody of eighteenth-century techniques in a Neoclassical vein, and the Third Piano Concerto (1921). The Piano Concerto, in particular, has enjoyed great popularity, and is an excellent blending of Classical and Romantic elements in a conservatively modern idiom. Perhaps the influence of the piano concertos of two earlier Russian composers— Tschaikovsky and Rachmaninoff—is present in the virtuosic flair and lyricism of the work.

In 1934 Prokoviev returned to Russia and as a Soviet composer suffered the same restrictions as other Russian artists of the time. One of his first compositions written during this period is the orchestral tone poem with narrator *Peter and the Wolf* (Op. 67, 1936). Perhaps his best-known work, it fits well with the esthetic ideals of the Soviet state in its broad appeal, morality, and Russian subject matter. At about the same time, while struggling to comply with the state, he also composed his *Concerto for Cello and Orchestra* (Op. 58) and his *Concerto No. 2 for Violin and Orchestra* (Op. 63), both important contributions to the solo literature for these instruments. His *Symphony No. 5* (Op. 100, 1944) and his opera *War and Peace,* based on Tolstoy's great novel, are also among the important works of this period.

Prokoviev was a fine pianist and contributed much to the solo literature of his instrument including nine sonatas (and an uncompleted tenth) and numerous incidental pieces such as *Visions Fugitives* (Op. 22). His chamber works include two string quartets, a number of ensemble pieces involving winds as well as strings, two sonatas for violin and piano, one for violin alone, a sonata for flute and piano, and a sonata for cello and piano. One of the best features of his style is the attractively simple lyricism that has been a hallmark of all Russian music. Occasionally, when his tunes or harmonies verge on the banal, one suspects him of deliberate irony—perhaps a hidden rebellion at the artistic strictures of the Soviet State? From the Western point of view, the Soviet composer has had a hard lot, and since we know of instances of Russian artists rebelling or defecting from the Soviet Union, it is quite conceivable that there exists unpublicized discontent among many of the most talented creative artists of twentieth-century Russia. That a major twentieth-century government could take an official position of condemnation against musical styles such as Viennese atonality or so called "bloodless" Neoclassicism is difficult for those of us in relatively free societies to comprehend.

Shostakovich, the best known Soviet composer of today, also had to cope with government disapproval, and during the early thirties was severely criticized for the un-Russian qualities of his music which up to that time had been strongly influenced by the Neoclassical movement. In particular, the style of his opera *Lady Macbeth of Mzensk* (1932) was condemned, and it was necessary for him to go through a period of reform from which he emerged in 1937 with his *Symphony No. Five,* a work which established him as one of the leading composers of the twentieth century. Since then he has brought the total number of his symphonies to well over a dozen, marking him as one of the major symphonists of the century. His *Thirteenth Symphony* (Op. 113) composed in 1962, once again brought criticism from official Soviet circles. Because of the censors it has remained banned and unpublished in Russia, although it was played there in 1963 and 1965. Based on the poetry of Yevtushenko, and scored for bass solo, male chorus and orchestra, the work courageously speaks out against Russian anti-Semitism and the repression of Russian spiritual life. First performed in the United States in 1970, it eloquently expresses Yevtushenko's powerful poetry. Shostakovich's other works for orchestra include numerous theater and film scores, and one concerto, the *Concerto for Piano and Orchestra* (1933).

Although the symphonies are the center of his output, he also composed a quantity of chamber music, including several string quartets and piano trios. Perhaps his *Sonata for Cello and Piano* (Op. 40, 1934) is his most popular chamber work. Its first movement shows Shostakovich's Romantic lyricism at its best, while the work as a whole demonstrates his Neoclassical tendencies and his incorporation of traditional forms into a conservatively modern idiom.

Although Sergei Rachmaninoff (1873–1943) left Russia in 1917 never to return, he is mentioned here as a composer of Russian descent. Although not a major composer, the style of piano writing in his Neoromantic concertos and solo works for the instrument have left their mark on this century. More significant are the Soviet composers Dimitri Kabalevsky (1904–   ) and Aram Katchatourian (1903–   ), both of whom have also been particularly successful as composers of concertos.

Ives and the American Scene

Charles Ives (1874–1954) is perhaps the greatest composer that the United States of America has produced. He is also the single composer who has most successfully assimilated truly American elements into his startling and exciting musical style. The composer himself attributed the great originality and freedom of his music in part to the nature of the early guidance he received from his father, a highly talented band director and music teacher in Danbury, Connecticut. George Ives, though not a composer, was a jack-of-all-trades in music, and not only insisted that his son learn the traditional ways of making music, but also encouraged him to experiment, as he himself did, with new ways of putting sounds together. Indeed, the source of nearly every musical innovation of Charles Ives can be found in the experiments and suggestions of his father.

In his totally natural and inherent desire to create new musical sounds out of old materials, Ives unknowingly anticipated many of the musical innovations of the three other most influential composers of the early twentieth century—Schoenberg, Stravinsky, and Bartok. In particular, his music is marked by polytonality, atonality, polyrhythm, polymeter, and various other effects of simultaneity; but he also experimented with less common devices such as tone clusters and quarter-tones. The fact that very little of his music was performed prior to 1950 tends perhaps to minimize the impact of its originality, but when viewed in the proper context of time (most of his major works were composed between 1906 and 1916), the innovative qualities of his music are strikingly and dramatically apparent.

There are many instances of Ives' use of indigenous American materials such as hymn tunes, folk songs, gospel songs, the sounds of camp meetings and parades, etc., but in addition there is an American philosophical overtone that is evoked not only by his music but by his very life style—that of New England Transcendentalism. This philosophy, with its emphasis on the meditative, intuitive, and spiritual life above the empirical, is most strongly associated with the figure of Ralph Waldo Emerson (1803–82). Ives considered Emerson a great poet and prophet, and in one of his monumental works, the *"Concord"* *Sonata* for piano, he named the first movement for him. The other three movements of this great work are entitled *Hawthorne, the Alcotts,* and *Thoreau,* also Concord Transcendentalists.

Realizing that his music would have little chance of conventional success, Ives very early gave up the idea of being a professional musician. After his study at Yale with Horatio Parker (1863–1919), one of the best of the few American composers of any distinction during the late nineteenth century, Ives went into business and devoted himself wholeheartedly to the development of insurance, both in business and in concept, reserving musical composition only as a well loved avocation. Transcendentalism was as much a part of his insurance work as it was of his music. It was typical of the man and his philosophy to do the best at anything seriously undertaken and he is still remembered as one of the prime moving forces in the early development of insurance. His writings on insurance theory and the training of insurance agents remain as important and standard guidelines to the business even today. He retired in 1930 at a time when his firm of Ives and Myrick had issued nearly fifty million dollars worth of insurance. He had earlier arranged for some of his works to be published privately (without copyrighting them, for he always insisted that all music was for everybody), and later some of his works were published in journals. But it was not until mid-century that his music began to be well known. He responded to negligence and distinction with equal contempt; in 1947 when he was awarded the Pulitzer Prize for his *Third Symphony* after a performance in New York, he responded by giving away the $500 and saying "prizes are the badges of mediocrity—Prizes are for boys, I'm grown up." His orchestral work *Three Places in New England,* published in 1935, was performed the year after by the Boston Symphony, and on this occasion he did not even bother to attend the performance. His greatest delight had been the creation of his exciting and innovative compositions. Recognition, timely or not, meant little to him.

To many listeners, one of the most baffling aspects of Ives' music is its quality of simultaneity and its multiplicity of seemingly incongruous ideas. In spite of what appears at times to be a devil-may-care piling up of diverse ideas, his music is highly organized. The universality of his music, a manifestation of his Transcendentalism, is seen in the manner in which he pulls together many conflicting and disparate elements into a meaningful whole. His five symphonies, many descriptive orchestral pieces, two piano sonatas, numerous chamber works including two violin sonatas, his choral music, and his 114 songs stand as eloquent testimony to his place as one of the greatest American-born composers.

Credit for recognition of the value of Ives' music must go in large part to his friend and biographer, the composer Henry Cowell (1897–1965). Like Ives, he too was drawn to folk music and to the use of complex combinations of sound. He wrote a great deal for the piano, experimenting with techniques such as reaching inside the piano to strum or hit the strings, percussive techniques on the keys, often in tone clusters—sometimes with a piece of wood or the forearm. His *Tiger* (1928) is a good example of his piano style. He composed a vast amount of music, in his later years drawing upon elements of Eastern music, particularly of India. He also experimented with notational devices, and must be viewed along with Ives as one of the great avant garde musicians of the American scene. He was untiring in his support of new music and was a founder of the *New Musical Quarterly,* which did much to advance unknown composers, including Ives.

Until the twentieth century, music in America was dominated by the influence of European composers and performers. Among the oases of excellence in a vast desert of inferior imitations of European models are the works of the colonial rustic William Billings (1746–1800) and Stephen Foster (1826–64). Dvorak, during his visit in the nineties, had stimulated some interest in the establishment of a native musical art, but it was slow in starting and often took wrong directions. In new England the only significant activity in the late nineteenth century other than that of Ives was found in a group known as the Boston composers, several of whom were students of John Knowles Paine (1839–1906). Because he was the first professor of music at Harvard (1875), and because he was one of the earliest American composers to achieve distinction in Europe and did much to further the cause of American composers, Paine has been called the "Dean" of American composers. The Boston group included George Chadwick (1854–1931), Horatio Parker, Arthur Foote (1853–1937), Henry Hadley (1871–1937), and a number of others of lesser distinction. Foote was unique among the group because he had been completely trained in the United States without any direct contact with European musical centers, although the European influence is there nevertheless.

Somewhat more distinguished than this group was Edward Mac-Dowell (1861–1908), who achieved considerable success not only in this country, but in the musical centers of Europe as well. Except for a few short piano pieces and the second of two orchestral suites based on what he conceived to be "Indian" themes, his works are nearly forgotten. He served rather unsuccessfully as Chairman of the newly formed Music Department of Columbia University from 1896 to 1904.

In the early twentieth century after MacDowell, the most widely known American composer was George Gershwin (1898–1937), who achieved fame as a composer of Broadway musicals such as George White's *Scandals, Lady Be Good, Girl Crazy,* and *Of Thee I Sing.* To fulfill his ambitions to compose in a more serious artistic vein than that of musical comedy, he began a collaboration in 1923 with the Paul Whiteman orchestra which resulted in the production of his famous *Rhapsody in Blue* for piano and orchestra which was orchestrated by Ferde Grofé (1892–   ), another successful semi-serious composer who was associated with Paul Whiteman. After this initial success in the realm of concert music, Gershwin undertook to complete his musical training by serious study with competent teachers, and in the remaining years of his life produced a number of works that have become successful standard repertory pieces, including the *Concerto in F* for piano and orchestra, *An American in Paris,* and the unique opera *Porgy and Bess.* Frequently underrated because of his association with Tin Pan Alley, Gershwin was one of the first truly American composers, and one who set precedents for later experimentation with the combining of jazz and pops with serious concert music.

A frequently overlooked American composer active past the mid-twentieth century is Carl Ruggles (1876–   ). Like Ives, he independently arrived at some of the same innovative musical devices adopted by the progressive European composers of the early twentieth century. Indeed, his counterpoint at times sounds very much like that of Schoenberg, and in one of his earliest works, *Angels* (1921) for six trumpets, the harmonic scheme is decidedly atonal. One of his last works is *Affirmations,* for orchestra, which Ruggles completed in his eighties.

There were a number of composers of Gershwin's generation, some of them still active, who have maintained the traditions of Western culture in serious but eclectic styles at the same time that they successfully incorporated indigenous American elements into their music. Many of these composers were or are associated with American colleges and universities as resident composers or as professors of composition; for the American institution of higher education in this century has become the haven and home for practitioners of the art of composing music. One of the earliest and most representative of these is Walter Piston (1894–   ), whose music is characterized by emphasis upon the Classical instrumental forms, a high degree of technical perfection, and balance of form and expression. Like many American composers of his generation, he studied composition in Paris with Nadia Boulanger (1887–   ), the famous teacher of music to whom Piston must be at least partially indebted for his superb craftsmanship and polished style. By consistently avoiding conscious Americanism such as the use of folklore, and by rejecting programmatic elements, he developed a Neoclassical style in the European tradition without being dominated by it. Some American elements do appear in Piston's music, but only as a natural and intrinsic part of his musical language, not as outgrowths of nationalism.

Piston served on the faculty of Harvard University from 1926 until his retirement in 1960 and has written a number of music textbooks which have been widely used. There is a serious and mature elegance in much of his music, and he frequently uses canonic and fugal devices in harmonic styles that show the influence of Schoenberg. But with his incorporation of jazz and popular elements into his music, a less serious side of his personality is apparent. The Third (1947) of his seven symphonies received the Pulitzer Prize. His other orchestral works include the *Concerto for Orchestra* (1933), the well-known ballet *The Incredible Flutist* (1938), and the *Violin Concerto* (1939). His chamber works have been frequently performed and include four string quartets, a piano trio, a sonata for violin and harpsichord, and numerous other works in various instrumental combinations.

Another distinguished figure in twentieth-century American music is Howard Hanson (1896–   ), who is unsurpassed as a champion of the cause of a native musical culture. His achievements as a composer parallel his career as teacher, conductor, and director of the distinguished Eastman School of Music of the University of Rochester, a position which he held for nearly forty years until his retirement in 1963. There he gave unstintingly of his time and energy to the training of the talented young musicians who attended the school. Many well-known American works received their premier performances at the Festivals of American Music founded by Hanson in Rochester, and many distinguished composers of today received their early training there.

In his own music the conscious application of American elements is the exception rather than the rule, although the opera *Merry Mount* (1934) based on a story of colonial New England is a case in point. The Fourth of his six symphonies received the Pulitzer Prize in 1946 and he has composed numerous other works for orchestra, including a single movement work entitled *Mosaics.* Throughout the early twentieth century he clung courageously to the belief in music for a mass audience—universality in the true Romantic sense. In this and other ways his style can be compared to that of Sibelius, and like Sibelius his ancestry is of the north of Europe. In recent years his Neoromanticism has been considered out of place in light of the new musical developments of this century, but this criticism, based as it is upon current fashion, may indeed be too harsh. In any case, his contributions to the cause of composers in America is of great historical significance, quite aside from the undeniable value and lasting beauty of his music.

Roy Harris (1898–   ) has endeavored to give musical expression to America's highest aspirations and noblest ideals. By means of assimilating Americana such as Civil War songs, hymn tunes, and cowboy songs into his musical style he succeeded to a remarkable degree in giving voice to the American spirit. Indeed, even when not employing indigenous material that is clearly American, his music evokes the idealistic yearnings and indomitable courage and tenacity that are among the best aspects of the American spirit. His career reached its peak in the thirties during a time when America was ripe for his kind of nationalistic expression, and for a while he was *the* American composer. Howard Hanson had helped launch him in 1926 with a performance of his *Andante for Orchestra* and he subsequently spent two years of study with Boulanger in Paris, but, perhaps because he undertook a musical career at a relatively late age, his style, even in his later works, was marked by crudities that could not be ignored, and his earlier promise of great musical achievement did not quite come to pass.

Harris' unique orchestral sound bears some resemblance to that of Sibelius and Tschaikovsky. Harmonically he tended, like many American composers around mid-century, toward diatonic and even triadic sonorities brought up to date by colorful dissonant added tones and polytonality as well as frequent modal passages. He employed contrapuntal devices a great deal, as did most of Boulanger's students, and had a particular affinity for streams of block-like chords moving dramatically in parallel motion. He was at his best in symphonic forms, and his Third Symphony (1938) is perhaps his best and certainly his most popular work. Among his chamber works, the Third String Quartet and the *Quintet for Piano and Strings* are the most significant, while his choral works *Song for Occupations* and *Symphony for Voices* are also well known. The Third Symphony, which is in one movement, seems to have set a precedent for similar works by other American composers. The idea of the one-movement symphony was used by later composers such as Samuel Barber (1910–   ) in his highly successful First Symphony.

Aaron Copland (1900–   ) was the first of the many American composers who studied composition with Boulanger in Paris. He studied with her from 1921 to 1924, and the Parisian environment of the twenties—which included Stravinsky and the French Six—undoubtedly encouraged his experimental tendencies. From the beginning, he seemed consumed with a desire to bring elements into his music which the listener would identify as being clearly American. In the twenties he was particularly interested in using American jazz and popular elements, particularly apparent in the *Concerto for Piano and Orchestra* (1927). Later he tended away from the influence of popular music toward older folk elements and American literature and poetry as seen in his three ballets of the late thirties and early forties, *Billy the Kid, Rodeo,* and *Appalachian Spring,* and in the opera *Tender Land* (1954). But a more abstract influence also crept into certain of his works in the early thirties and he produced a number of excellent instrumental works in the Neoclassical tradition, including sonatas for the piano (1941) and violin and piano (1943) and the Third Symphony (1946). The abstract musical thought apparent in these works was even more striking in the *Quartet for Piano and Strings* (1950) in which he made use of serial techniques, a practice which he continued in later works such as the *Fantasia for Piano* (1958) without, however, sacrificing the individuality of his style to the system. His most characteristic style is marked by not-too-daring though fresh and original harmonies in diatonic or modal passages in which triadic and quartal sonorities predominate. His contrapuntal textures are clear and usually rather simple, and he occasionally used polytonality, all welded together by an excellent grasp of musical form.

There are a number of early twentieth-century American composers who are particularly known as composers of opera and various types of music drama. Chief among these is Gian Carlo Menotti (1911–   ) who, although Italian-born, has lived in this country since 1927. His style is conservative but melodically very attractive, strongly influenced by the Romantic opera composers of his birthland, perhaps most of all by Puccini. Aside from *Amahl and the Night Visitors* (1951), a Christmas opera written for television which has become a traditional Christmas TV viewing event for children in the United States, his best known operas are *The Medium* (1946), *The Telephone* (1947), which inspired Poulenc's *La Voix Humaine, The Consul* (1950), and *The Saint of Bleeker Street* (1954). His *Help, Help, The Globolinks* (1969) was a relatively unsuccessful, though amusing, attempt to point an artistic moral as well as utilize electronic sounds in opera. He has written all of his own librettos and has also written them for his friend and associate Samuel Barber—for Barber's operas *Vanessa* (1956) and *A Hand of Bridge* (1959).

Barber, it should be noted, has been a successful composer in virtually all forms and media. His Neoromantic style has been tinged in his later works with a high level of dissonant tension, but his style is basically conservative and eclectic. Among his most successful instrumental works are the Neobaroque *Capricorn Concerto* (1944), the *Piano Sonata* (1949), *The Sonata for Cello and Piano* (1932), and the *Concerto for Piano and Orchestra* (1962). Two of his most popular works are *Dover Beach* (Op. 3), for voice and string quartet, and *Adagio for Strings* (1938), arranged from his first string quartet.

Virgil Thomson (1896–   ), known as a New York music critic and a composer in many media, composed two operas to texts of Gertrude Stein, *Four Saints in Three Acts* (1934) and *Mother of Us All* (1947). The distinguished former conductor of the New York Philharmonic, Leonard Bernstein (1918–   ) has emulated Gershwin with the success of his Broadway musicals *Fancy Free* (1944) and *West Side Story* (1957). Bernstein, who is a highly successful though conservative composer in other media as well, managed in *West Side Story* to create a moving music drama based on an updated Romeo and Juliet theme laced with social commentary which combines the best elements of the Broadway musical with serious opera. Chief among those opera composers who concentrated on truly American subject matter in their librettos is Douglas Moore (1893–   ). Composer of many operas and works in other media as well, Moore's best known operas are *The Devil and Daniel Webster* (1939) and *The Ballad of Baby Doe* (1956). His lyrical scores have something of the folk-like quality of singspiel as well as spoken dialogue in place of recitatives, and, because of their conservative appeal, have gained considerable popularity.

Wallingford Riegger (1885–1961), a composer whose talent was recognized only in recent decades, was one of the first Americans to undertake to compose with the twelve-tone technique. Some of his works dating from 1924 make strict use of the technique, while others use the row very freely, with modifications to suit the needs of his personal musical language. Among his better known works are *Dichotomy* (1932), *New Dance* (1942), and the *Symphony No. Three* (1948).

Ernest Bloch (1880–1959), a Swiss-born composer whose strongly felt Jewish heritage is apparent in his music, composed mostly in instrumental media, often with programmatic associations. He wrote two Neobaroque concerto grossos, and an abundance of other orchestral works, but his best-known work is the programmatic rhapsody for cello and orchestra, *Schelomo,* based on the life of Solomon. *Schelomo* and some of his other works employ quarter tones, the direct result of the subtle influences of Jewish cantorial singing, and the Hebrew influence is also seen in the moods of pathos, anguish, and resignation which can be heard in his music. He composed a number of excellent chamber works (notably a piano quintet which makes much use of quarter tones) and a frequently performed setting of the Jewish Sacred Service.

One of the first black American composers to make use of the music of his heritage in a style other than jazz is William Grant Still (1895–   ), who has employed slave songs and dance rhythms in a contemporary symphonic idiom. His *Afro-American Symphony* (1931) is his best-known work. Roger Sessions (1896–   ), a student of Ernest Bloch, is one of the outstanding abstract instrumental composers of twentieth-century America, but his music is difficult to categorize as to style or school. To a high degree it is esoteric and intellectual, but because of its harmonic style, it is charged at times with great emotional intensity. He has composed four symphonies, several concertos, and a quantity of chamber music.

William Schuman (1910–   ), a student of Roy Harris, has been one of the significant forces in furthering the cause of American music in this country through his directorship of the Julliard School of Music in New York, and as President of the Lincoln Center for the Performing Arts. His style can be described as the fusion of folk-like American elements with a Neoclassical technique. Schuman's colleague and associate at the Julliard School is Vincent Persichetti (1915–   ), a versatile musician who has produced notable works in all media, but particularly for piano solo. Both composers possess a remarkably fine melodic gift.

Because of the abundance and diversity of musical activity in this first great period of American music, it is impossible to discuss all the significant American composers during the early twentieth century. Certain of them, however, from the perspective of the latter part of the century, stand out for the significance of their artistic contributions, while others, because they are or were very much in tune with present-day developments, will be discussed in the next chapter.

Other Composers

The most significant composers of the early twentieth century have been discussed earlier in this chapter, but a vast amount of music was written by many other fine composers in England, Europe, and Latin America, and the problem of selecting a few for brief discussion here is most difficult. Many of them are still actively composing, and because we are so close to them, and their works have not yet stood the test of time, the choices must of necessity be based primarily upon personal taste and prevailing opinion.

The most significant British composer of the early twentieth century was Ralph Vaughn Williams (1872–1958), who represents the extension of Romantic nationalism into twentieth-century England. A symphonic composer of significant stature, he died at the age of eighty-five a few months after completing his Ninth Symphony. A group of British composers in the early twentieth century had collected many Irish, Welsh, Scottish, and English folk songs and, like the Russian and Bohemian composers of the late nineteenth century, began to use them or tunes like them in their compositions. Vaughn Williams was a member of this group, and the folk-song influence, along with a renewed interest in Elizabethan music, strongly colored his style throughout his career. The folk-song influence is clearly apparent in his *Norfolk Rhapsody* for orchestra (1906), while the modal melodies and Renaissance cadences of Elizabethan music left their mark upon his *Fantasia on a Theme by Thomas Tallis* for strings (1910). Another kind of folk element, the environmental sounds of the city of London —street cries, bells, etc.—are heard in his *London Symphony* (1914, rev. 1920).

Vaughn Williams was influenced by Ravel, with whom he studied for a short time in Paris, and his basically Neoromantic harmonic style at times sounds quite Impressionistic. In addition to the symphonies, he composed a large quantity of excellent choral music, including the *Mass in G Minor* (1922), the mystical oratorio *Sancta Civitas* (1925), and the comic choral suite *Five Tudor Portraits* (1936). He also composed a number of operas, including *Sir John in Love* (1929) based on the *Merry Wives of Windsor,* and *Riders to the Sea* (1927) based on the Synge play.

Gustav Holst (1874–1934) is another significant early twentieth-century English composer. In very recent years his orchestral suite *The Planets* (1916) has enjoyed renewed popularity, perhaps because of the new era of space travel. He too was influenced by English folk song, but there is also a mystical side to his musical expression seen in his use of Hindu subjects, such as in his *Choral Hymns from the Rig-Veda* (1912). He is particularly well known as a choral composer, both sacred and secular, and has set many texts of Walt Whitman.

William Walton (1902–   ) and Benjamin Britten (1913–   ) are the best-known English composers still living. Walton's best-known works are the *Viola Concerto* (1930), which was premiered with Hindemith as the soloist, and the oratorio *Belshazzar's Feast* (1931). All of the English composers discussed in this section, Walton included, have the common traits of a predilection for choral music and a strong interest in folk song, both of which seem to be national characteristics of British peoples. In addition, these twentieth-century English composers have the common characteristic of a musical style which, although expressive of twentieth-century ideas, is strongly linked to the nineteenth-century traditions of harmony, orchestration, and general approach to form. These Neoromantic tendencies and the delight in choral music are clearly seen in the music of Benjamin Britten, but in recent years Britten's successes, particularly in various kinds of vocal music, set him apart as the most distinguished English composer after Vaughn Williams. He is perhaps best known as an opera composer. *Peter Grimes* (1945), *Billy Budd* (1951), and *The Turn of the Screw* (1954) are among his best-known works in the operatic medium, but he has also composed numerous operettas, masques, and other works which fall into the general category of musical drama. In the persons of Handel, Purcell, and the Elizabethan madrigalists, England has had its great masters in the setting of English verses to music, and Britten can be viewed as the rightful heir to this tradition. His operas make excellent theater and are equally attractive from the musical viewpoint, while his many oratorios and other choral works demonstrate the same high talents. *A Ceremony of Carols* for women's voices and harp (1942) is one of his most popular works, and the intensely moving and dramatic *War Requiem* (1963) is an oratorio-type work of great distinction. He has composed purely instrumental works of value, but his greatest strength lies in his skillful orchestration combined with his idiomatic and evocative vocal settings of English texts.

Among the most significant German composers of the early twentieth century are Carl Orff (1895–   ), Kurt Weill (1900–50), and Boris Blacher (1903–   ). Orff's best known work in the United States is *Carmina Burana* (1936), a vast twenty-five-movement oratorio based on the Latin, German, and French texts of the Goliards. The work is a combination of impelling primitive rhythms, original use of voices and orchestra, and the curious but unmistakable influence of Viennese operetta. Vocal writing is his strongest point and he has composed a number of other oratorios, several with Latin texts, such as *Catulli Carmina* (1943), a distinguished work for chorus, four pianos, and a very large percussion section. He has written several successful operas, the best known of which are *Der Mond* (1938) and *Die Kluge* (1942), both based on fairy tales of the brothers Grimm. His style is marked by strikingly dramatic use of the instruments, particularly the percussion, often at shatteringly high dynamic levels. Harmonically he has in recent years departed from the conservatism of *Carmina Burana,* but his style continues to be marked by innovative use of the voices and experimentation with new sound combinations, including electronic sounds (in his Christmas play *Ludus de Nato Infante mirificus,* 1961).

He has also been interested in the musical training of children, and his five-volume work entitled *Das Schulwerk* (1930–54) has in recent years exerted much influence upon more progressive music educators in the United States. He believes in teaching music to children in such a way as to capitalize upon their innate creative and innovative abilities, rather than to stifle these talents as is often the case with more traditional approaches. *Das Schulwerk* contains folk songs of several nationalities, dances, ballads, etc., arranged for children to clap, dance, and sing to their own accompaniments on percussion instruments, recorders, etc. Zoltan Kodaly, discussed earlier in connection with Bartok, was also active and influential with similar ideas for encouraging children to make music in their own way and thus develop their personal creative talents.

Kurt Weill was active both in Europe and the United States and is best known for his *Threepenny Opera,* a modernized version of the eighteenth-century English *Beggar's Opera,* composed in collaboration with the playwright Bertholt Brecht. The work contains many elements of jazz and popular music, influences which were to lead to several musical comedies which Weill composed for production in the United States. He also composed a serious opera entitled *Street Scene* (1947) and a well-known folk opera, *Down in the Valley* (1948). His focus was upon music for the theater and he made definite contributions to musical drama in the United States after he settled here in 1935.

Boris Blacher has been particularly interested in the use of abstract mathematics as a means for organization, a feature of his style which has had considerable influence upon younger composers in Germany. He succeeded Werner Egk (1901–   ) as director of the Academy for Music in West Berlin, and collaborated with him on the composition of *Abstract Opera No. 1* (1954), a work which makes much use of complex mathematical serial techniques applied to both rhythm and pitches. One of Blacher's best-known students is Gottfried Von Einem (1918–   ), an Austrian composer who has been particularly successful in compositions for the operatic stage. It is apparent that opera and other forms of musical theater have been perhaps the most important medium in twentieth-century Germany. This may be attributed in part to the fact that there are over a hundred permanent opera houses in Germany and Austria, and in part to the influence of Wagner, which was still strong in the early twentieth century.

In France, Jacques Ibert (1890–1962) was quite popular during the early twentieth century, particularly as a composer of Neoclassical opera and ballet. More significant for his influence upon modern music is the French born Edgar Varése (1885–1965), who was a pioneer in the use of unorthodox instruments and instrumental combinations. Varése settled in the United States in 1915 where he composed his relatively short list of compositions, including *Ionisation* (1931) a striking work for thirteen percussionists, *Density 21.5* (1936), and *Poéme Electronique* (1958), a work composed for the Brussells World's Fair which utilizes electronic sounds and recorded sounds and which was performed at the Exposition on an incredible number of loudspeakers. Varése's style is marked by a steely-edged quality which comes from his predilection for certain metal percussion instruments, and which may also be the composer's expression of the urban environment in which he lived. In the twenties and thirties, when he composed his most innovative works, his experiments were not well received and he was thought to be an eccentric of little artistic importance. Today he is recognized as an important musical pioneer and a progenitor of *musique concrete* and electronic music.

Another French composer (who could as well be discussed in the final chapter dealing with the contemporary scene) is Oliver Messiaen (1908–   ), whose influence upon the younger avante garde composers of Europe has been profound. He was one of the first of the French composers to fully adopt the principles of serial technique, which he used in a unique way to control not only pitches but also rhythms through an extension of the principles of the twelve-tone system. But, unlike other European composers, particularly in Germany, he has not been dominated by the system, for he has brought many other influences to bear upon his music, including that of Hindu melodies and rhythms and Gregorian chant. He also is something of an ornithologist and has collected many bird calls for use in his music. This drawing upon the sounds of nature suggests a mystical side of his personality which is not unlike that of Scriabin. One of his best-known works is the *Quartet for the End of Time* (1941).

The only internationally distinguished composer of Spain in the early twentieth century is Manuel de Falla (1876–1946), whose style is marked by Impressionistic and Romantic traits cast in the characteristic rhythmic and melodic forms of his native land. This is seen most of all in Spanish dance rhythms and orchestration which often includes castanets and the guitar. His best-known work is the ballet *El Amor Brujo* ("Love, the Magician"; 1915) which has become internationally famous in various instrumental arrangements.

In Latin America there has been considerable use of folk music in serious musical forms, most apparent in the music of the Brazilian composer Heitor Villa-Lobos (1887–1959). The most striking aspect of his style is the manner in which he combined folk melodies and other indigenous Brazilian elements with classical European techniques. This is most apparent in his four works entitled *Bachianas Brazileiras,* which utilize the techniques of J. S. Bach in Villa-Lobos' unique musical language. The most famous of these is No. Two (1933) for eight cellos and soprano. He also composed fourteen works called *Choros* which combine folk and popular elements of Brazilian music. These nationalistic tendencies did not prevent him from composing in traditional instrumental forms and media, for he was a highly prolific composer who wrote excellent string quartets and other abstract instrumental forms, utilizing Brazilian elements to varying degrees.

In Mexico, Carlos Chavez (1899–   ) has worked primarily in the larger forms, introducing many native Mexican instruments, particularly percussion, into the orchestra. He too fused folk elements of his country to his personal style, which is marked by a high degree of dissonance and uniquely colorful orchestration. He has been prolific in all media, but particularly in ballet. The use of Mexican and American Indian elements is vividly heard in his *Sinfonia India* (1936).

18. The Contemporary Scene

Musique Concrete *and Electronic Music—Chance Music, Serialism, and Mathematics—The American Scene—Music of Commitment and a New Humanism*

It is virtually impossible to sift through the many musical occurrences since World War II and, with any assurance, arrive at the most significant trends in contemporary music. Many of the composers discussed in the preceding chapter are still active and remain relatively untouched by avant garde developments in composition, while others have kept their styles well in touch with contemporary trends. Thus, there is music being written today in every twentieth-century style, from the most conservative Neoromantic compositions to those progressive works which utilize new media and innovative compositional techniques. Inevitably, it is the new and different which is most demanding of our attention, simply because the older styles often require no further discussion. But this is not meant to suggest that the innovative music being written today is better or more important than the conservative, for without doubt there are works of great musical value being written today in the older as well as the newer styles of the twentieth century.

Musique Concrete and Electronic Music

Shortly after World War II, Pierre Schaeffer (1910–), a French composer and audio engineer, began to search for musical applications of everyday sounds. Such experiments were not totally new. There had been similar efforts earlier in the century—by Varése, by an Italian group called the Futurists, and others. Schaeffer used disc recordings of mechanical noises and sounds of the everyday world, many of which were standard sound effects in radio stations since the '30s, and manipulated them by speed change in playback, reversal, as well as by experiments in canon and polyphony using three phonographs at once.

Much of his work was frustrated, however, by the limitations of disc recording. Although the technique of wire recording existed at that time, it was not until the introduction of magnetic tape recording in 1950 that really diversified and artistic use of recorded sounds became possible. At that time, with the help of several other composers, including Pierre Henry, Schaeffer produced a number of works in a new art form which he dubbed *musique concrete.* The most ambitious of these was the "opera concrete" *Orphée* (1953) by Schaeffer and Henry.

Essentially, a piece of *musique concrete* is a work of art produced by the manipulation, mutation, and synthesis of recorded nonmusical and musical sounds realized in its final form as a recording. Often the origins of the sounds are not readily apparent, but the fact that the sounds were originally familiar sound patterns sets *musique concrete* apart from pure electronic music in which the sounds are generated only by electronic means. The range of sound sources available to *musique concrete* is virtually unlimited. Varése's experiments in the twenties and thirties with noise-like agglomerations of rhythms and timbres from unusual sources were important precursors of the new art, for any sound that can be recorded is considered suitable raw material for the new medium. There are numerous techniques for the mutation and manipulation of these sounds, including playing them backwards by reversing the tape, accelerating or decelerating the tape speed to change the frequencies, using filters to eliminate sounds in specific frequency ranges, cutting and reassembling tape segments by splicing, and recording sounds from several tape recorders simultaneously. To illustrate only one of many possibilities, a note on the piano which normally has a clean attack followed by a diminuendo, when played in reverse has the strange effect of no attack followed by an abrupt crescendo.

Electronic music began a short time later than *musique concrete* in 1950 with experiments in Cologne. There had been numerous earlier efforts to produce musical sounds by mechanical or electrical means. The science of acoustics had for generations been well informed on the true properties of sound materials, and it had become possible in the twentieth century to break sounds down into the overtone components which control their timbres. Leon Theremin (1896–   ), a Russian inventor who had studied music (theory and cello) at the University of St. Petersburg, invented the Aetherophone (also called the Theremin) in 1927 and presented many concerts on this and other instruments of his own invention throughout Europe and the United States. The instrument required a performer who regulated the pitch by moving his hand closer or further from an antenna—the closer the hand, the lower the pitch. Other experimental instruments included the Spharophon of Jorg Mayer (1880–1939), the Ondes Martenot of Maurice Martenot (1898–   ), and the Trautonium of the German engineer, Friedrich Trautwein.

As in the case of *musique concrete,* the first significant artistic attempts in electronic music were made possible by the introduction of magnetic tape recording in 1950. Herbert Eimert (1897–   ), a German musicologist and composer, was the moving force behind the experiments at Cologne, and the first compositional results were presented at an international new music forum in Darmstadt in 1951. Eimert officially became director of his electronic studio at Cologne Radio in 1951 and was soon joined there by other composers interested in the new medium, the most important of whom was Karlheinz Stockhausen (1928–   ), who took over directorship of the studio in 1963. The earliest experiments at Cologne were tentative and unsure, for the composers were indeed feeling their way into unknown territory. By 1950, however, their techniques had crystallized to the point that the studio (or laboratory as it is sometimes called) had most of the essential characteristics of the typical present-day electronic studio. These essentials include a number of electronic signal generators (oscillators) capable of producing at least three types of tones at any frequency within the range of human hearing. The basic tone is the sinus tone (sine wave), so named because its image on the oscilloscope is that of the sine curve. The sinus tone has a rather uninteresting timbre with no overtones whatsoever—in other words, a pure fundamental. More interesting in timbre are the sawtooth wave and square wave (also named for the images that they produce on the oscilloscope), which add certain overtones for more interesting colors. Another early addition to the electronic studio was the white noise generator, a device which produces a sound like radio static containing all or nearly all of the timbres in the entire audio spectrum. Definite pitches are not discernible in unfiltered white noise, but by using filters to select sounds from the total sound spectrum, remarkable effects can be achieved, many of which have highly percussive qualities.

These are the basic sound sources of pure electronic music and by using them in combinations of several tones of various frequencies and by using filters to achieve variety of timbre, the possibilities are very great. But the recording of these sounds after they have been selected, and assembling and splicing them in the desired combinations to produce a final tape was an arduous task. For this much additional electronic equipment, technical skill, and patience were required. Several tape decks were necessary to record sound combinations, and the various necessary pieces of accessory equipment resulted in an expensive and complex laboratory which could be organized for use only by means of a complicated control board or patch board—much like the switchboard of a telephone operator. There have been numerous attempts to develop an approximate notation for electronic music. One of the best systems, originally devised by Bulent Arel, is illustrated in figure 88.

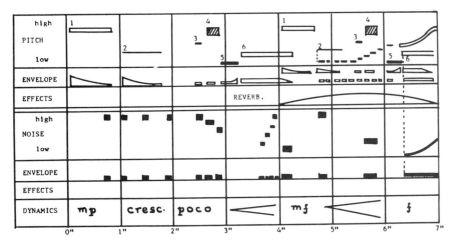

Figure 88. An Example of Notation for Electronic Music.

During the late fifties and sixties, electronic studios began to spring up in other places, such as Paris and Berlin and in universities in the United States. Several new devices were added which contributed to the resources of the electronic composer, including the envelope generator which made it possible to create a wide variety of musical attacks on a tone, and the synthesizer, an American development which permitted the composer to combine many sounds without prerecording them. A variety of types of synthesizers were produced in the United States in the sixties and seventies, some of which could be played almost like a keyboard, enabling the composer to do something close to improvisation with electronic sound combinations.

Meanwhile in Paris, Schaeffer was continuing his work with *musique concrete.* In 1958 he reorganized his studio and his methods of composition, and was joined by a number of younger composers, the most important of whom was Yannis Xenakis (1922–   ), a Greek composer who was trained as an architect and who had been Le Corbusier's assistant for a number of years. Xenakis produced his *Diamorphoses* (1957) at Schaeffer's studio. About this time Schaeffer expressed his preference for the term *experiences musicales* in place of *musique concrete,* although the latter term continued to be used.

Obviously, electronic music and *musique concrete* have much in common. Indeed, only the sound sources are different, for all of the techniques of reversing, changing tape speeds, splicing, using tape loops to produce ostinati, superimposition, canonic and polyphonic effects, use of resonators, etc., are common to both kinds of music. Although there were efforts at first to keep electronic music in a pure state (i.e., to use only electronically generated sounds), many later electronic composers have used natural, mechanical, and musical sound sources in combination with pure electronic sounds from signal generators. A typical situation might find an electronic composer striving for just the right kind of percussive sound at a particular point in his composition, and having tried everything in the way of electronic sounds, he picks up, say, an ashtray, taps it with a pencil, records it, slows it down so that it sounds something like a tam-tam, and uses it as a part of his otherwise purely electronic composition.

Thus, the fine line of distinction between pure electronic music and *musique concrete* has become less and less of a reality as composers use whatever means necessary to achieve the desired sounds. A highly successful method of using electronic sounds has been to combine them with conventional instruments in various kinds of ensembles. The invention of the synthesizer has opened up another possibility for electronic performances—the use of nonrecorded sounds from the synthesizer in actual performance, either improvised or planned ahead, alone or in combination with other instruments.

There are those today who believe that the history of music has seen a gradual but logical evolution toward dehumanization of the art. (The same point of view has been applied to the other arts as well.) The increasing importance of electronic music appears to support this theory, as does also the development of computer music. The Iliac computer at the University of Illinois (Urbana), for example, has been programmed under the direction of Lejaren Hiller Jr. (1924–   ) to produce music and perform other related tasks such as to extract orchestral parts from full score. Its best-known piece is the *Iliac Suite* (1957) for string quartet, the earliest piece of music produced entirely by computer.

Evidence of this dehumanization process can be seen throughout music history. As stated earlier, timbre was not an important element of the art of the medieval and Renaissance composer, for the first instrumental compositions originated simply as instrumental transcriptions of vocal pieces. Thus, the timbres of these early instrumental compositions were largely accidental, rather than resulting from careful choices by the composers. It was not until the eighteenth century that careful control of tone color began to be widely practiced, and even then there were a number of well-known compositions in which the instrumentation was not specified. Dynamics as an expressive element followed the same pattern, the first dynamic markings having been used in the late sixteenth century. The gradual increase in control of timbre and intensity parallels the development of instrumental music. If vocal music was the earliest form of music, then the relationship of instrumental to vocal music is similar to the relationship of electronic to instrumental music, and a de-emphasis upon the human element can be seen in both cases. Just as Bach's vocal lines were often written in an instrumental style, so contemporary instrumental writing seems often to be striving to emulate the sounds of electronic music. The analogy can be carried further: As Bach tried to make voices function as instruments, so some contemporary composers, consciously or not, try to make instruments sound uncharacteristic, unlike themselves, by using the most outré techniques imaginable—percussive effects on wind and string instruments, performing on disassembled parts of instruments, and many other outrageously unidiomatic devices.

But does this apparent dehumanization mean that our culture will ultimately see the disappearance of the vocal and instrumental performer? Certainly not, for this theoretical trend applies only to itself, to one kind of music in which can be seen a gradual evolution toward a music built of nonhuman sound sources and produced without performers. It does not apply to the bulk of our music, for the evocative immediacy of the human voice, and to a slightly lesser degree that of the instrumental performer, are as meaningful today as in the time of the troubadors and trouveres, and there is more music for human performers being written now than ever before. Vocal and instrumental music feels the influence of electronic music, combines with it--and our art is enriched by this fusion. But electronic music would itself become meaningless were it not for the coexistence of a continuing tradition of live music for vocal and instrumental performers using more or less conventional modes of performance.

Chance Music, Serialism, and Mathematics

Also significant on the contemporary scene are numerous experiments with the use of chance in the writing or performing of musical compositions. Chance music has in recent years been termed *aleatory* music, an expression derived from *alea,* the Greek word for dice. The American, John Cage (1912–   ), inventor of the prepared piano, and a highly controversial experimenter with all kinds of musical and nonmusical elements, coined the term *indeterminacy* to describe various aspects of his operations. In Cage's productions some of the indeterminate elements are controlled to varying degrees, others are left completely to chance. Readings and various other activities, some of them violently expressive of a desire to destroy music, often come into play, and silence is sometimes used for its expressive as well as "anti-music" qualities.

Perhaps the most extreme use of chance is the "happening," which combines dramatic and visual elements with music in a kind of theatrical production in which musicians, actors, and other persons relate randomly to each other, doing virtually whatever occurs to them. Presumably the artistic value or charm of such an event is found in the fact that it is a unique experience which could never be repeated. A more controlled use of chance is found in Stockhausen's *Piano Piece XI* (1956), the nineteen sections of which are notated on a large sheet in order that they may be played in various orders according to certain prearranged limitations. In this instance the performer is given certain alternatives from which he makes choices according to his own inclinations, but in other kinds of chance music the element of improvisation enters in. That is, a composer may notate only portions of the music, leaving its full realization to the performers themselves. When several performers are involved in such a performance, the chance juxtapositions of the various performers' improvisations can produce striking and sometimes beautiful effects, none of which can be reproduced. The German-born American composer Lukas Foss (1922–   ) has used techniques of this sort in his *Time Cycle* (1960) and *Echoi* (1963). Pierre Boulez (1925–   ), one of the most significant French avant garde composers, has used chance effects in his Third Piano Sonata (1957) and in other works. Stockhausen, in his vocal and instrumental *Momente I* (1962), uses chance elements in a large ensemble and uses audience applause as a part of the composition to capture something of the spontaneity of a happening.

Directly at odds with aleatory music are the attempts in the forties and fifties to totally control all of the elements of music through the application of the principles of serialism to every phase of the craft of musical composition. Webern is viewed as the progenitor of such practices, and, as mentioned in the preceding chapter, Olivier Messiaen was not only the first significant French composer to use serial techniques, but was also one of the first to apply them to the elements of rhythm and timbre. Two of his many students, Stockhausen and Boulez, are among the most significant younger composers to attempt total serialization in some of their compositions. The medium of pure electronic music is, of course, the most natural place for total serialism. There are no performers to make interpretive decisions, pitches can be measured to exact frequencies, all durations can be measured exactly in terms of the lengths of tape segments, and timbres and textures can be accurately controlled and reproduced. Stockhausen's early electronic works, *Study I* (1953) and *Study II* (1954), both use serialism applied to all of the musical elements. His *Zeitmasse* (1956) for wind quintet is an excellent example of an instrumental piece based on the precepts of total serialism.

In 1955, however, Xenakis, who was also a Messiaen student, took a stand against serialism in an article entitled "The Crisis in Serial Music." Here he advocated a return to a musical art incorporating intuition and emotion rather than exact mathematical relationships in what he called a "stochastic" approach to composition. His *Diamorphoses* and his electronic *Concret PH* (1960) both manifest these philosophies. Boulez also, earlier one of the strongest advocates of total serialism, backed off from the twelve-tone system in the mid-fifties and began to use controlled chance in many of his compositions. The two extremes in Boulez' approach are seen, on the one hand, in his most famous work, *Le Marteau sans maître* (1954) for solo contralto and chamber ensemble, which Stravinsky once referred to as the work by a younger composer most attractive to him; and, at the other extreme, *Pli selon pli* (1960) one of two cantatas based on the poetry of Mallarmé. The first is a serial work of considerable mathematical predeterminacy, while the second, although mathematical, makes use of chance, and exploits the phonetic and semantic properties of the spoken syllable. The Italian, Luciano Berio, (1925–   ) has used the voice in similar ways in a kind of *musique concrete* style in *Hommages à Joyce* (1959), which consists of electronic mutations of a woman's voice reading a passage from *Ulysses,* as well as in *Esposizione* (1963), a theater piece influenced by the theater of the absurd.

Chance itself can be approached mathematically, and this has been a part of Xenakis' "stochastic" approach. His *Strategie, Game for two Orchestras* (1959–62) uses a stochastic (probabilistic) structure in which the two back-to-back conductors select musical structures or "tactics" from the matrix shown in figure 89. The work will vary in length from ten to thirty minutes. The trend begun by the Russian-American composer and theorist, Joseph Schillinger (1895–1943) toward the increased use of mathematics in music was not reversed by the intrusion of chance or by a lessening of the importance of serialism. Indeed, judging by the nature of many articles written by composers in the sixties and seventies, mathematics continues to be an important tool in contemporary composition, often in combination with improvisation or chance.

STRAT
EGIE

MATRICE DES REGLEMENTS.
DUEL, (VALEUR DU JEU = 0).

CHEF X
(LIGNES)

◀ VENTS
● PERC. NORM.
H CORDES: PERC. CAISSE
∴ CORDES: PIZZ, ETC...
CORDES: GLISS.
≡ CORDES: TENUES

▲ (VENTS + PERC) SIM.

◢ (VENTS + PERC + CORDES PERC) SIMULTANEMENT

I. Xenakis
ST/VBNISE-101062

CHEF Y (colonnes)

	I	II	III	IV	V	VI	VII	VIII	IX	X	XI	XII	XIII	XIV	XV	XVI	XVII	XVIII	XIX	
I (I*)	116	10	84	-48	4	-52	-60	-40	132	-44	-8	-36	-22	24	-46	102	138	-38	32	2
II	-56	96	-44	-22	-24	52	-50	-14	12	28	6	-48	-20	-16	-10	-24	-36	-20	44	3
III	-110	-2	96	96	24	0	4	-56	-32	-24	4	-52	-48	-40	-16	-44	-16	20	72	1
IV	0	-20	24	84	4	-12	12	-12	-28	8	-8	-24	-40	4	22	-10	-16	28	-16	11
V	-110	-104	-86	4	104	-8	44	20	-8	4	8	-8	-38	-24	-16	40	8	20	-24	1
VI	24	44	12	-14	-6	64	24	-8	24	4	-24	-40	-52	-44	24	44	4	4	-48	3
VII	-56	-52	20	16	36	44	44	4	-52	-48	0	-46	-36	-12	-20	-40	-44	16	40	4
VIII	-32	-8	-52	-8	12	4	4	48	-44	-12	8	-52	-4	8	32	-36	-40	-16	24	3
IX	-36	10	-16	-32	2	4	-44	-52	52	44	2	48	-18	64	24	22	-36	-28	-52	6
X	-48	22	-22	4	-4	32	-46	-16	8	-36	-24	-4	8	32	24	4	-8	20	-32	4
XI	4	24	26	-4	4	-28	-36	-12	20	4	64	68	4	40	-12	-2	-24	-27	-32	10
XII	-36	-196	-188	-28	-34	-42	36	32	24	0	-32	74	76	-4	4	-32	-28	40	76	7
XIII	166	-20	-42	-40	-52	-44	14	-16	4	22	-14	80	72	-26	-58	40	-18	78	42	2
XIV	32	-14	-34	0	-32	-52	36	12	-12	36	24	-28	42	76	-42	-64	-30	-29	72	5
XV	-20	8	4	28	-28	14	0	20	2	-4	-32	14	26	-56	46	-36	12	-8	14	4
XVI	88	88	104	-28	20	16	-2	-16	20	-20	-50	-26	-8	-36	-40	108	-24	-33	60	9
XVII	32	92	52	-28	16	8	-44	-48	-32	0	-16	-16	-20	-32	24	-30	96	52	-36	8
XVIII	-36	-24	8	4	0	-2	52	78	-12	-4	36	-8	28	-24	-16	-14	42	-12	-40	9
XIX	-52	-52	-66	4	6	-6	-4	44	-66	-4	44	12	44	40	16	-46	44	-42	-32	4
	4	4	2	3	7	11	3	3	4	6	9	2	5	7	10	4	4	8	10	:100

Figure 89. Matrix of the Game for Two Orchestras, Strategie, Xenakis.

An older composer drawn to electronic music through its natural affinity for serial techniques is Ernst Krenek (1900–), who had been closely associated with the modern Viennese school during the early twentieth century. His jazz-opera *Jonny spielt auf* (1927) created enough of a sensation to cause it to be widely imitated in the late twenties and early thirties. Subsequently he came to live in the United States where he established himself as a distinguished and prolific composer, though one whose extreme mathematical tendencies and interest in total predetermination lend an esoteric quality to much of his music. His opera *Der Goldene Bock* uses electronic effects to evoke magical moods.

The American Scene

There are a remarkable number of American composers of the older generation who have to varying degrees kept up with the newer trends of twentieth century music. Three of them, Otto Luening (1900–   ), the pioneer of electronic music in the United States, and his two colleagues, Vladimir Ussachevsky (1911–   ) and Milton Babbitt (1916–   ), were responsible for the first real thrust in electronic music in America. They have been working since the early fifties at the Electronic Music Center at Columbia University, operated under the joint auspices of Princeton and Columbia Universities. All of them have, of course, composed in conventional media, and they have also experimented with *musique concrete. Poem in Cycles and Bells* (1954), composed jointly by Luening and Ussachevsky, combines electronic sounds with the conventional symphony orchestra.

Babbitt is as well known for his theoretical writings and speculations upon the theory of modern music as for his music itself. Among his works in conventional media are his *String Quartet No. 2* (1954), *All Set* (1957) for seven jazz instruments, and *Composition for Tenor and Six Instruments* (1960). He was one of the pioneers in the use of the synthesizer, and utilized it in his *Vision and Prayer* (1961), for soprano and electronic sounds, and in *Philomel* (1963), for soprano, recorded soprano, and electronic sounds. Such combinations of electronic media with electronic sounds have added a new element of human expressiveness to the medium that is a great improvement over the stylized bleeps, bubbles, and various other contrived sounds of early electronic music. One of the younger composers at the Columbia Princeton Center, Mario Davidovsky (1934–   ), has been highly successful with the combining of electronic sounds with instruments. His three *Synchronisms,* the first using flute, the second with woodwind ensemble, and the third for cello (all in combination with electronic sounds) are particularly successful works of the early sixties. Columbia University has become one of the significant centers for the performance of contemporary music, and so many composers are associated with the school that it is impossible at this point to assess their relative importance. Among them, Charles Wuorinen (1938–   ) and Harvey Sollberger (1935–   ) have attracted considerable attention, not only for their music, but for the concert series of contemporary music they have established at Columbia.

John Cage, mentioned in the preceding section, continues to wield influence on the contemporary scene, but in most instances his outré methods of composition and performance are more striking than the music itself. The experiments with the piano, preparing it, reaching inside it, etc., have been widely imitated by younger composers, while

his aleatory endeavors and mystical (Zen Buddhist) esthetic philosophies of music have increasingly caused him to appear to be consciously trying to destroy the traditions of Western music. Another
single-minded experimentalist is Harry Partch (1901–   ), whose total effort has been bent to the task of creating microtonal music. To this
end, he devised a scale and a special notational system in which the
octave is divided into forty-three equal parts. Like Cage, his innovative
ideas are more remarkable than his music.

Partch is only one of several twentieth-century composers who
have experimented with microtonal music. The Czech, Alois Haba
(1893–   ), inspired by the microtonal inflections of east Moravian
folk song, attempted to combine Viennese atonalism with microtonal
techniques. For the most part, microtonal music has not had much
impact upon Western music, perhaps because the ears of our audiences
have not yet reached the point where meaningful discrimination of
such fine pitch differences is possible. With composers experimenting
with such things as microtones, glissandi, chance elements, and prepared pianos, new notational systems have had to be devised. One of
the most common types is illustrated in figure 90, a line of score from
Music for Cello and Piano by the American composer Earle Brown.

Highly regarded among American composers of the older generation is Elliot Carter (1908–   ), who has enjoyed a long career as a
teacher and composer and presently resides at Yale University. Among
his early works which established him as one of the foremost American composers of the mid-twentieth century was his *Sonata for Cello
and Piano* (1948). One important aspect of this work is the manner in
which Carter effected rhythmic transitions from one tempo to another
by means of a system of accurately notating gradual accelerations or
ritards. The technique, which Carter has called "metrical modulation,"
has been used successfully in many of his works, but its importance

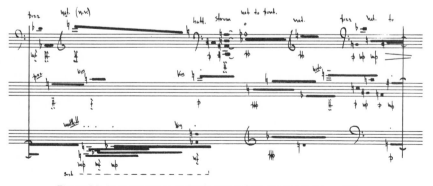

Figure 90. New Notation in Earle Brown's Music for Cello and Piano.

as a compositional technique has been overemphasized. Among his later works, the most successful has been his *String Quartet No. 2* (1959), which was given numerous awards, including the Pulitzer Prize.

Ross Lee Finney (1906–   ), for many years composer-in-residence at the University of Michigan, since 1950 has made considerable use of serial techniques, particularly in the last three of his eight string quartets. Although he has composed highly successful music in all media, one of his major contributions to American music has been his teaching of composition. Among his many talented and successful students are several who have won significant awards, including Pulitzer Prize winners Leslie Bassett (1923–   ), for his *Variations for Orchestra* (1965), and George Crumb (1929–   ), for his *Echoes of Time and the River* (1967).

Leon Kirchner (1919–   ), who teaches at Harvard University, is one of the most accessible among progressive American composers. His *Double Concerto* (1960) for violin, cello, winds, and percussion is worthy of note, but there are numerous other worthwhile compositions among his predominantly instrumental output. Karel Husa (1921–   ), a Czech-born composer of the Cornell University faculty, has gained considerable recognition in recent years, including the 1969 Pulitzer Prize. Gunther Schuller (1925–   ), although best known for his "third stream" efforts to integrate jazz and serious concert music, has composed in all media, including an opera *The Visitation* (1965) based on Kafka's *The Trial.* Another successful composer of opera is Robert Ward (1917–   ), whose four-act *The Crucible* (1962) received the 1962 Pulitzer Prize. George Rochberg (1918–   ), one of the most progressive composers of the older generation, has contributed much to the theory of serial music. His *Contra Mortem et Tempus* (1965) for flute, clarinet, violin, and piano, and his *String Quartet No. 2* are worthy of note. A younger composer, Salvatore Martirano (1927–   ), has shown real creative individuality in a number of works of which one of the best known is his *Cocktail Music* for piano composed in the sixties. Ben Weber (1916–   ) is a more conservative composer who has been particularly successful in his music for solo voice. Although there are many more American composers, young and old, who might well be mentioned here, to assemble a comprehensive list of significant contemporary American composers is beyond the scope of this book.

Music of Commitment and a New Humanism

This concluding section deals with those European composers who have felt and expressed in their music a deep concern for humanity and, above all, compassion for the innocent victims of political oppression. With rare exceptions, it has been characteristic of composers throughout history that—although deeply moved by social problems, and, through their music, expressive of this feeling–they have not themselves been actively concerned with politics or ideologies. For many composers prior to the Romantic era, this may have been partly due to their strong religious commitments or allegiance to their wealthy and distinguished patrons, which took the place of strong social commitments. But even Beethoven, committed as he appears to have been to brotherhood and equality, was not politically active. The same appears to be true of today's composers. It has been said that the artist feels deep emotions more strongly and expresses them more effectively and beautifully than other people–that this is what makes him an artist–and that this is why a powerful work of art can be the direct result of an external event perceived by the artist, but in which he plays no active part and for which his concern is indirect. It is generally true of composers that their strongest expression of commitment is through their music, rather than through their actions, but this is not an indictment, for this is the artist's nature, and it is important to remember that the value of a composer's music depends not upon the outward realities that may have colored his expression but upon the true value and meaning of the music itself.

From the Middle Ages to the Baroque, when religious music was obviously written almost entirely at the behest of the Church and when most composers of religious music were in one way or another employed by the Church, it was probably not difficult for the Church composer to feel a strong musical commitment to the glory of God. From the Romantic era to the present, however, such a commitment often came only from a composer's personal convictions without benefit of the patronage of the Church. This is undoubtedly one of the reasons why there has been relatively little religious music, good or bad, composed in the nineteenth and twentieth centuries. Churches still commission sacred music, but only a few works of our more distinguished twentieth-century compositions were clearly generated by deep religious feelings. Among these are the Folk Songs, Op. 12, of Webern, based on anonymous religious texts, and several other works composed throughout his life. Stravinsky, a devout Catholic, was undoubtedly motivated by a desire to express personal feelings in his various religious works from the *Symphony of Psalms* (1930) to *Threni* (1958), even though the means of expression underwent great changes during this period. Schoenberg's *A Survivor of Warsaw* (1948) and many others of his works express a deep religious feeling as well as anguish and compassion for the persecution of his race. Also in much of Messiaen's music can be heard a mystical beauty that is undoubtedly the unique expression of deeply felt religious feelings. This is apparent in his *Quartet for the End of Time* composed in a German prisoner-of-war camp and in several other works.

But there is a commitment of another, though related kind to be heard in the music of Luigi Dallapiccola. His *Quaderno Musicale (Variations for Orchestra)* discussed in chapter 16 is an abstract instrumental work concerned with the working out of purely musical problems, and although it may have emotional meaning for the listener, it is not, at least outwardly, expressive of strongly felt beliefs. It does show Dallapiccola—unique among Italian composers for his early adoption of the twelve-tone system—as one of the great twentieth-century masters of the craft of musical composition. Others of his works, such as the *Canti di Prigionia*, the opera *Il Prigionera*, and many later works are expressions of his concern for human liberty and a protest against Italian Fascism and the Nazi occupation of his homeland during and prior to World War II. Although they are committed works, they are not ideological in nature. Rather than a protest against any political faction, they constitute a universal appeal for freedom and for humanity.

Unlike Dallapiccola, his countryman Luigi Nono (1924–   ) has in his vocal works espoused a specific ideology, that of socialism. He is an Italian composer of the first rank, a serial composer who has experimented extensively with the expressive properties of words broken down into syllables and even letters. So fragmented does the text often become in his hands that the words are at times unrecognizable, a fact that detracts from the effective communication of his ideologies, although it in no way mars the purely musical qualities of his work. His *Il canto sospeso* (1956) is based on the last letters of resistance fighters, while his opera *Intolleranza* (1960) is a clear expression of his socialist beliefs. He and his colleague Bruno Maderna (1920–) are active in the field of electronic music through their work at the electronic studio of Milan Radio.

Hans Werner Henze (1926–   ), a German composer who has gone through various stylistic stages including one of strict serialism, has arrived at a synthesis or consolidation of several contemporary styles—chiefly serialism and the Neoclassical style of the pre-1950 Stravinskyites. The result is a musical language of conscious simplicity and great communicative powers. Around mid-century he composed a number of successful operas, including *Boulevard Solitude* (1951) and *Undine* (1956). In some of his latest works Henze, like Dallapiccola, has given expression to the ideals of a new humanism—freedom of thought and the rights of man. This is most apparent in his oratorio *Novae de infinito laudes* (1963), as well as in the opera *Die Bassariden* (1966), the libretto by W. H. Auden and Chester Kallman. The oratorio is scored for an ensemble of many voices, lutes, pianos, harps, English horns, trumpets, and trombones.

In Poland there are a multitude of composers producing music in highly progressive styles. Two of them, Witold Lutoslawski (1913–   ) and Krzystof Penderecki (1933–   ) stand out as the most gifted and creative, and both have been committed to a new expression of humanistic ideals. Lutoslawski in his early works integrated folk music into his style, but by degrees he also incorporated the serialism, aleatoric techniques, and speech-composition of Western Europe. His *Funeral Music* for string orchestra, completed in 1958 and dedicated to the memory of Bartok, is a serial composition which has become internationally known.

Penderecki is one of the most advanced of the European experimentalists, but in spite of his apparent intention to transform musical sound into noise, his music has a compelling emotional quality. His *Threnody for the Victims of Hiroshima,* composed in the fifties, bears the imprint of the nightmare experienced by all involved in the Second World War. Scored for string orchestra, it utilizes indeterminate pitches such as those produced by bowing between the bridge and the tailpiece or by blowing into the F holes of the instrument as well as the more conventional techniques of modern string writing such as *sul ponticello, col legno,* glissandi, etc. His *St. Luke Passion* (1963) has the same gripping qualities of torment and compassion as the *Threnody,* but at the same time it is a religious work which brings contemporary styles into the world of traditional church music. Commissioned by Cologne Radio, it was first performed in the cathedral at Münster. In two parts and over an hour in duration, it calls for soloists, a speaker, three mixed choirs, boys' choir, and orchestra. Its twelve-tone row incorporates the B-A-C-H theme, and various types of vocal sounds such as hisses and whispers are used to create an atmosphere that is at times emotionally chaotic, but nevertheless maintains both the humanistic and the religious traditions. The work has been performed frequently throughout the world and may well become a twentieth-century symbol of the new humanism.

In the course of music history we have discussed many musical works of the highest artistry and creative individuality. But some of them stand out above the others because they are also expressive of deeply held human feelings—values and truths that are as meaningful now as in the Middle Ages. It is these works, regardless of their theoretical or historical significance, which justify the study of music and its history. Perhaps Penderecki's *Passion*, Webern's *Cantata No. One*, or Carter's Second String Quartet will one day be counted among the most significant and universal works of the past along with Bach's *B Minor Mass*, Beethoven's Ninth, and Mozart's *Don Giovanni*. In the twentieth century, as in any period of music history, a multitude of currents and cross-currents tends to obscure the major trends. Only time will tell which major movements and which musical works will emerge as most significant to the evolution of musical thought and the communication of musical ideas.

Suggestions for Further Reading

Abraham, Gerald. *This Modern Music.* New York: Norton, 1952.

Apel, Willi. *Harvard Dictionary of Music* (2nd ed.). Cambridge: Harvard 1969.

Barzun, Jacques. *Berlioz and the Romantic Century.* Boston: Little, Brown, 1950.

Bauer, Marion. *Twentieth Century Music.* New York: Putnam, 1947.

Berger, Arthur. *Copland.* New York: Oxford, 1953.

Berlioz, Hector. *Memoirs.* New York: Knopf, 1948.

Blom, Eric (ed.). *Grove's Dictionary of Music and Musicians,* 5th ed. New York: St. Martin's, 1954, 1961.

Blom, Eric. *Mozart.* London: Dent, 1935; New York: Farrar, Straus, 1949.

Blom, Eric (ed). *Mozart's Letters.* Bristol: Western Printing Services, 1956.

Brown, Maurice J. E. *Schubert.* New York: St. Martin's, 1958.

Bukofzer, Manfred F. *Music in the Baroque Era.* New York: Norton, 1947.

Chase, Gilbert. *America's Music.* New York: McGraw-Hill, 1955.

Coates, Henry. *Palestrina.* London: Dent, 1938.

Cohen, Albert and John White. *Anthology of Music for Analysis.* New York: Appleton-Century-Crofts, 1965.

Collaer, Paul. *A History of Modern Music.* New York: Grosset & Dunlap, 1961.

Cowell, Henry (ed.). *American Composers on American Music.* New York: Ungar, 1962.

Cowell, Sidney and Henry. *Charles Ives and His Music.* New York: Oxford University Press, 1955.

David, Hans T. and Arthur Mendel. *The Bach Reader.* New York: Norton, 1945.

Deri, Otto. *Exploring Twentieth Century Music.* New York: Holt, Rinehart, and Winston, 1968.

Debussy, Claude. *Monsieur Croche.* New York: Lear, 1948.

Deutsch, Otto Erich. *Handel: A Documentary Biography.* New York: Norton, 1955.

Einstein, Alfred. *A Short History of Music.* New York: Knopf, 1947.

Einstein, Alfred. *Mozart: His Character, His Work.* New York: Oxford, 1945.

Einstein, Alfred. *Music in the Romantic Era.* New York: Norton, 1947.

Ewen, David. *The Book of Modern Composers.* New York: Knopf, 1942.

Fellowes, Edmund H. *William Byrd,* 2nd ed. London: Oxford, 1948.

Ferguson, Donald N. *Masterworks of the Orchestral Repertoire.* Minneapolis: University of Minnesota Press, 1954.

Geiringer, Karl. *Brahms: His Life and Work.* New York: Oxford, 1947.

Geiringer, Karl. *Haydn.* New York: Norton, 1946.

Grout, Donald Jay. *A History of Western Music.* New York: Norton, 1960.

Grove, George. *Beethoven, Schubert, Mendelssohn.* New York: Macmillan, 1951.

Hamburger, Michael (tr. & ed.). *Beethoven—Letters, Journals and Conversations.* Garden City, New York: Doubleday, 1960.

Hansen, Peter S. *An Introduction to Twentieth Century Music.* New York: Allyn and Bacon, 1961.

Hanson, Lawrence and Elizabeth. *Prokofiev.* New York: Random House, 1964.

Howard, John Tasker and George Kent Bellows. *A Short History of Music in America.* New York: Crowell, 1957.

Ives, Charles. *Essays Before a Sonata and Other Writings* (ed. Howard Boatwright). New York: Norton, 1961.

Kirkpatrick, Ralph. *Domenico Scarlatti.* Princeton University Press, 1953.

Kobbe, Gustav. *Complete Opera Book.* London: Putnam, 1954.

Lang, Paul Henry. *Music in Western Civilization.* New York: Norton, 1941.

Lang, Paul Henry (ed.) *Stravinsky. A new Appraisal of His Work.* New York: Norton, 1963.

Leyda, Jay and S. Bertensson. *The Mussorgsky Reader.* New York: Norton, 1947.

Liess, Andreas. *Carl Orff, His Life and His Music.* New York: St. Martin's Press, 1966.

Lockspeiser, Edward. *Debussy.* London: Dent, 1951.

Machlis, Joseph. *Introduction to Contemporary Music.* New York: Norton, 1961.

Morgenstern, Sam (ed.) *Composers on Music—From Palestrina to Copland.* New York: Pantheon, 1956.

Newman, Ernest. *The Life of Richard Wagner.* New York: Knopf, 1933–1946.

Parmet, Simon. *The Symphonies of Sibelius.* London: Cassell, 1959.

Pincherle, Marc. *Corelli: His Life, His Music.* New York: Norton, 1956.

Pincherle, Marc. *Vivaldi.* New York: Norton, 1957.

Redlich, H. F. *Alban Berg.* New York: Abelard Schuman.

Reese, Gustave. *Music in the Middle Ages.* New York: Norton, 1940.

Robinson, Michael. *Opera Before Mozart.* New York: Morrow, 1966.

Roland-Manuel. *Maurice Ravel.* London: Dobson, 1947.

Sachs, Curt. *The Commonwealth of Art.* New York: Norton, 1946.

Sachs, Curt. *Our Musical Heritage: A Short History of Music,* 2nd. ed. New York: Prentice Hall, 1955.

Schoenberg, Arnold. *Style and Idea.* New York: Philosophical, 1950.

Schrade, Leo. *Monteverdi: Creator of Modern Music.* New York: Norton, 1950.

Schulmann, Robert. *On Music and Musicians.* New York: Pantheon, 1946.

Schweitzer, Albert. *J. S. Bach.* New York: Macmillan, 1935.

Sitwell, Sacheverell. *Liszt.* Boston: Houghton Mifflin, 1934.

Slonimsky, Nicolas (ed.). *Baker's Biographical Dictionary of Musicians,* 6th ed. New York: Schirmer, 1967.

Slonimsky, Nicolas. *Music Since 1900.* New York: Coleman-Ross, 1949.

Sourek, Otakar. *Antonin Dvorak.* New York: Philosophical, 1954.

Spitta, Phillipp. *Johann Sebastian Bach.* New York: Dover, 1951.

Stevens, Halsey. *The Life and Music of Bela Bartok.* New York: Oxford, 1953.

Stravinsky, Igor. *An Autobiography.* New York: Norton, 1962.

Stravinsky, Igor. *Poetics of Music.* New York: Vintage, 1956.

Stuckenschmidt, H. H. *Twentieth Century Music.* New York: McGraw-Hill, 1969.

Sullivan, J. W. N. *Beethoven: His Spiritual Development.* New York: Knopf, 1947.

Thayer, A. W. *The Life of Ludwig Van Beethoven* (ed. H. E. Krehbiel). New York: Beethoven Association, 1921.

Thompson, Oscar and Nicolas Slonimsky. *International Encyclopedia of Music and Musicians.* New York: Dodd, Mead, 1953.

Thompson, Oscar. *Debussy: Man and Artist.* New York: Dodd, Mead, 1937.

Tovey, Donald Francis. *The Forms of Music.* Cleveland: World Publishing, 1956.

Toye, Francis. *Giuseppe Verdi.* New York: Knopf, 1931.

Ulrich, Homer and Paul Pisk. *A History of Music and Musical Style.* New York: Harcourt, Brace, and World, 1963.

Wagner, Richard. *Prose Works.* London: Kegan Paul, 1892–1899.

Weinstock, Herbert. *Chopin: The Man and His Music.* New York: Knopf, 1949.

Weinstock, Herbert. *Tschaikovsky.* New York: Knopf, 1943.

Westrup, J. A. *Purcell.* New York: Dutton, 1937.

White, John D. *Understanding and Enjoying Music.* New York: Dodd, Mead, 1968.

Wildgans, Friedrich. *Anton Webern.* New York: October House, 1966.

Index